THE WALL

THE PEOPLE'S STORY

Mine is not a pleasant story, it does not possess the gentle harmony of invented tales; like the lives of all men who have given up trying to deceive themselves, it is a mixture of nonsense and chaos, madness and dreams.

Demian,
Hermann Hesse

THE WALL

THE PEOPLE'S STORY

CHRISTOPHER HILTON

SUTTON PUBLISHING

First published in 2001 by
Sutton Publishing Limited · Phoenix Mill
Thrupp · Stroud · Gloucestershire · GL5 2BU

Reprinted in 2001 (twice)

British Library Cataloguing in Publication Data
A catalogue record for this book is available from the British
Library

ISBN 0 7509 2756 9

Typeset in 11/13.5 pt Sabon.
Typesetting and origination by
Sutton Publishing Limited.
Printed in Great Britain by
J.H. Haynes & Co. Ltd, Sparkford, England.

Contents

List of Plates		vii
List of Maps		ix
Acknowledgements		xi
Prologue		xv
One	Fault Line	1
Two	Saturday Night	25
Three	And Sunday Morning	37
Four	First Week of the Rest of Your Life	82
Five	Cold as Ice	132
Six	The Strangeness	181
Seven	The Bullet Run	208
Eight	Thaw	241
Nine	A Quiet Night Like This	269
Ten	Dawn	304
Eleven	Pieces	319
	Notes	355
	Bibliography	373
	The Death Strip: The Toll	377
	Index	381

List of Plates

Between pp. 108 and 109

1.	Division
2.	Building the wall
3.	The death of Peter Fechter
4.	Border Guards and Military Police
5.	Hartmut Richter's escape
6.	The destruction of the Church of Reconciliation . . .
7.	. . . and ten years on
8.	People

Between pp. 268 and 269

9.	East meets West
10.	The line at Invalidenstrasse Checkpoint
11.	Harald Jäger and Bornholmer Strasse Checkpoint
12.	The Café Adler and the Berliner Museum-Archiv
13.	Ordinary people
14. and 15.	Old friends
16.	The end of the wait

List of Maps

		page
1.	The wall, cutting across central Berlin	2
2.	The divided Germany	7
3.	Districts surrounding Berlin	14
4.	Bernauer Strasse	41
5.	The Teltow Canal	90
6.	The River Spree	139
7.	Exits and Entrances	157
8.	The death of Peter Fechter	166
9.	Tunnel 57	190
10.	The Steinstücken enclave	214
11.	The gateways to the West	270
12.	Checkpoint Charlie	280

Acknowledgements

Any book like this, balancing political and historical background against the first-person testaments of the foreground, draws to itself a lot of people and a lot of sources of information. I pay my due tribute to them all and offer my sincere thanks.

First, Birgit Kubisch, who started off as an interpreter but became an enthusiast, an organiser, a translator, a provider, and handled some interviews herself. To her I must add my neighbour Inge Donnell who moved doggedly through translating the paragraphs of those who died at the wall even though she found the task upsetting; and to her I must add Viktoria Tischer, of Haynes, who set herself to add to the store of knowledge on Peter Fechter, the teenager whose fate – he was left to bleed to death in 1962 – still lives, if I may use that word, in the domain of the grotesque and the barbarous which the Berlin Wall created.

I list the others who helped in no particular order. The book is, I hope, greater than the sum total of its parts – and many, many good people provided those parts, each in their own way. To people who insist that civility, courtesy and cooperation are vanished echoes of a genteel past, I say: wrong. Almost *nobody* I approached – in so many walks of life – was difficult. On the contrary, and for no reward of any kind, they went out of their way to help.

I owe a special debt to Hagen Koch, a former Border Guard who has, in his cosy East Berlin apartment, set up a museum to the wall because he feels there should be one place where people can find out about it. He has refused a great deal of money for some of the material he's gathered (including a unique set of photographs of the death strip) and I salute him for that as I thank him for maps, information, and advice. If you want to see for yourself, try http://www.Berliner-mauer.de. The Rt Hon. Lord Hurd of Westwell CH, CBE, then British Foreign Secretary, sent specific memories which were gratefully received. Millie Waters, a bubbly public affairs specialist at the HQ US Army, Europe, proved to be a one-person army in finding people and arranging things.

And thanks to the interviewees: Chris Toft, British Military Police; Bernard Ledwidge, British Mission, Berlin; the late Diane Loeser, who lived in East Berlin; Bernie Godek, Michael Raferty, Bill Bentz and Russ Anderson of the US military; former US Secretary of State Dean Rusk, Frank Cash, Dorothy Lightner (wife of Allan), the late John Ausland, George Muller, Al Hemsing, Richard Smyser and Frank Trinka of the US political and diplomatic services; Adam Kellett-Long (with particular thanks to his wife Mary who allowed me to use extracts from her diary), Peter Johnson (who also let me have his diary) and Erdmute Greis-Behrendt, of Reuters; Günter Moll and Roland Egersdörfer of the Border Guards; Peter Schultz and Ernest Steinke of the RIAS radio station, Berlin; Peter Dick, a Canadian and briefly a West Berlin resident; Peter and Daniel Glau of the Hotel Ahorn, which became a second home; Erkhard Gurtz, Gerda Stern, Bodo Radtke, Nora Evans, Mateus, Kurt Behrendt, Heinz Sachsenweger, Uwe Nietzold, Erhard and Brigitta Schimke, Lutz and Uta Stolz, Rudiger Hering, Klaus-Peter Grohmann, Martin Schabe, Horst Pruster, Birgit Wuthe, Jakob Burkhardt, Elli Kohn, Pastor Manfred Fischer, Marina Brath, Astrid Benner, Brita Segger, Katrin Mongau, Harald Jäger, Hartmut Richter, Janet and Jacqueline Burkhardt. E.L. Gordon kept watch on the US media. A friend and fellow enthusiast, John Woodcock, was a valued companion on trips to the city.

There is a Bibliography at the end, but for permission to quote I am indebted to: Edith Kohagen, Editor-in-chief of Presse- und Informationsamt des Landes Berlin for *The Wall and How it Fell* (1994) and the invaluable *Violations of human rights, illegal acts and incidents at the sector border in Berlin since the building of the wall (13 August 1961–15 August 1962)*, published in 1962 on behalf of the government of the Federal Republic of Germany by the Federal Ministry for All-German Questions (Bonn and Berlin). She also demystified the time gap between Berlin and Washington in August 1961, something not as straightforward as one might imagine. The extracts from *Berlin Twilight* by Lieutenant-Colonel W. Byford-Jones (Hutchinson), *Man Without a Face* by Markus Wolf (Jonathan Cape), *Goodbye to Berlin* by Christopher Isherwood (Hogarth Press) and *The Ugly Frontier* by David Shears (Chatto & Windus) are courtesy of the Random House Group Ltd.

I sincerely thank the following for extracts: Aufbau-Verlag, Berlin for *Der Sturz* by Reinhold Andert and Wolfgang Herzberg; Peter

Owen publishers for the quotation from *Demian* by Hermann Hesse (Panther); A.M. Heath & Co. Ltd for *The Ides of August* by Curtis Cate (copyright © Curtis Cate, 1978); the Orion Publishing Group Ltd for *Willy Brandt: Portrait of a Statesman* by Terence Prittie (Weidenfeld & Nicolson); Duke University Press for *We Were the People: Voices from East Germany's Revolutionary Autumn of 1989* by Dirk Philipsen; Continuum for the *German Democratic Republic* by Mike Dennis; the History Place (webmaster@historyplace.com) for the full text of John F. Kennedy's speech in Berlin in 1963; Rainer and Alexandra Hildebrandt for *Berlin: Von der Frontstadt zur Brücke Europas* and *It Happened at the Wall*; the University of Massachusetts Press for *The Wall in My Backyard* by Dinah Dodds and Pam Allen-Thompson; HarperCollins for *The Siege of Berlin* by Mark Arnold-Forster; Sanga Music Inc. for the lines from *Where Have all the Flowers Gone?* by Pete Seeger; Norman Gelb for *The Berlin Wall* (Michael Joseph, 1986); George Bailey for *Germans: Biography of an Obsession* (Free Press, New York) and *Battleground Berlin* (with David E. Murphy and Sergei A. Kondraschev, Yale University Press); the British Army HQ in Germany (and thanks to Helga Heine for smoothing the way) for the Friday 17 November 1989 issue of *Berlin Bulletin*, the magazine published by Education Branch, HQ Berlin Infantry Brigade for British Forces, Berlin; ITPS Ltd, on behalf of Routledge, for *Eastern Europe in the Twentieth Century* by R.J. Crampton; Christian F. Ostermann, Director, Cold War International History Project, The Woodrow Wilson Center for Scholars Project, for *Khrushchev and the Berlin Crisis* and *Ulbricht and the Concrete 'Rose'*; the Associated Press for their reporting of escapes and escape attempts in the 1980s.

I owe special thanks to Yorkshire Television, for allowing me to quote verbatim from their emotive and emotional documentary *First Tuesday* on relatives of those who died at the wall. The Bureau of Diplomatic Security of the Department of State, Washington, DC, has allowed me to use a memorandum exploring options before the wall was built, and thanks to Andy Laine for help there as well as the late John Ausland for providing it. Irene Böhme gave permission to quote from her book *Di da drüben* (originally published by Rotbuch Verlag, Berlin, in 1982) in a charming letter.

Prologue

Commander Günter Moll walked briskly across the concrete concourse which was carpeted by white light falling softly from the banks of tall arc-lamps. He was a small, neat man and, like many professional soldiers, his uniform seemed moulded to him. Five o'clock, almost to the minute, and his shift had ended.

He reached the car park at the far side of the concourse, eased himself into his Skoda, settled and fired the engine. He had no need to glance back at the checkpoint because he knew precisely how it was functioning, understood all the predetermined clockwork motions which kept it running as it had run twenty-four hours a day for twenty-eight years. It ticked at a slow, even, careful pace to regulations of great exactitude. He'd handed control to his deputy, Major Simon, a competent, reliable man, and as he drove away his mind was at peace. Another day had ticked by.

The checkpoint lay broad and deep, some 50 metres by 50, hewn out of a city centre and constructed in a clearing among ordinary streets. For the tourist who chanced upon it for the first time, the impression remained invariably the same: profound incomprehension that an armed encampment could be a few footsteps beyond shops and a corner café. At that first glance it all seemed bewildering – the wall, the watchtowers, the death strip – and only when you came to know it did the geography and the geometry make sense. The checkpoint was at the precise point where East and West met.

To Moll it was known as the crossing on Friedrichstrasse, the street it straddled. To most of the rest of the world it had another name altogether, although quite why the tourist would probably have been unable to say.

A generation before, the US Army decided that checkpoints should be designated in alphabetical order. To travel across East Germany one went through *Alpha* and *Bravo*, and now here was the third. The name had a simplicity, a resonance and an alliteration which made it and its connotation recognisable on every continent.

It was called Checkpoint Charlie.

The office Commander Moll left was on the second floor of a pastel-shaded building, and through a square, squat window he could survey the expanse of the checkpoint, his checkpoint, as it faced the West: successively the Customs offices under a vast roof covering the centre of the concourse; a plain area beyond that, then three watchtowers, then the wall itself, white, 12 feet high and of vertical slabs so smooth that they offered no grip to a hand. The wall flowed along the extremity of the checkpoint to the left and right like arms, flowed on mile after mile, making an encirclement so that it locked the Western half of the city in a military embrace.

The arms of the wall folded into the checkpoint and, lower here – only shoulder high – ran across in front of the watchtowers. Two gaps had been left in it like mouths, a narrow one for pedestrians, a broader one for vehicles. The gaps allowed the old road – Friedrichstrasse – to come through the checkpoint: same road, same width, same name but the different ends of it completely separated.

Even these fortifications had been tightened a month before by the erection of a hip-high forward barricade – three tiers of concrete laid horizontally and wire mesh fencing secured to the top – although it, too, had the two mouths for pedestrians and vehicles.

Daily, Moll controlled this geometry of division, and the leader of his country had, only months before, proclaimed proudly that – no matter how many people condemned it as primitive and inhuman – the division would endure for another hundred years, maybe more.

As Moll drove the small car to his apartment in the suburbs he was not only at peace, he was a man of certainties in a country of certainties. When he reached the apartment, while his wife Inge cooked the evening meal, he'd watch television.

And did.

And the world moved.

It was 9 November 1989.

ONE

Fault Line

The construction workers of our capital are for the most part busy building apartment houses, and their working capacities are fully employed to that end. Nobody intends to put up a wall.

Walter Ulbricht,
June 1961

Looking back on it, the mixture of madness and dreams seems logical, with each step leading inexorably to the next but, even so, dividing a major European city by a wall and for twenty-eight years killing anyone who tried to cross it without the right papers still stretches credulity and probably always will; but this is what happened to Berlin and this is what happened to ordinary human beings who lived and died with it.

The credulity is stretched even further because the division wasn't a neat thing: not Paris split either side of the Champs-Élysées, not London camped on either bank of the Thames, not New York riven into East and West of the Avenue of the Americas to make two separate, sovereign countries who hated each other. No: Berlin was bisected along ancient, interwoven, interlocking district boundaries so that the division zigged and zagged through sixty-two major roads, over tram tracks, round a church and through its cemetery, across the frontage of a railway station and, stretching the credulity to its absolute limit, clean through the middle of one house. Each day an estimated 500,000 people had circulated quite normally through what would become the two hostile, alien lands. To take a random year, every day in 1958 some 74,645 bus, tram and underground tickets were sold in the West to people from the East, and that didn't include the extensive overground rail network. Some 12,000 Eastern children went to school in the West.

There was a street called Bernauer Strasse where the apartments stood in the East but the road in the West so that, by opening their

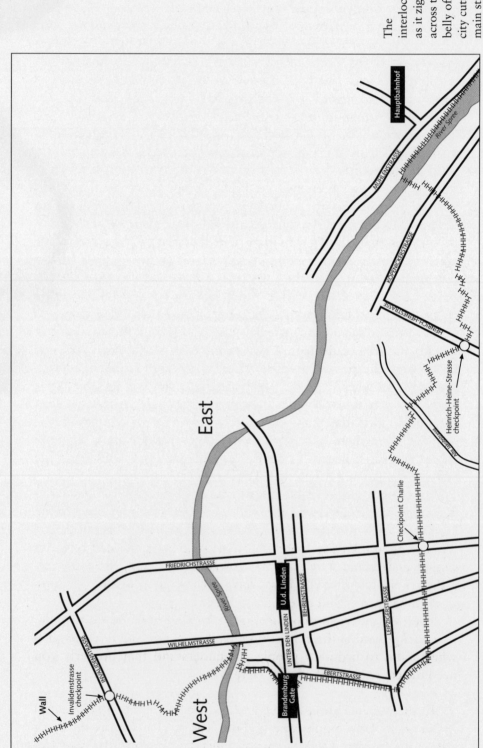

The interlocking as it zigzagged across the belly of the city cutting main streets.

front doors, residents stepped from one side to the other. There had been the subway network (U-bahn), a spider's web, serving the whole city, and the overground train network (S-bahn) fulfilling exactly the same function. Both were cut by the wall but still overlapped. There had been the sewage system, and electricity, and telephones, and postal districts as common to both sides as they would be in a capital city united since (depending on which date seems conclusive to which historian) at least 1230. There had been waste disposal and burying the dead and walking in the woods on a Sunday afternoon.

No city had ever been subjected to anything like this: a son being refused permission to attend his mother's funeral because he happened to live on the wrong side of the street.

Nor was that all. The dividing line represented the exact point where the two dominant political and financial systems of the twentieth century, each the opposite of the other, met. At Checkpoint Charlie in 1961 a jolly East German Border Guard called Hagen Koch had been given a bucket of white paint and a brush and told to paint a line across the road. It was, maybe, 6 inches wide but it held apart the equivalent of two tectonic plates: precisely *this* side was where the power of the United States and its allies ended, precisely *that* where it ended for the Soviet Union and its allies. That both were immensely armed with nuclear weapons, and that escalation towards their use could well begin with some trivial incident somewhere like here, made Hagen Koch's line a defining place. For three decades people came to gaze at it and what lay around it, and were frightened. They were not wrong.

What logic, what inescapable steps, led to this – both the beginning of it in 1961 and the end of it in 1989? The journey to the answer is itself tortuous and improbable but I am persuaded that without undertaking it – even short-stepping it, as we shall be – you cannot understand why the watchtowers went up or, those twenty-eight years later, why you could have owned one provided only you could take it away and give it a good home.

This book moves in two dimensions, background and foreground. The background is the story of the wall itself and the foreground is what it did to ordinary people. To understand that properly you need the context and the logic. Here it is.

When the war in Europe ended, at 2.41 a.m. on 7 May 1945, central Berlin resembled a moonscape, and that's as good a place as any to set out on the journey. There's a phrase which lingers down the years like an echo of the wrath which had been visited upon the city, *Year Zero*, as if, now that everything had been destroyed, the trek back to civilisation must begin from here. Few Berliners thought like that yet, because the future meant surviving until tomorrow.

The bombing by the Royal Air Force and the United States Air Force broke Berlin – not the spirit of the people but most of the infrastructure and a high percentage of the buildings. Statistics are useless to convey the scale. Imagine, instead, gazing down on an area of 2 or 3 square miles and *every* building there like a blackened, hollowed, broken tooth. Now imagine what that looked like from ground level.

The Soviet armies reached the city in the spring of 1945 and, fighting street by street, conquered whatever resistance remained. There are mute echoes of that still in the East, where the old stone buildings bear the scattered pockmarks of gunfire.

This Prussian city of broad avenues and heavy architecture, cathedrals and churches, embassies and opera houses, hospitals and universities, pavement cafés and naughty nightclubs – this widowed place – had been home to 4 million confident, cheeky people who'd walked the walk and talked the talk of a capital city; and now ate horsemeat if they could find it.

There's another phrase which lingers, *Alles für 10 Zigaretten*. It was the name of a stage review but it captured the plight of what remained of the 4 million: 'Everything for 10 cigarettes'. Money – the Reichsmark – had no value and the currency passed to cigarettes.

Hitler never liked Berlin but, from taking power in 1933, ruled from the Chancellery, a Prussian building – heavy and classical – in the city centre.[1] Dictators and diplomats came to its courtyard and walked down its marble gallery to the intimidating office where Hitler would inform them what he had decided for the world. The Chancellery was a partial ruin now: not a broken tooth but a badly beaten face. Its landscaped gardens, where his body had been burnt on the afternoon of 30 April, were cratered and grotesquely strewn with debris like a mini-moonscape.

Now the Soviets were here in their baggy uniforms, and the absolute power had passed to them. Soon enough they'd bring the exiled German communists back from Mother Russia and exercise the absolute power through them.

Major-General Wilhelm Mohnke, who'd commanded the government area, would remember[2] after his capture being driven out of the city and 'coming towards us column after column, endlessly, were the Red Army support units. I say columns, but they resembled more a cavalcade scene from a Russian film. Asia on this day was moving into the middle of Europe, a strange and exotic panorama. There were countless *Panya* wagons, drawn by horse or pony, with singing soldiers perched high on bales of straw.' He added: 'Finally came the *Tross* or quartermaster elements. These resembled units right out of the Thirty Years War [between Catholics and Protestants at the beginning of the seventeenth century]. All of those various wagons and carts were now loaded and overloaded with miscellaneous cumbersome booty – bureaux, and poster beds, sinks and toilets, barrels, umbrellas, quilts, rugs, bicycles, ladders. There were live chickens, ducks, and geese in cages.'

On the first days after the surrender, many soldiers in Berlin sampled the victors' spoils and no woman was safe. Four decades later, a sophisticated lady summed this up in a phrase: 'And the Russians had their fun.' She looked away when she said it. A shiver of fear had run through Berlin, and nobody knows for how many women – young, old – it was justified; but a lot.

The Germans had fought a barbaric war in the East and now the barbarism had come back to them.

The German communist leader was called Walter Ulbricht, a dour Saxon with a Lenin goatee beard who'd spent the war in Moscow. Several of his comrades had disappeared in the night as Stalin carried out mini-purges but he had survived by unquestioning loyalty and tacking in the wind. One of the men who would accompany Ulbricht, Wolfgang Leonhard, has described it graphically:[3] 'At six o'clock in the morning of 30th April, 1945, a bus stopped in a little side street off Gorky Street, in front of the side entrance of the Hotel Lux. It was to take the ten members of the Ulbricht Group to the airport. We climbed aboard in silence.' They were driven to Moscow airport and flown to Germany in an American Douglas aeroplane.

On the drive into Berlin 'the scene was like a picture of hell – flaming ruins and starving people shambling about in tattered clothing; dazed German soldiers who seemed to have lost all idea of what was going on; Red Army soldiers singing exultantly, and often drunk'. The Berliners, waiting in long queues to get water from pumps, looked 'terribly tired, hungry, tense and demoralised'.

Ulbricht, by nature a bureaucrat and organiser, set about creating an administration, and it would include non-communists to make it seem fully representative. He told Leonhard: 'It's quite clear – it's got to look democratic, but we must have everything in our control.'

The communism which the Ulbricht group brought was based exactly on the Soviet model and, with Stalin watching in all his suspicion and malevolence, would not deviate from that regardless of whatever happened. Leonhard put it this way. 'When he [Ulbricht] came to laying down the current political line, he did it in a tone which permitted no contradictions.'

The Soviet model which Ulbricht brought was already completed in every fundamental, because Stalin had done that through the 1920s and 1930s. It controlled *everything*. Built onto that was a further factor. No East European communist government came to power with the legitimacy of winning free elections, and each was pathologically suspicious of its own citizens. The logic of this, too, would play itself out.

Germany was no stranger to communism: at one point before Hitler seized power the Communist Party had 100 seats in the Reichstag. Many working-class Berlin districts remained solidly communist all the way to Ulbricht arriving. They believed that communism was a scientific path to peace, prosperity and justice for all and represented the only sane future. They had experienced market economics and had their life savings destroyed in the financial crash of 1929 (when inflation became so intense that diners paid for their meals in restaurants course by course because the price was rising as they ate). They had experienced democracy and it had brought them Hitler. Communism looked very attractive as the women of Berlin formed chains and began to clear the mountains of rubble by passing bricks from hand to hand, and the trek back to civilisation began.

Germany was carved into four Zones: Russian, American, British and French; and, mirroring that, Berlin was carved into four Sectors. The Soviet Union took the east of the city (and its 1 million inhabitants), the Americans, British and French fashioning their Sectors out of the west (and its 2.2 million). In retrospect, and even knowing where the logic would go, it is extremely difficult to imagine how such an arrangement could have endured untroubled, because Berlin lay 130 kilometres into the Soviet Sector. Air corridors were formally agreed but land links were not. The autobahn from West Germany to West Berlin stretched like an umbilical cord and Stalin could sever it at any moment he wished.

The Americans, British and French should have taken over their Sectors as soon as the war ended but the Soviets stalled them and it didn't happen until 4 July 1945. A Kommandatura was set up by the four occupying powers and the official statement said 'the administration of the "Greater Berlin" area will be directed by an Inter-Allied Governing Authority . . . and will consist of four Commandants, each of whom will serve in rotation as Chief Commandant. They

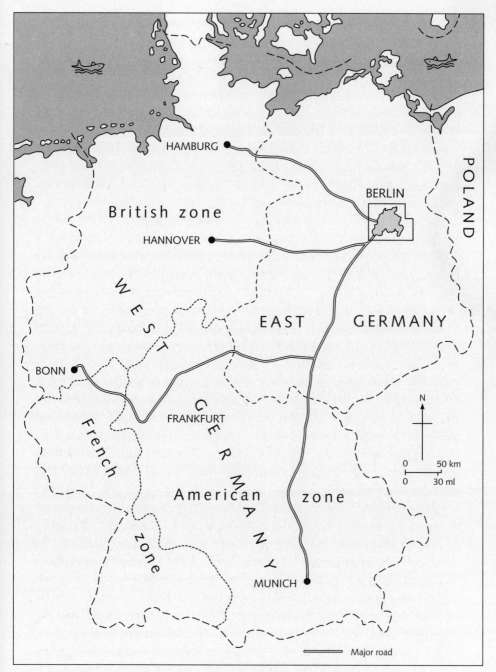

POLAND

HAMBURG

British zone

HANNOVER

BERLIN

W E S T

EAST   GERMANY

BONN

French

G E R M A N Y

FRANKFURT

N

0   50 km
0   30 ml

American   zone

zone

MUNICH

———— Major road

The division of Germany immediately after the war.

will be assisted by a technical staff which will supervise and control the activities of the local German organs [organisations].'

The population had other concerns. A 10-year-old called Peter Schultz, who would go on to become a distinguished radio reporter, lived with an uncle.[4] 'I remember destroyed houses and no traffic at all except the military. I remember a jeep with a very big black American sergeant and he lifted me onto it and he gave me American-Canadian white bread. This is all I can remember about West Berlin in 1945. It was important that I got white bread: American soldiers lived downstairs and they gave me a lot of bread, for me and for the whole family. So we had bread and – this was the most important thing – white bread. I will never forget that. I can still taste it.'

In April 1946 the Communist Party merged with the Social Democrats and became the SED, which would govern East Germany throughout its life, but there were elections that autumn and the SED did badly against the other surviving parties. In Greater Berlin they finished third with 19.8 per cent of the vote and, from this moment on, would never allow another free election in the area under their jurisdiction. There would be further elections, however, on 18 March – 1990.

In retrospect, the Berlin Agreement carried too many anomalies and too many practical difficulties, heightened when the political differences between the Soviet Union and the Allies reasserted themselves as the warmth of shared purpose – defeating Hitler – iced over. That Berlin was an island deep inside the Soviet Sector made it a nerve centre between what would become NATO in the west and the Warsaw Pact in the east.

R.J. Crampton sums it up neatly:

By 1947 the British and American Zones had separated almost entirely from the Soviet and in March of that year the division of Europe into two hostile blocs became much more rapidly focused. The communists left the governing coalitions of France and Italy, the Truman doctrine warned against communist attempts to expand into Greece, and in the summer the Soviets insisted that the east European states should not take Marshall Aid. In May 1948 the new currency introduced into the three western zones of Germany provoked the Soviet blockade of Berlin and the Berlin airlift.[5]

To pass across this terrain citing the steps is all too tempting, but it misses the human element entirely. A British Lieutenant-Colonel, W. Byford-Jones, visited the city in 1947 and wrote:

Epidemics were rampant. The water supply was polluted – there were 521 major breaks in pipes of over 21 inches in the British Sector alone, and 80 per cent of the sewage was not reaching the sewage works. All but one of the 44 hospitals in the British Sector were badly damaged, and the 5,817 beds available were all filled, with long waiting lists. There were no medical supplies, not even anaesthetics, heart stimulants, or sulphonamides. Food was poor and at starvation level. . . .[6]

Bodo Radtke, a Berliner who was to become a leading East German journalist, says that 'it wasn't until 1948 that you felt things were getting back to normal. Every day you saw or heard something: one day, two U-bahn stations are open again, *very good*, then three stations, then the bridge over the river Spree is open, *oh very good*.'[7]

On 20 March 1948, the Soviet delegates walked out of the Allied Control Council and never went back. They were unhappy at how Marshall Aid was affecting Soviet influence throughout Germany and, in an effort to force the Allies from West Berlin, Stalin threatened to sever the umbilical cord: from 1 April road, rail and canal traffic was hindered crossing the Soviet Zone to West Berlin. On 18 June, to Stalin's fury, the west replaced the worthless Reichsmark with the new Deutschmark. Almost immediately it brought an end to the black markets and stimulated industry.

The British and principally the American air forces were able to sustain West Berlin by an astonishing airlift which lasted until May 1949. The Allied pilots, some of whom had been bombing the city barely four years earlier, were now keeping it alive. Enemies were becoming friends.

From Moscow, the perspective was very different. The Soviet Union had been invaded by Hitler in 1941 and almost torn apart by cruelty on a scale unimaginable. It may be that 20 million people died in the Soviet Union: Stalin, and all his successors up to Mikhail Gorbachev, regarded their primary duty as making sure that this never happened again. Stalin constructed a buffer zone of states – Romania, Bulgaria, Hungary, Czechoslovakia and Poland – between the motherland and Germany; and would go further.

That same May in 1949, the Federal Republic of Germany (FRG), embracing the American, British and French Zones, was born, but the Four Power status of Berlin remained unaltered. In October, the Soviet Zone became the German Democratic Republic (GDR), so that now two German states, both insisting they were sovereign, faced each other. The GDR government, however, claimed that East

Berlin was their capital and called it simply Berlin. To them, West Berlin was *Berlin (West)* or variations of that, a severed limb at first then eventually left blank on their maps: a dead limb.

From Moscow, the Deutschmark, Marshall Aid and possible FRG rearmament represented great danger. Compounding that, Stalin demanded reparations from the Germans and made the East pay them. He stripped his zone of perhaps 26 per cent of its industry, dismantling it and shipping it to the Soviet Union. In May and June 1945, about 460 Berlin enterprises were 'completely dismantled and transferred'.[8] (Reparations, worth a total of 34.7 billion marks at 1944 prices were paid until 1953. It was a crippling disadvantage to the East just when the FRG's economy was racing.)

The postwar misery of Berlin could be expressed by many witnesses. One of them, Jacqueline Burkhardt, came to the city 'in 1949. I was born in Düsseldorf where my mother came from but my father was from Berlin. In my grandfather's will he left my father a big old apartment house in Schöneburg and we came to live in it. I was nine. Berlin was totally flat. I saw absolutely nothing here. It was total devastation, absolutely *down*. There were no cars, only military vehicles. Berlin had nothing to sell. There was nothing to eat. I was very small and always hungry – you couldn't buy food. I remember in the house was an old woman who had a ration card which got her extra rations and extra bread. For many weeks I ate the crust of the bread because this old woman had bad teeth and couldn't eat it. I lived on that and water. It was a horrible time. Then German marks were introduced and it was a chance to start anew.'

A flow of refugees began from East to West, some political and some economic. (For an explanation of the use of capital letters for East and West, please see the introduction to the Notes at the end of the book.) The total ran at over 2,000 a week in 1949, rising to 4,000 in 1950, dropping slightly in 1951 and 1952 then reaching 6,000 in 1953, when Stalin died and workers in East Berlin rose up over an increase in the work norms. That 'insurrection' had to be put down by Soviet tanks and for a moment the GDR's survival hung in the balance. It made Ulbricht's government even more pathologically suspicious of its own citizens.

By the time Nikita Khrushchev came to power the refugee flow had become self-generating. Professional, educated, trained people – the builders of the future – were leaving and their absence made conditions worse, and the flow increased. The East looked, and was, threadbare, the West looked, and was, increasingly affluent. *Berlin*

(West) beckoned magically from the far end of the street, across the park, a stop on the S-bahn or U-bahn. In Bernauer Strasse, you just opened your front door.

Because the city was under Four Power control, and open, whatever the GDR said, East Germans could make their way to the refugee centre in Marienfelde, a southern suburb of West Berlin relatively unhindered. From there they were flown to the FRG. And they kept on coming: 5,000 a week through 1955, 1956 and 1957. Despite that, Bodo Radtke says, 'this was the happiest time. You could see construction everywhere, apartment blocks going up for people to live in.'

The act of having fled remained sensitive for decades afterwards. The story of a man who would only describe himself as Mateus ('that should be enough') might be seen as typical.[9] His father had worked in the southern GDR town of Carl Zeiss Jena and 'in 1955 the family decided to move to the West. He took the chance of a congress in the West to stay there, and he organised a new life. My mother started to sell what could be sold discreetly, and sending parcels to the West. Then in 1956 we went over, my mother, my sister and I. My sister was five years older than me – I was seven. Mother did not explain to me what was happening but probably my sister knew. It was better that I didn't know, because my mother was afraid I'd start talking if I was asked questions about where we were going. We first travelled to my grandparents just north of Jena and from there to Berlin by train with two suitcases. She left these suitcases with relatives in East Berlin.

'I can't remember the crossing point. It seemed a sort of open border with guards who were on patrol and who controlled the passports of the people trying to go West. We simply walked across – people were moving across. My mother later told me the story: just before we crossed she slapped me, I started crying like hell and the Border Guard was pretty annoyed about this kid making all the noise. "Get him out of here!" So that went OK. She dropped us at American friends who had contact with my father and went back to get the suitcases. We learned later that she was arrested. We waited for two days for her and that was terrifying. My sister fully understood what had happened and that we might not see our mother again.

'She was in jail for the two days but then they had to release her because there was nothing they could actually do. They didn't have anything against her. Finally she made it but without the suitcases and the three of us flew out to Frankfurt on an old American military machine with metal seats like bath tubs. We avoided going into a refugee camp there because my father had arranged everything.'

The absurdities and anomalies of the future were largely unforeseen, but not everywhere. A young man called Kurt Behrendt,[10] just married in September 1957, needed an apartment. There were some in a scenic hamlet called Steinstücken, in the south of West Berlin not far from Potsdam and bordering Babelsberg, which had been the centre of German film-making before the war and was now in the East. He didn't know Steinstücken, he didn't know Babelsberg and he didn't much mind because an apartment was an apartment. 'I came on the day the Soviets sent up the first satellite: 4 October 1957.'

Although older residents naturally had family and friends in Babelsberg, Behrendt found himself living in what was now an enclave. 'It was difficult because, since the political division of Berlin in 1945, they argued whether it belonged to the East or the West. Then they recognised that it belonged to the West but one of the difficulties was getting to it. You came over a bridge which, prior to 1945, belonged to Potsdam but after 1945 belonged to the GDR. So you had to come through the GDR and only residents were allowed to do that. There wasn't even a street, only a path through the forest. You could get through by car but it was so narrow that if two cars met one had to pull onto the side. The school was in Wannsee [near a lake] and the children went along this path to the bridge and took the bus there. A little later the community had a school bus and my wife Helga drove it.'

The absurdities and anomalies would revisit Behrendt, becoming more serious each time.

In 1958 the refugees came at 4,000 a week, and in 1959 at 3,000. The overall total in 1959 stood at 143,917, of which 90,862 had passed through West Berlin and the rest from the GDR to the FRG. In 1960 the refugees came at 4,000 a week with a record 16,500 in May. The overall total stood at 199,188, of which 152,291 had passed through West Berlin.

This was the equivalent of losing a town a year, and no small country could survive it for long. Ulbricht saw this as clearly as everybody else and exhorted Khrushchev to staunch the flow. Khrushchev made several attempts to force the Allies out of West Berlin, threatening to sign a unilateral treaty with the East German government – but that would mean unilaterally ending the Four Power Agreement, and unilateralism was extremely problematical in a nervy, nuclear era.

And still the refugees came. After processing, most sat huddled shoulder to shoulder on mattresses in the centre at Marienfelde. Its interior was wide like an aircraft hanger, the children cradling their heads in their arms, already asleep. The women gazed ahead unseeing. Here and there a hand comforted a child, smoothing its hair in timeless rippling motions of warmth and reassurance. That masked anxiety. The Eastern Railway Police and Peoples' Police searched West-bound trains heavily now. Anyone with luggage might be hauled off, and any obvious family travelling together – father, mother, children – might be hauled off, too.

Friedrichstrasse station,[11] which itself would become an absurdity and an anomaly, was the last stop before the West. Twelve policemen tried to check all the compartments as each train stopped but even on Saturdays, when the trains were more lightly filled, they struggled to check them all. Getting across became a matter of luck, chance, ill-luck, averting your gaze from a policeman's glance, keeping your nerve, looking innocent, literally sitting tight.

Some families took precautions and split up, the father going with a child one day, the mother following the next, perhaps alone – less suggestive like that – or perhaps with another child. Some left their suitcases behind, as the mother of Mateus had done, and went back to retrieve them only when the children were safely delivered to the West.

In January 1961 John Kennedy was sworn in as President of the USA and six months later he met Khrushchev in Vienna. In the background and far away, the mute, anxious, exhausted refugees still flowed in at 4,000 a week and Khrushchev's aides were joking that 'soon there will be nobody left in the GDR except for Ulbricht and his mistress'.[12] In addition, the Soviets were concerned that their economic assistance to the GDR would 'end up in the pockets' of the Westerners because the Deutschmark had so much more purchasing power than the GDR's Ostmark.

At Vienna, Khrushchev went unilateral. Unless the Allies agreed to a German peace treaty within six months he would sign a treaty with the GDR 'normalising' the situation in Berlin. The Allied troops would have to go and West Berlin would become a free city with control of all access, including the air corridors, passing to the GDR.

'Mr. Khrushchev left no doubt as to his "irrevocable" determination to conclude a separate treaty with the GDR, with all attendant consequences for the west as already threatened. President Kennedy said the United States would regard any violation of vital rights of access and any encroachment on West Berlin as a breach of US rights and interests.'[13]

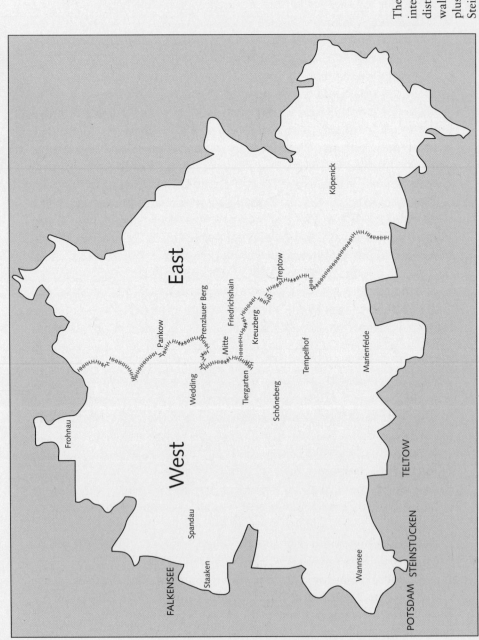

The bigger picture of interlocking Berlin: some of the districts on both sides of the wall and three Eastern towns, plus the Western enclave of Steinstücken.

Frank Cash, who worked for the US State Department's Berlin Task Force, says[14]:

> I think Ulbricht pushed Khrushchev and Ulbricht was right because they were haemorrhaging with the refugee flow: all of these people who were coming out were those that he needed most, the young, active, bright engineers and professional people and he really had to stop it in some way. I also had the feeling, having attended the Vienna summit, that Kennedy really was pleading with Khrushchev to help him find a way out. I think that that was *Khrushchev's* assessment of Kennedy and, OK, he – Khrushchev – could go ahead with a wall.
>
> There's another thing that emerged from the Vienna meeting. Berlin came up [on the agenda] and the White House made much of the fact that the Allied response to Khrushchev's demands took 45 days to appear. What actually happened – and I know this very well – was: McGeorge Bundy [Kennedy's National Security Adviser] asked if we could prepare a policy and we did but when we rang the White House they said 'what document?' They'd lost it, so ten of the 45 days were really due to the White House. I'm not sure if Khrushchev took the delay as a sign of weakness.
>
> We also looked back to other Soviet demands and our responses, and this was not an undue amount of time. All of Khrushchev's demands were a rehash of earlier demands and there was nothing new in it so we could go back to previous responses which had been agreed within the US government and say 'well, here's this point and here's our response'. But you want to get an answer out quickly. If you've got responses which have been previously cleared by the US government, the British and French, then you're going to have very little problem getting it cleared again and that's what we did.
>
> I think the comment to our response from the White House, when it finally arrived, contained only one new idea – submission to the International Court of Justice of Berlin's rights – and from that point the answer as it went out was essentially the one we had submitted three or four days after we got the original request.

Did Khrushchev read much into this delay? Nobody knows.

From Sunday 4 June 1961, when the Vienna Summit broke up in bitter disarray, the logic became more insistent and the steps were closer, were taken more quickly and were moving towards an abyss. Even now, in retrospect, when the consequences of the logic should be clear, it is all but impossible to evaluate which of these steps increased the sense of crisis more. They have a cumulative feel to them, a sense of something very powerful in play.

When Kennedy returned to the United States two days after Vienna he made a television and radio address: 'Our most serious discussions dealt with Germany and Berlin. I made it clear to Mr. Khrushchev that the security of Western Europe, and with it our own security, is intimately interlinked with our presence in and our rights of access to Berlin, that these rights are based on legal foundation and not on sufferance, and that we are determined to maintain these rights at all cost and thus to stand by our commitments to the people of West Berlin and to guarantee their right to determine their own future.'

The flow of refugees rose to over 4,000 that first week after Vienna.

The Secretary of State, Dean Rusk, said[15] that 'an attack on West Berlin would have moved rather quickly to a nuclear situation. Yes, I really think that. It was part of the Berlin planning all along, particularly since Khrushchev had given the president an ultimatum on Berlin at Vienna. So the British, the French and ourselves as well as the West Germans put our heads together to work out contingency plans and they were based on a gradual upping of the ante depending on the East German and Russian reaction. Kennedy had explained to Khrushchev that we could not accept an attack on West Berlin and, as a matter of fact, at one point during the conference Khrushchev said he was going to do *this* about Berlin and do *that* about Berlin and Kennedy said "there will be war. It's going to be a very cold winter." It was in the forefront of my mind that there was nothing we ought to try and do about East Berlin but any infringement into West Berlin would have set in motion the contingency plans.'

After Vienna, Khrushchev accepted Ulbricht's proposal that the Warsaw Pact countries should meet in Moscow as soon as practical.

The flow rose slightly above 4,000 in the second week.

On Saturday 10 June[16] Yuli Kvitsinsky, an attaché in the Soviet Embassy in East Berlin, 'learned in a meeting with E. Huttner of the East German Foreign Ministry's department on the Soviet Union that many in the East German leadership felt that it was "high time, at last, to sign a peace treaty and on that basis resolve the West Berlin issue. This measure is connected with a certain risk, but there is even more risk in the further delay of the resolution of the issue, since any delay assists the growth of militarism in West Germany which increases the danger of a world war. Thus, the danger of conflict in connection with the conclusion of a treaty with the GDR is balanced by the other danger. In this connection . . . Comrade

P. Florin, chairman of the SED CC International Relations Department, said that further dragging out the signing of a peace is a
crime." It was also assumed that at some point "the sectoral border
in Berlin would be closed."'

When Hope M. Harrison [see note 15] asked Kvitsinsky about
this in an interview, he said: 'There was not then on our part a real
readiness to conclude a [general overall] peace treaty with Germany.
We were not impatient. But the GDR was impatient and in a weaker
situation and Ulbricht used strong propaganda for a peace treaty.'

On Monday 15 June, Ulbricht called a press conference – itself
highly unusual – at the House of Ministries (in another life it had
been the headquarters of Hermann Goering's Luftwaffe) and, during
it, restated the position outlined by Khrushchev's ultimatum. Anna-
marie Doherr, a journalist of the western *Frankfurter Rundschau*,
asked 'Does the formation of a Free City in your opinion mean that
the state boundary will be erected at the Brandenburg Gate?'

'I understand by your question,' Ulbricht replied, 'that there are
men in West Germany who wish that we [would] mobilise the
construction workers of the GDR in order to build a wall. I don't
know of any such intention. The construction workers of our
country are principally occupied with home building and their
strength is completely consumed by this task. Nobody has the
intention of building a wall.'

Why Ulbricht said this is not known. One theory suggests that he
was simply telling the truth as he perceived it at the time, another
that he must have understood the effect his words would carry
within the GDR, particularly when the press conference was extensively reported in Eastern newspapers and on Eastern television.
Ordinary people, accustomed to reading the inner meanings of
doublespeak, would assume he was going to build a wall – provoking
a rush to Marienfelde. That would force Khrushchev's hand because
Khrushchev could not afford to let the GDR die.

On Wednesday 28 June, a senior GDR International Department
official returned from Moscow and told Ulbricht that the Soviet
Presidium would discuss the request for the Warsaw Pact meeting on
the following day. The steps within the logic were very short now.

In the third and fourth weeks of June the flow of refugees
continued at over 4,000 and by the month's end, only halfway
through the year, the overall total had reached 103,159, with 49.6
per cent under the age of 25. The future itself was flowing away.

Former Soviet diplomat Yuli Kvitsinsky wrote in his memoirs[17] at
the end of June or the beginning of July that Ulbricht invited him

and Soviet Ambassador Mikhail Pervukhin to his country house. There Ulbricht told Pervukhin to inform Khrushchev that 'if the present situation of open borders remains, collapse is inevitable' and that 'he refuses all responsibility for what would then happen. He could not guarantee that he could keep the situation under control this time [the haunting of the 1953 uprising].' Kvitsinsky is not more specific about when this took place but notes that after it nothing seemed to change.

Then, according to Hope M. Harrison, a political scientist who has researched this period exhaustively, 'one day' Pervukhin told Kvitsinsky to find Ulbricht immediately and bring him to Pervukhin. Pervukhin informed Ulbricht that Khrushchev had agreed to close the border and that Ulbricht should begin preparations in great secrecy. The operation was to be executed very quickly so as to be a complete surprise to the West. 'Ulbricht immediately went into great detail about what must be done. He said that the only way to close the entire border quickly was to use barbed wire and fencing. He also said that the U-bahn and S-bahn to West Berlin must be stopped and that a glass wall should be put up at the main Friedrichstrasse train station so that East Berliners using the metro could not change over to the train to West Berlin. Kvitsinsky noticed that Pervukhin was quite surprised at how much Ulbricht had already thought through these details.'

On Monday 3 July, Ulbricht spoke to the 13th Assembly of the SED. He said a peace treaty was imminent and assured the comrades that Khrushchev would act before the FRG had nuclear weapons. He outlined how action would be taken in Berlin against the so-called border-crossers: people who lived in one sector but profited by working in the other.

Next day, Pervukhin submitted a detailed sixteen-page report to Andrei Gromyko, the Soviet Union's Minister of Foreign Affairs, with his analysis of what signing a peace treaty with the GDR would bring. He wrote of 'the establishment of a regime over the movement of population' between the two halves of Berlin and felt 'it would be better at first not to close the border, since this would be difficult technically and politically'.[18]

The total that week was 4,000 again.

On Friday 7 July, Erich Mielke – head of the GDR secret service (the Stasi) – told his senior officials he was ordering immediate preparations so that 'operative measures can be carried out at a certain time according to a united plan' and demanded 'a strengthening of security of the western state border and ring around Berlin'.[19]

On Saturday 8 July, Khrushchev spoke at a military academy and said the demobilisation of Soviet armed forces had been halted. That second week the flow rose to 8,000.

On Saturday 15 July, an unsigned report to Ulbricht spoke of how, after the writer of the report had had conversations in Moscow, 'we should especially expect to deal with questions about West Berlin' at the Warsaw Pact meeting, now scheduled from 3 to 5 August.

Lutz Stolz and his fiancée Uta lived in East Berlin but went to visit Uta's aunt in the Black Forest. 'At this time you had to apply for an interzonal passport so I went to the authorities and applied for Lutz and myself,' Uta says. 'First, they only gave me a passport and wouldn't allow him to go. I applied a second time and, although I really don't know why, I succeeded. I remember the day well. I went along the little side street jumping up and down the kerb with joy waving the passport in my hand and saying "we can both go, we can both go".

'We went by train to Stuttgart where our relatives were waiting for us and they took us to their little village, Rohrdorf, a very romantic place in the mountains.' This happy, almost idyllic, time would haunt the couple. 'We had our work, our parents, the houses of our family all in the GDR, and the houses, even in the GDR, were worth something. We can never say whether we'd have stayed if we'd known. My parents-in-law could have sold up in the GDR and come as well, everything would have been done fast – but how could we know then? Would we really have stayed in the little village in the mountains, leaving behind the security of our family? Would we really have dared? When we were leaving we told my aunt and uncle that we'd try and visit them again the following year. It never occurred to us that . . .'

On Monday 17 July, the three Western Allies rejected Khrushchev's ultimatum to change the status of Berlin. That third week the flow rose to 9,000.

On Saturday 22 July, a secret telegram from the State Department in Washington went out to the London, Paris and Moscow Embassies as well as the US Embassy in Bonn and to Berlin. It was arranged in nine numbered paragraphs, phrased in a sort of cabalese, and it explored possibilities. It said that 'if refugee flood continues' the GDR could 'tighten controls over travel from Soviet Zone to East Berlin or by severely restricting travel from East to West Berlin', and added: 'We believe Soviets watching situation even more closely than we, since they are sitting on top volcano. Continued refugee flood could . . . tip balance towards restrictive measures.'

The telegram also contained a great truth: 'If GDR tightens travel controls between Soviet Zone and West Berlin there is not much US could do, other than advertise facts. If GDR should restrict travel within Berlin, US would favour counter-measures' – including economic.

Lutz Stolz and Uta came back from Rohrdorf. 'When I went to the authorities to get our identity cards back – we had had to leave them before our departure – I noticed that they were smiling in a strange way when they handed them over,' she says. 'It was like a scornful smile on their lips as if they were thinking: *these stupid people, if only they knew . . .*'

The German Protestant Church Synod, due to be held in West Berlin from 19 to 23 July, was banned by the East Berlin chief of police.

On Tuesday 25 July, Kennedy spoke on American television. He defended the Allies' rights in West Berlin and stressed that any unilateral action against West Berlin would mean war with the United States, but made no mention of *East* Berlin, a deliberate nuance, perhaps, which Khrushchev would deduce as giving him a free hand there.

On Wednesday 26 July, Ulbricht sent to Moscow a summary of the speech he would be making at the Warsaw Pact meeting there nine days later. He proposed creating a state border between East and West Berlin.

On Sunday 30 July, Senator William Fulbright, chairman of the Committee on Foreign Relations, said publicly that he could not understand why the East Germans were not closing the border, because they had every right to do it. Under the Four Power Agreement, the GDR had no rights like this, of course.[20] It may be, however, that Khrushchev and Ulbricht – who'd essentially spent the whole of their adult lives within totalitarianism – assumed Fulbright's words would have been sanctioned and were code for: do what you want in your own backyard.

Certainly Richard Smyser, a junior officer in the American Berlin Mission, thinks so. Smyser, an American born in Vienna (his father was a diplomat) had spent part of his childhood – 1939–41 – in Berlin and returned in 1960 to join the Mission. Smyser says that Khrushchev and Ulbricht 'took the Fulbright speech as the go-ahead. The Russians have told me that Ulbricht expected no military response.'[21]

That fourth week the flow fell slightly, to 8,000, but the total for the month reached 30,415, of which 51.4 per cent were under the age of 25. On 2 August alone the total was 1,322.

Many astute judges, particularly in the CIA and the State Department, had contemplated a division of the city as an abstract proposition and concluded that in practical terms it could not be done. At least one Stasi general, Markus Wolf – famed, fabled and feared spymaster – reached the same conclusion as he pondered dividing the East's 1,071,775 from the West's 2,207,984.

In the city, the halves interlocked intimately as they had for centuries and to prise them apart some sort of barrier would have to run for 28½ miles. From the north, and beginning in countryside, it would go westwards in a triangle at the first of the housing, follow a railway track with houses on both sides for 3 miles and embrace parallel railway tracks, one of them from the West but looping inside the line; then turn at a right angle into Bernauer Strasse; double back over the Western U-bahn line beneath East Berlin, follow a narrow canal bank and bisect a bridge, run directly behind the Reichstag to the Brandenburg Gate and on to the broad expanse of Potsdamer Platz. It would then corkscrew left and bisect five streets, zigzag across seven more streets until it reached twin, curved roads with sunken gardens between them; and turn to follow the banks of the Spree to the district of Treptow, itself a maze. There the barrier would turn westward, bisecting half a dozen streets. . . .

To seal the GDR countryside looping round West Berlin, the barrier would have to run 22.30 miles through residential areas, 10.56 miles through industrial areas, 18.63 miles through woods, 14.90 miles through rivers, lakes and canals, and 34.15 miles along railway embankments, through fields and marshes.

Could such a thing really be done?

George Bailey, a veteran American journalist who knew Germany intimately, wrote a feature in a magazine called *The Reporter* in which he said that the Soviet Union and 'its East German minions' have 'finally drawn the ultimate conclusion that the only way to stop the refugees is to seal off both East Berlin and the Soviet Zone by total physical security measures'. He foresaw 'searchlight and machine gun towers, barbed wire, and police dog patrols. Technically this is feasible.'[22] The feature was billed as 'The Disappearing Satellite' and, in Bailey's words, 'attracted a good deal of attention'.

One account[23] says Ulbricht flew to Moscow on the last day of July and was informed by Khrushchev that the peace treaty was not going to be signed yet but he could close the border. Ulbricht wanted to close the air corridors, too, which would prevent the refugees who did reach Marienfelde from flying on to West Germany, but Khrushchev weighed up the risks and said no. Ulbricht suggested building a wall around West Berlin *on East German territory* and Khrushchev said he would put that to the Warsaw Pact meeting. (For reasons of security, he cannot have done this in open session; rather, he sounded out various members in private.)

On Thursday 3 August, Khrushchev opened the meeting by accusing the 'Western powers' of receiving 'our proposal for a peace treaty with bayonets' and added: 'Kennedy essentially threatened us with war if we implement measures for liquidating the occupation regime in West Berlin.' He called for the meeting to work out detailed plans and gave the floor to Ulbricht.

In great and laboured detail, Ulbricht moved through the whole situation and made his pitch: how the peace treaty must be signed without delay and how the 'whole socialist bloc' must be ready to risk confrontation to protect the GDR, although he made no mention of a wall.

At some stage on 3 August,[24] Khrushchev seems to have added a proviso to closing the border. Ulbricht must give an assurance that his government could deal with any civil unrest (the haunting of 1953 again). Ulbricht flew back to East Berlin on Friday 4 August and satisfied himself that such an assurance could be given. The *New York Herald Tribune* prepared a front-page story headed ULBRICHT SAID TO SEEK ASSENT BY KHRUSHCHEV TO CLOSE BERLIN BORDER.

Their reporter Gaston Coblentz wrote that 'Ulbricht's move was . . . revealed by well-informed quarters.' He also noted: 'In addition to the highly reliable report of Mr Ulbricht's proposal to Mr Khrushchev, unconfirmed information said that he has made a secret flight to Moscow to put his plan before the Soviet leader.'[25]

That same Friday, the East Berlin Magistrat ordered that any Easterners working in the West – the border-crossers – had to register and pay their rent and bills in Deutschmarks. The three Western commanding officers protested about this to the Soviet Commander. The number of refugees for the day was 1,155, making a total of 11,000 for the week. Flood tide was near.

Dean Rusk flew from Washington to Paris for a meeting with the Foreign Ministers of Britain, France and West Germany. Before he left he spent an hour with Kennedy at the White House and said: 'There is peace in Berlin and there is no need to disturb it.'

On Saturday 4 August, Coblentz was reporting: 'The East German persistent "no comment" reply to all inquiries about Mr Ulbricht's movements since he was last seen in East Berlin Monday strengthened the belief he has been out of the country on a secret trip to the Kremlin.'

Ulbricht, as it seems, returned to Moscow on Sunday 5 August and gave the assurances. Khrushchev said the border could be closed with barbed wire – which could, if necessary, be removed as quickly as it was set down – and ordered the wire to be laid 'not one millimetre further' than the lip of East Berlin territory. There would be no incursion into the West. Ulbricht returned to East Berlin and summoned Erich Honecker, a trusted aide, and told him to draw up plans in the most laboured secrecy.

The total flow for the weekend was 3,268.

On Monday 6 August the West's Foreign Ministers in Paris called on the Soviet Union to provide a 'reasonable basis' for negotiating on Berlin. The meeting ended next day in what has been described as an atmosphere of calm confidence although, as they were sitting down to dinner in the private dining-room at the Quai d'Orsay (the French Foreign Ministry), news came through from Moscow of a 90-minute television and radio address by Khrushchev, during which he said he might call up military reserves.

The background to the Paris meeting remains important. Dorothy Lightner, wife of Allan – the minister at the American Berlin Mission – remembers[26] that 'there was a meeting of the Foreign Ministers in Paris and the American ambassador, Walter Dowling, and Allan went there. Allan was to put in a plea for Berlin but they were given very short shrift. Nobody wanted to hear what they had to say. They wanted to tell them that the allies were not about to fight, bleed and die for the East Zone, so there was no question but that it was only about access. And once you know that, you can see that a policy had already been established. Allan was mad about that, yes. The decision perturbed him and it perturbed everybody in Berlin.'

John Ausland, who worked at the State Department on the Berlin Task Force, described how 'there is always tension between the State Department and the White House but this was the worst I have ever seen during my lifetime, and I've seen a number of examples – [John Foster] Dulles [who wanted to destroy communism] was pretty bad but it was nothing like the Kennedy situation. It was very hard to deal with people, and that went from top to bottom. That lessened as time went on.

'Part of the problem was the bureaucracy, which we overcame by organising the Berlin Task Force. When I returned to Washington in July of '61 from Australia I was shocked by the chaotic way business was being conducted – you know, people all over town were making decisions and not talking to each other. Right away I started talking with Martin Hillenbrand [of the State Department's

German desk] and Foy Kohler [Assistant Secretary of State] and I said "we have got to get this thing organised". I am a kind of compulsive person who likes to organise things. I wrote a draft directive to take care of that but Kohler did not want to put anything in writing at that time. One day, as they were going off to Paris for the Foreign Ministers' meeting he called me in and said "I want you to go up to the Operations Centre and establish a Task Force." That was the beginning of it.'

Norman Gelb[27] has written that 'this Operations Centre . . . was set up on the seventh floor of the State Department building, not far from Rusk's office. Among other things, it was to house a service special "task force" whenever one was organised for the purpose of gathering all pertinent facts bearing on a specific problem in foreign affairs and producing recommendations for action.'

The Berlin Task Force would consist of Kohler running it with Hillenbrand as his deputy, Frank Cash, Ausland, Arthur Day, David Klein, Jerry Holloway from the State Department, and [Wilbur] Bur Showalter, liaison officer to Assistant Secretary of Defence Paul Nitze.

On Tuesday 8 August, the flow reached 1,741, the next day 1,926.

Marshal Ivan Konev arrived from Moscow on Thursday 10 August to take command of all Soviet forces in the GDR and word of this spread. The *New York Herald Tribune* carried the story and recorded: 'The East German news agency ADN made the move known shortly before midnight and reported that Marshal Konev conferred in East Berlin earlier today [this Thursday] with . . . Ulbricht.'

In East Berlin there were hints that special measures against the refugees might be taken at a meeting of the GDR People's Parliament the next day. Ulbricht, visiting a cable-making factory, warned his own people about spreading hostile propaganda. 'We will not tolerate revanchist agitation,' he said. All day, communist organisations within the GDR sent the government 'petitions' demanding action against the refugee flow and the ADN pumped this out. The total on this Thursday, most queuing in grey, sodden rain was 1,709 and the next day rose to 1,532. It was Friday 11 August 1961.

The GDR Ministry of the Interior kept private statistics. Fifty-five members of the People's Police fled in 1959, sixty-one in 1960 and, an official report stated, 'this year up to now forty. It is a characteristic that the proportion of desertions is increasing.' Those who fled included all ranks from cadets to senior officers, some after fifteen years' service. Who knew who would be next, who could be guaranteed to stay? Within one more day the overall total of refugees would reach 16,167 so far in August. Taken all together, it was flood tide.

TWO

Saturday Night

The Germans are a busy people

Peter Glau,
Owner, Hotel Ahorn, Berlin

12 AUGUST 1961

The first-floor apartment combined home and office. If the neat, busy man sitting at the typewriter gazed from the window over the rooftops opposite he saw an overcast morning, the light southerly wind pushing and prodding folds of cloud; saw at almost eye level the trains grunting and grumbling along the elevated rail in the middle of the road. Schönhauser Allee, a main artery from the centre of East Berlin, stretched long and broad and, like so many roads, remained tattered and exhausted all these years after 1945. The façades of darkened pre-war buildings loomed, guarding their memories.

Adam Kellett-Long worked for Reuters, a global news agency and the only one to have a bureau in East Berlin. He'd taken up the post in March and the GDR government, questing for international recognition, granted him more than usual access to themselves. Reuters had a bureau in West Berlin and for East Berlin to get one implied, to them, a step in the recognition process. Ulbricht called Kellett-Long 'my little shadow' as a term of endearment.

The day before, the People's Parliament had met in their chamber (it looked like an opera house) and Kellett-Long covered the meeting: 'A resolution was passed in effect giving the government the authority to take any action necessary to stop West Berlin being used as a propaganda hotbed ensnaring socialists and so forth.' [1] On the way out, Kellett-Long ran into a contact, Horst Sindermann, a bespectacled senior politician with the air of a businessman, his straight, short hair thinning over the crown of his head. Kellett-Long asked what the resolution really meant and

Sindermann replied he couldn't say exactly 'but I would advise you not to leave Berlin this weekend'.

A newsman with the instincts of Kellett-Long didn't miss the possible significance, particularly since Konev's arrival.

Kellett-Long sat at his typewriter weighing up Sindermann's cryptic semi-sentence and, perhaps, subconsciously weighing up something else. After the Volkskammer meeting he called in to see 'the chap who used to get our coal and all our supplies from the Diplomatic Service Bureau. He was a member of the Factory Fighting Groups [2] and he wore his uniform, he had his kit and his rifle.' Kellett-Long wondered why and the man said 'Oh, we are going off on an exercise this weekend.' The man didn't know where and, anyway, Kellett-Long thought, 'so what?' – but he'd never seen the man in his uniform before, and wearing it now seemed vaguely peculiar.

Kellett-Long reasoned that any steps to staunch the refugee flow would probably be taken during a weekend, when the tempo of the city was relaxed and most workers were at home. All else aside, that made a repetition of 1953 less likely. He composed a day-lead, standard procedure for Reuters correspondents. Usually a day-lead represented a synopsis of any situation overnight and a careful anticipation of what the day might bring. He wrote: 'Berlin is this weekend holding its breath for dramatic measures.' As he typed the words he understood 'I was sticking my neck out a hell of a long way but I trusted Sindermann.' The day-lead finished, he telexed it to London via the Reuters bureau in Bonn. London automatically processed it and fed it to subscribers all over the world.

The day-lead created an immediate effect. Reuters' News Editor in Bonn travelled to Berlin, arriving during the afternoon, and said 'We're right out on a limb, you'd better justify this.' Kellett-Long couldn't, because he'd constructed what he wrote on a tip and a hunch.

A news agency is, by definition, different to a newspaper. News agencies supply all branches of the media and are expected to provide probity, factual reporting and circumspection. Newspapers can write floral prose of their own and speculate as much as they want. Agency copy, as it is known, is used as a bedrock. Certainly newspapers from Australia to Singapore, Cape Town to Stockholm, Boston to Brazil would assume Kellet-Long's day-lead was based on hard fact – or he wouldn't have filed it. This is certainly what radio stations would have assumed, and broadcast it on the strength of that. If Kellett-Long had got this wrong, the error would be compounded by the fact that it was, quite literally, of global proportions.

The temperature climbed toward 20 degrees, and people took their leisure and their pleasure in the most ordinary way on this summer weekend which seemed so like any other. Heinz Sachsenweger, who worked in a railway factory, spent agreeable hours with his wife and son at his brother-in-law's at Brandenburg, a solid town 50 kilometres away. Journalist Bodo Radtke and his wife relaxed in a chalet south of the city. Diana Loeser, a believer in communism from England, had travelled to Birmingham to see her family. Hagen Koch spent a day off relaxing with his wife. Erhard Schimke, a policeman who drove radio cars, spent a day off relaxing, too. None knew each other but they had something in common. All resided in East Berlin.

And still the refugees came. As they reached Marienfelde a flat, nasal female voice counted them in over loudspeakers: '763 . . . 764 . . . 765 . . .'

Under the weight of these numbers Heinrich Albertz, town hall Chief of Staff to West Berlin Mayor, Willy Brandt, made a significant and worried telephone call. He rang George Muller, deputy political adviser at the American Mission, and asked if the US Army could provide field rations.

'When I got the call for food,' Muller says,[3] 'it contributed to the sense of crisis but we regarded our primary concern as safeguarding West Berlin and Allied access to it, so in a way the call was incidental to my other concerns. I did what I could to get food because the Reception Centre just couldn't handle the traffic. The refugees weren't allowed to eat in the dining halls until they'd been processed and with this stream of them the processing lines became so long people starved waiting. Part of Albertz's problem was to feed the people in line, especially the children.'

The nasal voice counted the refugees dispassionately in and the weight of numbers increased to a point where they overflowed into tents outside. Some wandered the centre's gardens taking the air, a father with a daughter hoisted over his shoulders walking and walking, the daughter constantly asking, 'When is Mummy coming?' To allay suspicion, she must have been travelling there by another route and was out there somewhere.

The dilemma in the West – of sensing that the East would have to respond to the situation but being unable to predict what that response might be – was a deep one. The CIA had seventy intelligence officers in their Berlin base. Donald Morris, who worked there from 1958 to 1963, has summed it up precisely:[4] 'We all knew something was going to happen. The border was too loose, there was a population drainage, a haemorrhage, from East Germany coming into the West. All of a sudden this haemorrhage assumed *arterial* proportions. Something of a panic had set in, there were 2,000 refugees on a Monday, 4,000 on Tuesday, 6,000 on Wednesday. Ulbricht went to Moscow and got permission to lower the boom – I'm not using the wall – came back and did lower the boom. We knew the boom was about to fall, we didn't realise it was going to take the form of a physical wall surrounding West Berlin – but that is the form it took.'

To predict the building of the wall, 'you would have had to have had one of the top three men in the East German government to get even twenty-four hours' warning that a wall was going up. We had requirements to get agents in practically every sector of the eastern bloc, [but] to tell us that the logistical arrangements were being made would have involved recruiting several people in masonry supply and truck services. They probably weren't on the list. . . .'

Tom Polgar, a CIA man in Germany from 1947 to 1961, puts this into a broader perspective:[5] 'The United States government as a whole was not alerted to the possibility that something drastic was going to happen in Berlin which required an immediate American counter-action one way or another, whether physical or just oral [and] political. So in that sense it was certainly an intelligence failure but I think we have to be careful where we want to pinpoint the blame.'

To reinforce this, a British author – Terence Prittie – quotes Robert Lochner, head of the United States-sponsored radio network in West Berlin (RIAS), as saying that no United States official had the faintest idea that a wall was about to be built through the middle of the city and adds an intriguing postscript of his own. On 30 July, Prittie had written to a 'very senior member of the British Intelligence Staff in Berlin' to voice concerns about a 'report that there was considerable movement on roads leading into East Berlin . . . mainly of goods packed in large lorries'. As a journalist, Prittie wanted to know if the report had any significance. The reply, written on 3 August, had reached Prittie on the 10th and assured him that there was nothing to worry about. The writer said 'I believe the present crisis will end in anti-climax after the [upcoming] Federal elections.'[6]

Lutz Stolz, the trainee civil engineer who'd been with his fiancée Uta to the Black Forest, fully intended to go across, but tomorrow. Lutz Stolz savoured the prospect of a football match. Although he and half the team lived in East Berlin the side was based in the West. They scarcely thought of the difference. Which city team would? Stolz tried never to miss a match in the crowded fixture list – matches were on Tuesdays, Thursdays and Sundays. The rendezvous for all eleven had been designated the most convenient place, the Lehrter station, first stop in the West after Friedrichstrasse in the East.

Willy Brandt was campaigning during the Federal elections and he had a party of people with him, including Klaus Schultz, his campaign manager. In the market square at Nuremburg, Brandt made a speech laden with emotion and foreboding which strayed from ordinary electioneering. He demanded a plebiscite for all Germans and added: 'Tonight refugee number 17,000 of the month will arrive in Berlin. For the first time we shall have taken in 2,500 refugees in twenty-four hours. Why are these people coming? The answer to this question is that the Soviet Union is preparing an attack against our people, the seriousness of which is apparent only to a few. The people in East Germany are afraid that the meshes of the Iron Curtain will be cemented shut. They are agonisingly worried that they might be forgotten, sacrificed on the altar of indifference and lost opportunities.'

Brandt had been toiling hard in this election – more than 500 speeches since May – and had hired two maroon railway carriages (a sleeper and a lounge car) as mobile headquarters. That evening they would be hitched to the Munich–Kiel express because Brandt's next destination was Kiel.

In the northern city of Lübeck, Chancellor Konrad Adenauer, also electioneering, appealed to East Germans not to panic and stampede, before returning to his home on the banks of the Rhine.

At 4.00 p.m., Ulbricht summoned Erich Honecker to the House of Ministers. A Politburo meeting had already been held in this building, Ulbricht chairing it. His level Saxon tones stroking the words, he gave a situation review and revealed the decision taken in Moscow. Reportedly no discussion took place and no dissenting voice rose. The fate of a city was sealed, and a decisive event of the century was enacted, in virtual silence.

Ulbricht signed an order and it assumed the authority of law. He instructed Honecker to enforce it. Self-doubt had been remote from either man for decades but it cannot be known if they suddenly felt it then. The Politburo meeting, the signing ceremony and the summoning of Honecker were simply a way of making the border sealing, already decided by Khrushchev, official. Since Honecker had previously been ordered to make preparations, what had just happened gave a cloak of legality and the sort of quasi-legitimacy GDR propagandists could wield like a sword in front of the cloak.

Even at this late moment the sealing was held tightly within a small circle of people. Some senior members of the Stasi did not know, Markus Wolf among them. 'At the risk of damaging my reputation as the man who really knew what was going on in East Germany, I have to confess that the building of the Berlin wall was as much a surprise to me as everyone else . . . I can only conclude that Erich Mielke, who handled some of the covert planning of the operation, kept this information from me out of malice.'[7]

The CIA, with their payroll of seventy, also did not know. The American Mission did not know. The West Berlin police did not know. And Wolf did not know.

However, the FRG security service, led by the spider-like Reinhard Gehlen, claimed to know at least the outline. 'Many items of information', Gehlen subsequently wrote,[8] 'showed that it would not be long before the communists had to take vigorous steps. Then we learned from a reliable source that the Russians had given Ulbricht a free hand so that only the date was left open to conjecture. We received and passed on further reports of an imminent sealing of the sector boundary, particularly within Berlin itself, and of the stockpiling of light materials suitable for the construction of barriers. We could not predict the actual date they would start. It was known only to a handful of top Party officials.'

At Hyannis Port on the Massachusetts shore in the USA, Kennedy rested at his summer house with family and personal friends. White House Press Secretary, Pierre Salinger, said no business visitors were expected. Kennedy spent part of the morning reading official papers brought overnight from Washington, and he received his daily intelligence briefing from his naval aide, Commander Tazewell Shepard. A time difference, of course, held the United States' east coast and Berlin apart: the United States would be constantly and inescapably six hours behind.

While Ulbricht and Honecker spoke, Kennedy savoured the prospect of the cruise he and his wife Jacqueline would take off Nantucket Sound at midday, their time, in the family cruiser the *Marlin*.

Honecker left the House of Ministers and was driven across East Berlin to the Police Headquarters, a tall, shorn, 1950s building behind the Alexanderplatz. He walked briskly in and along anonymous corridors. He'd taken over an office with secure communications during the week and laid the plans detail after detail. Now, shortly after 4.00 p.m., Honecker issued orders of his own, one to the Politburo member running the region from the Polish frontier to East Berlin, another to the Politburo candidate running the region which covered the arc round West Berlin, cumulatively a vice holding the whole city:

I ask you to arrange for the necessary measures to be taken on 13 August from 1.30 a.m. on as agreed. I will send the documents you already know about during the course of the evening. I enclose a draft of the alert order to the heads of operations.

With socialist greetings,
E. Honecker.

Instructions would spread out from this moment but still only at the highest, most secure and trusted level.

None of the 4 million Berliners heard the faintest whisper of a rumour, a single word of warning. Superficially the morning, afternoon and early evening of 12 August 1961 melted into another summer's day playing itself out in the innocence of ordinariness. The Reuters office secretary, Erdmute Greis-Behrendt, visited her aunt in West Berlin. Rudiger Hering, a factory worker who lived in the countryside, went to see his uncle and cousin in the West Berlin district of Spandau, a couple of stops away along the S-bahn. Why not?

Along the Ku-damm,[9] girls in light summer dresses oscillated past the pavement cafés where patrons from East and West sipped a beer or mountaineered through cakes and cream. Easterners bought subsidised tickets to see the latest American films.

A woman (who many years later still preferred anonymity) sat in a sunlit garden in the West raking over the future with her son, her daughter and a lifelong friend. She lived in an apartment in Treptow, just beyond the line to the East. Her son had been arrested a few days earlier, helping a friend push a hand-cart across. The Stasi took him and when they released him he looked haggard, complained they'd treated him without dignity and announced he was going West, which he did. Now they all tried to persuade the woman to stay here in the West, too. Her friend even offered to go over and get the woman's papers from her apartment, eliminating the risk of anything happening if she went back to get them herself.

If only it could have been so easy. The woman felt attached to her parents over there, attached to the apartment over there, her friends, the familiar haunts of a life. Her son suggested that grandpa and grandma could follow later and they'd be reunited. The woman said no, she'd go home. After all, she could nip across to see her son whenever she wanted.

Some fulfilled domestic duties. A woman from the homely Eastern hamlet of Muggelheim helped repaper her sister's apartment in the

West. If she'd time, she'd visit her mother nearby before going home. Her husband stayed in Muggelheim, gardening.

In a red-brick barracks south of Muggelheim, a manual typewriter clacked laboriously, its echo travelling down linoleum-laid corridors onto a parade ground fringed by lawns. A high, distempered boundary wall screened the barracks and almost concealed it. Pätz, a hamlet like Muggelheim, was hard to find even on a map, just a place down a country lane with a lake glimpsed through trees; quiet, rural, typical of so many hamlets beyond the tentacles of the city.

The typewriter clacked out (extract):

Command of the Border Police.
  Order No. 002/61
  Command Post Pätz
At X-hour + 30 minutes, an increased border defence has to be organised at the State border West to prohibit border violations in both directions and to avoid further provocation of the territory of the German Democratic Republic.

Staff officers are to be employed to control and instruct units about their tasks.

The heavy Border units are to be put on readiness for action and be prepared to move to trouble spots.

The greatest density of men and material is to assemble where the main flows of border trespassers take place and on the flanks of the border crossing points. In those sectors prone to provocation, camouflaged Border Police are to be installed. Motorised reserves are to be ready for back-up.

Political-ideological instruction is to be increased for all policemen, other ranks and officers by the Commanders and political units in conjunction with The Party.

It is to be ensured that all orders and instructions are obeyed correctly and conscientiously and the secrecy of all measures is maintained.

The reconnaissance units of the Border Police are to be given the task of identifying the enemy and his actions. All results are to be continually evaluated.

First situation report at X + 4 hours, further reports every six hours.

(Signed)
Peter, Colonel.[10]

Erich Peter commanded the three Border Police frontier forces, north, centre and south. X-hour remained unstated. The secrecy enveloped it. Further orders followed, some extremely specific: ninety-seven men, thirty-nine of them for construction, to go to the Friedrichstrasse crossing point and establish inter-state control. The ninety-seven gave a density of one man per square metre – the planning had been as specific as that.

Friedrichstrasse, a long street, remained battered and exhausted just like Schönhauser Allee. It was a backbone of East Berlin, stretching over the River Spree for half a mile due south to a crossroads, which was the sector boundary between East and West. The railway station which bore its name – a cold glasshouse of an arched roof, long platforms and long tiled corridors leading to them – was up near the Spree. Here twelve policemen searched the trains.

This Saturday afternoon, a cinema near the station showed *All Quiet on the Western Front*.

People boated and rowed on the lakes around Berlin; many walked in the woods, a favourite pastime; Rudiger Hering took coffee with his cousin and Erdmute Greis-Behrendt took coffee with her aunt.

Through these careless hours Adam Kellett-Long waited and waited. Reuters had the wire service of ADN, the official GDR Press Agency, and the ADN teleprinter chattered in his office, but it was normal traffic, nothing to justify the day-lead. The news editor from Bonn returned to his hotel in West Berlin and waited, too.

At the Police Headquarters a Lieutenant-General Schneider dictated a timetable and phrased it so that, step by step, it reached down in a pyramid:

7.00 p.m.: the summoning of leading Police chiefs to Room 5614 to be informed of the operation; **8.00**: a consultative meeting in the same room, sealed orders to be opened, senior officers to be briefed on specific tasks. Headquarters section heads ordered to meet in the room at **9.00** for instructions; **10.00**: the heads of special Police sections to be given instructions; **11.00**: officers running police stations to be told to attend the room at **12.00**.

It ended X + 30 minutes although X-hour remained unstated, the secrecy still enveloping it; X-hour would be added later, swiftly and by hand but, that aside, a timetable had been set out and a countdown had begun.

At 6.00 p.m. in Berlin, the city was sprucing itself up to take the pleasures of a Saturday night; it was noon in Hyannis Port, USA.

Under a hot sun, Kennedy and his family set off on the 52-foot *Marlin,* moving out into Nantucket Sound.

Around this time, in slightly scrawled writing, X-hour was added to the orders from Police Headquarters in Alexanderplatz: X-hour = 1.00 a.m., Sunday morning 13 August. That meant X + 30 would be 1.30 a.m.

The wallpapering complete, the woman from Muggelheim refused her sister's invitation to stay the night but she'd see her next week as usual. She travelled back to the apartment in the East, on the S-bahn through to Friedrichstrasse station, and noticed it was strangely quiet.

A West Berliner, Klaus-Peter Grohmann – like Lutz Stolz a football fanatic although not a player – wrestled with a common human problem. His mother-in-law, also a West Berliner, had visited and 'We wanted to get rid of her, we wanted her to go home.' Grohmann and his wife began yawning very deliberately but the mother-in-law didn't go.

Stolz himself had a two-room apartment in his parents' house in the East. His fiancée Uta lodged with Lutz's grandparents across the courtyard. 'Usually I stole away to see Lutz carefully so that his grandparents didn't notice. We were not married yet.' She crept across the courtyard and they made love, but 'since his bed was too small for both of us I went in to the other room to spend the night there'.[11]

Around 11.00 p.m., Kellett-Long took the Reuters office car, a reddish-orange Wartburg, and drove to the Ostbahnhof, the East Berlin station serving the south of the country.

I had a system whereby for a few West marks I could get an advance copy of *Neues Deutschland* [the official newspaper], which was useful if you suspected something was going to happen. All decrees and promulgations came out in *Neues Deutschland.* The paper didn't actually appear on the streets until the morning but they shipped off the provincial copies in the late evening, so in effect I got a first edition. I looked at the paper and to my horror – nothing. That really shook me. I was aware, however, of an awful lot of Railway Police at the station. They wore their black uniforms and the place swarmed with them. That was the only unusual thing. I reeled away from the station feeling a bit nervous and went back to the office thinking I'd write the day-lead for the morning.

Which, however he phrased it, would have to be an admission that he'd warned the world of dramatic measures and they hadn't happened.

Al Hemsing, who handled press relations for the American Mission, was at home.

Late in the evening I got a call from the European representative of *Readers' Digest* based in Paris but on a trip to Berlin. He called to sort of check in with me and see what was going on. He added that he'd been to the Brandenburg Gate, he'd noticed a lot of milling around and something seemed to be afoot. Then I had a call from the son of one of the big shots in Reuters who'd been assigned to their West Berlin bureau. He said he'd been across and seen far more than the normal number of People's Police around; he felt some kind of tension in the air and what did I know about it? I said I knew nothing. I had a dedicated (secure) phone to the Mission and each time I had these calls I reported it, which ordinarily I wouldn't have done. We kept a permanent 24-hour staff in this period and I'd tell the duty officer and ask him what he knew. Each time, the duty officer said, 'No, we don't have any reports.'[12]

The man from the *Readers' Digest* and the Reuters cub reporter experienced the very beginning – X-hour was now only 90 minutes away. What they'd glimpsed represented a discreet increase in police presence but not enough to announce the operation and set off serious alarms.

Rudiger Hering said goodbye to his uncle and cousin and waited for the S-bahn to pull into Spandau from its long loop across the city. He boarded the train and it crossed into the countryside of the GDR, delivering him to the administrative area of the prospective Politburo candidate who, in an office in Potsdam 12 miles away, had issued many orders of his own and waited for X-hour.

The train sighed and stopped at Falkensee, a worn, worked station in the middle of a solid village beside a lake – one of those favoured for boating, and surrounded by the woodland favoured for walks. The town itself consisted of substantial pre-war houses hugging narrow, cobbled streets. At the station, Hering noticed the controls were a bit harder than usual, more Railway Police in those black uniforms, but he thought no more of it. He lived in a little community outside Falkensee, on a cobbled roadway angled at a steep camber. It had pastures at the end and a farmhouse in the distance. The roadway narrowed to a track through the pastures and a small bridge took it over a brook where a couple of houses stood. He knew a girl in one of them because he went to school with her. The track wandered on towards the farmhouse.

Hering made his way home and went to sleep. He was 15 years old and would return to Spandau again quite normally to celebrate his uncle's 60th birthday; but that would be in 1988, when he was 42.

A small, wiry former prisoner of war, Martin Schabe was a farmer who'd built the farmhouse with his own hands. Although his land was in the West he'd regularly motored to Falkensee nearby to do his shopping. He had friends there, too. He hadn't been able to go to Falkensee for years, however, because a crude fence blocked the track as the first tightening of the borders began. Schabe was 41 years old; he would return to Falkensee again to do his shopping, but not until 1990, when he was 70. Some of the shops were still there and, although many of the people working in them had changed, some hadn't.

At midnight the Marienfelde Reception Centre drew up its total number of refugees for the day: 2,662, the second highest it had ever recorded. How many would tramp and shuffle in on the morrow? How many were already starting their journeys, as fugitives in the darkness? How many families would be reunited? How much more food would the centre need? The flow might rise to anything.

After midnight, Willy Brandt and his party turned in. Someone had brought bottles of Scotch and it softened the journey as the night train went north on its long journey to Kiel. The Nuremburg speech had gone well and the mood on the train had been slightly euphoric. They'd had a drink. Now they slept.

THREE

And Sunday Morning

I am a camera with its shutter open, quite passive, recording, not thinking. Some day, all this will have to be developed, carefully printed, fixed.

Christopher Isherwood,
Goodbye to Berlin

Adam Kellett-Long sat in front of his typewriter trying to compose the day-lead for Sunday. 'I suppose I was in the third sentence when the phone rang. I picked it up and a man's voice I didn't recognise said in German "Don't go to bed this night." He hung up. At that moment the ADN service closed for the night as usual, *End of Transmissions*, but because of this extraordinary call I stayed there wondering.' Kellett-Long couldn't know that the *Neues Deutschland* he'd bought deliberately contained no news, or that a compact group of journalists prepared a special edition, or that it would fulfil a specific, pivotal function in the operation.

Al Hemsing's phone 'started to hot up but nothing firm, just enquiries'. George Muller's phone 'started to ring all the time. Around midnight Albertz called to tell me that something curious had happened to the S-bahn system. At the Mission, we'd been concerned that because the East Germans owned the S-bahn they could infiltrate large numbers of Factory Fighters through the stations in the West but this seemed contrary to that – a decrease in the traffic. The trains ran into the East and weren't coming back again. It created considerable confusion and one explanation might have been to reduce the number of trains refugees could use.'[1]

West Berlin taxi drivers caught the wind, passing and relaying a message among their fraternity, 'Don't accept fares to the East.'

The anonymous woman who'd sat in the garden got a lift back to Treptow with her daughter. They were dropped on a corner and walked the two streets to their apartment. They didn't see or hear anything unusual and went to sleep.

The policeman Erhard Schimke also slept, and so did a woman called Brigitta in her apartment near him. In time they would marry and live facing the twin curved roads and the sunken gardens, the dividing line running along the far side. She'd cross it very normally again to catch the bus to work – but not until 1990.

In Hyannis Port, Kennedy returned from his cruise and loaded a white golf cart with people: a friend, Jacqueline – chic in a blue blouse and red slacks – his 3½-year-old daughter Caroline and four of her cousins. He drove a block and a half to the neighbourhood candy store and the friend took the kids in to buy ice cream. Kennedy turned the cart around, inadvertently swerving onto some grass. He made a quip to a woman watching, collected the party outside the store and drove back with Caroline, who wore a blue and white bathing suit, sitting on his lap. It was an innocent day, as six hours before it had been in Berlin.

At 1.00 a.m., two orders chattered from the Police Headquarters, centralising the command structure:

(a) The first brigade of the Riot Police is subordinated to the Police Commander of the district of Berlin.
(b) The Security command, Berlin, is subordinated to the Commander of the First Brigade of Riot Police.

At 1.05 the lights at the Brandenburg Gate were switched off and Border Guards began to arrive there.

Grohmann's mother-in-law finally left for the Botanical Gardens station to take the S-bahn home, a journey entirely within West Berlin. 'She came back after about ten minutes and said, "It's very peculiar but the S-bahn is not running, it's all blocked up." She and we didn't understand why but we wondered.'

At 1.11, the ADN teleprinter in Kellett-Long's office 'suddenly opened up again and began to run a generalised Warsaw Pact communiqué from Moscow. We also had the Reuters service and I saw we were running it so I thought it was useless me filing the same stuff.' Kellett-Long studied this communiqué carefully:

The present traffic situation on the borders of West Berlin is being used by the ruling circles of West Germany and the intelligence agencies of the NATO countries to undermine the economy of the German Democratic Republic. Through deceit, bribery and blackmail, West German bodies and military interests induce certain unstable elements in the German Democratic Republic to leave for West Germany. In the face of the aggressive aspirations of the reactionary forces of West Germany and its NATO allies, the Warsaw Pact proposes reliable safeguards and effective control be established around the whole territory of West Berlin.

Kellett-Long rushed into the bedroom and said to his wife Mary, 'The Germans have closed the border – but don't worry.' She'd remember 'leaping' out of the bed.

This Sunday would be spread into a vast mosaic of images, of currents, of moments; but all that was in a sense governed by the timetable. East Berlin, slumbering, would become a prisoner of this timetable in a very few minutes as massive movement stirred in the battered, exhausted street and overgrown bomb sites, at canals and bullet-riddled bridges, on the broad and brooding avenues and cosy little alleys, in fields and allotments and back gardens; movement played out under pallid street lamps making many thousands of uniformed men into flitting ghosts. And, as shadows within the shadows, the Stasi lurked, charting the moments, reading the currents.

Horst Pruster was an Eastern policeman who'd been in Berlin from January 1956:

That weekend I was working in the Interior Ministry in Mauerstrasse but I had some free time – I was alerted at midnight. I lived in Prenzlauer Berg with my wife and my little girl, who was two. I had a telephone and they rang – the Ministry commanded all the police in East Germany. The headquarters at Alexanderplatz was for East Berlin only.

I did not know the wall was going to be built. In the Ministry there had been about fifty officers – Majors, Lieutenants, Lieutenant-Colonels – and they were always in a locked room. We knew they were working on something but not what, and I can't remember for how long they had been working on it. I must say also I was a very little man [in terms of importance]!

After the telephone call, I came from my house and I saw a lot of movement, Soviet army, GDR army, police, Factory Fighters [*Kampfgruppen*]. I had to get to the Ministry and I had no car so I hitch-hiked. I was there in thirty minutes. I was working in a centre where all the police reports came and were distributed, a very big room. We were eight and we had five, six telephones. The switchboard had buttons which lit up so you knew where the calls were coming from.

Within the coming hour and a half Pruster 'understood that the border was closed although at the moment that happened the police were not standing in the front line. They were the *Kampfgruppen* and, in Berlin, the Riot Police. We thought the closure was temporary. . . .'[2]

At 1.30 a.m., senior officers of the Factory Fighting Groups in every district were alerted by Police Headquarters. The Fighters, organised in units of 100 subdivided into three platoons of three squads, could only be deployed by the police under instruction from the Ministry of the Interior.

At 1.40, a general alert went from the senior officers to every Factory Fighter in the districts of Mitte, Treptow, Prenzlauer Berg, Pankow and Friedrichshain. The general battalion at Weissensee and the reserve battalions at Lichtenberg and Köpenick were alerted, although these districts did not share a sector border with West Berlin. Cumulatively the timetable set in motion the massive movement.

The Fighters, activists drawn from each factory, were difficult to assemble quickly away from their workplace, so a system had been devised. If a Fighter lived in an apartment block but had no phone – an extremely scarce commodity – a designated contact in the block who did have one would be rung and told to go and wake him. Such a system could not be completely efficient and the police themselves went round and roused as many as possible. At the same time, the police moved towards many of the eighty-one crossing points, reinforcing officers who were already there.

Within the next hour 25,000 Fighters pulled on their baggy uniforms and joined the operation. Not one knew of it a minute before 1.40 a.m. and that they achieved what they did remains an enduring testament to their discipline and their belief. If they'd faltered, the operation risked disintegration – and that might have taken the GDR with it. An abortive attempt at sealing the border would compel hundreds of thousands to Marienfelde, and which East German would ever trust the government again?

The GDR army moved to positions back from the sector line except at carefully selected strategic and sensitive places like Bernauer Strasse. The GDR wanted the operation to appear as civilian as possible but the army served interlocking functions. Its presence intimidated any thoughts of insurrection, it stood poised if that happened, and it was in place if the Allies used troops against the operation.

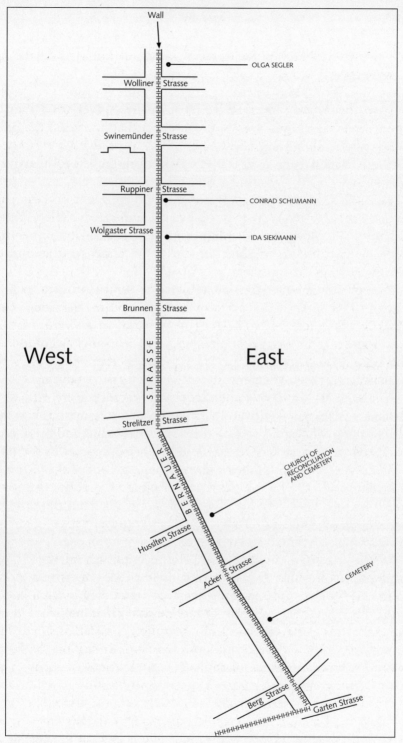

The unkindest cut – Bernauer Strasse showing where Olga Segler jumped to her death, Border Guard Conrad Schumann jumped to freedom, Ida Siekmann jumped to her death, and the Church of Reconciliation, which was blown up.

Three divisions of the Soviet Army moved out of their barracks in Potsdam and a member of the American Military Liaison Mission there, hearing heavy metallic treads grinding, ventured out to investigate. A policeman held him motionless until a column of tanks moved into the darkness towards the Berliner Ring autobahn which snaked round the whole city.

North of Potsdam, at a barracks in a village called Rontgental, a platoon of the Border Police was woken and sealed orders read. They understood they were to take part in the division of Berlin and their Sergeant, Rudi Thurow, heard a member of the platoon wonder if the Allies would stand for it. The platoon was to go and take control of the mainline station at the town of Bernau, well beyond the city limits but a direct connection to West Berlin: East Germans boarding at Bernau arrived in the West very quickly. Thurow's platoon set off to be there before the first train of the morning came in.

The embrace of the operation spread, touching indiscriminately. In the Western district of Zehlendorf, a young radio reporter, Peter Schultz, and his wife Astrid – in the seventh month of pregnancy – slept. They looked forward to making her parents, who lived 50 kilometres into the GDR, grandparents. 'My telephone rang. It was RIAS calling. They told me to get up and dress, they said the radio car would be there in ten minutes and I should be ready to go by then.'3

So far away – now – in the other half of the city, Erhard Schimke, the policeman on a day off, was sleeping but 'a car came and I was told I had to serve, I had to do my duty. I was driven to the Police Station at Lichtenberg and they put me on standby.'4

Kellett-Long wanted to see for himself. On a hot night, and with the streets deserted, he drove towards the Brandenburg Gate. 'Up to then you'd been able to just drive through it into West Berlin. As I approached, a red torch waved at me and I stopped. A Border Policeman came up and said "I'm sorry, you can't proceed, it's closed." I didn't ask him too many questions. I turned the car round and started to dash home.' Kellett-Long had confirmation that the Moscow communiqué contained more than verbal sparring, and that his Saturday day-lead had been right after all. More than that, he had a world scoop on his hands.

At Marx-Engels-Platz, the broad, cleared area where the old Imperial Palace had stood (the GDR blew it up in 1950 because of its militaristic associations), 'another red torch waved and a policeman stopped me. I sat while a column of lorries went past, a very, very long column and the lorries seemed to be towing gun carriages. It was pitch dark because the street lighting in East Berlin was pretty minimal and I didn't find out until later that what I thought were army troops were in fact Factory Fighting Groups and the gun carriages were field kitchens. The column took about twenty minutes to pass as it moved towards the Brandenburg Gate, then the policeman waved me on. I didn't know what to do. I was half-tempted to follow but, if I did, I wasted time. I really needed to get to the office and put the snap message out that the border had been closed.'[5] [A snap, in journalist jargon, is a blunt and staccato sentence announcing that something important has happened.] Because Kellett-Long did not follow, he missed the lorries fanning out to their appointed places along the line.

His wife Mary would remember: 'When Adam returned I think I was [back] in bed and he said, "Don't you worry about it, you go to sleep", that kind of thing, but I spent the night punching copy for him [onto the teleprinter].'

She'd write in her diary: 'Adam came back white to the lips and said the streets were full of soldiers, and lorries pulling guns. The soldiers and police all had sub-machine guns. Of course this frightened me but I managed to control myself and get over it in a short time. Soon after the announcements over the teleprinter, the streets filled with lorries and motorbikes. Police cars rushed along with their sirens sounding.' Mary Kellett-Long witnessed the direct result of the order from Pätz beginning: X + 30 minutes, *closure of the crossing points.*[6]

A reporter with another international news agency, United Press International (UPI) felt the consequences of the order. Three times he tried to drive east through the Brandenburg Gate and three times he was turned back. A West Berlin policeman told him 'they've shut it tight. Cars can't go through in either direction and neither can pedestrians.'

Kellett-Long filed the snap, 'by which time more stuff ran on ADN. We were lucky because within a hundred yards of our office in Schönhauser Allee a very large Police Station doubled as a headquarters for the Factory Fighting Groups. By then, that buzzed with activity, people coming and going, the whole place mad.'

The tempo quickened across the city as the timetable gripped. At 1.54 a.m., an S-bahn train stopped at Staaken in the West – not far from Falkensee, but on a different line – and the Railway Police ordered it to turn back. Because the GDR controlled the whole S-bahn system the police had the authority to do this; they also made all the passengers alight and returned their fares. The empty train reversed into the East. A minute later the police in the Western district of Wedding reported no S-bahn trains com-ing through Gesundbrunnen, an important rail intersection, from the East.

At 2.10, a Factory Fighting Group reached the street linking the Brandenburg Gate to Potsdamer Platz, disgorged from lorries and hoisted down roll after roll of barbed wire. At the same moment the Factory Fighters in Treptow reported that they were ready.

At 2.15, the chief constable of West Berlin put the entire police force on alert.

Already photographers caught images and froze them into permanence. Among the first: in the headlamps of a truck, uniformed men shifted into silhouettes as they unloaded the wire. A distant torch played over a young man wearing a camouflage jacket, an automatic weapon slung across his chest. Under the moulded steel helmet, his sallow face was startled by the sudden light. It looked morose, defiant, charged with mistrust.

Fifteen minutes after RIAS had rung him, Peter Schultz reached the line 'at a place where there had been a crossing point between Zehlendorf, a southern district of West Berlin, and Kleinmachnow, a small village in the East. Previously only a sign said you were leaving the American Sector: this was an ordinary street where people crossed and re-crossed normally. Now heavily armed men stood and they held torches. They'd laid barbed wire across the road but they weren't doing anything except line up behind it, looking.

'In a sense, they closed the crossing point with the barbed wire and their bodies. I saw they were Border Police and the Factory Fighting Groups. The light from their torches fell onto the street and that looked eerie. I couldn't imagine what was happening. *I could not.* From the radio car, I tried to explain this to the listeners, whilst I couldn't grasp it myself. I noticed no civilians on the Eastern side and the Factory Fighters appeared to be old men. I stayed for a few minutes making my report and moved to other places in Zehlendorf, and each time I saw the same thing.'

Bernard Ledwidge, political adviser to the British Mission, attended a party at a military mess near the Olympic Stadium.

They held dances on a Saturday night, that sort of thing. I'd come home and I was just getting ready for bed. I took a telephone call and the Military Police said some funny things were going on along the section border. 'We have heard from the West Germans that the late night trains have been stopped, communications with the west suspended and groups of People's Police at crossing points are closing the roads, so I thought I ought to report it.' I said, 'Well, ask the Commander of the Military Police to come and see me at my office at the Stadium.' I hadn't undressed so I went down there in my dinner jacket. In London a resident clerk is always on duty. I rang him and said, 'I am sending you an important telegram' and immediately that is what I did. I added 'Further Information Follows' and then telephoned my American and French colleagues in the city.

Ledwidge's telegram was the first official notification to the outside world that 'the balloon had gone up'.[7]

It had indeed.

The British Minister in Berlin, Geoffrey McDermott, acted, too. 'The first thing was to report these events by short, immediate telegram to the Foreign Office and (our embassies) in Bonn, Washington, Paris and Moscow. An alternative which I used on another critical occasion was a telephone call to the Ambassador in Bonn. The service through the GDR was quick and efficient and I hope they enjoyed listening in to what was said.'[8]

The operation did not take Ledwidge, an urbane and experienced man, particularly by surprise, nor perhaps McDermott. (The British Foreign Office, having in its time seen Napoleon and Hitler dispatched, operated on phlegmatic principles.)

'We felt something was bound to happen but I don't think anybody guessed exactly what,' Ledwidge says. 'We did get intelligence reports and we didn't quite believe them. They came from the Norwegian Military Mission in Berlin a few days earlier and the Norwegians told us they'd heard orders were issued for the closure points on 6 August but the order was cancelled at the last minute. We had not heard anything as specific as that from our own sources.'

Still the timetable gripped. At 2.20 a.m., the Factory Fighters at Prenzlauer Berg reported ready. Ten minutes later Albertz, as Willy Brandt's town hall Chief of Staff, telephoned the Allied commanders to ask 'What are you going to do?' At that moment, the West Berlin police at the Brandenburg Gate radioed that *twenty-three armoured personnel carriers have taken up position just to the East but are not under the columns of the Gate.*

At 2.50, the Factory Fighters at Friedrichshain reported ready, at 2.55 those at Pankow, Köpenick and Treptow.

The GDR designated each of the eighty-one crossing points with a number, starting with 1 in the north. At 2.55, at crossing point 34 –

the Brandenburg Gate, within clear sight of the West Berlin police who'd just reported the arrival of the armoured personnel carriers – a People's Policeman radioed that its force of 100 fellow policemen had closed it to traffic.

Five minutes later, the district of Weissensee reported that 10 per cent of its Factory Fighters had arrived and contact had been established with the Border Guards. As that came in, the district of Mitte reported ready and Police Headquarters made the first of their hourly reports to the Ministry of the Interior: two copies, one for the Ministry, the other for their own files.

In Kellett-Long's office 'ADN were running communiqués from the East German authorities about all sorts of rules and regulations, some underground stations closed and so on, although they described these as temporary measures. People couldn't, however, go to the West without special permits. On GDR radio the communiqués reeled out, too, in between western jazz which they never ordinarily played. You'd get a proclamation, then jazz, then another proclamation and all done while people slept. They'd wake to a *fait accompli.*'

Around 3.00 a.m., the Bonn news editor arrived from West Berlin so, Kellett-Long concluded, the border couldn't be completely sealed. The news editor added material to what Kellett-Long filed and returned to West Berlin.

Allan Lightner of the American Mission in Berlin got a call at the 'beautiful house' he and his wife Dorothy lived in. 'It came on the red phone, on my side of the bed,' Dorothy says. 'I picked it up and handed it to Allan. I didn't talk to whoever rang because it was the red phone. The Mission had tried to alert the political officer, Howard Trivers, an eccentric who didn't want his red phone by his bed because thinking about it being there would keep him awake. He'd put it out in the dressing room. His wife Millie would have heard it but she happened to be away for the weekend. Howard slept peaceably through the whole business! Allan immediately got up. I don't remember his exact words but he told me what was going on.'[9]

Lightner dressed and drove the ten minutes to the Mission. The tempo among the Americans quickened as the timetable embraced them. George Muller rang Richard Smyser, a junior officer, briefed him and said they needed first-hand information. Smyser and another junior officer, Frank Trinka, were to provide that. Trinka was bilingual: he'd been born in the United States but studied in Europe, particularly Austria. He'd come to Berlin in the summer of 1960 after a training programme in California.

Smyser rang Trinka, who'd already been woken by Muller, and they made their arrangements quickly. Smyser owned an open-top Mercedes and 'I took that because I judged we'd be able to see more. I picked up Frank. Being with the Mission, we didn't have a uniform, of course, and I was actually wearing casual clothes. We had a special licence plate, enough to guarantee us access to the East. If ever we were stopped we didn't show documents but pointed to the licence plate.'[10]

At 3.25, UPI felt confident enough to put out a snap, no doubt partly based on the three refusals at the Brandenburg Gate and partly on the mounting evidence: *Strong units of the Communist People's Police have blocked off the sector border between East and West Berlin during the course of the night.*

'It was still dark when Richard picked me up,' Trinka says. 'We drove to Potsdamer Platz and when we reached it there were shadows around, trucks with their lights going. The East Germans unloaded the trucks and strung wire.' The night ebbed into the half-light although sunrise wouldn't come until 4.48. 'The effort was to erect some sort of barrier to pedestrian and automobile traffic. It appeared rather makeshift and improvised, there didn't seem to be anything permanent about it. We had an exchange with them. . . .'

Smyser remembers this exchange. 'People's Police – not Border Police – stood in a line and stretched coils of barbed wire. One stopped us at the wire and we demanded access. He was very reluctant. He consulted with what seemed to be an officer and they pulled the wire back and we drove through. I assume they were under orders to have no direct confrontation.' The open-top Mercedes motored across Potsdamer Platz. Other vehicles would motor across it quite normally, too – but not until 1990.

The half-light revealed the full scope of the operation.

At 4.00 a.m., Willy Brandt's train reached Hannover and the two maroon carriages were decoupled from the Munich–Kiel express. 'There a friend wakened us with the news,' Brandt would remember. Deputy Berlin Mayor, Franz Amrehn, had found a way to have Brandt woken; he 'dressed as quickly as he could' and shook campaign manager Schultz awake, 'telling him to get the others out of bed' while he went to call Berlin from the stationmaster's office.[11] Brandt returned from making the call and found his party in the restaurant car eating rolls and drinking hot coffee. He looked composed and not hungover. He'd been informed during his telephone call that a special emergency meeting of West Berlin's Senate had been called for that morning and the Kommandatura – the Allied body – would meet afterwards. Schultz set off to get taxis to take them to Hannover airport.

French President Charles de Gaulle slept at his weekend retreat at Colombey-les-Deux-Eglises, far to the south of Paris. When his Foreign Minister, Maurice Couve de Murville, was informed of what was happening by telephone he said, 'Well, that settles the Berlin problem.'

British Prime Minister Harold Macmillan and his Foreign Secretary, Alec Douglas-Home – they'd been engaged in the traditional pursuit of shooting, although in different parts of the United Kingdom – were still sleeping.

Erdmute Greis-Behrendt, the Reuters office secretary, caught the first U-bahn from her aunt's around 4.00 after a lot of talking. She sat, paying no particular attention to anything as the train rattled across the River Spree and stopped at Warschauer Strasse 100 metres further on. It was the first station in the East. She walked the 5 minutes to her apartment, noticing nothing unusual and went to sleep. Greis-Behrendt would always wonder about this, whether some administrative error temporarily overlooked Warschauer Strasse. Of the 4 million inhabitants, Greis-Behrendt and the others on that underground train must surely have been the last to cross the line quite normally. Others would again, too – but not until 1989.

At 4.00, all People's Police units established lines of communication, some using coded radio messages. The highest density along the border had been achieved and that allowed redeployment to support the Factory Fighting Groups. Within a few moments, jackhammers beat holes in the roads to take concrete posts. Pneumatic drills gave Berlin its dawn chorus.

George Bailey, the American reporter, was 'awakened by a telephone call from my friend John Daly, who happened to be visiting Berlin. His message was short: "They have closed the sector boundary." I arrived at the sector boundary at 4.00. It was already light and the morning was clear. Members of the People's Police and East German troops had already strung barbed wire across Leipziger Strasse where it enters Potsdamer Platz from the east. To the left soldiers were sinking concrete pilings and stringing more barbed wire across them. Beyond, where the sector boundary runs through Ebert-Strasse to the Brandenburg Gate, People's Police and firemen were ripping up a strip six feet wide in the middle of the street. A police Captain in a plum-colored dress uniform was applying a pneumatic hammer to the pavement. With a cigarette in the corner of his mouth, he smiled as he worked. The rest of the city was still asleep. . . .'[12]

Smyser and Trinka toured the centre of East Berlin and noted a large number of police. 'We snaked in and out of about a dozen, maybe fifteen, crossing points trying to establish the policy line, what they were trying to do and how all of it affected Allied rights,' Trinka says. 'At the crossing points we saw plenty of activity, basically pretty much the same everywhere. The People's Police and Factory Fighting Groups were armed with automatic weapons, mostly sub-machine guns. We crossed at the most frequented places. Obviously we didn't go down side alleys or narrow streets. They were still open. We were looking at the main arteries. We went north to Bernauer Strasse, although we didn't notice as much activity there as at the other crossing points where dozens were busy stringing the wire.'

When Smyser and Trinka scanned Bernauer Strasse they saw a typical Berlin street: a terrace of dark stone apartments leaning together like elderly widows of the bombing so long ago. Some were seven storeys, their windows decorated by ornate pelmets and cornices; tiny balconies jutted like jaws from a few. Several shops, on the ground floors of the apartments, fed the community by selling groceries and milk and meat, and these shops had the same feel of survival about them. Their pre-war signs, painted on the stonework in old script, had faded. One said simply *Lebensmittel* – Food. It was the way the world had been, and the way it still was, here. Behind a white façade nearby a sort of boutique proffered porcelain.

Bernauer Strasse was a homely place. Members of the same families lived on both sides – a widow on one, her son on the other so he could tend her, carry coal across to her and help with the shopping. It had never mattered, and surely never could matter, that the house fronts on one side marked the precise boundary line of the district of Mitte in the East, or that as residents stepped from their front door they were in the Western district of Wedding. Bernauer Strasse was the sector boundary.

Tram tracks flowed up and down Bernauer Stasse and trams cranked along quite normally. At the southern end, the entrance to an S-bahn station was in the West but the station itself and platforms were in the East.

Two cemeteries butted onto Bernauer Strasse from the East. Old people, particularly widows, often moved to the apartments to be near the graves – heavy, inscribed headstones in rows shaded by trees. Posies of flowers, constantly renewed, decorated the graves and racks of watering cans hung on hooks in special sheds to refresh them. At the rear of both cemeteries, family mausoleums charted the generations.

Six side-streets went across Bernauer Strasse: not unusual in a city centre street almost a kilometre long but, by definition, they bisected the sector boundary. It had never mattered, and surely could never matter.

Smyser and Trinka might have glimpsed a young army Sergeant, Conrad Schumann, who guarded the corner of one of the bisecting streets with a platoon of six men. 'Nothing was organised. We had to find ourselves somewhere to sleep in the empty houses,' Schumann would later say. 'Now and again we were able to take turns for a few hours' sleep on old blankets. We had nothing proper to eat, only a plate of soup.' Schumann would give the world one unforgettable image and Bernauer Strasse would give many.

At 4.30 a.m., Adenauer was woken at his home in Rohndorf, on the banks of the Rhine not far from Bonn, by the West German Minister for All German Affairs, Ernst Lemmer. He was told what was happening. Adenauer did not care for Brandt and did not care for Berlin. He fully intended to go to mass at 6.30 as usual.

Smyser and Trinka continued their reconnaissance and 'we got the impression of something major because they were out in such large numbers and they had brought up trucks,' Trinka says. 'When we penetrated further into East Berlin we could see quasi-military units in position with dozens of trucks and all kinds of engineering equipment – although nothing in the way of tanks or artillery indicating an intention to engage in combat.'

They went to Friedrichstrasse station. 'Dozens if not hundreds of people – women, children, the aged – tried to get up the stairs and out onto the platforms but the police pushed them back,' Trinka continues. 'They must have felt this was their last opportunity. A lot were in tears because they realised it was all over.'

'Plastered on the walls of the S-bahn station,' Smyser says, 'was a decree from the Central Committee which contained a whole host of regulations. It was very carefully phrased. Frank and I read it while, around us, the most striking thing was the total confusion which reigned. These dozens of people, some with suitcases, had no idea what was going on and they were asking the Railway Police. I don't remember any anger, only bewilderment. I didn't notice any popular resistance or any shouting but I do remember the tears pouring out. They seemed to realise they were a day too late. They read the decree and tried to figure out what it meant because it did not say travel was completely prohibited. It did say there were a lot of procedures. We took note of all that.'

The announcement, dated 12 August and signed by the Minister of Transport, was set out in two columns of small, dense type under headings:

Long distance trains between East Berlin and West Germany run as per the timetable but the service now begins and ends on platform A at Friedrichstrasse station.

Direct S-bahn lines between the East and West of the city are discontinued: Pankow-Gesundbrunnen, Schönhauser Allee-Gesundbrunnen, Treptower Park-Sonnenallee.

The S-bahn remains open at Friedrichstrasse as a connection to and from West Berlin but the trains now begin and end on platform B. Suburban Eastern trains terminate at Friedrichstrasse and only on platform C.

It did not state that police manned controls barring platforms A and B to all East Germans without the right papers, which meant virtually the whole population. All the platforms faced each other like any station and would open again quite normally – but in 1989.

The announcement churned on, specifying which U-bahn stations were closed and noting those stations on Western lines underneath East Berlin where trains no longer stopped, Bernauer Strasse among them. Paragraph after paragraph methodically forbade each outlet to the West. That's why so many studied it and, the police shoving them, why so many didn't have time to understand the immediate complexities.

'We drove back to Potsdamer Platz to try and go out,' Smyser says. 'By that time the wire lay all the way across and, although I didn't count them, there must have been ten rows, no way I could take my car across. The moment when they were going to part the wire, at least on Potsdamer Platz, had gone.'

Trinka expands on that. 'They were already *squeezing* certain areas they had closed but the full implication only became clear later.'

This dawn, Potsdamer Platz already offered a stark image. The wire was attached to a crude post, and the street behind this post – where once the fashionable of Berlin shopped and drank and scanned the girls parading by – was empty save for a small, white car parked in the distance. The wire travelled in front of a group of low, saucer-like flower pots and a knot of policemen shuffled nearby. A Volkswagen moved gently up to the wire from the Western side, the driver expecting to continue as he always had. He stopped, then steered the car away while a policeman scrutinised him. The policeman's face betrayed no particular hostility, just traditional authority.

Smyser headed to the Brandenburg Gate. 'A uniformed man said "hold on". We always had difficulty there because somebody would try to score points, I guess to impress their superiors. We identified ourselves and they wanted the identification in their hand but we were members of the Allied presence and the Mercedes bore the licence plate. We had a verbal exchange and the man said "We are the German Democratic Republic, we are a sovereign state and the Soviet Union is not involved in controlling our borders." There are two side-pieces to the Gate a bit like folded wings. The man disappeared into the wing on the right, large enough to contain offices. I heard later a member of the Politburo was in there because the Gate was so sensitive. After a while the guy in uniform came out and said "OK, you can go" and we did.'

'At the Mission we told what we had seen,' Trinka adds. 'The Task Force gathered: operational staff and a large number of people called in, and I'm only talking about the State Department element. I wasn't aware of what others – the intelligence, the military – were doing.'

Al Hemsing, the Mission's press officer, was not among those present. 'I couldn't leave the phones that long. The other frustrating thing was that I kept asking, "Has the General in Berlin [Major General Albert Watson Jnr] been notified that barbed wire is being put up?" I couldn't get an answer but they hadn't called him. I said, "Dammit, if you don't I will!" They were reluctant to wake the General, especially if it proved to be nothing, but when I said I would they did. It was obvious he had to be notified.'

Smyser and Trinka presented a report orally then hand-wrote it. 'By then', Smyser says, 'a lot of information flowed in and of course everyone waited for instructions. We sat saying, "Well now, what is Washington going to do?" We were concerned about where the Russians were and their role. One report spoke of Russian tank movement – something not actually unusual, however.'

The report of that came from the man at the US Liaison Mission in Potsdam who'd been held motionless by a policeman while the column of tanks went by. It said:

The Soviet 19th Motorised Rifle Division, combined with 10th Guards Tank Division and possibly the 6th Motorised Rifle Division, moved out early this morning into position around Berlin. Elements of the 1st East German Motorised Rifle Division moved out of Potsdam and are presently unlocated. Soviet units deployed and moved off the autobahn, deploying the units into small outposts and roadblocks composed of three or four tanks, an armoured personnel-carrier and several troops. These outposts are established about 3 or 4 kilometres apart and appear to ring Berlin completely.

By moving to surround the city, Marshal Konev proclaimed how seriously the Soviet Union regarded the operation but, because the units remained in a ring away from the sealing, Khrushchev could claim that the GDR controlled its own borders as an independent state. This was the sovereignty thrust at Smyser and Trinka at the Brandenburg Gate.

Dawn spread purest blue sky over the city, and the first of the East Berliners who worked in the West made their way to their usual crossing points.

Sergeant Thurow, guarding the mainline railway station at Bernau, north of Berlin, found almost none of the people wanting to board a train knew anything about the official announcements. He refused them entry and one called out, 'Act like a human being, will you?' Thurow did allow a woman through whose face seemed familiar but, suspecting the Stasi watched him, made no further exceptions. He told the crowd to go and buy newspapers (*Neues Deutschland* had printed a special edition, remember) where everything would be explained. Some drifted away to do that.

The role of the little *Neues Deutschland* team assumed its pivotal importance. Briefing every policeman, every Factory Fighter and every soldier on how to explain the operation to distraught, enraged and bemused fellow citizens hadn't been a practical possibility in the time available, the more so under the duress of the secrecy. A single instruction, a brilliant coup, solved it: tell the people to buy a newspaper. The Berliners, notoriously irreverent and independent, might prise a concession or wring a response from anyone in uniform but they couldn't do that to a newspaper bearing ponderous announcements which carried the force of law.

At 5.00 a.m. in Berlin, it was 11.00 on Saturday night in Washington. John Ausland of the State Department's Berlin Task Force, in bed early in his house just beyond the district line, slept blissfully. The timetable hadn't gripped him but it would within the hour and wouldn't release him for days, or years.

East Berlin seethed with movement, men working, trucks rumbling, jack-hammers beating, phones ringing in the Police Headquarters and, in every police station, orders being given and received. The swell of noise woke many East Berliners and they peered from their windows and wondered; and maybe went back to sleep thinking it was just some sort of night exercise for the military. Many slept clean through, the way people do.

At 5.30, Pioneer Platoons of the army in Potsdam, to be used for construction work, were alerted.

Outside Bernau station the crowd in front of Sergeant Thurow showed hostility and he requested reinforcements. Thirty reached him at 6.00 a.m.: men from a Factory Fighting Group and women from the Free German Youth. They threaded into the crowd to dilute the hostility. Thurow is reported to have heard someone call 'No-one can expect me to do a thing for the state if they are going to bar my way to my own mother.' A man, possibly a member of the Stasi, approached Thurow, reprimanded him for lacking resolution and ordered him to tell the crowd the sealing was really 'an anti-fascist protective wall'. Thurow said no, he'd do his duty but not use phrases like that when they kept a son from a mother. Later he'd remember one of the platoon washing his hands to cleanse them.

Bernard Ledwidge stayed in his office. 'Everyone came to the headquarters and enquiries came in from London. The head of the Central Department at the Foreign Office became involved and Alec Douglas-Home's private secretary did, too. Home was already up in Scotland shooting grouse, as Macmillan was in Yorkshire.'

Adenauer went to Mass.

Kellett-Long decided to have another look. 'Factory Fighting Groups and the police, miles and miles and miles of them with their guns at the ready, were putting up barbed wire. They lined the whole border. I only found out later that their guns weren't loaded, although their officers' guns were.' (The Factory Fighters and the police had clips of ammunition, but in their pockets.) A policeman told Kellett-Long nobody had been allowed through 'for a period of about an hour while we got into position, but now things are working as we mean them to and someone with papers like yours will not be prevented. You must take no East Germans with you.'

This initial and supposedly total sealing 'while we got into position' probably lasted no more than a few minutes, not an hour, and cannot have been total because the Brandenburg Gate remained open until 2.55 a.m. and Kellett-Long's Bonn news editor found a way across around 3.00. Erdmute Greis-Behrendt rode the U-bahn at 4.00 to a station where no controls yet existed.

But that misses the point. The scale of the operation carried within it inevitable confusion and improvisation because so many men had been dragged from their sleep to seal off the two interlocking halves of the city, all 28.5 miles (45.8 kilometres) of it. However, the seemingly innocent fragment of conversation between the policeman and Kellett-Long implies that there was an attempt at a complete border sealing, an action in absolute violation of the Four Power Agreement. Would that have provoked a counteraction from Washington, London and Paris if they'd known? It remains academic because they didn't know. Smyser and Trinka had the wire pulled back around 4.00 a.m. when the operation was assuming its shape, and by then the thousands of soldiers, Factory Fighters and police were in position. The moment of being off-balance had gone and any physical counteraction now risked escalation to the nuclear level. Perhaps it always had.

Kellett-Long says that 'for the first few hours the British passport didn't matter and that was scary – it lasted from about from 2.00 to 6.00 – but after that they did let us through.'

While Kellett-Long drove on looking and noting, John Ausland's phone rang in Washington. It was midnight there. The call came from the State Department's Operations Centre and the caller said 'Press agency tickers indicate something is going on in Berlin but it's not clear what.' Ausland told him to 'call me when he had an official report and I went back to sleep'.

Those East Berliners who'd slept through woke into a nightmare. In the Stolz household Uta switched the radio on and tuned it to RIAS as she habitually did. 'RIAS said the border had been closed overnight and you could only cross at certain points.'

It might have been Peter Schultz broadcasting these words which Uta heard. Schultz had worked the whole night and 'I didn't leave the office because we had to do so many reports, Willy Brandt returning from the Federal Republic, calls from radio stations in Switzerland and Austria wanting information, colleagues at the Brandenburg Gate and at Potsdamer Platz sending in reports, *everything*.'

Uta 'rushed to the other room to tell my boyfriend, "The border is closed! The border is closed!" He told me off for waking him, and this after a wonderful night. "Don't talk rubbish," he said. I was very offended. I sat on the edge of his bed and I kept saying, "The border is closed; you can't cross anymore." He didn't believe me, he did not really grasp it. He was not keen to get out of bed and a little fight between us followed. He only grasped it when RIAS broadcast the next news bulletin.'[13]

Lutz felt 'stunned' as he heard that. Even when his disbelief hardened to recognition of the reality, 'I couldn't digest it, I couldn't judge the implications.' Lutz and Uta wondered about the direction their lives might have taken if they'd stayed in the West after their holiday in the Black Forest three weeks before.

'We talked with his parents about what had happened and they were filled with consternation, they couldn't digest it either,' Uta says. 'What really hurt Lutz immediately was that his sporting contacts had been broken.'

Stolz would remain a football fanatic and savour particular memories of a match, Stuttgart versus Bayern Munich in the West, which – of course – he watched on television. He'd remember a news flash at half-time and know he could now go quite normally to the Lehrter Stadium again – but that was 9 November 1989.

Around 7.30 a.m. the doorbell of the anonymous mother who'd returned to Treptow rang furiously. She opened the door and a neighbour gripped her arm, blurting, 'The border's closed, the border's closed.' The woman, sleepy, muttered, 'But that's impossible.' The neighbour led her to the window and she saw the barbed wire along the canal bank at the end of the street.

Also at 7.30, Colonel Ernest von Pawel of the US Army went to the Emergency Operations Center to report. He'd been out to Potsdam and seen the Soviet armaments on the move. Now he wanted to inform Major-General Watson that West Berlin was in effect surrounded. The noose went all the way round.

In Bernauer Strasse, Sergeant Schumann had three orders: 'In our sector we were not to allow anyone to proceed from East to West, we should not react to provocation from the West and we should not open fire with live ammunition.' He and his men patrolled behind the wire across the side-street. On the Western side a crowd hurled abuse, calling them concentration camp guards. A daughter on the Eastern side handed flowers to her mother over the wire. 'I heard the daughter wish her a happy birthday and say she wouldn't be able to come across any more because *those here* [Schumann and his men] won't let me.' This disturbed Schumann more than the abuse. He started asking himself questions and wasn't getting any answers.

Brigitta Schimke awoke, gazed from her apartment to the twin-curved roads and sunken gardens, then over to the Western district where her parents lived. Between here and there she saw the barbed wire and she burst into tears. She'd cry for two days.

Klaus-Peter Grohmann woke up in the Western district of Lichterfelde and switched his television on. 'It cost a fortune, 998 marks, and only received what they called the Second Programme. I earned around 180 marks a week with the Berliner Bank so the TV really represented something. It was an ugly affair, enormous, a bit like "Big Brother Is Watching You" but I felt ever so proud because it was ours – although I had to pay for it on hire purchase over three years and the guarantee only lasted six months. We saw the first pictures of people at the border and troops and streets being blocked. It was genuinely incredible because all the streets connected right through the city. Try to think of that in terms of New York City or London or Paris. The men in uniform looked pretty grim. We wondered and we were scared. It seemed like war, you know.'[14]

Rudiger Hering woke in his hamlet north of Falkensee and found he lived 150 metres the wrong side of a closed border. He went into the cobbled street with the angled camber and 'a lot of people stood watching the Factory Fighting Groups putting up barbed wire. They had come in trucks.' He turned away, embittered, I strongly suspected, and would never quite shed that bitterness.

At 8.00 a.m., Kellett-Long rang Erdmute Greis-Behrendt. 'Adam said, "Get out of bed and come to the office quickly because they've sealed off West Berlin, but before you do that tell your relatives." My grandparents lived close and I went there then I caught the tram. It stopped at Eberswalder Strasse, not very far from the office, because barbed wire had been rolled across the tramlines.' Eberswalder Strasse formed part of the northern tip of Bernauer Strasse. 'I got out and thought I was dreaming. People jumped over the one roll of wire and made fun of it like a game even though they were told not to. They thought it was a joke but as another roll uncoiled the seriousness dawned on them. Many hung around jeering as one lot of wire unrolled after another. People watched from windows. They thought the three Western allies would help them by doing something about it. I walked to the office.'[15]

By 8.00, several miles of wire had been laid and the noose tightened.

During the morning Greis-Behrendt found herself 'trapped but I couldn't believe it, I couldn't believe that that was it. All the people I spoke to said, "Wait for the Americans to come, they will help us. The Allies will help us."' Only in 1976 would she be able to cross to West Berlin again quite normally, and then by visa because she worked for Reuters. She wondered about staying in the West and talked it over very seriously with her husband but by then she had a six-month-old son. Of course she'd return East, and did.

A journalist called Peter Johnson had set up the Reuters bureau in Schönhauser Allee but, this Sunday, was finishing a tour of duty in Moscow. He'd learned of the border sealing from a Reuters service message alerting all correspondents, and by the BBC *World Service*, which was broadcast on short wave and could be 'received without jamming'. Johnson lived in Bonn and 'I was dying to get back home to my family but at the same time sorry to be leaving Moscow after my first taste of life and work there.' A friend drove him to Sheremetevo airport to board an Aeroflot TV-104 jet for East Berlin where he'd catch a connection to Bonn. While he waited for the flight he bought a gramophone record of a popular Russian song, *Evening near Moscow*.[16]

From about 8.00, people began to gather at the wire, milling gently, staring at it, discussing it. At 8.15, Eastern bureaucracy began to function, officially recording the first escape – although that compressed the fate of human beings to lines on an incident sheet. The escape took place at crossing point 22, the street next to where Schumann patrolled:

Date	Time	Command Post	No. of Groups	No. of People
13.08	08.15	22	1	1

The second took place at

Date	Time	Command Post	No. of Groups	No. of People
13.08	09.20	22	1	3

The bureaucracy added incidents during the day, however massively incomplete such an exercise would have to be. Many fled before 8.15 – over wasteland and allotments, or stepping from their front doors into Bernauer Strasse, or slipping into alleys and stealing across an unguarded corner. Some strolled over before the wire uncoiled and the police were too preoccupied to stop them. By contrast, a *Washington Post* reporter saw a man visibly agonising for about fifteen minutes while the wire rolled towards him. He hesitated too long and the noose constricted. And further afield, in the countryside around West Berlin where, as Rudiger Hering points out, woodland masked movement, 'in the first few days after 13 August many tried and 90 per cent made it'. How many did that before 8.15?

At 9.00, crossing point 48 – close to where Brigitta Schimke lived – reported that the number of people gathered on the Eastern side had increased to 100, but a platoon of police cleared the street. Crossing point 18 reported a crowd of 150 and requested reinforcements. The first crisis for the GDR government might be within the next few minutes or it might be now. Would the soldiers, police and Factory Fighters keep their nerve as more and more people, anger rising, were drawn to the line? Who knew what isolated squads of Fighters would do if an enraged mob advanced, or a daughter begged to be let through to her mother? Who knew what the population on the Western side would do? It might all turn on a horribly simple yet horribly brutal question: would Germans shoot Germans and, more specifically, would Berliners shoot Berliners?

At 9.11, a report from near Bernauer Strasse said 'three more persons went West at 9.02', implying previous escapes. The incident sheet represented a concerted and serious effort to record the number of East Berliners who, for whatever reason, came to somewhere along the 28.5 miles at any time after X + 30 hours, picked their moment and fled to the West.

Willy Brandt landed at Templehof. When he'd reached Hannover airport there'd been a delay to the PanAm flight he'd been able to get on and he'd phoned from the PanAm office to be given fuller details of the sealing. Brandt reported to his party that 'there are only a handful of people who know what's going on'. Now, from Templehof, 'I proceeded immediately to the sector border at Potsdamer Platz and at the Brandenburg Gate. The incredible and yet not totally surprising was under way. East Berlin was being cut off from us by a huge military force. Giant posts were being rammed into the ground and roll upon roll of barbed wire stretched between them.' It would become 'one of the saddest days I have ever lived through. Fear, desperation and rage were written on the faces of my fellow citizens.'[17]

The Eastern police monitored every move Brandt made, reporting he left the Brandenburg Gate at 9.05 and misspelt his name, Brand. The report added that 'the eighty persons who have gathered around him are about to disperse'.

At 9.15, crossing point 52 – the bridge Greis-Behrendt had crossed on the U-bahn so long ago – noted 'the American officer who came from West Berlin and was reported at 7.00 had a look at the tanks in Warschauer Strasse and left again'. This may well have been a colonel captured by a photographer's camera as he walked, hand in pocket, past a policeman. Tanks, parked nose to tail, formed the backdrop to the print and, on the pavement opposite, passers-by glanced furtively at them.

Another crossing point recorded the defection of a riot policeman, reported at 6.27, but this proved to be untrue. At 9.20, a report from Bernauer Strasse said people were trying to smash the doors of houses so that they could reach Bernauer Strasse itself and step in to the West. Reinforcements had already been dispatched. At 9.20,

Police Headquarters noted the arrival of a convoy of army heavy vehicles at a goods depot at Wriezen some 40 miles east. The commanding officer requested a police escort to bring them in, and a motorcycle left to do that at 9.30. The bureaucratic machine clicked out the strength of the Factory Fighting Groups:

District	Motorised	General
Friedrichshain	82	102
Köpenick	95	214
Lichtenberg	187	0
Mitte	274	782
Pankow	0	120
Prenzlauer Berg	69	81
Treptow	127	103
Weissensee	0	81
	834 = 22.5 per cent	1483 = 14.1 per cent

These totals constitute an immense force but the real significance is in the percentages of their full strengths. Some Fighters only heard on the radio – perhaps RIAS echoing over from the West – and hastened to their groups wearing sandals or ordinary shoes; some broke off holidays, some left the bedsides of pregnant wives, and their numbers rose during the morning, reaching 63 per cent. To assemble and deploy so many people without warning from a standing start remains an extraordinary achievement.

At 10.00 a.m., Kellett-Long's phone rang and this time he did recognise the voice, Ivan Shishkin, a Soviet Embassy spokesman enquiring how he was.

'I'm fine.'

'Not nervous?'

'No, not terribly, but it would be nice to know what's going to happen.'

'Well, don't worry because if things turn very nasty we'll get Mary out through Prague.'

Kellett-Long judged those words as being 'obviously part of the psychological warfare. Through me (and Reuters) he wanted to give the West the impression the Soviet Union really backed Ulbricht and this was a no-nonsense situation, this was for real. I'll never forget his words – *If things turn very nasty, we'll get Mary out through Prague*. He did not say he'd get me out through Prague!' Kellett-Long disregarded this psychology, although he found the ploy an 'interesting facet'.

While Kellett-Long fielded this call, in Washington John Ausland's phone rang again. 'The duty office at the State Department said a CIA message had arrived bearing an indicator that called for awakening the President in Hyannis Port.' It begs the questions: Why did the first notification to Ausland come from press agency ticker-tape and why, now, did the first official message reach him eight hours into the sealing of East Berlin from West? The answers demonstrate the difficulty of collating reliable information and communicating it in the era before computers, mobile phones, and satellite links; and before television channels like CNN were able to transmit live news globally and continously.

The timetable in play was in fact two timetables, one in Berlin and the other those six crucial hours further back in Washington.[18] No doubt Ulbricht and Honecker had calculated this. The laying of the barbed wire began after 2.00 a.m. Trinka and Smyser didn't get back to the Mission to report until around 6.00 a.m. (midnight in Washington) and, when they did so, they had to observe procedures.

Frank Cash of the State Department's Task Force, explains it.

We had secure lines but they didn't always work and we could never compete with the wire services, who were sending everything in 'clear' [uncoded] and instantaneously. From an Embassy or Mission, a message needed clearance among a number of people in a number of offices and it would almost always be coded. That didn't involve an elaborate procedure because it was mostly done mechanically, but all of these things take time and, of course, a message had to be decoded at the other end and so on. That's why the news media can always beat any Department and why the Government is frequently behind the news media. Dick Smyser was in Berlin, he had to return to the Mission, make his report, put his message in writing, have it cleared by two or three people, then it's encoded . . .[19]

This does not alter the great truth that Berlin was essentially sealed while, as a phrase at the time went, Washinton slept.

Like Bernard Ledwidge and Willy Brandt, Ausland did not find himself totally surprised. Shortly before, he'd drafted a telegram on the theme that the Soviet Union would have to act but '"We're not quite certain whether they'll do it by cutting off all of Berlin or stopping movement within the city." Our Bonn and Washington and Moscow embassies commented on the telegram so it wasn't as if we didn't foresee something drastic, but there were no plans to cope with this because maintaining our access preoccupied everyone.'

And nobody knew. British minister McDermott wrote in his memoirs:[20] 'With hindsight it is clear our intelligence was not too good. British intelligence, which a few years back had greatly flourished in Berlin, had taken a hard knock as a result of the activities there of George Blake, the double agent, which had only recently been exposed. No doubt our allies' intelligence was affected to some extent, too, by his skilled treachery; but what is more surprising is that the West Berliners' own information was not more complete: with families divided between the West and East Sectors, and more than the usual supply of agents and informers in the city, one might have expected someone to have got wind of Ulbricht's intentions.'

The tempo in Washington quickened. Ausland phoned Cash, who lived in Maryland, and Cash said he was taking his wife to the airport but would join him at the State Department as soon as possible afterwards.

Cash remembers it clearly: 'Martin Hillenbrand, Director of the Office of German Affairs, Secretary of State Dean Rusk and I had just returned from a quadrapartite conference in Paris. Hillenbrand immediately took off on holiday and I was the guy left in charge of the Task Force. My wife and two children had scheduled a vacation in Florida with her mother and my parents, and their plane was due to leave at 7.00 that Sunday morning. It was somewhat after 4.00 a.m. when John called me. As I had to take my family to the airport and he was headed to the office I didn't see any point in going, then coming back to take them. It was at least a twenty minute drive each way. I told John that I'd be in shortly after 7.00.'

Ausland drove to the State Department.

In Moscow, Soviet diplomat Arkady N. Shevchenko sensed that 'in many offices of the Foreign Ministry a crisis atmosphere prevailed as we waited to see what kind of countermeasures Kennedy would take'.

Markus Wolf, running the Stasi department infiltrating the West, had heard rumours 'but nothing precise and above all no discussion. The decision had been taken in a military way and in the most absolute secrecy and, I swear, even I didn't know in advance. It created real difficulties because this barrier became uncrossable for us, too. We'd prepared people to be sent to the West under their real names as we always had but now that would be impossible. We couldn't furnish our agents with operational orders which the soldiers and police at the frontier would accept' – for security reasons.

Many others had more personal concerns. Bodo Radtke, the journalist on holiday, heard about the situation on the radio. 'I called my office and asked what's happening? What will happen tomorrow? They said, keep quiet, take your holidays and when you come back we will tell you.'

Heinz Sachsenweger, the railway worker on his family holiday in Brandenburg, also heard it on the radio and, as chairman of a Factory Fighting Group, knew he must go home. To get to Brandenburg, he'd ridden the S-bahn from East Berlin as it looped across the Western half of the city and re-emerged in the East at Potsdam. There he'd changed to an inter-city train. Now he returned to Potsdam but had to work his way round the outskirts of West Berlin on the slow country line because the S-bahn loop had been severed.

The timetable ticked. The police achieved more than 53 per cent of their full complement, although significantly higher (63 per cent) in Treptow where so many houses and apartments were close to each other and the word could be spread.

At 10.15, the Western newspaper *Morgen Post* distributed a special edition, like a poster, with its headline screaming THE CITY IS CUT BY BARBED WIRE and a photographer froze an image of that: a lad in his Sunday best – white shirt, tie and braces, hair neatly combed – reading the poster in front of the wire. Concrete posts were in place and the wire was being stretched between them by two Factory Fighters.

Crossing point 55, in Treptow, reported that 'young people have swum the canal in the direction of West Berlin. A patrol has been brought into action.' The swimmers were two men who stripped down to trunks, so that they brought no possessions at all, not even the clothes they stood up in. Later they posed at the Marienfelde Centre draped in blankets. Both were smiling.

The American Mission required an update, and Smyser and Trinka drove to the East again. During their 4.00 a.m. visit, Trinka had judged it 'prudent for the East Germans to pull the wire back, give us a dressing down and, after telling us they were a sovereign state, allow us through – same thing on the way out. We'd had something to eat after making our report, now we'd gone back and we could see everything. The scenario had changed. Very obviously they were serious about putting something in the way of a permanent barrier up. They had barbed wire in place, we had to identify ourselves and in some places wait a while to pass.

'They were acting *de facto* contrary to the Four Power Agreement but it's the old question: when do you decide your national interests are seriously involved? The confusion was so great and what did it all mean? Is it going to result in a military confrontation? Are we going to be overwhelmed in West Berlin? Will there be an uprising in East Berlin like 1953? What if it breaks down into civil war and thousands and thousands flee into West Berlin? How do we cope with that?'[21]

While Smyser and Trinka toured, the Police Headquarters received a report that 'about a hundred persons have gathered on both sides of the street at crossing point 48. They are provoking the Border Police and trying to break through the barrier. Operational staff in the Mitte district have sent two Groups of a hundred Factory Fighters each.' Five minutes later a telex chattered out to the police commanders of all Eastern districts: 'To maintain order and security, the battalions of the Factory Fighting Groups have to be brought into action in closed formation. It is once again pointed out that vigilance has to be increased.'

A loss of control might lead to Soviet Army intervention, bringing tanks back onto Potsdamer Platz like 1953, firing into a mass of civilians within full view of western cameras. Could Khrushchev survive that politically?

The Kommandatura met at 10.00 a.m. with Major-General Watson in the chair, and McDermott wrote that 'we discussed possible countermeasures, both local and further afield. The Americans would have liked to put on a show of force but we and the French questioned whether this would improve matters with large Soviet forces at the ready all round Berlin. I suggested that, as the Warsaw Pact countries had announced their support of the East Germans' action, reprisals might be taken against them or their allies, and it was agreed to refer this idea to our governments. Nothing came of it, so far as I know.'[22]

Willy Brandt went to the Kommandatura at 11.00 and was astonished to see an empty seat still there for a Soviet delegate, although none had attended a meeting since 1948. Brandt was preoccupied. Was, he wondered urgently to himself, the laying of the barbed wire 'only the first step? Would an attack on West Berlin follow? Would there be outbreaks of mass fury and attempts to break through to West Berlin? And what would the Allies do? Would they tolerate this violation of the Berlin treaty or merely react with protests? If they did not, would there be any way out except war?'[23]

George Muller remembers an atmosphere of 'consternation' throughout the meeting, nobody knowing GDR and Soviet intentions. 'Brandt was very, very taciturn although he wasn't a morning person anyway. He'd been taken off his train and flown to

Berlin. He didn't say much of anything. My British counterpart and I were drafting the first cut of a protest but the Commandants couldn't say anything without instructions from their governments.'

'To be honest,' Brandt would say, 'we were very unhappy when it became obvious our friends, our protecting powers, were not able to change anything as far as the other part of the city was concerned.' The Allied representation told him they would issue a protest but he commented if that was all they were going to do 'people will laugh themselves sick from East Berlin to Vladivostok'. He said: 'scanning the faces of my American friends I could imagine what had happened. They had alerted the Pentagon, the State Department and the White House, only to be told that ungovernable reactions must be avoided at all costs.'

McDermott remembered:

Brandt joined us by invitation with Amrehn and other colleagues. He was grave but statesmanlike. He never demanded any rash actions nor reproached us for lack of firmness, though some of his colleagues later tried to make scapegoats of us. In reply to some criticism of bad Allied Intelligence which a Christian Democrat spokesman made I did not hesitate to express my surprise that the Berlin government's own information had not been better. But these disagreements came later and were never serious. On August 13 we were all concerned together to devise the best measures we could against the communist outrage which it was clear to us might have incalculable consequences. Far away in their capitals, officials and politicians began to think. In Berlin the first reaction was to call a committee meeting, which was hardly calculated to terrify the enemy. The Allied troops there, all 10,000 of them, were put on alert.

After Willy Brandt had arrived to join our deliberations we went on discussing for hours what effective practical counter-action we would launch. The fact is we were all stupefied and almost as much taken by surprise as everyone else. We decided to meet early the next day, and a French diplomat's suggestion that a quarter to eleven would be early enough was overruled.'[24]

The time-gap between Berlin and Washington is misleading. In fact Ausland arrived at the State Department, a ponderous and dignified building in the museum style of architecture near the Potomac River, around 5.00 a.m. his time – which was 11.00 in the morning in Berlin, as Brandt joined the Kommandatura meeting.

There had been no time for the Pentagon, the State Department or the White House to say anything.

At the State Department, the Task Force occupied offices on the sixth floor where they had the secure phone, a detailed street map of Berlin and methods of seeing incoming communications traffic. Ausland felt very alone, a junior who'd returned from Australia only the month before. Dare he rouse Secretary of State Rusk at such an hour? He called Showalter, liaison officer to Paul Nitze (Assistant Secretary of Defence), but also a member of the Task Force. Showalter immediately phoned the US Army Command in Paris, and they said 'Well, we don't know any more than you.'

For a while, Ausland explains, 'we just lacked information, nothing we could do'. Meanwhile, he 'talked with the duty officer at the White House and gave him the points that he could pass along to the President's Press spokesman. I gave him three points . . . this, this and this. I was a rather junior officer. At that point Frank Cash is on his way to the airport and Martin Hillenbrand was on holiday. I tried to phone Foy Kohler, Assistant Secretary of State, and couldn't get a reply. I was too new back in Washington. If I'd been there longer I would have called Rusk directly, but I didn't feel at ease calling him. The irony is that I didn't hesitate to give guidance to the White House.

'A little later I had a call back from Walt Rostow [Deputy National Security Adviser] and he said the three points I had given to the White House looked all right but he wanted to add a fourth – so I know that both the duty officer at the White House and Rostow knew something was happening. I must assume they passed that on to Hyannis Port. Now what happened after it got to Hyannis Port is a matter for speculation . . . but the reality is that Kennedy had already decided in such a contingency not to do much, so in that sense it only mattered as far as appearances are concerned. It's this problem you always have: When do you wake the President? When do you bother the President? There was nothing he could do.' Ausland did manage to reach Kohler, who said, 'Well, you and Frank Cash go ahead and handle this.'[25]

At 11.00 a.m. in Berlin, the Aeroflot TU-104 jet landed at Schönefeld, the East's airport, with Peter Johnson of Reuters among the fifty passengers. He wrote cryptically in his diary: 'I should have arrived home after the flight via East Berlin but world events decided otherwise.' He saw a lot of soldiers with sub-machine guns in and around the airport, and he reacted like a newsman. He forgot his connecting flight and headed for the Reuters office in Schönhauser Allee as fast as he could.

A telex chattered out to police commanders that Factory Fighters could carry live ammunition but must be issued with blanks as well, and added that the use of water cannons and smoke canisters was permitted according to local situations. The noose was tightening further and Kellett-Long would witness the full consequences later because the Reuters office stood only about 300 metres from the line at Bernauer Strasse and 'as the morning went on people gathered and the Factory Fighters gradually pushed them to create a dead zone. The line of Factory Fighters came back very slowly during the morning.'

The timetable ticked and although it brought no insurrection, crowds were beginning to gather on both sides as the realisation settled into the reality. On the Western side near the Brandenburg Gate, some youths made noises and a (Western) policeman took their names. At 11.15, the crossing point at Wollankstrasse, two stops from Gesundbrunnen and where the line lay under a stout old bridge, reported 350 people on the Eastern side, adding that Westerners were 'trying to establish contact with them' – this meant, perhaps, waving to your parents, glimpsing your children, or saluting a lifelong friend. A photographer froze just such an image: a mother tentatively holding a baby across the wire so that the grandmother on the other side might lightly kiss the forehead.

A report near Wollankstrasse gave 200 people gathered on the Western side and 300 on the Eastern but the latter were being dispersed. At the same time, a crowd of 150 had assembled at Treptow on each side but didn't touch the wire and, again, the Easterners were being dispersed. A report said a senior West Berlin official arrived at the bridge opposite Warschauer Strasse and gazed across. He talked to people but on his own side and went away.

These were the last moments when the fury of a people might have prevailed. If enough thousands from the East had marched to the wire and begun tearing it down, what could anyone have done against them? Try and drive them back? Form cordons, arms linked? And what if the thousands were too strong, wanted it too much and were enraged by any attempt to deny them? But the moments were passing and each moment was a moment further away.

At 12.00, the Factory Fighting Groups achieved 40 to 45 per cent of their full complement but reports of desertions began. Eighty-two police officers and constables would also be punished for drunkenness and thirty-six discharged for refusing to obey orders. Did they let people through? Did they stand aside in disgust?

Also at 12.00, US press spokesman Hemsing felt able to leave his phones. He drove to the Brandenburg Gate and the Friedrichstrasse crossing point and found 'lots of police and Border Police patrolling the other side of the wire. Openings still existed, it wasn't shut off entirely. Some people showed their papers and mostly they'd be allowed through.' These included Easterners who'd finished the night shift at their jobs in the West and were going home as they'd done for years.

A male friend of the anonymous woman in Treptow arrived from the West around the same time and, as she remembers, 'he talked about something indescribable. All the U- and S-bahn stations were crowded, the stairways and escalators packed, nobody could change trains and he'd taken hours to get here.' The talk turned, inevitably, to the conversation of the afternoon before in the garden, and the question: Why hadn't she stayed? It was too late. The shape of so many lives – and nobody can ever know how many – were forever altered by decisions which, it seemed, could wait a while longer on Saturday 12 August and had assumed a ghastly finality on Sunday 13 August.

Johnson arrived at the Reuters office and snatched something to eat with Kellett-Long, who he found 'slim and tired out after about thirty hours on the go'. Johnson took the 'new orange office Wartburg to have a look at the scene. Adam had earlier reported East German police and Factory Fighting Groups armed with rifles and sub-machine guns forcing back sullen crowds in some places away from the closed sector border.

'I went to view ten East German tanks parked in a square not far from the border in a drab working class district about a quarter of a mile from our office [the street was one of the six bisecting Bernauer Strasse]. I asked to see an officer and was presented with a stern-faced young blond Captain who stood with his battle overalls over his grey-brown uniform. I asked him what the tanks were doing and he said, "You'll find it in the newspapers and on the radio." The tanks had been roped off and small groups of people stood around talking about the situation. One man said to me, when I asked him what was going on, "It's unheard of." An elderly woman said, "I was absolutely staggered when I heard about it." Other people looked out of house windows.'

At 12.00, the Border Police reported two escapes in Treptow.

It was dawn in Washington, and Washington would begin to catch up. Frank Cash found the State Department very quiet when he arrived at 7.00 a.m. – 1.00 p.m. in Berlin.

As I recall, only John Ausland and the routine duty officer in the Operations Centre were present. We didn't have a clear idea but we knew something was happening because we kept getting reports from Berlin. John was concerned about contingency plans but he didn't have the combination of the safe. I did and I opened it. John pulled them out and it is true there were no specific plans to deal with a barrier across Berlin. All of us had concluded the East Germans would have to act but, almost to a man – well, I know I did – we thought they would do it by stopping the refugees coming from East Germany into East Berlin: do it where they exercised complete control. None of us really conceived they'd erect a wall down the centre of Berlin. We started drafting a statement to be released by either the Secretary of State or the President.

Dean Rusk got a call. 'What I was told was more precise than just something strange in Berlin. It was obviously a restraining barrier even though in those first stages it was simply a matter of barbed wire – although, anyhow, the barbed wire was there to keep people from crossing.'[26]

By now in Berlin, the Factory Fighters pushed the crowd – a 'pretty angry' crowd, Kellett-Long noted – 'back about quarter of a mile. It was a highly tense situation they absolutely had to handle with kid gloves. I did not see anybody being hauled away, because anything could have set it off. They were being, and I have to say this, extremely gentle, amazingly so because normally anyone speaking to an East German in uniform the way these people were speaking to them would have been manhandled out instantly. Around the middle of the afternoon the Fighters reached a crossroad in Schönhauser Allee and lined up. They'd pushed the people right back, they thought, until nobody in the West could see them. They forgot our office and us sitting watching it.' Kellett-Long went down to ask some questions.

His wife Mary watched from the window. 'Suddenly I saw masses of policemen and then three or four great flashes and clouds of smoke. My first thought was that they were grenades and Adam was in the middle of it.'

'They tear-gassed them and told them all to go home. It was a ten minute rumpus, absolute chaos,' Kellett-Long continues. 'When I first heard the bangs I thought they were shooting. I got to the chap who seemed to be in charge and I said, "What the hell's going on?" and he said, "We are dispersing the crowd. Everything is calm. Remain clam. We are not shooting."'

In Washington, Ausland was told that Dean Rusk would arrive at 10.00 a.m., his usual time, and speak to the President in due course.

Rusk seems to have been a man disinclined to panic or nurture panic in others. Ausland waited for Rusk to come in.

Frank Trinka waited in Berlin but 'like the crowds, in anticipation that an event might take place, a confrontation of some sort or a breakout or an uprising. It never came. We'd gone over a third time and a psychological moment came in the early afternoon when the crowd could have gone either way after, I guess, they realised the Allies weren't going to do anything. These guys – the police and Factory Fighting Groups – had guns and the people weren't about to test them head on because the few that did were hauled off immediately. Violent verbal exchanges took place and then the people were grabbed or moved on. Whether they were taken to prison or put in holding pens I don't know, but the police were quick to focus in on and grab the outspoken ones, those trying to whip up some sort of opposition.

'We went to the Alexanderplatz [a big square in the East] where thousands of people remained until late afternoon, and government agitators, planted in the crowd, decried the West. The crowd waited and anticipated but the crowd-control was effective. If people said anything the Factory Fighters took them out and took them away. The Fighters also lined up with their guns and forced the people back. We visited various crossing points and saw thousands hoping, I guess, to flee. The women carried handbags and pushed baby carriages but I don't remember anyone holding suitcases. Maybe they'd liquidated everything into money.'

At 3.40 p.m., the Border Police reported a group of fifty had escaped between the Brandenburg Gate and Potsdamer Platz but gave no further details. At 3.45, they announced an arrest at Wollankstrasse. Ten minutes later a group of six escaped near Treptow and, ten minutes after that, two escaped north of Wollankstrasse, sprinting across the railway line in a strong, desperate burst of movement. Some escapes were only reported to the Western media: a man grasping a soldier's sub-machine gun and running over the line brandishing it; a man impulsively swimming a canal fully dressed; a man clambering a cemetery wall and dropping into the West.

Johnson and Kellett-Long decided to test their own rites of passage and drove to the Friedrichstrasse crossing point. They were allowed over but 'of course our office Wartburg had East German number-plates and the West Berliners were very, very angry – they didn't know who we were,' Kellett-Long says. 'They spat at me. We tried to hold up our British passports and we lived through tense moments until we got clear. These people shouted and shook their fists.'

He made another sweep during the afternoon and took Mary. 'We went round the border', she wrote in her diary, and 'by this time large crowds stood and watched and goaded the policemen. The police and Factory Fighters closed all the streets near the border and they all had guns. We thought that there might be demonstrations but on the whole the mood of the people was peaceful. They lacked a leader. Watching the border seemed to be the new Sunday afternoon pastime.'

One journalist noted that 'at one time, in a one-square-mile area . . . at the Brandenburg Gate and East German government headquarters, there were 25 tanks, 70 armoured troop carriers and 200 trucks filled with combat-clad police and soldiers. As they roared down Unter Den Linden [the avenue in the centre of East Berlin which ran from the Brandenburg Gate] the catcalls of East Berlin crowds were so loud that they could be heard hundreds of yards away.'

Another journalist saw the road leading to a crossing point at Spandau 'jammed with West Berlin cars heading East for a look'. Easterners would form mighty queues for a look in much the same way, too – but that was on 10 November 1989.[27]

At 4.00 p.m. it was 10.00 in the morning in Washington. Kohler arrived at the State Department and so did Rusk, unhurried, certainly unflustered. 'I think I'm a calm man under pressure and I'd been through many crises in my day,' Rusk told me. 'My limousine came and picked me up at my house in Quebec Street and I was driven in.' He went to his office on the seventh floor – plush, as those of bureaucrats go, he insists. 'It had a sofa and paintings on the wall which came from the Museum of Modern Art in New York and were rotated by them.' Rusk gathered 'as much information as I could and I reminded myself that what the East Germans and Soviets did to their own people had never been a case of war and peace between NATO and the Warsaw Pact. Yes, I reminded myself of this.

'We anticipated the East Germans and Soviets would take some action but we didn't know exactly what. The erection of the wall came as a bit of a surprise to us all. It should have been included in the possible action they would take. The wall was a monstrous monument to the nature of the East German regime and we knew at once that its purpose was not to keep people out but to keep people in, that it was directed against the Easterners rather than the Westerners. So we did not take any military action against the wall – it was defensive on their part. No member of NATO, including West Germany, recommended that that action be taken because it might have been World War Three, oh yes. Moreover, we didn't take action because of the nature of Berlin's location and the nature of the forces surrounding it. A military response would have been futile and self-defeating and did not figure in our estimates.'

For a precise update, Rusk asked Kohler to ring the Mission in Berlin on an open line. 'Not a risk, really,' Rusk says, 'because the East Germans and Soviets knew what they were doing. We wouldn't be giving any information away.' Kohler spoke to Allan Lightner, who briefed him, but the telephone conversation did not end there – and the dividing of the Americans began.

Rusk forbade anyone in Berlin to issue a protest to the Soviet Union. 'What comment would come would come from the President. That was my decision. This was a serious situation and it would be perfectly natural for the President to be personally involved in any action we took or any statements we made. It was not a situation in which underlings – and in that I include the Secretary of State, myself – could do so on their own.'

Hemsing remembers Lightner getting the call. 'I was supposed to make some sort of statement and that was a terrible time,' he says. 'In addition to being the spokesman for the US Mission we had a system of rotating the Allied spokeman, and the US was in the chair. Therefore I'd also become the Allied spokesman. Rusk said, *Hold up on everything, no statements, the statements will be made here in Washington.*' Hemsing would have to live with that but, leaving statements aside, what about a protest to the Soviet Union? 'Altogether, I believe, it was fifty-six hours from the time the East Germans actually infracted the Four Power Agreement to the time a protest came, which as you may imagine had a terrible effect on the Berliners. They all knew the drill and previously an incursion by, say, an East German military vehicle would get a protest in a matter of hours and we'd present it in person at the Soviet headquarters at Karlshorst. Now a wall was going up in dead silence and Lightner and I were absolutely outraged.'

Muller also remembers Lightner getting the call. 'Foy Kohler phoned him with Rusk standing there dictating what Lightner could and could not do. My British counterpart and I had our protest drafted and Rusk said *no statements at all* because it was so serious a matter. The Allies wanted to deliver the protest in Moscow and the West Berliners said, "My God, what's happening?" Before this, any little infringement met with an immediate protest to Karlshorst and now nothing's happening, now here is the real thing surrounded by silence. In Berlin we felt handcuffed.'

This friction ran like a theme into the days ahead. Washington took the global overview, with Rusk constantly reminding himself and Kennedy of nuclear conflict. The US community in Berlin took the emotive and personalised view, insisting the overall significance of the border sealing hadn't been appreciated and the mood of the West Berliners hadn't been appreciated, either. The friction built itself upon an already existing friction: Kennedy believed the situation in Berlin so emotive that it affected the judgement of Americans there: 'They go to the city', he'd say, 'and come back Berliners.'

George Muller of the Mission says 'the attitude of Washington was well nigh incomprehensible. We were always tainted with the brush of "Berlinitis" and there was inevitable tension between the diplomats on the spot and the foreign office at home, but in this case it was particularly striking because a number of our senior and otherwise highly respected diplomats argued nothing should be done. Their reasoning ran: "Khrushchev and Ulbricht cannot tolerate this blood-letting of East Germans, they had to do something, the wall was what they did and it will defuse the crisis." We in Berlin argued the opposite: that if Khrushchev got away with it, the operation would be a two-stage thing with much tighter controls to come.'[28]

The intensity of the friction only became clear after a couple of days. Now, on Sunday morning in Washington, 'Kohler turned up and disappeared into Rusk's office,' Ausland says, 'then he came back and told us "We've agreed to issue this" and it was basically the points I'd worked out, plus one Kohler added when I'd spoken to him on the telephone. Only later did I learn of the telephone conversation between Kohler and Lightner in which he told Lightner to lie low while we took care of this. Kohler read out this press release. I said, "Well, OK, now we know what we are going to say but some people are going to wonder what we are going to do" and Kohler said something to the effect of "Well, let's not be in a hurry on this. After all, that refugee flow is causing a lot of problems and we need to think about it. You call a meeting of the Task Force for tomorrow morning and let's take a look at the problem then."'

Rusk needed to talk to Kennedy 'because there was a chain of events that demanded I did. Cable communication was sent to the White House and then to Hyannis Port as a matter of course, as a matter of information.'

At 10.00 a.m., Kennedy attended mass in the Church of St Francis Xavier and changed for a cruise on the *Marlin*. As the cruise began, a message (presumably from Rusk) arrived at his mobile communications centre in a local yacht club. It was placed in a sealed envelope and taken to Kennedy's military aide, Major-General Chester V. Clifton, who opened and read it. Clifton used a walkie-talkie to reach Kennedy's secret service agent on the *Marlin* and the yacht returned to shore. Kennedy telephoned Rusk, they reviewed the situation and Kennedy approved the statement.

In part it read:

The authorities in East Berlin and East Germany have taken severe measures to deny their own people access to West Berlin. The refugees are not responding to persuasion or propaganda from the west but to the failures of communism in East Germany. The pretence that communism desires only peaceful competition is exposed. The refugees, some half of whom are under 25 years of age, have 'voted with their feet'. . . . Limitation on travel within Berlin is a violation of the right of free circulation throughout the city.

To emphasise that, Rusk cited the Four Power Agreement signed in Paris on 20 June 1949; but the words seemed predictable and impotent to a population feeling isolated, violated, frightened and abandoned. Rusk had to address broader considerations. 'An uprising in the East and the unpredictable consequences of that was in my mind when Kennedy rang,' Rusk says. 'We simply did not know what the East German people thought and whether there would be any demonstrations or action which might force Soviet action to suppress it. We had to keep that in mind as one possibility.' Rusk could give Kennedy dispassionate advice.

I saw Kennedy many hundreds of times but my relations with him were strictly business, they had to do with the business of government and did not involve his personal circumstances, his family circle or anything like that. He always called me Mr Secretary and I was the only member of the cabinet with whom he used that term. Jacqueline Kennedy once said at dinner, 'It's very significant my husband always calls you Mr Secretary' but she didn't explain the significance and I didn't ask her. It could have been a sign of respect or it could have been a sign of distance. I preferred it that way myself because I'd learned from George Marshall [of the Marshall Plan aid scheme fame] that you ought to keep at arm's length from the people who are working under you and are working over you.

How did Kennedy handle it over Berlin? Well, there wasn't much handling to be done except to fortify the morale of West Berlin and that was the real problem we had. Kennedy was pretty cool throughout the several crises through which we lived – he did not get flustered and he did not get emotional. He kept his eye on the main theme of the problem rather than be diverted by extraneous incidents of various sorts. He was a very impressive man, cool and calm in a crisis, very well informed, a rapid reader from a technical sense.

He was very conscious of the fact that he was the first President to be born in the twentieth century and he thought that gave him a mandate to review the bidding on all sorts of conventional policies to see whether they still made sense. We probed all sorts of conventional wisdom – and yet he was fun to work with. He had a sardonic sense of humour which he used first of all on himself so that, when he used it on you, you didn't mind. He'd look at a situation in a balanced way.

We knew that some action would be taken but we didn't know what: we didn't know that they were going to drive trucks up with barbed wire in them. We didn't get any indications of that at all ahead of time. I would have to say that tactically we were caught by surprise but strategically that wasn't the same thing.

Kennedy decided on no panic and no suggestion of panic. Rusk was due to attend a baseball game in the afternoon and he was advised to go to that. Kennedy would resume his cruise. The President's press spokesman said the President would not return to Washington until Monday morning as scheduled, when he'd have a pre-arranged meeting with the US Ambassador from Moscow, Llewellyn Thompson.

While this prudent but placid strategy unfolded in Washington, the timetable ticked in Berlin: incident sheets were filled, crowds gathered and dispersed, little flurries of movement stirred and died. The current of resentment did not, however, find a central, cohesive means of expression; did not find, as Mary Kellett-Long observed, a leader. How could it? All opposition had been rigorously suppressed since 1949. In the late afternoon Frank Trinka toured East Berlin again and judged the psychological moment for insurrection had gone.

Bernard Ledwidge journeyed to see from the Western side and noted the barbed wire but 'no signs of a wall. One did not know exactly what was going to happen at that stage. It was pretty clear they had sealed off East Berlin for German traffic but not Allied traffic – a very important point because, by doing that, they kept the crisis below boiling point. We could not have accepted exclusion from East Berlin. They took care to build all their obstructions on their own territory about five yards back from the actual line and we had no authority to attack those positions under the existing arrangements. However, if we'd been refused passage the fat would have been in the fire.

'The Brandenburg Gate looked quite different from normal because on the Western side the police erected barriers to keep the crowds back. The crowds were not allowed anywhere near the border line and the Soviet memorial [just on the Western side of the Gate] was given a special British guard so the locals couldn't get at it. We kept the temperature down in that way. Our Deputy Commandant, a new man, drove into the East in an official car to see if he actually could. Our Military Police were doing it all the time: they sent regular patrols round East Berlin and all those were admitted. The police looked them over but didn't prevent them.'

By coincidence, the famous and respected American broadcaster, Ed Murrow, was due to visit Berlin. 'As luck would have it,' Hemsing says, 'Murrow, then Director of the US Information Agency, had a long-planned trip. I asked someone to go and meet him at the airport and said I'd see him when he was installed in his guest quarters. Instead, Murrow immediately requested he be taken on a tour of the border, which he did for several hours.' Murrow's presence would assume particular significance.

Heinz Sachsenweger reached East Berlin after the difficult journey from Brandenburg.

I went to the factory and said here I am. The Fighting Group I commanded were in Treptow and we had to stand there for the first fourteen days after August 13, sleeping a few hours in the factory. I came from a very anti-Fascist family. I don't say that so people will admire me, it's just a fact. My father was a communist put in a concentration camp under Hitler. In 1961 we thought the wall was necessary. We stood in Treptow with machine guns and rifles because at the very beginning it wasn't even wire everywhere, it was only the men of the Fighting Groups. None of my hundred defected and I don't remember any people shouting at us.

We were stationed by some small gardens near a canal, and the gardens were typical of what Berliners had, chickens and rabbits. One member of the Group stole a rabbit to cook but we took him to the local police station. We arrested him because we did not want the people to think of us as thieves. We were convinced we were doing something good, we thought the GDR was a genuine alternative to German history and, of course, the international situation was very complicated then. Some in my Group even said 'Why not a barrier earlier?' in order, they thought, to calm that down.[29]

Such sentiments were scarcely reported in the Western media and have been barely covered in many subsequent studies. The coverage understandably pumped enormous moral indignation from the developed, fixed images recorded quite passively – that baby held tentatively across the wire and the grandmother's kiss bestowed so lightly on the forehead; the tanks along an ordinary street like Warschauer Strasse; handkerchiefs dabbing at swollen eyes, then waving to a loved one, then dabbing the eyes again – but, this late Sunday afternoon, many in East Berlin experienced an emotion far removed from the immediate and unavoidable suffering. They felt relief.

No understanding is complete without examining that, because it explains why the Factory Fighters and the police held steady. They were obedient but not blindly so, and although the number of ordinary citizens who shared their beliefs cannot be quantified, it may have been substantial. The whole of East Berlin, after all, did not fall enraged upon the wire and rend it asunder.

On an everyday level, East Berliners were tired of being humiliated by the power of their Western neighbours with their Deutschmarks which had to be balanced against the relative worthlessness of their own East mark. Mary Kellett-Long encapsulated that when she wrote in her diary a few days before: 'Hairdressers are plentiful and cheap. The great majority of clients had been West Berliners able to have a good hairdo at a fifth the price due to the exchange rate, but because of a clampdown any who come over now to the tailor or furriers must pay in D-marks at a rate of one to one. The majority of East Berliners are pleased by this move because it was annoying for them to have to wait weeks for a dress or hours in the hairdresser while Westerners got priority. On the black market, they got East marks for nothing, really. Within a week of 13 August you could buy butter, buy all sorts of things you couldn't before because – no doubt about this at all – I know lots of West Berliners would come over and do their weekly shopping.'

A 21-year-old, 'Jakob' was representative of this. 'We always went to the East side, my father also, to the gasolene station because it was very cheap.' He had experienced the clampdown before the wall.

'There were Stasi at parking places, you couldn't have any contact with the people and you could never offer someone a cigarette. The Stasi watched constantly. Someone might come up and try to talk but even traffic wardens watched out for that. I felt it very strongly. Once my car was broken into while they searched it for Western newspapers or anything else. They took the insides of the doors off.'

Gerda Stern, a Communist Party member since 1932, endured the frustrations of the hairdresser (something she emphasised to illustrate the humiliation). 'The Westerners came to buy everything because we were very cheap for them.' She welcomed the border sealing.

Elli Kohn, a Communist Party member since 1928, says that 'honestly I wished the wall would come because I saw the state of the area I lived in – terrible. Even the workers were divided. Some had jobs in the West, earned West-marks and lived like kings here compared to Eastern workers being paid in East marks. Like everybody else, I didn't know about the sealing but the question was, how could the situation be stabilised? We wanted action to staunch the brain drain and stop the young people, the highly qualified people, from leaving. We were trying to rebuild the country and this prevented us doing it.

'I lived in Karlshorst, I heard the news on the radio and I saw tanks in the street moving towards the city centre. My reaction? *Now we will be left alone, we will have our peace and we can continue to rebuild properly.* I don't know, of course, if most thought this but I do know a lot did because it had reached a point where it could not go on. We did not realise it would assume such tragic proportions. For example, part of my family lived in the West and I couldn't see my brothers and sisters.'

Horst Pruster, the policeman hard at work in the Interior Ministry, says at first 'we didn't recognise the whole extent of the measure but we knew things couldn't go on as they were. Many people worked in West Berlin, and they were millionaires – they lived here in the East in cheap flats, they didn't pay taxes because they didn't work here, but they took all the social advantages.'[30]

Sachsenweger re-emphasises his own words: 'Although it must have been difficult to keep the operation a secret, East Germany was very well organised, even in the first years of its existence. We had a lot of committed people and, to the majority of the politically active, the wall meant something good.'

Heiner Muller, a playwright, said retrospectively: 'We were pleased about the wall. We thought we'd be free to discuss our own problems at last.' And Stefan Hermlin, a writer, looking back, remarked, 'I repeat, the wall was not a crime. The wall was an action taken by the state in an extreme emergency. Don't forget the cold war, don't forget the postwar period. Millions in the GDR were in favour.'

At the time, however, Hermlin relayed a disturbing anecdote to Muller that 'while we had been happy about the wall Otto Gotsche, Ulbricht's secretary, was saying, "We'll crush anyone who's *against* us, against the wall."' He concludes, 'We were so innocent, we never thought anyone could think like that.'

Honecker himself said later that 'the Cold War had reached its height. A mass exodus from the GDR was being organised. As a result the Political Consultative Committee of the Warsaw Pact met in Moscow in July. By unanimous decision the GDR was charged with taking the frontier with West Berlin and the FGR under its control. Of course there were human tragedies, but the main issue was to safeguard peace because instability in central Europe meant a danger to that.'

Easterners knew the haemorrhaging threatened the basic fabric of their lives but they also understood that the Soviet Union would not tolerate the country melting into West Germany, with the spectre of a vengeful, wrathful Fourth Reich rising someday. It simply didn't matter how uneasily this knowledge had to coexist with empty shelves in the shops. The knowledge recognised the fact. (By something of an irony, Lenin himself defended the violence of revolution by saying 'You can't make an omelette without breaking eggs', but he didn't mention what happened if you didn't have eggs. . . .)

On yet another level, every East German remained acutely aware of the desirability of peace at virtually any price and East Berlin, still trying to rise from the rubble of war, was a daily reminder of that. Each overgrown bombsite, each broken building, each street corner with its stonework gouged by the bullets of 1945 whispered what the alternative to peace looked like.[31]

Nor did every citizen regard the Soviets as oppressors, something else largely unreported, and Gerda Stern – the communist since 1932 – captures aspects of that. 'Many people worked with the Soviet Union to defeat Hitler. We thought we had to have the Soviet Union and only the Soviet Union to do that, to stop Hitler and then make a better world.'

Sometimes history seems to have been written in and by the West, and the East *seen from the East* remains an unknown, darkened place – the way it goes.[32] What went on from the 1940s through the early 1960s all too often gets lost in the refugee totals at Marienfelde and the kisses on the baby's forehead.

But a large number of people were communists because they were determined to make the world better. They saw themselves as liberators. Leaving aside innate German discipline, one cannot imagine *this* quantity of Factory Fighters holding the line in the uncertain night unless they were believers. They could have turned over and gone back to sleep. The Factory Fighters were not seeing the future flow away, they were taking the first steps towards creating it, in public, on camera with, here and there, the most distressing abuse being shrieked at them; and they stood and they took it.

Nor were the communist leadership crazed tyrants, as they were portrayed in the West. If you seek power you go where power is, and this is exactly where the communists of the 1930s did not go. After 1933, if you sought this power, or even a taste of it, you joined the Nazi party and *ruled*. You did not go, as Ulbricht did, on his own tortuous journey from Berlin to Moscow where he'd spend each moment, especially the hours of darkness at the Hotel Lux, utterly at the whim of Stalin: Ulbricht, a German exile even as the German Army was tearing the Soviet Union to pieces. Consider it. Stalin, most malevolent of men, killed his friends as well as those who might be enemies; and in the last convulsive twist of paranoia thought that even he himself might be a counter-revolutionary, and logically *an enemy of himself*. What might he have done to Ulbricht, the German? He did it to other Germans in the Hotel Lux, the ones nobody saw again.

Yet still Ulbricht believed.

You did not go, as Erich Honecker did, to Nazi prison camps. There are disputes and contradictions about the evidence of this, and understandably so, but that does not disturb the central tenet. He was in the camps and if you sought power, and that was all you sought, you'd have been somewhere else, *anywhere* else.

These communists, who ultimately did get the power, can be imputed with all manner of failings, and have been, and will continue to be. The failings are writ large, and larger now the documentary evidence is in and all the witnesses can be called, but they cannot in all conscience be accused of insincerity.

It's a different argument as to whether communism was inherently flawed. In a sense, *that* logic had a chance to work itself out from 13 August 1961, and did, climaxing on 9 November 1989 by destroying itself across the white line Hagen Koch had painted, and thus ending precisely where it began.

To his last breath Honecker made no apologies because, in his eyes, he had nothing to apologise about and he remained sure that history would judge him well.

Until you understand this, you cannot understand the wall.

Perhaps the last word should go to Diana Loeser, the English-woman who'd gone to live in East Berlin. She was, as previously mentioned, visiting her home town of Birmingham, England when she heard the news of the wall going up and she prepared to return. 'If you lived in Berlin it was different to living in Frankfurt or wherever because the border was just up the road and you saw the smuggling, the black marketeering and the currency exploitation, and all of it was damaging the economy. We could have gone on trying to persuade people to stay through conviction but there was no chance. In West Berlin you saw the shop windows full, and you couldn't win economically on those grounds, so I was pleased when it went up. I thought at least we'd a chance of building socialism in this part of the world and, given a fair crack of the whip, it would go along at a galloping pace, we'd be all right and catch West Germany. The need for toing and froing across the border would go.'

Whatever, the toing and froing had gone now, gone for the dreamers, the believers, the disciples and the bloke in the corner bar wondering what it meant. He'd find out the hard way. They all would.

FOUR

First Week of the Rest of Your Life

When will they ever learn,
When will they ever learn?

Pete Seeger,
Where have all the flowers gone? *

That Sunday afternoon, a small boy in a cardigan, arms upraised, beseeched that he be allowed to cross, and a policeman adjusted the top of the wire so that he could. The policeman's head twisted away to see if anyone was watching him – someone was, and he was arrested immediately.

Another fixed image, taken quite passively, was of two soldiers positioned at a broad crossroads beside a lamppost and a litter bin, with a rambling web of the wire in front of them. Behind, a crowd lingered on the pavement not daring to go near. They formed the eternal backdrop of history, curious and uncomprehending.

At another place, where the wire hadn't yet reached, a Western motorist emerged from his car, advanced and an Eastern policeman pushed him in the chest. A soldier, bayonet fixed to the barrel of his rifle, prodded it towards the motorist. The portals of a tall, broad church loomed behind all this, eternal against the foibles of men. Was the motorist going there to worship, as he always had, and now found his church in another, forbidden, country?

Two soldiers faced a crowd at a crossroads while a third had gone among the people to silence or intimidate them. Beyond the crowd, two elderly women in summer frocks chatted, arms folded. The other part of their own street was less than 40 metres away and now it, too, was in another, forbidden, country.

Two Factory Fighters in shirt sleeves walked with a coil of the wire wrapped in a ball round a stout stick, a Fighter holding each end of the stick. As they walked, the wire automatically uncoiled and another Fighter, kneeling, lifted a strand of it and hammered it into a concrete post using cleats, gathered another strand and hammered that in, then another – row upon row, neatly spaced – until the wire was head high.

An elderly couple were escorted from the wire by a policeman, the sadness and the powerlessness expressed by the stoop of their shoulders.

A family of four smiled and smiled and explained how they'd managed to scramble over because some incident diverted the police.

An Eastern policeman said to a photographer: 'This is Free Berlin, taking photographs is not allowed here.'

On a street bisected by knee-high wire, people milled on both sides. In the East, a young man had his hands in his pockets; nearby, a plump woman held a baby and two women stood next to her. A policeman strode by, automatic rifle on his back. On the Western side, a very young girl wearing a frock trampled the wire down with her foot, presumably to step over it. Her mother, one of the two women standing together, scolded her for risking tearing the frock. A man in shirt sleeves went by on the Western side and made a joke so that suddenly everyone was laughing. Did the child step over? Did the mother step over? Did the policeman stride back and hold them apart? The moving camera had stopped filming by then, and what it had taken would be developed, carefully printed, fixed into the montage but giving only the present, not past, not future.

'Toasts of good luck were drunk by some of the East Germans who arrived in West Berlin but some women in Marienfelde wept quietly', Kellett-Long filed to Reuters. 'They said they waited in vain for husbands or children who had arranged to cross by another route for safety.'

At 5.52 p.m., a report to Police Headquarters noted 'several young people rampaging near the National Council building but armoured cars dispersing them', At 6.00, a police radio car announced, 'About 300 people are at the Unter den Linden– Friedrichstrasse intersection but do not show any negative attitude. Eighty per cent of them dispersed by the Factory Fighting Groups at 6.05 and the dispersing is being continued.' The Brandenburg Gate remained a place of potential insurrection, and that gave the Unter den Linden a particular importance.

Several reporters saw the dispersal at the intersection, Kellett-Long among them. 'A line of ten steel-helmeted black-booted policemen with rifles slightly down but at the ready faced the silent crowd. The atmosphere was tense in the centre of the crowd for a moment, but people gradually began to drift away while others took their place, and the moment was gone. The police, who also carried their usual pistols, were especially armed with automatic rifles.'

A *New York Times* reporter sensed 'a note of fury building up. Hundreds of young men moved down Unter den Linden. Two troop carriers drew up to reinforce the police. A line of rifles was raised slightly towards the crowd who made a slow backward movement.'

A report to Police Headquarters said 'security forces and water cannon deployed in the passage under the Brandenburg Gate by 6.20. The water cannons are not in action.'

Armoured cars, which had arrived earlier, moved fractionally through the Gate. A long cordon of men from six different services – the six to demonstrate solidarity – arranged themselves shoulder to shoulder in front of the armoured cars because the sector line bulged there. One of these men, a Factory Fighter, wore his uniform but white socks and sandals, betraying the haste in which he had come.

The sector boundary was a white line painted across the roadway but none of the uniformed men in the cordon put a boot – or a sandal – on it; they stayed fractionally behind. Above them, by the old stone charioteer on top of the Gate, a soldier with field glasses scanned a British Military Police jeep parked 100 metres away. The officer behind the jeep's steering wheel spoke into a walkie-talkie. A helicopter from the West skimmed by far overhead and banked, monitoring.

The GDR did not pass up a chance to fix images. From their side a photographer moved behind the cordon and took a picture through it so that the cordon appeared as a protective bastion against the threatening mob of Westerners in the distance who bayed abuse, shook their fists and chanted. A middle-aged man, seeing this Eastern camera recording him, cupped his face in a hand to mask it. Did he have relatives over there, did he fear retribution being visited upon them if he was recognised? Was he from over there and he'd made it? The images posed questions as well as answered them.

Kellett-Long saw 'a working party of police erecting six-foot high concrete posts for a wire fence across open ground in Potsdamer Platz and then the Brandenburg Gate'. The noose was still tightening. A crane with a grab would clear this obstruction away in a straight-forward demolition job – but this would be on Sunday 12 November 1989.

At 6.10 p.m., a report to Police Headquarters said a West Berlin senator would make a speech at the Potsdamer Platz at 7.00 – a possible incitement to insurrection. A reserve Factory Fighting Group of 162, stationed just off the Unter den Linden, was dispatched to cover that and, at the same time, an order went out to deploy water cannons in Potsdamer Platz. At 6.20, the Factory Fighters cleared the road between the Brandenburg Gate and Potsdamer Platz – 'No people gathered on the western side at the moment but several little groups in West Berlin.'

At 6.30, a report from Treptow said young Westerners had trampled the barbed wire. Another from nearby announced that 'Citizens can still go to West Berlin unhindered. The situation cannot be changed with our own forces. Measures will be taken.' The noose had not tightened there yet.

At 6.40: 'The situation at Potsdamer Platz is unchanged as a whole although West Berlin television has put up a second camera.'

Two minutes later, a report noted 'about 500 persons gathered at Wollankstrasse, mostly young and undisciplined. Two platoons of Factory Fighters and one platoon of police brought into action.' Five minutes later, the number on the Western side grew towards 800. They shouted across, 'Have you a ticket for the Walter Ulbricht Stadium [a few streets away]? They're showing the last piece of butter there.'

At 6.50, a report from Treptow said a crowd of 150 in the West and 100 in the East 'whistled from both sides' and a batallion of Factory Fighters 'normalised the situation'.

Peter Johnson of Reuters spent 'much of the evening on different sides of the Brandenburg Gate. On the Western side a crowd of several thousand collected and for a time got partially out of hand because the West Berlin police precautions had not been strong enough. Some groups made dashes onto the road in front of the Gate – the road itself was East German territory – and were driven back by water cannons mounted on armoured cars. [These were the ones deployed at 6.20.] Later, the police confined these people behind ropes. A section of the crowd, perhaps two or three hundred strong and composed mainly of teddy-boy-type youths, shouted rhythmically such slogans as "Berlin stays free" and "Away with the Goatee Beard"— Herr Walter Ulbricht, the East German leader, sported one.

'A British Army Corporal keeping watch in a radio jeep was critical of the West Berliners who, he said, were causing the tense situation at this spot. The left-wing Social Democratic Mayor of the [Western] district of Kreuzberg asked a police officer to move back the crowd to reduce the danger of a clash. One police officer, I was told, said that a member of the West Berlin Senate had been on the spot and said, "Let the people stay, it's good like that." While I fully understand genuine feelings of anger at the East German action, I think it is wrong to let it be manifested in this dangerous way and mainly by a lot of louts who have little political sense anyway.'[1]

Mary Kellett-Long noted in her diary that 'later in the evening big crowds gathered at the Brandenburg Gate at both sides and reinforcements were called in and water cannons used and someone threw a Molotov cocktail. Eventually everything quietened down without any serious incidents.' She added: 'I've been worrying about the Berlin crisis ever since we came here but, funnily enough, apart from about five minutes I've been quite calm and relaxed. What is the point of worrying really? If there is a war we shall be as safe here as anywhere because both the Allies and the Russians have great numbers of troops. My own feeling is that there will be no war.'

The water cannon were framed into the images: a youth rushed forward to throw the Molotov cocktail and long jets of spray from the nozzle of the cannon engulfed him; someone else rushed forward and turned at the furthest limit of the spray then scampered back with his arm raised in the most temporal triumph.

Westerners called out, 'Why don't you go and dig your own graves?'

Round the House of Ministries, six tanks, three armoured cars and six trucks filled with troops stood guard. 'The helmeted tank drivers were perched in open turrets ready for action.'[2]

At Hyannis Port, Kennedy cruised gently on the *Marlin*. It's worth restating at least one of the reasons why he did not return to the White House. As Frank Cash says:

Berlin was a very special place, the only cosmopolitan city in West Germany. Munich might be big, Stuttgart might be big, Hamburg and Frankfurt might be big but none of them were the cosmopolitan centre which Berlin remained even though cut off from the West. I think Kennedy thought those who worked in the Mission and those of us in the State Department working on Berlin over-emphasised its importance, but to us it was the crucial point of confrontation between East and West. Perhaps we were gung-ho about it although, incidentally, nobody in the Department recommended knocking the wall down.

Kennedy never really committed himself to the whole of Berlin and you'll notice that all of his statements emphasise West Berlin. He constantly said, 'We will maintain our rights in West Berlin and our access to West Berlin.' Prior to that we, the Department, used the term Berlin because we felt that as an administrative area our rights were in the whole city. I think Kennedy felt if West Berlin was secure that was the main objective.[3]

The possibility that access might be cut in a second phase of the wall operation concerned Kennedy a great deal, but what could the United States physically do until that happened? So Kennedy waited and, in the meanwhile, did not intend to risk provoking an insurrection. It was an awesome power that one man, barely middle aged and on a cruiser off Nantucket Sound, might incite – by an inadvertent phrase, an innuendo, a hasty action – thousands upon thousands of total strangers a continent away to take to the streets and shake the world order; and it carried an inescapable conclusion. If they did, he would be powerless to help them.

He operated, too, within the nuclear constriction, that iron lung through which every United States President has had to try and breathe since September 1949 when the Soviet Union exploded their first atomic bomb. Each President would have to learn controlled breathing, even when he was running fast.[4]

Precisely to maintain visible calm, Dean Rusk prepared to attend his baseball game, Washington versus New York at Griffith Stadium in the north-west of the city, with his wife and 12-year-old daughter Peggy.

This measured approach found full endorsement and active promotion by the British Foreign Secretary, Douglas-Home, and also Prime Minister Macmillan, whose thinking had been conditioned by the slaughter of the First World War in which he served. The dictum was, better that grouse be shot on the Yorkshire moors than people in Berlin. The British did make a statement, a Foreign Office spokesman saying that 'restrictions which have been imposed on the movement between East and West Berlin are contrary to the Four Power status of the city and therefore illegal'. As an exposition of the obvious this is hard to fault, but it offers nothing more. The British, however, were in a harder situation than Kennedy because at least he could decide when to breathe out: they must hold their breaths until he did – unilateral action by the British belonged to the vanished imperial age. (GDR propaganda sensed the weakness of such statements and announced that, far from dismantling the barriers, they were here to stay.)

At 7.00, it was reported that 'a hooligan driver' burst through 'in a Trabant, colour white-red, number plate could not be seen and number of people in it could not be seen'. They may have been the first to escape using a vehicle, which was an obvious thing to do against barbed wire. Already, on some bridges, obstacles were being placed to prevent this.

Before dusk, Ulbricht – this portly man who'd been a believer since before Gerda Stern and Elli Kohn, who'd survived the Spanish Civil War and the Nazis, survived in Moscow at Stalin's whim and would survive into the decade beyond Khrushchev – made a tour of his own. He wore a white shirt, a tie and a light-coloured overcoat. Honecker, in a dark suit, walked behind. GDR television filmed the tour (although it was not shown for a week) and recorded a segment of dialogue:

Ulbricht: 'All the orders have been carried out on time, yes?'
Factory Fighter: 'Yes, yes sir.'
Ulbricht: 'Everybody was where he should have been at the right time, yes?'
Factory Fighter: 'Yes, sir. In the factories and our National People's Army.'
Ulbricht: 'The People's Army, yes . . .'
Policeman: 'The Factory Fighting Groups, their squads were there, too.'
Ulbricht: 'The Factory Fighters. And for support there are several tanks of the Soviet Army in reserve, yes, so that there won't be any misunderstanding on the part of our enemy, yes?' [Laughter]
Citizen: 'And we know those tanks . . .'
Ulbricht: 'Isn't that true. We know them, yes.'
Factory Fighter: 'Obviously the whole thing got to them [the West] because all day long a helicopter has been cruising around, they are burning up quite a bit of gas on behalf of us.'
Ulbricht: 'Yes, yes, ha, ha . . . well, I suppose everything is all right now, yes.'
Factory Fighter: 'I don't think they are going to say the "so-called GDR" any longer.'
Ulbricht: 'You see everything has simply been carried out on time, yes? Everything has simply been carried out. Everything is all right. There is no doubt everything is in order. The barbed wire is in place.'[5]

There is a certain awkwardness in these stilted words but the imperfections give authenticity, even as we hear ordinary people mouthing words they think Ulbricht wants to hear; but Ulbricht was under more pressure than anybody, including Khrushchev and

Kennedy. They might lose a round in the long tactical struggle sprawling across the globe; he might lose everything. How did he withstand this pressure? How did he cope? What did he think, *really* think? Did he have doubts and, more pertinently, self-doubts about a wall across a city? The answers are entombed with him in a Berlin cemetery and the only other person who could have told us lived in a plain, neat house with a modest garden a couple of streets from where the border, which her husband built, stood. She was called Lotte Ulbricht and when I asked for an interview in the early 1990s I got a polite refusal, typed on what seemed to be an ancient typewriter.

Darkness was drifting in and Al Hemsing spent a hectic evening because 'we'd planned a dinner with Ed Murrow and Mayor Brandt and, of course, Brandt got completely caught up. The phone kept ringing saying *he's coming, he's not coming, he's coming*, and eventually he didn't come. You can hardly blame him. That night a group of us sat around and Murrow said he needed to draft a telegram direct to the President, telling him what was going on from his [Murrow's] point of view. Murrow reverted to being a reporter, so to speak. He sent the telegram, it had a clear message and I have always felt it was one of the ones that "got through". The brunt was *a terrible thing has happened, not only for a violation of the Agreements but because so many people go back and forth every day, and this is a tremendous blow to the morale of West Berlin. Something needs to be done.* I've subsequently had confirmation that that message was taken very seriously by the President.'[6]

(Earlier Murrow had given an interview to RIAS and forged words as only Americans can. 'There is no Berlin crisis, it is Khrushchev's crisis. He has, in the vernacular of our western movies, told us to get out of town by noon tomorrow. We do not choose to depart.')

At 9.00 p.m., a photographer froze an image on the corner of a street bisecting Bernauer Strasse: five uniformed men stood under one of the stone arches bearing the burst of bullet marks of 1945, men who looked morose and gazed in mistrust towards the photographer. One of the five angled his face away. What did he fear? Was it shame?

No photographer froze what would have been an equally telling image. Two young East Germans undressed completely and swam across the Teltow Canal.

By evening, a portrait of two cities began to emerge, not Berlin and Washington but Berlin and Berlin. On one side lay the worked-for affluence which was being dispensed down the Ku-damm, enjoyed in shady clubs, eaten in international restaurants, and sat

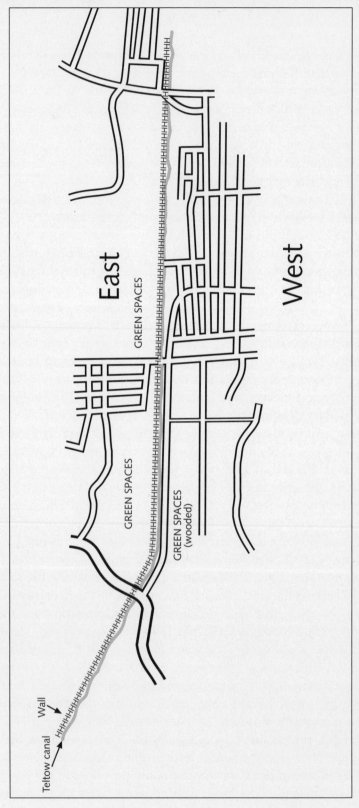

East

West

GREEN SPACES

GREEN SPACES

GREEN SPACES
(wooded)

Wall

Teltow canal

This is the Teltow Canal south of the city centre and, because of the green spaces on either side, a favourite place for early escapes.

through comfortably in the soft lighting of new apartments in futuristic buildings. Every smooth-tarmacked street was heavy with cars, many of them new cars. On the other side lay the worked-for poverty of waiting lists for accommodation along cobbled, potholed streets in pre-war apartment blocks so darkened and damaged they seemed to mourn what they had once been. People drank in little bars on the corner and played cards through the cigarette smoke across worn wooden tables.

These little bars, intimate by their cosiness, might be safe enough for a local to speak his mind and the natural forum for him to do it. If an insurrection came it would either be an impulse gripping a crowd at the wire or something explored, calculated and initiated in one of these little bars snuggled all over East Berlin. But as darkness drew its veil over the first day neither happened; and then it was too late.

At 10.30, a crowd of 4,000 lingered on the Western side of the Brandenburg Gate but for an insurrection to occur would mean bursting past their own police, then the cordon of Factory Fighters, then the armoured personnel carriers with the water cannons, then the Eastern police, before reaching Unter den Linden; and Unter den Linden had been cleared, anyway.

At 10.45, a report came in that 'a male person' had swum the Teltow Canal.

Towards 11.00, the radio reporter Peter Schultz finished his shift of seventeen or eighteen hours. 'I went with a colleague to the Brandenburg Gate because I'd been reporting about it all day but I hadn't seen it. I got a very destructive impression because what I saw was even worse than I'd imagined, the light of arc-lamps and, nearby, wire and soldiers and the Factory Fighting Groups and the street torn up. They bored holes in the surface with pneumatic drills. The West Berlin police had to work hard to push back protesters.'[7]

At 11.45, a report to Police Headquarters said the situation at the Brandenburg Gate 'remains unchanged. There are still young people on the Western side in green spaces in the area of the Tiergarten who are agitating against us.' Between 11.20 and 11.40, a report announced 'about 3,000 young people who had gathered at the Gate were dispersed by Western police using truncheons. During this, the young people shouted "you are beating the wrong side".'

By midnight, the passions and pulses of the day were ebbing and a report caught that: a gathering of 150 people in the East dispersed. It isn't clear where in the East and somehow that doesn't matter any more. They melted into the cobbled streets, walked uneven pavements under pallid lamplight, and they were gone just as the moment had gone.

The true numerical scale of what had happened was subsequently expressed in dry language in a Western publication:[8]

Before August 13, 1961, the Sector Boundary dividing West Berlin and East Berlin was crossed by 500,000 Berliners every day. Eight to ten million inhabitants of East Berlin and the Soviet Occupation Zone visited cultural and sporting events in West Berlin every year. Until August 13, 1961, the metropolitan railway (S-bahn) and the underground railway (U-bahn) were public conveyances for inter-sector passenger traffic.

The communist sealing-off measures, however, ended the through-traffic of eight metropolitan and of four underground lines. In the Soviet Sector, all the 48 metropolitan railway stations were closed for inter-sector traffic, and, of the 33 underground stations in East Berlin, 13 were closed completely. For the inter-sector traffic of foreigners and citizens of the Federal Republic of Germany, a special platform has been established in East Berlin both at the metropolitan and at the underground station in Friedrichstrasse.

The sector and zonal border round West Berlin cuts 193 Major roads and by-roads, 62 of them leading into East Berlin and 131 into the Soviet Zone. Before August 13, 1961, the sector boundary between West Berlin and the Soviet Sector could be crossed at 81 crossing points. On August 13, 1961, 69 crossing points were blocked by barbed wire or walled up. Twelve specially marked crossing points remained open for the purpose of entering the Soviet Sector.

By midnight, the reports coming in to Police Headquarters altered. An order went out that the Factory Fighters in Prenzlauer Berg must be relieved at 2.00 a.m. and replaced by two units of 100 each from the Mitte district. The order recorded those to be relieved: 'the second battalion motorised (101 comrades) and the seventh General battalion (46 comrades)'. A report said the Factory Fighter at crossing point 49, towards Treptow, 'who was injured by a smoke bomb has been taken to hospital and is being treated'. The Fighter thought he had time to pick it up and return it, and misjudged that.

A policeman recorded he'd picked up 180 cigarettes tossed to him from the West to entice or provoke him.

At crossing point 68, south of Treptow, a police inspector reported that the Factory Fighters 'have not received any provisions today. They do not have any torches and some of them have no blankets. They are in a bad mood.'

The incident sheet recorded a total for the day of sixty-six escapes and one caught; and although there must have been many more, the tightening of the noose produced an almost complete reduction in the number of refugees reaching Marienfelde, where the total of 150 registered compared to 2,662 on the Saturday. It is not known the numbers of those who got across and, bypassing Marienfelde, went to a mother, a father, a brother or sister, an aunt, a friend and slept there, and went looking for the rest of their lives on the Monday.

There must be 4 million postscripts. Here are just two. 'I can honestly tell you,' Lutz Stolz says, 'that Sunday 13 August 1961 passed normally for us, at least without us panicking. I tried to reach all my friends by telephone and they were as filled with consternation as Uta and I but we did not go anywhere near the border. We didn't panic because we were young and we hadn't realised what it all really meant.'

Geoffrey McDermott wrote: 'So August 13 ended after more than the usual quota of telegrams had been sent off to distant capitals asking for instructions.'9

Meanwhile, at 11.45 p.m. Michael Moore, a corporal in the 4th Royal Tank Regiment, had slotted his tank into position on the Western side of the border behind a railway station and wondered how he'd keep himself awake.

MONDAY 14 AUGUST 1961

At 1.00 a.m., the Border Police stopped a party of two at crossing point 45 and entered it on the incident sheet using the same headings as the day before. At 1.30, X + 24 hours, 5.96 miles of wire barriers on concrete posts had been erected.

Before dawn, Corporal Moore could see nothing of the street where his tank stood – Invalidenstrasse, not far from the old disused Hamburg main line terminal. A canal curved to the right and a bridge lay directly ahead. The East began at the other end of the bridge and the buildings there stretched away like sentries guarding the past. 'Every now and again I would search around visually using the episcopes [optical projectors] and binoculars, but if the image is black, magnifying black seven times doesn't really improve it.' At dawn, a shape revealed itself, a tank which he identified as a T34-35 and bearing Soviet markings. Headquarters wanted to know how far away it was and he said, 'about fifteen yards'. Incredulous, headquarters queried that and he confirmed it: 'Our gun barrels were more or less five yards apart.'

Moore decided he'd have a mug of the tea which the radio operator had already brewed (egg sandwiches were coming in a minute). He took the mug, popped up from the observation hatch and placed it on the flap in front of him. 'Till then there had been no sign of life from the T34. It could have been an empty hull but – and I nearly spilled my tea – the Commander's hatch opened and a head appeared wearing one of those super Soviet helmets and a pair of binoculars. All I could see was him looking at me and me looking at him. I suppose he was probably intrigued about the tea more than anything else.' Corporal Moore leaned forward and gave him a 'gentle wave'. The Soviet commander ducked down, shut his hatch and was seen no more.

Invalidenstrasse was one of the twelve crossing points open and the Soviet tank was fully entitled to be there on the very lip of the Soviet zone, but Moore's experience provides a curious historical footnote. Very few Soviet tanks were deployed within the city and this is one of the few sightings.

Mary Kellett-Long wrote in her diary, 'I woke this morning feeling considerably rested to find that everything had quietened down somewhat. Of course everyone except the Grenzgangers [who lived in the East but crossed daily to their jobs in the West] was at work.'

An artificial normality had returned. Shops opened, factory shifts clocked on and off, and trams creaked down their tracks but no longer continued into the West. The S-bahn did still run West, but only from that one platform at Friedrichstrasse station, of course. The *New York Times* reported that: 'On the elevated train several hundred stiffly quiet people rode towards East Berlin. A blonde woman sobbed and tears creased her make-up. She breathed hard and forced herself to stop crying. At Friedrichstrasse, a middle-aged couple argued with mounting anger only to be pushed aside from the turnstiles by the policeman. As East Berliners, they cannot go West.' The same journalist noted 'thirteen tanks in an empty lot near the station. The crews were putting up tents and operating cook wagons.'

The GDR government methodically cleared up any overnight confusion. They issued a situation review and inserted into it brutally simple instructions:

The measures taken were successful and the enemy so completely surprised he was not able to take effective countermeasures.

There are attempts at the moment to go to West Berlin on a legal basis. Yesterday, for example, several thousand people tried to get permission and applied at police stations. It is to be expected that the number of these persons will increase. It is not the task of the police to support these attempts by giving the relevant information.

The Ministry of the Interior announces that the issuing of such permits and the regulations governing that will be given in a special announcement. This demonstrates without question that the exact time for issuing these permits is not yet fixed.

Every person who appears with such an application has to be told with no possibility of misunderstanding that an application is useless at the moment. They must be told they have to wait for an announcement. No exceptions can be made.

It is no longer permitted to shunt applicants from one authority to another because nobody wants to take responsibility. It is also necessary for our comrades of the People's Police to show their class-related standpoint over this.

There is no reason to raise people's hopes of getting permits out of sympathy or indecision.

The blame for the harshness resulting from these measures rests with those who for years have rejected the serious proposals of our government to banish the danger to peace arising from West German militarism.

The measures taken by our government serve to protect democratic Berlin and its people. They are an effective blow against the illegal, subversive smuggling of human beings organised by the extremists in Bonn. This means that the security bodies have the task of preventing the citizens of our Republic and its capital being made into victims of unscrupulous slave traders. This entails preventing the entry of our citizens into West Berlin.[10]

The impact fell upon ordinary policemen behind counters in ordinary police stations who had to turn away distraught humanity, weeping no doubt, pleading no doubt, a mother to see son or daughter, a man to resume his job – the shock hit West Berlin hard because 53,000 Easterners couldn't report for work and never would again – a widow to visit a grave. The human consequences of wrenching Berlin apart fell upon these policemen now instructed to behave unlike human beings.

The police had been shunting people away because, up until the instructions, it must have been easier than refusing them outright.

Whatever feeling the police had, the words 'no exceptions can be made' forbade equivocation. The noose was a tourniquet now.

During the morning an American journalist, Norman Gelb, went through the Brandenburg Gate. He recognised a policeman because when he'd gone through the previous Thursday they'd exchanged some banter about Gelb giving him a ride to the Ku-damm for a cup of coffee. This time, as Gelb says,[11] 'I stopped to be cleared and that same man, whose double-take indicated he recognised me, stiffly asked for my passport. He looked at it, handed it back, scanned the floor of the back seat of my car for any unauthorized passengers, saluted and briskly waved me on.'

Even now, the Brandenburg Gate remained a place for possible trouble. Peter Johnson wrote in his diary: 'Another example of how dangerous letting louts loose on the Western side can be came this morning when a youth in a small crowd, which the West Berlin police had ill-advisedly allowed to approach the border, again threw a Molotov cocktail onto the East German road in front of them. These weapons – a bottle filled with petrol – were used in profusion during the anti-communist revolt in June 1953 and could, in the mind of a communist East German policeman, have provoked a savage reaction. No wonder the West Berlin police used a certain amount of rough technique to hustle the youths away from the spot.'

Before Bodo Radtke, the journalist who'd returned from holiday, went to work 'I travelled to the border with my wife. We wanted to see with our own eyes. We saw barbed wire and at the Brandenburg Gate the people on both sides calling to each other "What's going on? Can we come? Can we go?" Nobody knew what the future held. Everybody was saying it's only for a couple of weeks, maybe a couple of months but not longer than that.'[12]

Mary Kellett-Long 'went through in a car and I must say it was quite a sight with Factory Fighting Groups all carrying sub-machine guns and about six armoured cars at strategic positions. There were also tanks in the side streets and water cannons on the Western side of the Gate. Apparently the number of forces has been increased and we wondered what was going on.'

Shortly after, an order chattered from Police Headquarters (extract):

Content: measures to be taken against provocation at the Brandenburg Gate.

Because of continued provocation, and particularly because of the agitation carried out at midday today by representatives of the

West Berlin Senate and the government of Bonn as well as the irresponsible demands of the broadcasting stations Free Berlin and RIAS to violate the border at the Brandenburg Gate and prepare for other dangerous acts, I order

(1) The crossing point is to be closed with effect from 14 August 1961, 2.00 p.m.

(2) The traffic from democratic Berlin to the Gate is to be diverted at Friedrichstrasse. The drivers and passengers of these vehicles will have to be given the reason for this measure. The forecourt of the Gate, which belongs to democratic Berlin, has to be sealed using construction equipment. The passages under the Gate have to be kept open to guarantee our special vehicles and security forces can get through for swift and effective protection of the barriers which the construction equipment is putting up.

On the Eastern side, the closure was announced by loudspeakers on vans, the voices flat and nasal.

Mary Kellett-Long remembers coming back by train 'and that was all right. There were fears that you weren't going to be allowed to go through at all.' She'd write in her diary: 'I came back on the S-bahn. It took ages. I had bought cigarettes and chocolate, newspapers and books. The trains now have to be emptied at Friedrichstrasse and everyone go through controls. I was stopped at least six times, once by a customs man who, I am glad to say, did not ask if I had any goods as I should almost certainly have lost all our cigarettes.

'We'd been wondering what the increases in forces meant and we found out when the Ministry of the Interior closed the Gate temporarily because of incidents. I don't know where all the people in cars come from. Usually the streets are empty but today a thick stream of traffic went up towards the Gate and hundreds of people just stood and looked. On the other side were tremendous crowds. The traffic was so awful I was glad I wasn't driving. The Berlin police were out in full force, including the riot police wearing tin helmets. There were film cameras and tourists gaping but everything quietened late in the day, and the West Berlin police moved the crowds right down to about half a mile away and the East Berlin police did the same. We think the Gate may be opened early in the morning.' It would be opened again, though not for traffic – and not until 1989. Now, in mid-afternoon, a curve of barbed wire snaked round the front of it in large, loose coils.

Brigadier Godfrey Hamilton, Commander of a British Infantry Group, stationed himself near the Gate on the Western side and watched the police keeping civilians away. When a reporter questioned him, he said as far as he was aware 'there are no Soviet forces in evidence in East Berlin but we know they alerted two motorized divisions in the area of Potsdam.' (Presumably he didn't know of the tank which Moore saw or perhaps regarded its solitary presence as legitimate and not worth putting into the equation.)

Al Hemsing dropped in on Reuters' West Berlin office near the Ku-damm to see the bureau chief, 'a wonderful guy. He and I had a very close personal relationship, we'd chat and say, "What do you know, what do you know?" A young lady cried at her desk and I asked her why. "I was away in West Germany and I gave my cat to my aunt in East Berlin to look after for the weekend and I'll never see it again."'

When Mary Kellett-Long reached the Reuters office in East Berlin she found that husband Adam, Peter Johnson and Erdmute Greis-Behrendt had been under arrest.

'Adam and I were slightly worried that Miss B. [Greis-Behrendt] hadn't returned from the Town Hall in Prenzlauer Berg where Adam ill-advisedly sent her to enquire about the numbers of East Berliners with jobs in West Berlin who had now registered for work,' Johnson would write.

He and Kellett-Long went to the Town Hall and 'at the wicket gate Adam and I presented our documents and explained who we were. A young man in plain clothes took us inside and showed us to a room where people were registering. He invited us to ask questions of them if we wished. Just then we saw Miss B. who told us she was waiting to see the top official, at present at lunch. Another man came along and offered to take us to the Major on the first floor. We walked upstairs and waited outside the Major's room. Three green-uniformed police officers came with several Factory Fighters and one of the police officers snapped, "You are temporarily under arrest."

'He immediately told us to get moving and to reinforce his order gave me a push. I protested at his rudeness. He took my passport and hit my hand when I said he had no right to take it and tried to get in back. He barked viciously, "Don't lay hands on me." We were taken back to the wicket gate, during which time Adam and I explained several times that we had declared our identity and that we were accredited to the East German authorities and all he need do was to ring the Foreign Ministry to check on that. Instead, after we had phoned from a cubicle, we were placed in the back of an elderly black BMW police radio car, where we giggled and joked for about ten minutes. Once I wound the window down a little and one of the policemen standing outside made me wind it up again.

'Then, with two policemen in the front seats, we were driven at breakneck speed to the borough police headquarters. After several furious corners I asked the driver if he was a racing ace. He replied with a grin, "I always drive like that." In the police headquarters, which is a few doors down the road from our East Berlin office, we were ushered into a barred room occupied by an artificial platinum blonde, a West German girl from Duisburg, who told us she'd been there since 8 a.m. – it was then 2.30 p.m. – after being picked up for entering East Berlin without a permit. They had not offered her a chair, but they brought three for us. I asked that they gave one to the girl, too, but she said she would rather stand. The door of the room was left open.

'Through the barred window we could see onto a wired-off yard, beyond which was a cemetery. I passed some time reading inscriptions on graves – *Meine Lieber Frau* [My Dear Wife] – and then Miss B. pointed out a coiled rope in the yard, which she opined was the hangman's rope. None of us had brought a nail file so we could not go to work on the bars! Instead, I spent some time convincing the police that they should ring up the Foreign Ministry, and asking them repeatedly to give us something to eat. First I was told, "You have to be here eight hours before you are fed" but after they became tired of my nattering, or had received instructions from higher quarters, we were told we would get something. Then, about an hour after we had been brought in, an elderly police officer entered with our passports and said, "You are free. . . . It was a mistake." We asked him what kind of mistake and he mumbled something about them having to be vigilant in the present situation. Just at that moment our lunch arrived – three large white porcelain bowls full of meat-and-noodle soup. We stayed to eat it up and Miss B. even congratulated the white-uniformed police cook who had been working overtime to supply the members of the *Einsatzgruppen* – the operational squads of police brought in to stop the refugee flow and stand by in case of disturbances.'[13]

Mary Kellett-Long wrote that 'as far as I can gather they took their arrest as a great joke and mystified the police by joking with them the whole time. Of course they came back and did a story about it and everyone was very amused. Someone from ADN rang Adam and congratulated him on his liberation.'

Johnson, also liberated, roved to the Brandenburg Gate. 'During the course of the day, apparently as a result of an order from the British occupation authorities in whose sector the road leading to the Brandenburg Gate lies, the West Berlin police pushed the crowds to about half a mile behind the barrier, thus relaxing the situation. Brigadier Hamilton, who made observations through battered field glasses, told me he thought the crisis was completely over.' As an aside, Johnson added in his diary: 'On the Eastern side there have been some clashes with police but no-one has been hurt as far as we know. They have happened when police have cleared away crowds who stood near the border looking sullen. There have also been minor brushes with people openly complaining about the new clampdown.'

The escapes went on, a group of four getting across in the south at 4.00 p.m. and, 90 minutes later, two more in the south. North of Bernauer Strasse, where the train ran along the border and no wire was yet in place, a youth sprinted but was caught by three policemen who wrestled him to the ground. He wriggled, seized one of their rifles, held them off with that and ran over the line. The policemen caught him again. A bayonet went into his knee and he lay in agony while the policemen backed off. He crawled into an allotment crying for help; fortunately someone heard and he was taken to hospital.

Klaus-Peter Grohmann, the young banker, felt drawn not to the Brandenburg Gate but the Potsdamer Platz. 'The barbed wire was already up, of course. I went to Potsdamer Platz because that used to be *the* place in Berlin. It had been bombed during the war and there was still evidence of that, but somehow it remained the place to go.' He surveyed this vast, emptied expanse so full of memories for every Berliner. He had friends and relatives over there but 'telephones were cut, everything was cut, you couldn't communicate with anybody'. He would visit his relatives again – but not until 1972 and only for one day, the maximum time permitted. (It felt 'like an adventure, travelling into a strange country'. There'd be small talk and then many, many tears.)

Kennedy flew to Washington from Hyannis Port and met the Ambassador from Moscow, Thompson, for fifty-five minutes during the morning and Deak Rusk for seventy minutes during the afternoon. 'Secretary Rusk and I went over to see the President in the family quarters of the White House and talked to him about countermeasures we might take,' Frank Cash says. 'I suggested two: first to get the West Germans to stop inter-zonal trade with the East and second to stop East Germans travelling to the West. Kennedy immediately dismissed these and implied they were minor and ineffective. The actual word he used was Cajan [from a small French-speaking community in Louisiana] – *picayun*.

'As I've subsequently read, the cessation of inter-zonal trade and the serious effect on the East German economy was one of the main concerns Khrushchev had in mind in letting Ulbricht put up the wall. The other measure was to cut off the only people the East Germans gave exit visas to, because they were the ones the government wanted to travel. The East Germans worked very hard to gain respectability and recognition and a lot of their efforts involved sending officials, musicians and athletes to Western countries.

'Kennedy appeared relatively relaxed because I think deep down he had made up his mind World War Three wasn't going to start in Berlin. Rusk and I recommended that he himself go to the city. We had had a lot of messages from Al Lightner saying how morale in West Berlin was plummeting. Kennedy said, "I'll think about it." I came away with the impression he was not overly upset with the situation as we all saw it but he also knew we had a morale problem and he'd consider somebody going to reassure the West Berliners. If we got to a direct confrontation with the Soviets, and nuclear weapons were to be used, he was the guy to have to do it and that's a very sobering responsibility.'[14]

Kennedy's thinking centred on Vice-President Lyndon Johnson and also on a resident of Chatham, Massachusetts, military (retd), Lucius D. Clay. There's a tale that Napoleon, when a young soldier, saw the storming of the Bastille and a biographer wrote that, had Napoleon been in charge of its defence, 'he would have known what to do'. If Lucius D. Clay had been in charge of the defence of West Berlin on Sunday 13 August 1961 he would have known what to do. Retrospectively, that terrified most of the State Department and many other people, too.

The Task Force met but moved among uncertainties. Would the barrier be permanent? Was this the initial move on a big board, with Allied access denied next? Was it only a clinical, surgical operation now completed?

That evening Peter Johnson spent an hour with his wife Elfi's relatives in West Berlin and 'found there Richard and Erna, Elfi's fiftyish cousins. We visited Richard's aged mother who is in hospital after a fall. We had a warm-hearted chat about the Berlin situation. They don't seem really worried. Usually the most worrying thing in such situations are the headlines in the London papers.'

That evening, too, a cameraman fixed an image which holds its poignancy: a hip-high stake in a pavement and those loose coils of wire undulating from a wooden door out across the street, the stake supporting it. A soldier stands, left arm folded over his chest nursing the muzzle of his rifle. He looks ahead, but away from the camera. The building behind him is typical East Berlin, two basement windows but the ornate façade decayed to expose the bricks. Faded script proclaims the place is a hairdresser's. A burst of machine-gun fire from 1945 has chattered into the masonry and the pockmarks remain. At the doorway a dark-haired, attractive young woman wearing a creamy dress has laid her canvas shopping bag against the wall. Her right hand is raised to her mouth, the index finger resting on her lower lip in the universal gesture of contemplation.

The photographer had chosen his angle carefully: in sequence the stake and the wire, the soldier, the woman fractionally to the right of the soldier. Was she looking over the wire for a husband, a lover? Was she in love with the soldier, waiting for him to finish his stint? Had she brought him bread and sausage in the shopping bag? Did she just stop and look and wonder? She must be old now and so must he, if they are alive, and whatever happened to them in between?

Ulbricht visited an army tank group, no overcoat this time but a panama hat and a light, baggy suit. He shook hands with a tank commander. Nearby, two gunners stood to attention in the hatches of their tanks. Other tank personnel, moving in around Ulbricht, wore pull-down headgear, the flaps drawn over their ears. They looked boyish and serious, he looked relaxed. He must have known he'd got away with it.

In the West there was a different image to be developed, fixed: a crowd behind a cordon of rope brandishing banners: GERMANY REMAINS GERMAN. THERE'S ONLY ONE GERMANY. It was true and untrue, all in the same moment.

In her diary Mary Kellett-Long wrote that 'telex and telecommunications have been cut with West Germany and we heard a story that post had been stopped but the East Germans denied it. We got into a great flap thinking about our teleprinter connection with Bonn but were able to telex and telephone London. In the evening we went to dinner and when we finished drove to the Brandenburg Gate. Things seemed to be quieter, not so many troops and all the tanks disappeared. When we got home we found a new decree issued saying West Berliners must get permits for their cars and motorcycles before driving them into East Berlin.'

The incident sheet clicked through its machine, adding and adding.

Time	Crossing Pt	Fled the State		Prevented from Fleeing	
		No. groups	No. people	No. groups	No. people
5.45	67	1	2		
6.15	11	1	2		
7.25	22	1	1	1	1
8.10	40	1	2	1	2
8.20	31	1	1		
8.30	68/69	1	3		
10.10	12			1	2

The Ministry of the Interior fleshed out these statistics in a curiously rambling report to Ulbricht:

In the time between 7.45 a.m. and 11.00 p.m. about one thousand West Berlin people concentrated near the barriers in the area of Potsdamer Platz. Around 11.00 p.m. there were still about two hundred people on the square, who then gradually dispersed.

The riot police erected an iron barrier at crossing point Adalbertstrasse [the twin curved roads and sunken gardens] at 1.00 p.m. and prepared for similar measures at the crossing point at Köpenickerstrasse [further up the curve].

At the same time another barrier was erected at Kellerbrücke.

Around 11.15 p.m. an estate car, number could not be seen, did not respect the halt sign given by the Border Police and drove through to West Berlin at crossing point Wollankstrasse. Other hooligan drivers at this crossing point have been trying to break through. Measures to change the situation radically at Wollankstrasse are to be taken on 15 August.

A *Bilt Zeitung* reporter who made provocative statements and took photographs of military vehicles was arrested at crossing point Bornholmer Strasse at around 2.20 a.m. He was brought to the People's Police station at Prenzlauer Berg [and was no doubt at this moment in Kellett-Long and Johnson's barred room. Was the platinum blonde still here and, if she was, what did the reporter say to her?]

At crossing point 45, Heinrich-Heine-Strasse, a driver was told the new regulations and had to go back and the vehicles following him were not allowed through by the Riot Police.

One hundred and sixty-six persons have been brought to police stations for checking and sixty-one have been released.

All the offices of the Berlin police have received instructions from the district leadership of The Party to enable them to answer questions from the public [the order to refuse all applications without exception].

It has to be pointed out once again that the majority of the wives of our People's Policemen have a high degree of understanding of what their husbands are doing.

A battalion of police brought from outside Berlin have been accommodated in a schoolhouse in district Lichtenberg and another battalion in a slaughterhouse.

The mood of the population on the basis of previous reports: no new information resulted from the reports given during the night.

2,365 daily permits were issued to West Berlin citizens from 7 a.m. to 8 p.m. on 14 August. One hundred and twenty of the two hundred and fifty-five applications to travel out of Berlin into the area of the GDR by West Berliners have been granted. 9,851 permits to go to West Berlin have been applied for by the citizens of democratic Berlin on 14 August.

The incident sheet recorded its total for the day: fifteen escapes, seven caught. Marienfelde recorded its total for the day, forty-one. The noose had tightened.

TUESDAY 15 AUGUST 1961

The GDR government used the night again, tightening and tightening.

'Shortly after midnight,' Peter Johnson wrote, 'they announced that West German cars would be banned from East Berlin without special permits because such cars had been used for "spying". Doubtless some have smuggled refugees and goods, because so many cars cross from the West that only a minority are subjected to check, but this measure shows how worried the East Germans are about the atmosphere in their own population and are determined to go to extremes to stop people fleeing.

'Another restriction banned East Germans from holding identity cards issued by other countries or authorities, including West Berlin. Penalty: at least three years' imprisonment or a fine, or both. This is designed to prevent people fleeing by showing the identity card of another country because, at present, foreigners, West Germans and

West Berliners can still move to and from East Berlin after showing documents.'

The clearing of woodland in the country began, swathes sometimes cut to a depth of 60 or 70 metres. It kept Rudiger Hering far from the brook and the bridge and the farmhouse nestled over the meadows. 'They came at 3.00 in the morning with lorries, a Factory Fighting Group from Falkensee. The people living in the two houses on the border were told they had to leave immediately. I knew where some went but not others. Then bulldozers destroyed the houses completely.'

'Much quieter this morning', Mary Kellett-Long wrote, 'and lots of the troops and tanks have been moved. The Brandenburg Gate is still closed and barbed wire has been put up all along the front of it. Ulbricht says the West has seen that East Germany is quite capable of defending its borders and the East Germans have shown how quickly and well they can move without anyone getting any idea of it until afterwards.'

Half the tanks went back to their bases, more evidence that normality had returned and insurrection was no longer a concern. The FRG Minister of Posts and Telecommunications confirmed that the GDR had cut all links.

The Allied commanders delivered their protest to the Soviet commander, Colonel Andrei Solovyev, who dismissed it by adopting the primary position: the Soviet Union did not interfere in the internal affairs of the sovereign state of the GDR. What else could Solovyev have said? But he must have known that if the Four Power Agreement could be negated unilaterally like this, then anything could, which itself was a nightmarish prospect in the nuclear age.

'It was a great shock for Berliners that such a division of the city was possible but they believed it would be removed by the Allies,' the radio reporter Peter Schultz says. 'The disappointment began when the Berliners realised the Allies weren't doing anything about it. The first Allied Ambassador who came to the city was the British and he invited the Press to meet him in the Royal Navy Officers' Club. I remember what he said, in English: "Ladies and gentlemen, whatever happens in East Berlin we are staying in West Berlin." He only spoke this one sentence and it had been coordinated with the other Allies. It became clear they wouldn't do anything against the wall.'[15]

The Western morning newspapers carried a photograph of Macmillan in country shooting uniform – plus fours and cap – on the moors near Swinton, Yorkshire, looking serene and unconcerned; and it did not please West Berliners.

Al Hemsing provides a telling aside. 'On the Monday and Tuesday, the West Berlin newspapers were treating it very much like a police story, you know, what was happening in street so-and-so. They had more or less given up on us.'

Allied access remained unaffected – as yet. 'We'd go over on the U-bahn but Friedrichstrasse was the only station open and a control point there constantly checked identifications,' Frank Trinka says. 'If you were suspicious, or anything like suspicious, you were hauled off. Then the concrete blocks started to go up and you sensed a permanency, you sensed that this was really going to happen: a wall. It was a methodical but relatively slow-paced undertaking because they could only spare so many people to do the job and I guess they had to consult constantly with the Soviets.'

This was the beginning of the wall proper, something far more symbolic than the Brandenburg Gate, and a mystery endures: how did nobody notice the enormous stockpiling of material for it? The first barrier was the barbed wire, easy to store – one can put an awful lot in a warehouse – but the wall? The answer is both obvious and unexpected, and Adam Kellett-Long gives part of it: 'The wall was rubble at the beginning, any old rubble and there was plenty of rubble in East Berlin. It still makes me wonder if they thought they were going to get away with it. Apart from the barbed wire, they didn't seem to have any proper building materials for a wall but no mystery exists about assembling it because there was nothing to see.'

Not all the wall consisted of rubble, however. 'An American journalist came to Berlin later in August,' Hemsing says, 'and asked me how many apartments you could build with the material they'd made the wall from – the slabs were the same as the East Germans used for apartment blocks. I put him in touch with the Western building trades coordinator and they figured out about twenty thousand small apartments initially. It explains how they got their hands on so much so quickly. You could ask how they stacked up all this in East Berlin without anybody noticing but there were a lot of building sites.'

The Allied bombing had seen to that and by 1961 the immense task of rebuilding was simply continuing, as it would for many years afterwards. To build a wall, all one had to do was to go to the sites, load slabs onto trucks, ferry them to the line and lay them.

The crude, makeshift edifice was constructed out of whatever lay to hand: breeze blocks, concrete pillars one on another, the housing slabs, ordinary bricks, lintels; and that gave an image, such as a street bisecting Bernauer Strasse, a truck with a winch lowering a block and workmen steering it by hand into position. The wall would be laid on no foundation: its own weight would hold it. Elsewhere breeze blocks were cemented in tiers like bricks, and that also gave an image: a craggy old workman in overalls, cigarette clamped in his mouth, spreading the cement with a trowel while an armed soldier watched him carefully.

Another timetable had begun to tick, of long range and monumental. The events of the weekend of 12–13 August 1961, and the days immediately after, were only the beginning. Within a calendar year, 7,874 cubic yards of blocks would have made a wall 7.5 miles (12 kilometres) long where the city centre interlocking was closest and most intimate; the remaining 91.7 miles (137.5 kilometres) round West Berlin – the countryside, meadows, woodland and lakes – would be cut by twin rows of coiled wire. Sometimes they were as far apart as 70 metres, sometimes – depending on the contours of the land and the proximity of dwellings on either side – considerably narrower, but always fashioning a death strip between the rows once a chain of watchtowers had been put in place. Someone calculated that if all the strands had been stretched in a straight line they'd measure 6,313 miles. The total area of the death strip would measure between 49,000 and 55,000 square metres, the equivalent area of a town.

The wall would separate 10,000 Westerners from their allotments and weekend houses. These people were helpless victims of accidents of history and geography, and in time they'd have to find ways of accepting their losses. Many owners kept whatever legal documentation they had proving ownership, although that would become progressively more remote and more futile as the years solidified the division. Not until after 9 November 1989 would owners be able to come back to reclaim their property.

In Bernauer Strasse, Conrad Schumann challenged six men near the wire on his side and appealed to an officer to help him. The officer approached the men who produced Stasi identity cards and one said they 'just wanted to make sure you are awake, comrades'. Schumann judged the checking of one's own army a curious thing to be doing. Towards 12.00 midday, he heard sounds of protest and calls for 'freedom' from a square behind Bernauer Strasse. The protesters moved up towards him. He had orders not to open fire and thought he'd be overrun, but armoured vehicles and soldiers poured from two side streets. The soldiers drew their bayonets and forced the crowd back. 'I will never forget how some of the people stood their ground with their arms crossed and cried out, "Go on, shoot, you cowards."'

After 12.00 Schumann saw the first of the lorries lumber up with the slabs and someone told him a wall would be built. He could postpone the decision he'd been weighing up a little longer, but not much. Around 2.00, keeping a wary eye on the other soldiers, he repeatedly sidled towards the wire and fingered the top strand. A soldier noticed but Schumann passed it off saying 'the wire is starting to rust already'.

A Western photographer, who'd been taking images of Bernauer Strasse since Sunday, sat in his car and noticed Schumann. 'Every few minutes the soldier went back to the same piece of wire and pressed it down, a bit more at a time. *My God*, I thought' – Schumann seemed to be preparing to jump the wire. The photographer emerged from his car and watched, his camera poised.

Schumann saw him but 'suddenly a young man came up right close to me on the Western side of the wire. I went towards him and shouted loudly so that my comrades could hear, "Get back immediately!" but I whispered, "I am going to make a run for it."' Schumann had no way of knowing if his comrades would shoot him in the back *after* he'd jumped the wire.

The young man understood and walked briskly to the nearest police station. A moment or two later, four policemen arrived in a Volkswagen minibus and stationed it as if they were just patrolling and had stopped for a moment. Other photographers deliberately pointed their cameras at the other soldiers, who twisted their faces away.

Schumann selected an instant when the soldiers were at their furthest point from him and their faces still turned away. He was trembling. He flipped the magazine out of his rifle so it wouldn't go off if he fell. He sprinted the few paces to the wire and a film crew captured his right leg coming up in a vaulting motion, both arms out like wings for balance, rifle on its strap tight over his shoulder. The image of him, when one frame of him in mid-air had been taken from the film and developed, fixed, became globally symbolic and, like all great photographs distilling so much, it required no caption.

Schumann cleared the wire and landed awkwardly but on both feet, letting the rifle fall from him. He sprinted on, leaving behind him not just the soldiers who had been his comrades that instant before but, in the middle distance, three men and a woman who were chatting on the pavement and were now, also, startled witnesses. Schumann ducked into the minibus and a Western policeman in a white cap trotted to the rifle to pick it up.

One of the most potent symbols of the twentieth century, stark and forbidding. *(Photo: Kazuhito Yamada)*

The line, at left, which Hagen Koch drew at Checkpoint Charlie. Here the two dominant systems of the twentieth century rubbed against each other. Everything to the right of it is in the East including the pedestrian and this vehicle, presumably returning from a patrol. *(Photo: Berliner Mauer-Archiv)*

Building the wall at Checkpoint Charlie. Koch's line is out of picture on the left. Note that the wall is being made of ordinary construction material. *(Photo: Berliner Mauer-Archiv)*

Peter Fechter lies bleeding to death within sight of Checkpoint Charlie – and the world. This was taken by a cameraman from the West peering over. *(Photo: Ullstein Bilderdienst)*

Below: Fechter's body has been taken through the barbed wire at the far side of the death strip and is now carried away down a side street. *(Photo: Ullstein Bilderdienst)*

Dennis L. Bark, now a Senior Fellow at Stanford University, California, heard Fechter crying for help and it changed his life. *(Photo: Dennis L. Bark)*

Hagen Koch (right) as a Border Guard instructor. *(Photo: Berliner Mauer-Archiv)*

American Military Police taunt the Border Guards in a watchtower by brandishing a pin-up. *(Photo: Berliner Mauer-Archiv)*

Some women taunted the guards by exposing themselves. Both these photographs were used by the GDR to prepare Border Guards for what they might see. *(Photo: Berliner Mauer-Archiv)*

The canal along which Hartmut Richter escaped, looking from East to West. The right bank is now a caravan park. Beyond them is the watchtower he had to get past. *(Photo: Birgit Kubisch)*

He got into the water at the bridge (left). There were only patrol boats around then. *(Photo: Birgit Kubisch)*

The watchtower, seen from the patrol road behind it. The canal is out of view to the left. *(Photo: Birgit Kubisch)*

Hartmut Richter today, where he works at the Church of Reconciliation (see following page) *(Photo: author)*

The Church of Reconciliation on Bernauer Strasse. The Church stood in the death strip. *(Photo: Landesarchiv Berlin)*

Below: The Church is blown up in 1985, removing it as an obstruction to the Border Guards covering the death strip. Note the cross falling from the steeple into the cemetery behind, where it would be hidden. *(Photo: Landesarchiv Berlin)*

The aftermath. Westerners (left) gather and many watch from the observation platform (centre-right bottom). *(Photo: Landesarchiv Berlin)*

The death strip ten years on. The wall has gone, litter is everywhere and this is the patrol road the Border Guard jeeps used. At right is the futuristic Church of Reconciliation – on the same spot as the old. *(Photo: Birgit Kubisch)*

The cross ten years on and now placed near the Church. The impact of landing in the cemetery must have bent it to this shape. *(Photo: author)*

Worlds apart: President Richard Nixon visits the wall in 1968 *(Berliner Mauer-Archiv)*, Roland Egersdörfer, the Border Guard who could see into a Western shop from his watchtower *(Roland Egersdörfer)*, and Marina Brath, who was imprisoned for trying to emigrate West *(Daniel Glau)*.

He was a 25-year-old tailor and, in 1961, he tried to swim the canal (behind this memorial) to the West. He was shot to death. The photograph was taken in 2001. *(Photo: author)*

Reports of escapes kept coming in, two at 3.47 p.m., and a flurry when people finished work: at 5.20 three, at 5.30 two, at 5.50 two caught. Shots were fired at a couple swimming the Teltow Canal – the first recorded instance of shoot-to-kill intent. As the echo of the shots died, everyone who could hear them understood the true nature of the wall. It was, in modern jargon, a defining moment as well as a hard one.

The shoot-to-kill policy haunted even Honecker, and nearly three decades later it pursued him to exile and the Chilean Embassy in Moscow, then back to Berlin and forty-nine charges of murder; then pursued him to Chile itself. Many dead at the wall – nobody can know the definitive total – lay in between.

'The border security installations between the socialist and capitalist worlds from the Baltic Sea to the Black Sea were all the same at the time,' Honecker would say in self-defence.[16] 'Incidentally, it is interesting that people talk much less about the border security installations, for instance, between the USA and Mexico than those which were normal between the Warsaw Pact and NATO. The shoot-to-kill order did not differ at all from that of the West German Border Guards. Basically it was the same order and anyway it was nothing secret.'[17]

In Washington, General Clay formally volunteered his services to Kennedy, although that might have served to heighten and broaden the friction because Clay was a Republican who'd thrown his weight behind Richard Nixon in the last election.

This Tuesday, the friction between Washington and Berlin rubbed, too. 'We didn't know what went on in Washington,' George Muller states. 'We kept sending in our reports but Kennedy said afterwards he hadn't heard from the Mission, which was really disingenuous because we'd reported the East German decree and by Tuesday, when morale plummeted, we sent in a recommendation that some high-level representative should come, the President himself or Dean Rusk. We didn't think of the Vice-President. We also suggested reinforcing the Berlin garrison or some other commensurate measure.'

Kennedy considered the latter option carefully because the dangers of dispatching reinforcements along the autobahn to West Berlin were immediately obvious and profound. If Soviet or GDR forces severed the umbilical cord, what then? They need only say a bridge was closed for repairs, as they had done in 1948 when Berlin had had to be sustained by the air lift. Worse, if Soviet or GDR forces deployed on the autobahn and blocked it, what would the American reinforcements do?

Kennedy waited.

That night Peter Johnson 'returned to Bonn at last' to see his family. 'I was captivated by the beauty of the clouds from the aeroplane but at the same time saddened as I looked at the lakes, fields and forests of East Germany thinking of the unhappiness suffered by people forced to live under an alien system. It was dark when we landed at Wahn, the home airport for Bonn. It took Elfi and the boys some time to recognise me – although I was the first in the queue beside the stewardess as we walked to the terminal building – but, when they did, I saw a flurry of waves from their shadowy figures. Soon we were all together chatting excitedly.'

How many Berliners wanted that, and only that?

At midnight the incident sheet recorded its total for the day: four escapes, fourteen caught.

WEDNESDAY 16 AUGUST 1961

The timetable ticked on. At 3.20 a.m., Police Headquarters made their first entry of the day: one escaper caught in the south. The tightening tightened.

'We woke this morning to find everyone has to have new passes to cross and we got in a great state thinking we were shut in,' Mary Kellett-Long wrote, 'but it seems they only apply to East Germans because Adam went through without any trouble at all. We had an electricity failure which lasted half an hour and the water has been cut off. Really this place seems to be getting worse than ever now the border has been closed.'

All through the morning reports of escapes came in, at 9.00, 10.00, 10.15, 11.35, 11.45.

Mary Kellett-Long, who knew nothing of this, added in her diary:

The West Berlin police have kept people about half a mile back from the Brandenburg Gate but they are still making a nuisance of themselves at the other checkpoints. We find driving into West Berlin we get more stares than usual but not really any hostility. Yesterday we were waiting at some traffic lights, a big lorry drew up beside us and the driver leaned out of the cab and said to Adam, 'Oh good, you got a pass, then.' When Adam explained we were English he said, 'Oh good' again and we had quite a little chat.

West Berlin police at the border are funny, too. When they see our passports they smile and look rather puzzled, but they are charming. The East German police are still polite but thorough.

I think they are all fresh and full of enthusiasm for the new rules and regulations but they will get tired, we hope, because it takes such a long time to get through on the way back. They searched thoroughly and looked in the car. There was a newspaper on the floor and they asked to see it. Luckily it was *Neues Deutschland* so they couldn't say anything.

Rudiger Hering, living out in the country immediately west of West Berlin, says that 'during the first few days many people tried to escape and about 90 per cent of those who tried made it. Around Falkensee there were forests' – ideal cover for a sprint across at night. 'Afterwards nobody tried because the space between the two walls was so wide and so open. At the beginning the electricity which the Border Guards used was connected to the local grid and when they switched on searchlights the picture on television went small because they were using so much electricity.'

In Bernauer Strasse, ground-floor residents were ordered to surrender their front door keys to the police. Because the road was in the West, no East German – whether army, police, Factory Fighter or bricklayer – was entitled to stand on it to guard the front doors. Police lurked in corridors and in the apartments to prevent escapes. On 17 August, workmen would begin bricking up all the 1,253 windows, starting with the ground floors. An evacuation of 2,000 residents would be forced through the following month, and – later – every building except the Church of Reconciliation would be demolished and cleared to create the death strip. The wall cut across the front of the church and elaborate patterns of tank traps would protect its rear.

But on this Wednesday, a resident of No. 47, within sight of where Conrad Schumann vaulted the wire, was caught letting the wife of a friend use his front door to escape. Police arrested him but somehow he persuaded them to release him, returned and with a spare key let himself and his family out, stepping into the other country and taking nothing with them.

Students at Bonn University sent Kennedy an umbrella echoing Chamberlain's pre-war appeasement and included a message. 'Sorry to say that because of your reserved reaction you have become the most worthy possessor of this symbol of fatal policy.'

The escapes went on, at 2.55 p.m. , 3.30, 4.10, 4.15.

In the afternoon, 200,000 people gathered at West Berlin's town hall to hear Willy Brandt address them. Brandt looked almost a businessman in a dark suit, his hair swept back and perfectly in place. A thicket of microphones awaited him. Deputy Mayor

Amrehn made the opening speech and then Brandt, using his right
fist for emphasis, said:

> The people of Berlin have a right to know the true situation. The
> people of this city are strong enough for the truth. Today we must
> be the voice of our fellow countryman who can no longer speak
> out or come to us. In this hour I address myself particularly to
> those of my countrymen who work in government offices and
> organisations in the zone [the East]. Don't let them make fools of
> you! Conduct yourselves with manly restraint whenever possible.
> Above all, do not shoot at your fellow countryman.
>
> I deem it necessary to lodge a protest with the world forum of
> the United Nations against the perpetrators of this act of
> inhumanity on the soil of Berlin and of Ulbricht's state. Our
> concern is not with the rights of the Western Powers but with
> human rights which must be restored. We Berliners have some-
> thing to say to our protectors. This city wants peace but it is not
> capitulating. There can be no other city in the world that desires
> peace and calm and security more than Berlin, but peace has
> never been won through weakness. There is a point where you
> can't retreat even a single step. This point has been reached.

It was a speech of anger but its impotence could not be concealed.

Brandt had also written to Kennedy because Kennedy had invited
him to do that whenever Brandt thought it necessary or important.
The letter, telegraphed, included these words:

> The danger above all is that inactivity and defensiveness might
> create a crisis of confidence vis-à-vis the Western Powers. We fear
> the Ulbricht government might interpret a wait-and-see attitude as
> a sign of weakness, a licence for further attacks. The Soviet Union
> has achieved half of its 'free city' proposals. If a second act should
> follow, what remains of Berlin would become a ghetto. Instead of
> refugees moving into West Berlin, a massive flight from Berlin
> would begin.

Brandt said that at the United Nations he wanted to accuse the
Soviet Union of 'tampering in the crudest fashion with the
Proclamation of Human Rights'. He finished:

> After suffering an illegal Soviet *démarche*, and considering the
> many tragedies taking place today in East Berlin and in the Soviet
> Zone, we must take the risk of assuming a firm stance. It would

be desirable to reinforce the American garrison as a show of force. I consider the situation grave enough to write to you, Mr President, with the ultimate frankness that is possible only between friends who trust each other utterly.[18]

This letter evidently irritated Kennedy as an admonition – and some in Washington perceived it as an attempt to dictate American foreign policy – but its overall effect cannot be doubted.

George Muller says that, 'Ed Murrow called up Brandt and the criticial thing was that Brandt met Murrow on the Wednesday when Brandt was sending the telegram. Murrow had already sent his and Kennedy probably placed more weight on that than ours. It's not quite clear whether Murrow was the catalyst for action or Brandt, or whether it evolved in Washington during joint discussions.'

Kennedy waited.

In Bonn, Peter Johnson wrote:

There are only half our usual staff because of the Berlin crisis and the holiday period. As a result I had no day off but worked a long evening shift tonight with the Berlin story still humming along. Main thing was a televised speech by Brandt at a rally in West Berlin in which he announced he'd sent a letter to Kennedy demanding 'not merely words but political action'. Most of us regard this as an attempt to lift Berliners' morale because scarcely anyone thinks there is anything the West can do in the present crisis. I impressed colleagues by being able to take almost a verbatim of Brandt's speech (in English but with partly German word order, which was straightened out by a deskman) direct onto a typewriter.

Later I found myself listening to Adenauer, apparently as well as ever, speaking to a Bonn election meeting of several thousands in a trolley bus shed. He had rowed back from his immediate reaction to the East German measures, in which he called for an economic boycott of the communist countries, and is now talking of what has happened as only the pre-crisis. He spoke out in favour of negotiations and said he did not think there should be war – this seems to be his election line, to soothe people after he has opposed negotiations all along in the past. He repeated an earlier smear of Brandt by referring indirectly to his illegitimacy and directly to the fact that Brandt changed his name from Frahm – something being exploited as a suspicious act by the Christian Democrats.

Adenauer did not like Brandt, and almost incredibly did not visit Berlin until 22 August.

That evening a report of an escape came in at 6.45, two in different places at 6.50, one at 7.40 and the last at 9.45. The incident sheet recorded its total for the day: 21 escaped, 13 caught. However incomplete, the dehumanised statistics charted a trend: 66 gone over on Sunday, 15 on Monday, 14 on Tuesday and now 21. The Wednesday of the week before, 1,926 refugees had registered at Marienfelde.

The barbed wire, and the wall now rising, fulfilled a most primary Germanic objective. It worked.

THURSDAY 17 AUGUST 1961

The GDR government used the night again for further tightening of controls. At 3.00 a.m., five truckloads of material drew up to Potsdamer Platz and workmen busied themselves constructing a 5-foot high wall. This would happen elsewhere, too, and where the wall already existed it would be heightened, sometimes with barbed wire strung along the top. The statistical trend shifted because, moment by moment, escape became more difficult and – with the shoot-to-kill order operating – became potentially fatal, too. Thirty-five minutes after the trucks reached Potsdamer Platz, police caught the first escapee of the day, at 4.20 two more, at 5.10 two more again, at 7.35 one. The first successful escape was reported at 8.23, where a cemetery wall formed the frontier.

In Bernauer Strasse workmen swarmed the ground floors of the apartment buildings, bricking up windows from the inside. Residents called to people in the West for help and clambered onto window ledges to drop to the pavement. The West Berlin Fire Brigade hurried there with safety nets anticipating that, when the bricklayers reached the upper floors, residents might jump.

Some windows already had necklaces of wire nailed over them and they framed another image: an old man in shirt sleeves and braces gazing through a window from the third floor, his face heavy with finality, his hands resting on a strand of the wire.

At the north end of Bernauer Strasse the police positioned tall sheets of wood in a screen behind the wall so that people on either side couldn't see each other. At the side roads with intersections on Bernauer Strasse, West Berliners scaled lampposts to wave. Others brought stepladders. Some pressed their faces against the breeze blocks, searching for a crevice to peer through.

Elsewhere, workmen pulled up S-bahn tracks which straddled the line and that isolated a famous old terminal, the Gorlitzer Bahnhof. It stood in the West but the track to it threaded through the East. Western trade unions retaliated by demanding a boycott of the whole network, which of course the GDR ran and was a source of hard currency. Over 260,000 people used the S-bahn every day and now demonstrators carried placards saying 'Don't give your money to Ulbricht' outside Western stations. Posters reinforced the message, 'Don't travel the S-bahn', and the 260,000 fell towards 25,000.

The GDR Ministry of the Interior issued a decree that 'no permits for West Berlin will be issued to East Berliners until the conclusion of a Peace Treaty' – the treaty to incorporate West Berlin into the GDR or declare West Berlin a 'free city', negating Allied rights.

The East German's Free German Youth called for 'voluntary service in armed units' and formed Regiments of Volunteers who took down television aerials which could receive Western broadcasts.

The Protestant bishop of the Brandenburg district and the Administrator of the bishopric of Berlin, both Westerners, were refused entry to East Berlin and an Easterner, the chairman of the Governing Council of the Protestant Church in Germany, was refused an exit visa.

Loudspeakers on vans and poles poured out the GDR's official line and within days the loudspeakers totalled 216. The West responded, Brandt speaking vehemently and vans relaying his words: 'The East German police and army units stationed at the West Berlin border have received orders concerning the use of their weapons. They have been ordered to fire aimed shots at anyone attempting to cross the border even if the bullets strike West Berlin territory. Nobody should believe that when he is one day brought to justice he will be able to say, "I was just following orders." Murder remains murder.'

People could no longer cross but words could, and in both directions.

A carefully printed photographic image showed Brandt in Berlin, a van relaying his speech through four speakers to a string of soldiers on a bridge in the East. They seemed mildly amused, mildly contemptuous, one poised to gesticulate towards the van but he changed his mind, smiled and turned to a colleague. They talked.

Was it this day, out in the country, that a man rushed the wire and wriggled under, a young woman running hard behind him? The top row of the wire caught her jumper and wrenched it up under her chin, felling her as if she'd been decapitated. Hands reached out, grabbed her and pulled her through.

Was it this day that, at a similar place, a family rushed the wire, the woman scrabbling through on all fours after hands from the West lifted the baby she'd held? What looked to be her husband, following, stumbled between the two rows of wire. A soldier rushed up and gave him a final prod with the butt of a rifle.

Was it this day that a photographer froze the image of a cobbled road, now decorated with stakes in the ground supporting the wire, and a group of children standing either side of it? One of them, in the West, steadied a bicycle. They gazed towards each other as pals do. Did they ever meet again?

If they did they'd be middle-aged then, because within the tortuous and improbable journey the wall acquired a logic of its own, which demanded that it be a complete border sealing. That led to 116 watchtowers within a year and successively refined walls numbered the first generation, second, third and finally fourth which was extremely difficult to scale. It was made of high-density reinforced concrete and its L-shaped segments were 3.60 metres (11.8 feet) high and 1.20metres (3.9 feet) wide.

The fourth generation wall would be the one which fell.

The logic led to electrified fences, dogs on leashes trained to attack even their own handlers, scatter guns triggered by trip wire which flung 90 jagged iron fragments in a conical pattern (though between the two Germanies, not at Berlin), tank and vehicle traps, searchlights and arc-lamps, a constant chemical spraying of the dead zone so no blade of grass grew, jeeps patrolling twenty-four hours a day, special permits if you lived near it, and sometimes forced evacuation, as in Bernauer Strasse.

At 4.00 in the afternoon, the British made an exquisite move. Geoffrey McDermott wrote:

Although we did not find it easy to devise an effective riposte to Ulbricht's outrage, this is not to say we were powerless. It occurred to me that we had in the British Sector the Soviet war memorial, guarded always by Soviet soldiers and regarded by them as sacred. I suggested we should surround the memorial with barbed wire, inside which the Soviet guards might parade like animals in a cage, and station a small British contingent nearby. All this would be done, of course, in order to protect our Soviet ally.

Jumbo Delacombe [Major-General Rohan Delacombe, British commandant] warmly welcomed my little scheme. A Soviet Colonel came over and confronted our Chief of Military Police. Quivering with rage he asked what the hell we were doing to his memorial. The Chief of Military Police replied suavely that we wanted to ensure the safety and properly respectful treatment of the memorial and its guard against those who might wish to molest them. The Soviet Colonel said it was an outrage; no such measures should have been taken without consultation with the Soviet authorities. The Chief, gesturing at the Brandenburg Gate in its new condition, said that the Soviet authorities seemed to be taking quite a lot of action themselves without overmuch consultation. The Colonel departed, apparently heading for a coronary. This ploy proved a useful sanction on several occasions in bringing the Russians to heel when their provocations tended to go too far.[19]

The geometry of division found expression in Hagen Koch, the jolly young Eastern army volunteer from Dessau, a town south of Berlin. He joined up 'because I was nineteen and I wanted to wear a uniform'. Newly married, he and his wife lived with her parents near the twin curved roads and the sunken gardens. This Thursday he was on duty at Friedrichstrasse – the crossing point, not the railway station. He'd just been paid but hadn't given his wife his wages yet so a bundle of Ostmarks nestled in his breast pocket. He was issued with a brush, a bucket containing white paint and told to set down the precise line across Friedrichstrasse. Moving backwards he painted the line and the bulge of the banknotes rubbed against his arm as he did. The line, he reckons, took about twenty minutes to finish.[20]

In West Berlin, the loss of morale produced panic buying and hoarding of sugar, flour, canned food, oil, soap, and potatoes, but a spokesman for the Senate tried to calm this by announcing that ample stocks existed for between six months and a year. This was a legacy of the 1948–9 blockade and airlift. As a precaution against anything like that happening again, vast warehouses contained an inventory adequate for sustaining West Berlin: fuel for industry, caviar and castor oil, even hops, barley and malt for beer. The spokesman added that wholesalers had been instructed to speed distribution of all goods to retailers to 'mollify worried customers'.

In Washington, the full realisation came perhaps slowly. 'The key is that Foy Kohler and all these people had been off to Paris worrying about access to Berlin, what to do if the East Germans took over access,' John Ausland said. 'Their minds had not really focused on this problem of sealing East Berlin from West. Foy said in a Task Force meeting, "I hope we can get this out of the way so we can get back to planning for the crisis." There were about sixty people in the room and, me being junior, I wasn't going to say anything but afterwards I did say to Dick Davis, Foy's deputy, "You've got to explain to Foy Kohler that this *is* the crisis." They finally began to focus on it after the alarming telegram from Ed Murrow about the ugly mood and the angry letter from Brandt. There was a real danger West Berlin crowds would take matters into their own hands. On the Thursday there was a meeting at the White House and a decision was taken to send Vice-President Johnson and an armed Battle Group from West Germany.'[21]

Lucius Clay would go, too, and Frank Howley, a former US military commander in the city, and Charles Bohlen, a State Department Soviet expert.

Richard Smyser of the Mission in Berlin explores the context. 'Memories of 17 June 1953 haunted the East Germans but in a sense haunted us, too. What if we created a furore and the East German people responded, and rose, and we were able to do nothing to help them? I know it was a factor in Washington because it emerged when LBJ and Clay were coming. Young Kennedy had just gone through the Bay of Pigs [debacle] in Cuba and the Vienna Summit, and the feeling was we'd done something in Cuba which called for a popular uprising and it didn't happen – but in East Berlin we might have one, and Kennedy was very, very worried about it.'

George Muller in Berlin probes further into the context. 'Then we were told Johnson was coming and also General Howley, one of the old tank heroes who had a tremendous reputation with the Berliners for standing up to the Soviets, but the real brains trust was Johnson, Clay and Bohlen.'

To dispatch a Battle Group was highly unlikely to provoke uprising in the GDR of itself, but it represented a decisive move which may or may not meet with an equally decisive response. Some 1,500 men of the First Battle Group of the Eighth Infantry Division, stationed in Mannheim, would move – exposed – along the umbilical cord from West Germany to West Berlin. At each moment they would be vulnerable and become like West Berlin, symbolic. Neither could be defended except by the implied threat that any attack on them would move towards the nuclear scale.

It created more friction in Washington. Ausland said:

No consideration was given to the rules of engagement. The Berlin Task Force met and Martha Mautner from the State Department's Intelligence leant over and said to me, 'Ask Kohler what we are going to do if the Russians won't let the Battle Group through.' It sounded like a good question and I did ask. The reply was that we would implement our contingency plans. The meeting went on and then Henry Owen from Policy Planning says, 'Foy, what are our contingency plans?' and Foy looks over at Dave Grey who represented the Joint Chiefs of Staff and asked, 'Dave, what are the rules of engagement?'

Grey said, 'I'll get them.' He later brought them over and I well remember we all looked at them and realised that if the Russians tried to stop the Battle Group there could be some shooting. I was sitting in on the meeting with Kohler and Paul Nitze when Rusk appeared at the door and said, 'Paul, have you seen these rules of engagement?' He said yes. Rusk said, 'Do you realise there could be some shooting if the Russians try and stop us?' Nitze said, 'Yes, we realise that but I'm satisfied they won't try.' Then there was a little discussion. Rusk said, 'Well, I just want to be sure you understand that' and went back to his office. What this makes clear is that, as so often, these sorts of decisions are made but the consequences are not examined.[22]

At least two generals cautioned against sending the Battle Group because it could be construed as a provocative act whose only practical effect was to feed a few more troops into a place which, by definition, was indefensible anyway. The 1,500 raised the US contingent to 6,500. The British had a permanent contingent of 4,000 and the French 3,000. Leaving the Soviet forces aside, the GDR army numbered 110,000, the police 78,000, the Border Police 45,000, the police reserves 30,000 and the Factory Fighting Groups 300,000. Rusk said, 'An attack on West Berlin would have moved rather quickly to a nuclear situation, yes, I really think that, it was part of the planning all along.'

Kennedy understood how much the Battle Group would reassure West Berlin and, at the same time, quieten the American right wing which vehemently objected to the United States being pushed around in front of the world audience by communism. He intended the Battle Group to cross three days hence, the Sunday, and by then Johnson would be present to welcome it, creating a fusion of America's military and political strengths for every Berliner and the world audience to see. All week Kennedy had said virtually nothing in public but now he justified sending Johnson and the Battle Group because 'recent developments including the movement of East German military forces into East Berlin' dictated it.

During the evening, Kennedy summoned Johnson from a dinner party and told him he was going to West Berlin the following day.

Johnson initially refused but Kennedy explained he wasn't issuing an invitation. This was an order.

At midnight in Berlin the incident sheet recorded its total for the day: five escapes, fifteen caught.

FRIDAY 18 AUGUST 1961

And still the escapers came, but more rarely, the first an hour after midnight, a couple at 2.15 a.m., someone caught at 3.50 but no further entry until 11.00 By then the houses along the Eastern side of Bernauer Strasse were being sealed. Behind each window workmen placed bricks and cemented them in, sometimes the moist cement spilling and falling in plump droplets onto the West.

Simultaneously, at Potsdamer Platz, the entrance to the S-bahn station (which ran underground from the West) was sealed. Down there, the long platforms curved as they had always done and the station nameplate – in old, spiky script – remained set into tiles on the wall but the little kiosk, plastered in advertisements, shut. Shadows and semi-darkness fell upon this station which had once carried the same bustle as Times Square and Piccadilly Circus and the Place d'Etoile. Workmen cleaned it up and modernised it for a re-opening – but not until 1992. Until then the kiosk remained closed.

Outside the station on this Friday morning, a shop which had generated a handy livelihood for its owners by selling leather goods to Easterners – luxuries to them – shut its door forever.

Nearby, but on the other side, members of the Free German Youth manned sections of the border, releasing the Factory Fighters and demonstrating that the East German government judged the moment for insurrection absolutely gone.

In Bonn the Bundestag met and 'sharply' condemned the border sealing.

Alec Douglas-Home returned to London from Scotland 'inter-rupting' his holiday for, as one newspaper noted, 'emergency talks' with Western Allied ambassadors. It was very late for that.

Soviet commandant Solovyev restated the primary position, castigating 'the illegal provocative measures and subversion against the GDR', and damning protests as 'completely unfounded. As has already been stated several times the Commander of the garrison of Soviet troops in Berlin does not interfere in the affairs of the capital of the GDR.'

Noises off, really.

Kennedy, due to fly to Hyannis Port for the weekend, delayed that until Saturday and later delayed it again. He intended to be on hand as the Battle Group crossed. The time of sealed envelopes and walkie-talkies to the *Marlin* in Nantucket Sound seemed, and was, already a long way in the past.

And still they came, one at 5.15 in the afternoon then a gap until three at 10.45. At midnight the incident sheet recorded its total for the day, twelve escapes, eleven caught.

SATURDAY 19 AUGUST 1961

Lyndon Johnson took off from Andrews Air Force Base in the President's jet Air Force One at 9.14 in the evening of what was still Friday in Washington, 3.14 a.m. in Berlin. As the plane lifted and moved across the pastures of Maryland towards Chesapeake Bay and the Atlantic, the Battle Group – 300 trucks towing artillery but no tanks – lumbered from their barracks in Mannheim and strung out on the autobahn, settling to an average speed of between 30 and 40 miles an hour. The Soviet Union had been officially notified and, from Moscow, Pravda denounced it as 'military provocation'.

The first of the weekend civilian traffic was already on the move and flowed past the Battle Group which, travelling so slowly among it, faced a journey up past Frankfurt and out onto the plains to Hannover, then Brunswick [Braunschweig in German] where they'd pitch camp for the night. That was 20 miles from Helmstedt, the crossing point into East Germany.

On board Air Force One, now out over the Atlantic, Frank Cash found 'a big difference between this and a normal visit, very hectic but I'm not sure that wasn't easier than one of those visits pre-arranged six months ahead because then you have plan A and plan B and all the other plans. We simply made it up as we went along. On the plane over we worked on LBJ's speech and it proved to be exactly what was required. On a pre-arranged visit it can never be the same because speeches are written weeks in advance and everybody has to clear them.'

In Berlin, George Muller and Al Hemsing worked on this same speech all night.

Air Force One landed at Bonn in mid-morning and Adenauer greeted Johnson and the others. They travelled to Adenauer's official residence overlooking the Rhine. Johnson shook hands with some bystanders, went in and the men conferred for 90 minutes.

'We called on Chancellor Adenauer to discuss Berlin and we asked him would he like to come along,' Cash says. 'They were building up to an election in Germany, Willy Brandt was the opposition candidate and we did not want to get involved. It ended up with Adenauer not coming on Johnson's plane. The German Protocol Officer, Sigismund von Braun – Werner von Braun's brother, incidentally [the rocket man] – did, however, accompany us. The visit to Bonn was really one of protocol to check in with the Chancellor before continuing to Berlin. Adenauer and LBJ got on all right although there was no great rapport between them, I think. Of course Adenauer was an elder statesman and LBJ very much a practical American politician: they were from completely different backgrounds and with almost nothing in common.'

Johnson changed from the big jet to an Air Force Constellation for the 80-minute flight to Berlin. From it he saw what Peter Johnson had seen: the misty forests of the GDR, the patchwork of enormous collectivised fields, and traditional olde worlde villages sunk into the countryside, forever slumbering. Johnson landed at Templehof airport on a grey, overcast day threatening showers. He inspected a guard of honour and seven tanks fired a salute.

Brandt, welcoming him, said, 'It is a great day for Berlin. We are deeply grateful that you came at just this moment.'

Johnson immediately confirmed that the Battle Group was coming, too.

'We landed at Templehof Airport and we took a motorcade,' Cash says. 'That really was a very moving experience because up to that moment West Berliners had been so deeply concerned about what was going to happen to them. Mobs of people came out, old ladies up on balconies waving their handkerchiefs. It was a kind of triumphant motorcade.'

Johnson stood next to Brandt in a modest open-topped saloon car, the choice of vehicle removing any remoteness. Brandt waved his hat while Johnson flicked outstretched hands from the crowd. Muller rode 'in one of the cars behind. Johnson was delighted, he loved the adulation. Much to the consternation of the Secret Service people he stopped the car, got out, waved and shook hands as if he was running for office in Berlin. One of his bodyguards said, "You're taking a risk" but he said, "No, I'm among friends here." Johnson had his own photographer who took hundreds of pictures of him and always with the right profile. . . .'[23]

The motorcade moved much slower than the Battle Group was going, although it was nearly on the plains headed towards Hannover.

Johnson went first to see the wall at Potsdamer Platz. The saloon parked less than 10 metres from it and he and Brandt went walking beside the wall along roads glistening from a heavy shower. East German soldiers clambered onto the wall and took Johnson's picture, for official use.

Johnson did not reach the Town Hall until 6.20 p.m., 80 minutes late. Muller, meanwhile, tried to 'meld' the speech he and Hemsing had prepared with the speech created on Air Force One. 'Most of ours was discarded.'

Some estimates put the crowd filling the square in front of the Hall at 300,000. A line of children stood near the front, each supporting a giant white letter propped on the ground. *Freiheit*, the letters said when they were arranged: Freedom. Johnson was introduced to the crowd and so was Clay who raised his right arm to greet a great roar. His face opened into a brief smile. Clay said, 'What you and I started together several years ago we will finish together and the world will be free.'

Geoffrey McDermott wrote that 'the vast crowd was in that emotional mood when it would cheer every mention of "freedom" and "independence" and all the cliches of public speech. When General Clay came to speak they nearly went berserk. Here was the man who had saved Berlin over ten years before come back to save its people from an even graver threat. They remembered; and they would not disperse for many hours.'[24]

'Willy Brandt made a speech,' Cash says, 'and he had tears running down his face. . . .'

Then Johnson, bespectacled, almost sombre, spoke. Clay was positioned behind him and certainly sombre. Brandt was slightly to one side and had regained his composure. Johnson placed his speech on his lectern below the microphones and his head dipped to reach for the words. A mood seized him.

'To the survival and the creative future of this city, we Americans have pledged what our ancestors pledged in forming the United States, our lives, our fortunes and our sacred honour.' These were the final words of the Declaration of Independence. Johnson's growl of a voice deepened. 'The President wants you to know that the pledge we have given to the freedom of West Berlin and of Western access is firm.' The faces of the 350,000 Berliners had been sombre themselves but at this another great roar went up, the faces consumed by release. 'This island does not stand alone. Your lives are linked not merely to those in Hamburg, Bonn and Frankfurt, they are also linked with those of every town in Western Europe, Canada and the United States and with those on every continent who live in freedom and are prepared to fight for it.'

'LBJ made a speech,' Cash says, 'and he ended with tears in his eyes. They played the German national anthem, a moment of absolute silence followed and then the Freedom Bell [which Clay had brought in 1950 after the airlift] rang out from the tower above and I must confess that is when I had tears in my eyes, too. . . .'

Johnson went in to address the Senate and after that, wearing a light summer overcoat against the showers, worked the crowds again. With Brandt at his side he moved through endless corridors of people, flicking more hands, beaming, beaming, beaming. And images were fixed: a child hoisted to see him; an old lady in a headscarf – she'd just had her hand flicked – looking suddenly serene; a young man laughing, his anxieties stilled.

Pravda stabbed out its alternative view. 'Prussian marches rang out from amplifiers on special vehicles. From time to time appeals were heard from motorised propagandists. "Assemble to meet the American Vice-President Johnson, who is coming to defend Europe and Berlin."'

In the East on this Saturday, compulsory evacuation orders were served on the 2,000 residents of Bernauer Strasse – a turn of the tourniquet – and it brought the first of the killings:

<u>19 August 1961</u>   *Rudolf Urban, 47, and a friend were in number 1 Bernauer Strasse while workmen bricked up the doors and windows. When the workmen stopped for lunch, the two men lowered a rope from a first-floor window and their wives climbed down it to safety. People in the street called out in support and although Urban's friend made it, Urban himself evidently heard Border Guards or police rushing to the room, let go the rope and, the onlookers screaming, fell some 3 metres – almost 10 feet – and landed with what one report describes as 'an ugly thud'. He seemed to have no more than a broken ankle but was taken to hospital for examination and died there on 17 September.*

In a technical sense, if you can describe a human life as technical, Urban was the first person to die at the wall or, more accurately, because of the wall. The killing ended with another escapee, Chris Gueffroy – but that would be 5 February 1989, and Gueffroy was not born until seven years after the building of the wall.[25]

In the chronological sense the first named person to die would be a frail-looking widow living on the third floor of No. 48 Bernauer Strasse. How did she spend her time this Saturday afternoon while

West Berlin surrendered to LBJ? Shopping? Fussing about her apartment? She had four days to live.

The bricks encircled the front of the Church of Reconciliation and were laid high enough to mask its door.

Clay went to look at the wall at a point where it consisted of eight layers of horizontal concrete slabs. A photographer captured him levering himself up using both hands to peer over, his feet off the ground. It gave the GDR a propaganda opportunity, what you might call a reverse image. They reproduced the photograph on posters with a caption, 'Why so uncomfortable? You'd see more, you'd find out the truth, you'd be able to report objectively when you yourself visit the capital of the GDR, Berlin!' (The West had propaganda just as potent: a photograph of a labourer laying breeze blocks with a soldier covering him and – on the Western side, mounted on two metal supports – a placard showing Ulbricht and a quote from his speech at the press conference on 15 June: 'Nobody intends to build a wall.')

Clay did visit East Berlin, as he was fully entitled to do under the Four Power Agreement, and when he returned he did report objectively that almost no people were on the streets but 'I have never seen quite so many soldiers in a town' – more, he added, than when he'd been in Berlin at the end of the war.

That afternoon Ursula Heinemann, who'd been a waitress in a West Berlin hotel, went walking with her mother and they reached the Teltow Canal. Not far away Heinz Sachsenweger must have been on duty with his Factory Fighters, guarding the weekend chalets with their little gardens, their chickens and rabbits. The canal formed the border before it turned inwards to the Eastern district of Treptow. There, chalets clustered on either side of the line.

Heinemann and her mother reached them and Heinemann said the equivalent of 'Hold on a moment'. She opened the gate of a chalet and walked into the back garden. Wire had been uncoiled behind it. She crawled under the wire but found another coil in front of a drainage ditch. She crawled under that, crossed the ditch and saw 'a plume of cigarette smoke'. The smoker, a man, announced that she was in the West, congratulated her and gave her a cigarette. Added to her identity card and a handkerchief, that made her possessions three. A passing woman offered her a couple of marks and she caught the bus to the hotel to begin work.

The Battle Group crawled onto the plain towards distant Hannover and still, in constant profusion, the weekend civilian traffic flowed past it. Just another convoy, they must have thought.

Peter Johnson spent long hours at the Reuters office in Bonn. The day before, he'd covered a story about a British yacht sunk in the Elbe, 'a terrible story, three adults saved and their five children presumed drowned while their yacht was cut in two by a freighter in pitch darkness. I have the painful task of interviewing one of the survivors by telephone.' On this Saturday he was commended by Reuters' general manager for his 'indefatigable' work on the story and 'because LBJ was Berlin-bound I am being referred to in the office as the Vice-President'.

The first of the Battle Group stopped at Brunswick and began setting up an overnight camp. The rest were strung back down the autobahn.

At midnight, the incident sheet recorded its total for the day: three escapes, three caught.

SUNDAY 20 AUGUST 1961

And still they tried to come, one caught at 15 minutes past midnight, a second at 1.00 a.m.. At almost exactly this moment the last of the Battle Group reached the camp, but they wouldn't be able to sleep for long.

Peter Johnson was woken by 'a call telling me that an American Battle Group which President Kennedy has ordered to West Berlin was leaving earlier than expected from its night camp near Brunswick. This meant I had to rise again at 4.00 to be in the office for 5.00 to start up the story by phoning the frontier just before Alfred Kleuhs [a Reuters reporter] arrived there from Berlin to travel with the convoy.'[26]

A report of the first escape came in at 2.40.

The Battle Group was roused from the darkness and ate their rations while army radio patrol trucks set off for Helmstedt and positioned themselves near the crossing point to act as a relay station for the convoy. Moment by moment the Battle Group would give a running report which, via the radio trucks, would go to the US Command in Heidelberg and, moving upwards and outwards, to the Supreme Allied Command near Paris, the Pentagon, the White House and US Army headquarters in West Berlin.

Major-General Clifton, Kennedy's military aide, went to the Situation Room in the White House around 10.00 in the evening Washington time (4.00 a.m., in Germany) and prepared to spend the night listening to the running commentary. Kennedy was to be woken immediately if any incident developed. Clifton reached the Situation Room pretty much as the Battle Group broke camp.

A reporter at Brunswick noted the American soldiers were armed with M1 rifles, recoil-less rifles and 3½-inch rocket launchers although 'officers said the weapons would not be loaded' and the 49-year-old commander, Colonel Glover S. Johns Jnr, added: 'We are not anticipating any trouble. We told the Soviets we were coming.' He explained to the Battle Group that he'd travel at its head and deal with formalities at the crossing point. No one else must have any contact with East Germans or Soviets. The Battle Group set off along the autobahn again, through pleasantly rolling countryside and woodlands.

In West Berlin, George Muller established direct contact with the US Army headquarters and prepared to listen to the running commentary himself.

General Bruce Clarke, US Commander Europe in Heidelberg, had made the decision to give the Group live ammunition, albeit not to be loaded into the weapons. If the Soviets started shooting and the Battle Group couldn't return fire, well, what kind of a strategy was that?

Washington sources estimated the chances of an incident at 'a thousand to one'. Those odds might be short enough in a nuclear age.

The first couple of trucks carried bulldozers to remove any obstacles, but what would their use involve and would there *be* obstacles? Would the GDR or Soviets stand and watch as bulldozers cleared a path on their territory?

John Ausland gave the State Department thinking which, they believed, answered those questions. 'Khrushchev had problems on his hands, too. He and Ulbricht wanted to stop the refugee flow but they didn't want a big fat crisis about it and, having stopped it, they'd achieved what they wanted. Foy Kohler said "they've got that, they don't want to escalate it" and he was a Soviet expert, but I can tell you there were a lot of people listening to telephone conversations with Colonel Johns as the convoy went across, and a lot of nervousness. We faced the first potential flashpoint.'

Frank Cash, with the Lyndon Johnson party in West Berlin, emphasises that. 'The reinforcements crossing was a very emotional time because everyone wondered what would happen and it was essential from our point of view in reiterating our access to West Berlin, because without land access we faced another airlift. So we were all asking: Will the East Germans block the autobahn?'

The Battle Group reached Helmstedt at 5.00 a.m. Helmstedt was, in fact, a small town on the border with the autobahn flowing past

its outskirts and on towards the Eastern hamlet of Marienborn, and
the names betrayed the division: in the West the crossing point was
known as Helmstedt, in the East as Marienborn. The crossing point
itself was in open countryside with a small Allied hut on the Western
side but formidable fortifications to the East.

A *New York Times* reporter watched the Battle Group 'crawl
down the two hundred yards of no man's land' and halt at the
Eastern control huts. Colonel Johns, anxious to get through the
formalities as quickly as possible, made a tactical error. Under the
Four Power Agreement, he was obliged to inform a Soviet office
how many men he had and he gave that, but when the Soviet officer
counted them – they were in their vehicles – the number differed.
The Soviet officer counted a second time and still the number
differed. Johns ordered the Battle Group to dismount in order to
simplify the count. Instantly it became a precedent and, in future,
every convoy would be made to do likewise. The Soviets would use
this as an irritant, spending as long as they wished counting,
especially in the cold of winter.

Muller heard 'reports that the Battle Group was held up because
of the size of it. That amount of men hadn't happened in a long,
long time.'

The leading vehicle was cleared in 16 minutes and the Battle
Group moved off along the same autobahn but now, of course, in
the GDR. The autobahn was empty because far from erecting
blockades the GDR had kept all other traffic off it. They, too, were
nervous about incidents particularly, perhaps, civilian traffic getting
in the way or people trying to board the American trucks as
sanctuary.

A Soviet fighter plane flew over low and circled.

On the old bridges spanning the autobahn, police and soldiers
watched the Battle Group move slowly beneath them.

This autobahn was a curious, eerie, slightly unreal place. Its
surface was badly maintained so that vehicles bounced and rattled
their way along it, even at slow speed. Many of the stone bridges
had been destroyed in the war and not rebuilt, so that only stumps
of the uprights remained, standing at either side of the road like
sentries guarding the past. In many places, the autobahn was
hemmed by woodland – the trees up to either side – and that gave
the impression of screening out the light even in daytime; gave the
impression of a country hidden, a country you couldn't penetrate.
The autobahn did not go near towns: the spires of the cathedral at
Magdeburg, the first town in the East, could be seen far away. It

passed near a village or two but the old houses and streets in them seemed empty. It passed over country lanes of pre-war cobbles and sharp cambers. The fields seemed empty, too.

On this autobahn there was always a frisson of the forbidden, a sense you were taking a risk, a feeling of a deserted place locked into another time.

At 7.00 a.m., and with no fanfare, a British military train carrying eighteen armoured cars and sixteen scout jeeps pulled into West Berlin. The vehicles unloaded and drove to the barracks at the Olympic Stadium.

At 9.00, a report of one escape came in.

In East Berlin, Adam Kellett-Long went to St Mary's (the Marienkirche), the second oldest parish church in the city. 'Normally the Bishop of Berlin took the sermon but this was an unknown pastor. The church was absolutely packed. He said, "The theme of my sermon today will be 'God forgive them, they know not what they do'." He was one of the bravest men I have ever heard. I don't know what happened to him afterwards.'

At 10.55, a report of two escapes came in; at 11.00, a party of three got across; at 11.10, two but this time near Wollankstrasse.

The Battle Group crawled slowly on.

The *New York Times* reported that West Berlin was 'like a boxer who had thrown off a heavy punch and was gathering stamina for another round'.

For a week Brigitta Schimke's only contact with her parents had been waving to them across the twin curved roads, the sunken gardens and the wire from her apartment. Her sister, who lived in West Berlin, had a simple idea, although dangerous. They looked alike. Her sister went to the police in the West, said she'd lost her identity card and they issued her with another so that now she was armed with two. On this Sunday, she crossed – Westerners still could, of course – and journeyed to Brigitta's apartment. She gave Brigitta one of the identity cards and her sister used it to cross. She stayed three days with her family before making the decision which she suspected would alter the direction of her life, perhaps irrevocably, although deep down she thought – as so many others did – that the wall could not be and would not be permanent. She decided to return to her husband and their apartment.

She would not re-cross to the West again until 1977 for her mother's funeral and, even then, only after she'd proved the deceased was her mother and was indeed deceased. Permission to attend her father's funeral two years later was refused. She would re-cross a second time, but that was in 1987. 'It was for my sister's fifty-fifth birthday. They made an exception because normally you could only go for the "ten" birthdays: forty, fifty, sixty and so on. I was allowed but not my husband. I had three children and they knew I'd come back because of them. I found West Berlin very exciting, hectic. I noticed a very big difference.' She re-crossed regularly – but after 1989, when she walked over ground where the inner wall, the death strip and the outer wall had been, to catch the bus to work.

At 1.30p.m., a report came in of one escaper caught.

The Battle Group crawled slowly on. 'We spent,' Muller says, 'a very tense time because we didn't know what the Soviets might get up to. On the theory that you always fight the present crisis on the basis of the crisis before, much of our thinking was directed to a possible blockade.'

The first vehicles of the Battle Group neared Dreilinden, the checkpoint on the autobahn between the GDR and West Berlin. Thousands of Westerners waited to cheer them. Many among the thousands had picked bunches of wild flowers on the way and held them. Lyndon Johnson visited the wall again and set off for Dreilinden but the crowd became so great that his motorcade couldn't get through. It halted some distance back. As Colonel Johns led the Battle Group in after it had emerged from the checkpoint, the crowd closed on it, giving the flowers to the soldiers or casting them affectionately towards the trucks. Johns said, 'It's the most exciting and impressive reception I've seen all my life, with the possible exception of the liberation of France.'

The Battle Group stretched far, far back into the GDR but the vehicles were coming through surely and safely.

In Washington, just before dawn Major-General Clifton, Kennedy's military aide, left the Situation Room and drove to his house nearby. He changed clothes, returned and briefed Kennedy at 8.00 a.m. (2.00 p.m. in Berlin) that all was well.

At Dreilinden, Johnson stood on a very temporary reviewing stand to take the salute and at one point walked over to an armoured car and handed the driver a bouquet of the flowers he'd been given.

At 3.45, three reports came in from different sections of the border: two escaped, two caught. Ten minutes later a party of four escaped, again near Wollankstrasse.

The last Battle Group truck had come in by late afternoon. The US commander in Berlin, Major-General Watson, stopped it and said, 'The Vice-President of the United States wants to talk to you boys.' Johnson thrust his head through the window and said to the driver, 'My name is Johnson and I'm from Texas. Where are you from?' and the driver said, 'Brooklyn.'

At this moment Kennedy attended Mass at St Matthews Cathedral six blocks behind the White House and when the service finished he flew to Hyannis Port.

The Battle Group paraded down the Ku-damm past the broken-toothed Kaiser Wilhelm Memorial Church and another massive crowd celebrated their arrival.

The mood of West Berlin lightened and heightened.

The mood in East Berlin was reflected in silence, and in the reports which kept coming: one escaper caught at 7.35 that evening; a party of seven at 8.00; a couple at 10.00; three people at 11.45. The incident sheet recorded its total for the day: seventeen escaped, seventeen caught.

It was still afternoon in Hyannis Port. President John F. Kennedy and Jacqueline boarded the *Marlin* and cruised Nantucket Sound just as they had on the Sunday before.

FIVE

Cold as Ice

He who lives on an island should not make an enemy of the ocean.

GDR propaganda

By now, a week after the border sealing, a measure of clarity had settled over the confusion. The refugee flow had been almost completely staunched and, with the stability this brought, the GDR could begin to build a future. Part of that future would be in creating a distinctive society utterly unlike the West, part in establishing their right to run East Berlin as their capital, something precluded by the Four Power Agreement which, to the Western Allies, was still in full force. The GDR had already begun this process with the decrees of the previous Tuesday. They would increase them on the Wednesday of this second week. Here was another logic to work itself out: in the years to come East Germany would seek international recognition as a sovereign country and expend a considerable amount of money and effort to achieve that.

Inevitably, given so many complexities, that would create frictions of its own and one of them would not be long in coming – two months – when, it seemed, a single errant shot might have moved everything towards the nuclear escalator very quickly indeed.

Inevitably, too, the sealing was still imperfect this second week, and would be for months. The trauma of what amounted to captivity drove dozens to risk escape and the days were studded with the deaths of many of them. Shoot-to-kill became more than confirmed policy: it was happening with a terrible frequency. These escape attempts resembled a stampede and only when the wall had been refined to the point where it was extremely difficult to cross did this slow and virtually stop. To cover that, a lot of individual details are given which, cumulatively, become a broader picture. The slowing and stopping happened towards the end of 1964 and by then – in fact within a calendar year of the sealing – 116 watchtowers had been built, as we have seen, 84 round Berlin and 32 through it.

The attempts to cross still came, often using the full range of human ingenuity; and still the escapees died. Most, of course, did not try and for all the obvious reasons. Soon, East and West began to settle – however reluctantly – to their different normalities and one could feel the two halves moving at different rhythms and obeying different impulses; but not quite yet. When they did settle, the feeling would be that the Western half was searching out personal satisfaction in their lives, and the Eastern half was locked into some sort of vast communal endeavour. Each half would have its own centre of gravity and its own self-sufficiency; and soon enough the contrast would take your breath away, but not quite yet. Nor, in these comparisons, must anyone forget that the Western half was massively subsidised by the Federal Republic and the Eastern half had spent years repaying debt to the Soviet Union. The talk in the East, officially anyway, would be of overtaking the West but, as one swarthy Eastern worker said cryptically enough, 'Let's hope if we ever do they can't see the holes in our trousers. . . .'

22 August 1961   *Ida Siekmann, 58, jumped from the third floor of 48 Bernauer Strasse at 7.00 in the morning. Evidently she had been agonising over how to get to the West to celebrate her fifty-ninth birthday due the following day – the front door of the house was now bricked up. She heard knocking on apartment doors. Soldiers? Police? Stasi? She tried to make a rope out of bed sheets but couldn't. She threw her mattress out and jumped, aiming to land on it, but missed. She died of her injuries.*

Thirteen people crawled through the municipal sewers to the West.

On 23 August, the GDR closed five of the twelve checkpoints, leaving: Friedrichstrasse, for foreigners, diplomats and Allied forces; Bornholmer Strasse; Heinrich-Heine-Strasse, for West German citizens and goods; Chausseestrasse; Invalidenstrasse; Oberbaumbrücke; Sonnenallee, for West Berliners who worked in the East and who had a special identity card – about 6,000 people. The GDR also introduced compulsory permits for West Berliners wanting to go to the East, and instructed people 'in the interests of their own safety to stay a hundred metres away from both sides of the borders between the capital of the GDR and West Berlin'. The three Western commandants protested over that and, to counter any notion that people could not go within the hundred metres on the Western side, drove military vehicles up to the wall.

George Muller, Deputy Political Adviser at the American Mission, says:

We in Berlin argued that if Ulbricht got away with this [building the wall] it would be a two stage thing, the 13th and the 23rd. The decrees of the 23rd were much more stringent because they realised they'd got away with it. They'd stuck a finger in our teeth and it went right through, and God knows where it would happen next. General Clarke said stay a baseball's throw from the wall and you know how far you can throw a baseball. It meant go easy on border patrolling. I argued the opposite, that maybe increased patrols wouldn't have made them take the wall down but it might have prevented the next Berlin crisis. We were a victim of our own propaganda and our own newspaper coverage, because Berlin was still a remnant of the fabric of a whole city before the wall.

The people in Washington and elsewhere saw it as a city which had been divided since the end of World War Two. They were saying, 'What's all the fuss? All they are doing is tightening up their zone of control in their sphere of influence. We're only there to protect the security of West Berlin. Why is it our business to go after them for what they are doing to the East Germans?' The other argument was that World War Three could start in Berlin. We felt the opposite – that it wouldn't because this was a very controlled action on the part of the Kremlin. And we were not holier than the Pope: we could not do for the Germans something which they themselves did not advocate, and neither Adenauer nor Brandt advocated any kind of strong countermeasures like tanks.[1]

Mary Kellett-Long wrote in her diary: 'Once the official announcement of the measures was out we felt much better as what they boil down to is East Germans are not allowed to go into West Berlin. The West Berliners and West Germans and foreigners are allowed in and out of East Berlin as before. A lot of the overhead and underground trains now stop at the border. I have never seen so many policemen and soldiers in my life. There are also the Factory Fighting Groups dressed up in uniform toting machine guns. Adam was the first person to drive into West Berlin in an East German car after the new regulations. Adam went rushing round all the borders to see what was going on.'

Al Hemsing remembers that 'early in the week after the border was sealed I crossed and my wife Esther crossed. It was getting dicey then because they [the *Volkspolizei*, often abbreviated to *Vopos* –

People's Police] didn't know their orders. My wife told me she'd said to a *Vopo*, "Now I'm going in, will you let me out?" and the *Vopo* replied, "I can't tell you that" – in effect he had no orders. What I always thought was outrageous on our part, on the part of the Western Allies, was this: when there was an East German announcement which we got via radio – one of our sources of information was RIAS – saying that, in order to protect the GDR from chicanery and incursions from the West, henceforth the Allies would be restricted to crossing at what became Checkpoint Charlie, nothing was done. Now, the East Germans having accomplished their original purpose, I think that if we had insisted, we could have kept some of those other crossings open.'

24 August 1961 *Gunter Litwin, a 24-year-old tailor, was shot at 4.15 in the afternoon swimming the Humboldt Canal, after he had passed the middle of the dock basin, by a master sergeant of the Transport Police. His body was recovered at 7.10 and hauled crudely onto the quayside by five uniformed policemen, while a group of soldiers watched.*

There is a grotesque photograph of this. They are hauling him up by his left arm, the right lifeless at his side. The hauling distorts the jerkin he wears. His head hangs forward, the jerkin encircling his neck.

29 August 1961 *Roland Hoff, 27, was shot at 2.00 in the afternoon swimming across the Teltow Canal. He was fired on by rifles and automatic weapons and sank in the middle of the canal. An unnamed man swimming with him turned back and was arrested.*
2 September 1961 *Hans-Joachim Rassmann, 21, died at the wall.*
3 September 1961 *Axel Bruckner, 28, a lieutenant in the People's Police, was shot at the border trying to cross. His mother was told by the police only that he had had a fatal accident.*

However, 'during the night between 9 and 10 September, a married couple swam across the Havel, pulling an 18-month-old child in a bath-tub with a rope behind them. They reached West Berlin territory unharmed in the neighbourhood of the Glienicker Bridge.'[2] That same day three men broke through in a lorry at the sunken gardens. One man was slightly wounded in the right hand. A week later three men hijacked a postal truck and drove it through the barbed wire. They were shot at after they crossed.

By mid-September some 2,665 people had been escorted to police stations in East Berlin for 'state crimes', which were defined as 'rabble-rousing propaganda and state slandering' – euphemisms, presumably, for complaining about the wall. Preliminary proceedings had begun against 1,085 of them.

President Kennedy decided to appoint Clay as his special representative to the city, which was shrewd in terms of lifting West Berlin morale but might be more problematical if incidents developed and, the GDR pushing to assert what they claimed were their rights, incidents seemed inevitable. By nature, Clay preferred confrontation to compromise and his status was unclear, anyway. As Gelb writes: 'The White House was sending Clay to Berlin to reassure the Berliners; he was going there to take on the Russians.'[3]

Clay arrived on 19 September and moved quickly on three fronts. He ordered that a mock section of wall be built so American troops could practise knocking it down; he resumed military patrols along the autobahns in the GDR which had been suspended; and he turned his attention to the enclave of Steinstücken.

Kurt Behrendt, the amateur radio operator who'd moved there in 1957 soon after his wedding, remembers that 'General Clay came in September 1961. At that time, in fact, he wasn't a General any more. The first day he was in Berlin he came in a US military helicopter because they wanted to show him the American Sector and he was the inventor of the air bridge. They showed him the sector and, since the American helicopters were the only ones who were allowed to fly over the GDR, they came to Steinstücken as well and said, "OK, this belongs to the American Sector." There is a railway through Steinstücken and at the other side of it there is a big area, a field, and the helicopter landed there. He walked round Steinstücken and some of the residents accompanied him. At that time, I had a job where I worked at night so I was asleep. My wife woke me and I got my camera and took pictures of the whole thing.'

Next day the GDR began the process of forced evacuation of properties on the border line. This was at Harzer Strasse in the southern district of Treptow, a place which was as much an anomaly as Bernauer Strasse. The line followed one side of the road through a built-up area of four- and five-storey houses, running along Harzer Strasse, turning geometrically left into another street then geometrically right along the street after that.

Harzer Strasse had already provided a montage of its own photographic images: the wall made of stacked concrete lintels so close to the houses that, at one point, it passed under a balcony; two bricklayers positioning square stone blocks while three Border Guards monitored them; two young women holding hands and talking across a concrete block while a Border Guard surveyed them from three paces away; a crowd on the Western side watching a solitary bricklayer lift the stone blocks into place. The front door of No. 118 was the actual border line and, although the wooden door itself remained in place, the hall behind had been crudely bricked up. Now 20 houses and their 250 occupants were moved out.

25 September 1961   *Olga Segler, 80, jumped from the second-floor window of 34 Bernauer Strasse at 9.30. She landed in a blanket held by the West Berlin Fire Brigade but died of injuries.*

There would be other images in this street, of a 77-year-old called Frieda Schulze[4] who survived. Al Hemsing 'witnessed at Bernauer Strasse the old lady being held by the *Vopos* and it was a tug-of-war until the people in the West finally got her'.

Wearing a plain dress, she climbed out of a window and stood on a little ledge. Someone from the West leapt up and tried to pull her onto the blanket which the Fire Brigade held, spread taut, below. He gripped her shoe and it came off. In all her fear, she held on to the window ledge with her right hand. Just then an arm came from the window and grasped her hand, trying to haul her back in. She was on her knees facing the window and now the man held her with both his hands while, just behind him, a capless policeman threw a small smoke bomb into the crowd below. The woman wriggled off the ledge so that the man trying to haul her back had to hold her whole bodyweight. He did, but someone from the West leapt up again and tried to seize her left ankle; someone else already had her right ankle and pulled.

This was the precise image which would be developed and carefully printed, fixed: two men at a window pulling the arm of a white-haired woman, and two men on the ground pulling her ankles. *This* symbolism was so precise that it remains deeply evocative four decades later. She tumbled down into the blanket and the crowd raised their fists towards the window and shouted in triumph.

'I was standing right on the other side of the street and it was very emotional,' Hemsing says. 'Above all, my reaction was: can this be happening on an ordinary street? You just weren't ready to see that sort of thing. The people on the Western side were all shouting although I can't remember if I was shouting, too.'

Between 24 and 27 September, nearly 2,000 people living along Bernauer Strasse were forcibly evacuated. The GDR intended no more jumping from windows and ledges, but that would have to await complete evacuation. Elsewhere, however, a 35-year-old woman got across the border with two small children at 10.15 one night. They were fired at as they crawled under the wire but made it unhurt; and at the very end of the month further houses were evacuated in Treptow. The GDR resolved there would be no more holding hands over the concrete blocks down there.

> 4 October 1961   *Bernd Lunser, a 22-year-old student, died when he jumped from the roof of 44 Bernauer Strasse and missed the Fire Brigade blanket. He had been discovered and was shot at by the Border Guards. An unknown man planning to escape with him was reportedly beaten to death in the attic of number 44.*
>
> 5 October 1961   *An unknown man tried to swim the River Spree at 11.50 at night. Border Guards shouted warnings and fired warning shots. A police boat pursued him and shots were fired from it when he was about 6 metres from the Western bank. He disappeared under the water and, at 1.02 a.m., the West Berlin Fire Brigade found a body in the water.*
>
> 5 October 1961   *Udo Dullick, a 26-year-old engineer, tried to escape by swimming the Teltow Canal at 11.50 at night. His body was founds hours later – he had been shot and then he'd drowned. An unknown man, making the escape attempt with him, was fatally hit and drowned, too. A third man met the same fate, although whether he was with the other two is unclear.*

A pattern began to emerge, escapers working out that the waterways – the Humboldt basin, the Teltow Canal and the Spree – were weak points in the wall; and darkness might be their friend. If water equalled vulnerability so did the earth itself and that would bring the tunnellers. These early days, however, the tightening of control was still incomplete. For example, an underground passage carrying clear rainwater ran under a street in East Berlin to the West and, to reach it, all anyone had to do was lift a grating and lower themselves down. So many escapers used this – twenty-eight in one night alone – that a quota system had to be instituted to maintain its secrecy.[5] It was discovered after fifteen days and the grates replaced by bolted manhole covers.

> 12 October 1961   *Klaus-Peter Eich, 21, who'd hidden on a Westbound goods train, was seen by the Transport Police between the stations of Potsdam and Babelsberg. Two Border Guards fired four*

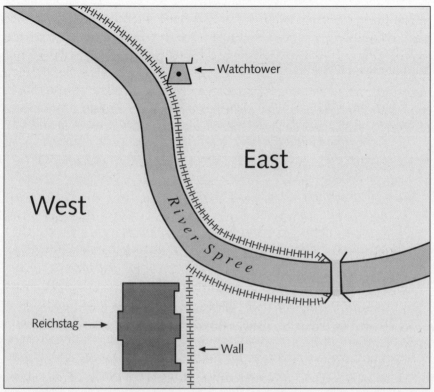

The River Spree, where tragic and very public escape attempts were made.

warning shots in the air and then four aimed shots. Eich died later in hospital. A man with him escaped by shaking off tracker dogs.

Bernauer Strasse was now evacuated further, and so were houses within 150 metres of the wall in the side streets off it. The area became a ghostly place of silences and blinded windows. The tramline along it was bisected by the wall so that the West Berlin trams had to stop and go back; and a television crew interviewed a conductress one day, framing her against the wall and the wooden screen behind it. (The screen had been erected so that people could not see each other, or wave to each other, over it. Bearing in mind that Bernauer Strasse had been one street with friends and families on both sides, the screen was almost more inhuman than the wall itself.) The conductress spoke a few words, gesticulated in a stunned sort of way and broke down. Bernauer Strasse lived on with its ghosts and its memories until the following August when the GDR began to demolish the houses. In time, they would all go, making a long, broad death strip with only the Church of Reconciliation left standing, and in time that would be demolished, too.

Between 23 September and 13 October 1961 an estimated 150 people escaped through a drainage canal before it was discovered.

<u>14 October 1961</u>   *Werner Probst, a 25-year-old transport worker, tried to swim the Spree. Twenty-one shots, including warning shots, were fired at him and he was hit in the head, heart and lungs.*

<u>18 October 1961</u>   *An unknown man was shot by Transport Police between Potsdam and Babelsberg after boarding a Westbound goods train. He died of his wounds the next day.*

Of necessity, many people tried to maintain normality as best they could and, as a consequence, Allan Lightner of the American Mission and his wife Dorothy prepared to enjoy themselves on the evening of the 22nd. In the background, however, the GDR were beginning their process of assertion. 'There had been a series of incidents with the *Vopos* stopping American, British and French cars who were testing the free access to the East,' Dorothy Lightner says. 'These incidents were usually on the weekend. About a week before the 22nd I got a call from Allan's general services officer – named Earle Cleveland – inviting Allan and I to a Czechoslovakian performance in Eastern Berlin. I said to Allan, "Would you like to go?" and he said "Oh, Sunday evening, there are always the incidents." I said, "Earle has to know if we're going or not" and Allan said, "OK, we'll go."

'We had house guests [including] an army officer from Frankfurt up for that weekend. They were going back on the train which went from West Berlin to Frankfurt. We went down to see them off – they'd already been to East Berlin with George Muller [of the Mission] and they'd had some difficulty, but the *Vopos* finally let them through. They reported to us that it seemed to them the *Vopos* were trying to make trouble but would, in the end, chicken out.

'Cleveland thought the performance was something wonderful – an amazing combination of lantern slides and live action and projected pictures. I've never seen it, I only know it was evidently a terrific thing to watch and it was just something Cleveland thought we'd want to go to. We weren't in the business of provoking but we were not just about to give up anything, either. We'd dropped our friends off at the station. We debated whether we should get something to eat or go right to the show and we decided we were already eating too much, we were too fat and the Clevelands had invited us to have something afterwards – so we headed off to Friedrichstrasse.'

They reached Checkpoint Charlie and moved past the Allied control, a white hut in the middle of the road with US ARMY CHECKPOINT written above it. They reached the white sign as big as a hoarding with YOU ARE LEAVING THE AMERICAN SECTOR written on it. They continued to Hagen Koch's line, now just in front of them, and when they crossed that they were technically and physically in the East. The checkpoint had not yet grown into the finesse of fortifications it would later be: Friedrichstrasse, broad and straight, had, just over the line, a 'chicane' of concrete sleepers laid three deep to slow traffic, and then much further on a couple of sentry boxes. More than that, the area had a battered feel to it. The façades of the tall buildings – six storeys, some of them – still bore the familiar pockmarking of gunfire from 1945. There were vacant lots where the bombed buildings had been taken down. The road itself had been patched and so had the pavements along either side of it.

Dorothy continues, 'When we got there the *Vopos* demanded to see our papers and, according to established procedure, my husband was supposed to demand a Russian officer. We were not negotiating with the *Vopos*. When, after an interval, there was no Russian officer and it was apparent that they hadn't even called one, Allan said, "I have a right to go ahead, I am taking advantage of my right."'

Al Hemsing, Press Officer at the Mission, explains it. Someone from the Mission had gone over 'in a dark Chevrolet and Al Lightner and his wife went over in their Beetle. The dark car was waved through just on a show of ID cards but Lightner, immediately after him, was held up and to this day I'm quite convinced that had he been in the Mission car he wouldn't have been, but the idea of the Chief of Mission going over in a little Volkswagen and driving himself probably struck the *Vopos* as being strange. He said, "I don't show papers." The *Vopo* was simply behaving like any Corporal would.'

Dorothy Lightner says that 'Allan was driving my car, which was a little Volkswagen and it had the licence plate one thousand. So although it was mine – well ours, Allan normally used an official vehicle and I was the one who really drove it – he was driving it at this point. He switched into first. Now if you know anything about those Volkswagens you know they make a terrible noise when they go into first gear – well, the 1959 version I had did. There were two *Vopos* in front of the car and they sprang back. We were not about to run them down but they didn't know that. So they sprang back and we went ahead and it was a very short distance that we went ahead through this No Man's Land. They chased after us, stopped us and they thumped on the car with their batons – which really made me mad because they were denting it. They said, "This time you've really done it, now we're going to put you in jail." They made various and summary threats which we ignored. We sat in the car. Meanwhile the American lieutenant on duty at Checkpoint Charlie came walking over to us . . .'

Lieutenant: 'Is there anything I can do, Mr Lightner?'

Lightner: 'No, we're in no trouble, let's wait and see what's going to happen.'

The lieutenant clearly sensed the possibility of an incident and went off to telephone the American Operations Centre in Clayallee (named for General Clay, and in the west of the West). Clay himself was at the Operations Centre and he, too, sensed an incident. He fully intended to demonstrate how you dealt with incidents. He ordered soldiers, four tanks and two personnel carriers to the checkpoint.

Word had gone to Howard Trivers, Political Officer at the Mission. He and his wife were sitting in their living-room and the red phone rang, which was an alert. He answered it, spoke briefly, replaced the receiver and put his hat and coat on.

Mrs Trivers: 'Howard, what's going on?'

Trivers (turning and looking at her): 'They've got Al.' He headed for Clayallee.

Operations Centre

Trivers arrived in time to hear Clay saying into a telephone, 'Tell Mrs Lightner to get out of the vehicle.' That would have been to the lieutenant at the checkpoint.

When Clay put the phone down Trivers said to him, 'General, I think you're going to have a little trouble with that.'

Clay, an old and good friend of Dorothy Lightner, said nothing.

Checkpoint Charlie

She sat very calmly in the stationary Volkswagen and the lieutenant walked over to it again.

Lieutenant: 'Mrs Lightner, would you please come back with me? They've asked me to ask you to return to Checkpoint Charlie.'

Mrs Lightner: 'I certainly will not. My husband and I are in this together.'

She remembered they had a package of chewing gum, the only thing edible in the car, and they chewed it. The lieutenant walked to the checkpoint and telephoned the Operations Centre to report that Mrs Lightner refused to leave the vehicle.

Operations Centre
Clay: 'Tell her I *order* her to leave it.'

Checkpoint Charlie
The 'poor lieutenant' (her phrase) came back a third time.

Lieutenant: 'Mrs Lightner, General Clay has ordered you to leave the car.'

Dorothy Lightner: 'Well, I guess I have to if it's General Clay, but tell him from me that I think he's very mean to ladies to order them out of vehicles.' Neither she nor her husband had felt in any danger except when, in the gloom, she could see *Vopos* coming up with dogs. She walked back with the lieutenant, leaving her husband still sitting and the car still stationary. He was certainly not about to turn it round. When she reached the checkpoint she heard why she had been ordered out.

Lieutenant: 'Mrs Lightner, the reason this is happening is that they [the soldiers Clay had despatched] want to do something and what they are going to do is make a forced entry with fixed bayonets.'

By now, the *Vopos* had reported the incident to their superiors. As Hemsing says, 'then it went up the line in the East and I think what happened is they thought this is as good a time as any, let's hold him up and make him show his ID. And it escalated. There were higher officers there by the time I arrived.'

Lightner didn't move until the lieutenant and the squad of Clay's soldiers came up. As they marched ahead of the Volkswagen, the lieutenant said, 'Boys, watch your throats', because of the dogs. Dorothy Lightner watched Clay's soldiers deploy to both sides of the Volkswagen with fixed bayonets. They all moved through the checkpoint into the East and Lightner drove symbolically for a couple of blocks before he came back. She waited and when he did come back they talked.

Lightner: 'We'll try again. For heaven's sake, the whole point of this is to prove our right of entry.'

Dorothy Lightner suggested somebody should go with him 'because it was a lonely thing in the car by yourself and he chose Al Hemsing to go. I felt that history had side-swiped me. I felt we should have been in it together because you can't fight Anglo-Saxon womanhood!'

Hemsing remembered her saying, 'No, it's not fair, I was in the car and it ought to be the way it was', but finally she agreed and Hemsing got in.

The Volkswagen set off again, the *Vopos* challenged it again and the soldiers came out again. Hemsing says, 'He and I then set off, him driving and me on the passenger side. Members of the Berlin Brigade with rifles and drawn bayonets and hand grenades escorted us. The drill was that we'd go forward and they'd hang behind and we'd inch our way in. There was one *Vopo* who always gave us a hard time and he did pull back a little bit. Lightner advanced but he let the clutch out too fast and hit this guy in the shin. Lightner and I were hardly as calm as we might be and this guy let out a string of curses. Lightner had German but he didn't have gutter German – as I did – and I was happy about that. I'm glad he didn't get the full brunt because I think he would have run the *Vopo* down or something. The *Vopo* was saying things like, "You bastard, I'll make mincemeat out of you" – maybe not those exact words but that sentiment. So we did go in. We went in maybe a couple of hundred feet, maybe a hundred yards, something like that, and then we turned around and came out again. We were emphasising our access to East Berlin.'[6]

Howard Trivers arrived. He was official liason with the Soviets; he crossed and he spoke to[7] the Soviet political adviser at the checkpoint, Lazarev (presumably Anatoly Ivanovich Lazarev, who was also involved in espionage).[8] Lazarev expressed surprise at the incidents, leading to the supposition that Ulbricht had taken this further and started the assertion without Soviet knowledge.

But 'we had established our rights,' Dorothy Lightner says, 'and after the second time they didn't stop Allan.' Lightner went across a third time later on, unescorted and unmolested.

The next day, however, the GDR – no doubt this time with Soviet approval – announced that now uniformed Allied personnel could not go across without showing their identity papers. Hemsing says 'it was tried a number of times again next morning, this time with army officers as civilians doing the same drill, and that's what caused the tank confrontation'.

Clay decided to confront the challenge at Checkpoint Charlie and cleared it with Kennedy personally. This was delicate, Kennedy breathing inside the iron lung. Against that the niceties and formalities of showing ID papers at a distant checkpoint seemed fantastically *picayun*. Clay was thinking parochially, maybe, but he knew if you gave anything to Soviets they'd take that, and then take more, on and on. An evocative name had been coined for it: salami tactics. The difficult question was where and when you said 'no more slicing' and meant it. Clay was not troubled by such indecision. The slicing ceased here and now. The problem, as Hemsing explains, was that Clay had retired: 'Didn't belong in the military chain of command and he didn't give a damn. He was the personal representative of the President.'

On Wednesday 25 October, two American military police officers wearing civilian clothing drove an Opel with official licence plates across. The *Vopos* flagged them down and they returned, picked up an escort, went back and went through. Ten American tanks arrived near the border. The Opel now made repeated passes at the checkpoint. Each time it was flagged down, each time it sought the escort. The Americans continued to maintain their rights.

On Thursday 26 October, they did this again. The Soviets decided that for them, too, it was enough.

'When they'd stopped Lightner coming through I wasn't there and I didn't know anything about it but I read it and in the subsequent days they began these forays through Checkpoint Charlie up to Unter den Linden. They'd turn round and come back again,' Kellett-Long says. 'Things had got quieter then and we had been to the cinema with our office secretary, Erdmute. Mary and I were driving her home after the cinema and we went along Warschauer Strasse. We crossed over one of the main roads leading into the middle of Berlin and she said to me, "Mr Kellet-Long, there's a soldier standing on that corner." I said, "Don't be silly, you're imagining things." We went on, we dropped her and on the way back I said to Mary, "I think we'd better have a look. Perhaps she wasn't seeing things after all." So we stopped the car on the crossroads and sure enough there was a soldier standing there.

'I went up to ask him what he was doing and at that point he stepped out into the middle of the road to halt the traffic coming both ways. A column of tanks roared by very fast bound for the middle of Berlin and I recognised them as Russian tanks because they had Russian markings on. I watched them go past and, being an agency man [Reuters filing to the world did not have deadlines], I rushed to the office and put out a "snap" saying "Column of Soviet tanks moved into the middle of East Berlin tonight". I sent out this one sentence, got back into the car and drove down to Unter den Linden to the Staatsoper [the opera house, bombed during the war and reopened in 1955] where I saw these tanks disappearing into a courtyard. Again they were shouting to each other in Russian as they were backing the last of them in, so that confirmed to me what and who they were. This was about eleven o'clock at night, because people were actually coming out of the Staatsoper – the opera performance had just finished – as the last of these tanks was being put in. The Pentagon issued a statement saying they were aware of this but they weren't Russian tanks they were East German tanks.'[9]

The Soviets were fully entitled under the Four Power Agreement to move their forces around their sector, but any movement of GDR tanks would have been a clear and serious violation.

Kellet-Long continues. 'I filed all that and overnight – again – somebody came up from Bonn to say, "We are in trouble here because you say they are Russian and the Pentagon says they are definitely not Russian." I said, "I'm sorry, but I speak Russian, I've seen them and they had Russian markings on them which I recognised and I've heard them shouting to each other in Russian. There is no question that they are Russian." They were quite invisible.'

It was Friday.

27 October 1961   *Gerhard Kayser, 21, was found at 4.25 in the morning caught in the barbed wire near a station in the north. He'd been shot. 'The severely injured man was brutally dragged 30 metres through the barbed wire and was left lying for an hour before he was taken away.'[10] He died in hospital.*

'About three o'clock that afternoon,' Kellett-Long says, 'the usual foray came through from Checkpoint Charlie, went back and five minutes later there was a rumble and the column of tanks went down Friedrichstrasse and stopped on the border. At this point I was standing at the border and I was very pleased to hear the American Commander on the other side, whoever he was, saying, "By God, they *are* Russian." The Americans quickly marshalled their tanks and they were facing each other across the checkpoint. I can very much remember the relief on the American side at the fact that they were Russian but it was extremely tense because who the hell knew what was going to happen?

'If they had been East German tanks there would have been a real problem, and that's why I'm always convinced that the man who was running Checkpoint Charlie on the East German side was a Russian although he was in a *Vopo's* uniform. Before this, I'd been down to the checkpoint and I was told to get the hell out of it – "You can't stay here, you've got to go back." I went to see the Soviet Second Secretary handling press and I said, "They've just told me I can't be near the border." His reaction was astonishing. He went out of the room, returned and said, "Come with me." We got into a Soviet Embassy car and we drove down to the border. I felt a bit embarrassed and I didn't know what was going to happen. At the checkpoint he spoke to this alleged East German who was in charge for a couple of minutes, and then he said, "All right" and he disappeared. That showed me who was in control of that operation. I mean, this was the Russian Second Secretary telling them, "Let this chap stay here." He'd been too far away for me to hear whether they were speaking in Russian. Anyway I was convinced that whatever the inital situation might have been the Russians had taken control of it.'

Hemsing says 'our tanks went up to the line at full speed, there was a great screeching, a bobbing of the guns – and at that point there was a man in his early sixties on the Eastern side. The tanks came eye-to-eye and he bolted to our side and went right past me. I said, "Hold it!" but he kept yelling, "I'm free! I'm free!" Some reporters caught up with him, but that was a street and a half past Checkpoint Charlie because only there did he stop running.'

Richard Smyser, as junior officer at the Mission, explains that 'it was always understood on our side that Western military would not go into the East except on patrols. That was proved during the Checkpoint Charlie confrontation where our tanks went up to the border but not across it. Curiously enough the East Germans were not sure and they put up an anti-tank barrier. Our principle was always that we would not go East just as we told the Russians that their military could not come to the West, and there were all kinds of arguments about that.

'During the confrontation I was in the Operations Centre situation room. Situation rooms have a kind of common appearance: no windows, a lot of tables, a lot of telephones and one large table where all the people sit. It was in the basement. Clay was in it, too. He was a very remarkable man, quite different from what I had expected. I'd been told he was a tough guy – which he was – but he was also a very human, sympathetic man.

'Actually, even as the tanks faced each other, it wasn't a tense time. One of the great mythologies of the Berlin confrontation, which has been permitted to go on and on, was that it was tense. It was tense *only* until the Russians came, and when the Russians came Clay said, "OK, from now on they're in control. The status quo has been restored." The press wrote some of the most nonsensical stuff about this great confrontation. Garbage, utter garbage. We knew very well, Clay knew, I knew, everybody knew that the Russians had instigated this exercise. They had done it perhaps reluctantly – I was never sure and I'm still not sure – but they were certainly not the people who were pushing it. It was being pushed by Ulbricht and I think that Khrushchev had far different fish to fry. He had many things he wanted in Germany and I don't think sealing off Berlin had been an ambition, but – whatever it was – it became a situation where American and Russian tanks faced each other. Neither was going to shoot: we were certainly not going to start World War Three over some goddamned incident at Checkpoint Charlie and the Russians weren't going to start World War Three there, either.'

(The ordinary population didn't know this. Jacqueline Burkhardt, who'd moved to Berlin in 1949, was now 21. 'The tanks came to the demarcation line – Russian tanks, American tanks – and people who lived nearby went to see what was going on. I was nervous, I didn't know which tank would fire the first shot.')

Smyser accepts that 'it may seem a sophisticated interpretation but I think it is an accurate interpretation to judge that the wall was to consolidate – or save – East Germany and when the Checkpoint Charlie thing happened we were, in a sense, playing games. Clay figured that once we got our tanks there, "We'll see what happens." Through intelligence – and we had patrols over there, don't forget – we knew that the Russians were sending tanks. One of our patrols came back and told us that there was a platoon of Russian tanks.

'We were fascinated by what the Russians would do and, of course, when the Russian tanks came in it was calm but the wire services were churning out the confrontation. At that point Clay talked to the White House because Kennedy called – he must have had people running around saying, "What's happening?" Kennedy called and got Clay and must have said, "Now what's going on?" Clay replied – I can't remember the exact words – "The situation is calm, don't worry because the Russian tanks have arrived." The sentiment was "Relax Mr President, the status quo has been restored." [George Muller confirms this: 'I was with Clay when he called Rusk on the scrambler at some ungodly hour to report to him that Soviet tanks had drawn up and that was that.']

'Then we did a delicate manoeuvre in withdrawing because the rest was all face saving. When you have a confrontation you always have that problem and what you do is back off a little way. Then if the other guy doesn't do anything you go forward again, but if the other guy says "Ah ha, thank God" and also pulls back a little bit then you understand he's not trying to shoot you.' And you back off a bit more, and he backs off a bit more, and you back off a bit more . . . [11]

In fact, 'Kennedy and Khrushchev quietly defused the situation by agreeing that the Soviet tanks would withdraw first.'[12]

Frank Cash of the Berlin Task Force in Washington, expands on the context:

Kennedy was far less than the public thought he was in terms of morality, principles, beliefs – in almost every respect. I never was as overwhelmed with Kennedy as the general public, because having dealt with him on Berlin I was somewhat sceptical. I didn't know about the amount of sex – God, he was almost an obsessive with it. His brother and his father, too. It all comes from old Joe [the father] who probably learned it in London![13]

It was not evident to me. This was early on, you see, and there were some mild rumours but nothing like what is documented now. It's rather sad because Kennedy was such a hero to so many, and it really makes cynics out of people when their heroes are destroyed.

The nuclear aspect was what Kennedy had to keep in mind and that's what Rusk was constantly reminding him of when we were urging the President to be tough on Berlin, but he was the guy who was going to have to press the button if it came to it. I think the closest thing we had to Cuba was when the tanks pulled up to each side of Checkpoint Charlie. I remember we had a meeting in the White House and the Berlin Task Force were urging that our tanks stand firm and the White House staff were urging that they withdraw. We kept saying, 'If we stand firm the Soviets will back down' and Kennedy listened to this for about half an hour. Finally he got up, shook his head, turned to us and said, 'OK, but you'd better be right.' Then he walked out of the room.

We [Allied personnel] would hold our passports up to the window so the East Germans could look at them to see that we were indeed the guy in the picture but we refused to hand over our travel documents to the East Germans. It almost sounds ridiculous to make a point like that to the President of the United States: that we can't hand our documents over. Once again he'd say, 'That's *picayun*.'

At least the wall removed the threat of instability, and I think the strong stand we took – maintaining freedom in the West – wasn't only realised in East Berlin and East Germany but it went on back through the satellites and ultimately to the Soviet Union. I believe you can draw a direct line between the freedom in West Berlin and the end of the cold war. If we'd let West Berlin go, they'd have consolidated and maybe 1989 wouldn't have happened . . .'

John Ausland of the State Department gave another view from Washington:

The problem really became Clay. I think it's important to understand that no-one wanted to do anything against the division of the city. And another thing. I'd been watching the division of the city since 1951 so in a way it was only the completion of that ten-year process. Once it was agreed to accept that, our problem became one of dealing with the Germans, not the Russians, you know, because of the Germans' reactions. I'm talking now mainly about the Berliners but to some extent about the West Germans, too, because at that time Brandt and Adenauer were preoccupied with an election campaign and on different sides.

Our problem was how to calm down the West Berliners and to reassure them that we weren't going to desert them, and the [immediate] decision had been, of course, to send the Vice-President, the Battle Group and Clay. All right, now we'd got through the Battle Group problem [a possible challenge on the autobahn] very quickly, the Vice-President went and left, and then we had Clay. He stayed in Berlin for some time and he became the problem. Basically Kennedy was following a very cautious line and Clay and Lightner wanted to be very aggressive. We were caught in between. Clay couldn't afford to blame the President so he blamed us, and you have kind of a merry-go-round going on. Kennedy was warned he would have problems, although whether we had problems in the long run was not important, I think, in terms of reassuring the West Berliners. Clay being there and the tank incident were very reassuring.

The only thing that became a reality was the tank confrontation and that was not a thing that was welcomed in Washington. Everyone was very glad when it was over, and it was quite clear there was some communication between Kennedy and Khrushchev that ended it. No, we didn't have a hot line but we had ways of communicating. The useful thing, from my point of view, that Clay did was quiet down the Steinstücken problem that had been troubling us for years. He just took a couple of soldiers, put them on a helicopter, flew them out, put them there and the whole problem went away. I welcomed that one. So, in retrospect, having

Clay there was very good but at the time it was a pain in the neck because we were caught between this cautious President and this aggressive bunch in Berlin.'[14]

The Clay 'problem' became a strange thing to Geoffrey McDermott, the British minister in Berlin. Alec Douglas-Home, the Foreign Secretary, came on an official visit and only after it did Clay return, from a visit of his own to Washington. 'Others beside myself could not help wondering whether he had deliberately avoided Lord Home's visit. In my curiosity I asked to be allowed to call on him to exchange views. I was snubbed. From then onwards General Clay mingled very little with his Allies, even socially, and I have reason to believe that he also became increasingly difficult towards his compatriots. Reconstructing this curious episode, I can only conclude that Clay wanted to press on with the forward policy he had so clearly pursued in the October tank confrontation' – while, presumably, Douglas-Home would have advised extreme circumspection and caution.'[15]

Kurt Behrendt, the resident of Steinstücken, saw all this from ground level, as it were. 'When they started to build the wall, the Americans were passive but General Clay gave the order after the day he visited us that a company of American soldiers would be deployed here in tents. At this time we had the conflict at Checkpoint Charlie with the tanks and nobody wanted to risk a similar sort of conflict in Steinstücken. The order was that after two or three days the soldiers should be withdrawn but, three days later, Clay gave the order to deploy three American soldiers in order to demonstrate that Steinstücken was in their sector. These soldiers rotated after two or three days by helicopter and we called it the "little airbridge". [The 1948–9 airlift had been known as the 'airbridge'.] Except for residents, it was not allowed for anybody – even Americans, even politicians – to come here using the path [through the GDR] and so they had to come by helicopter. Even our relatives weren't allowed to use the path.'

<u>31 October 1961</u> *An unknown man was fatally shot at the wall.*
<u>17 November 1961</u> *Lothar Lehmann, 20, tried to swim a lake to the west of West Berlin and was shot. His mother was told he died 'through an accident in the Army'.*

After the tank confrontation, Berlin quietened into a sort of muted, choreographed dance. Frank Trinka of the Mission describes how 'we'd go to Karlshorst [the Eastern suburb where the Soviet headquarters was] to protest and they'd say that whatever had happened was in line with their policy and the GDR was a sovereign state. It was a Mexican stand-off, as we say. All people hold their positions and nothing happens. I was at Karlshorst frequently with Howard Trivers – he was the man who generally went over, the senior officer – to make the protests or to receive them. I accompanied him. It was a Soviet headquarters and there were troops everywhere so I'd say it was more a military headquarters. You couldn't compare it to the US Mission in Clayallee. On their side it was much more evident that the military were in charge.

'You had to go through a check-in procedure although there had already been prior contact, so they knew you were coming. We'd phone and they'd say, "Yes, we expect you at such and such a time." We'd go there and we'd register formal protests. The effect was probably that they'd tell the East Germans to back off and not be so aggressive, but it would not change their policy to us. We still maintained that freedom of access in Berlin encompassed all of Berlin and all of the civilian population. We generally had an interpreter along, and the way we did it was either English-to-Russian or German-to-Russian. Some of the Russians spoke German so German was fairly frequently used. Most of our people were quite competent in German, Smyser too.'[16] (Trinka, incidentally, was transferred to Prague towards the end of 1961 and so his Berlin story ended then.)

And still they came. One mid-October morning at around 5.00, nine men in a lorry burst through two rolls of barbed wire at Kleinmachnow, where radio reporter Peter Schultz had watched in consternation and disbelief as the wire had been laid on the night the wall went up, but were halted by the third roll of it. They abandoned the beached lorry and, under a hail of fire, sprinted.

In early November a West Berliner smuggled his 19-year-old Eastern fiancée out in the boot of his car. When the customs officers at the checkpoint started to search it he accelerated away, breaking the wooden barrier, and although six shots hit the car they made it. Four days later a 28-year-old engineer and his wife duplicated this in a highly original and perceptive way. The date was the anniversary of the October Revolution (but falling in November in accordance with the Russian calendar). A Soviet military convoy moved up towards Checkpoint Charlie to cross and proceed to the war memorial in the West. The engineer bought a wreath and tied it to the roof of his car, then simply joined the convoy and was waved through with it. Two days afterwards, an unnamed 33-year-old went to a theatrical costume shop in East Berlin and hired a uniform which resembled that of an American soldier. He walked across Checkpoint Charlie. Four days after that, a car with two men and three women in it broke through near Bernauer Strasse. The Border Guards fired what one report suggests was about a hundred shots at it but the car had been reinforced with steel plating and concrete.[17]

<u>17 November 1961</u>   *An unknown person died at the wall, possibly drowning.*
<u>20 November 1961</u>   *An unknown person, thought to be a man, may have been fatally shot and drowned.*

That first Christmas was the bitterest, with families separated by a street or two and without any contact at all. The wooden screens at the end of Bernauer Strasse, as an example, had taken care of that. How those in the GDR government could justify such conduct to themselves and their families – at the same time as they were proclaiming to the world that they had established the first and only humane society the world had ever known – remains a complete mystery. Possibly, according to the size of their ambitions for humanity, they were prepared to sacrifice individuals for the collective whole. It was the most unChristian of ethics but then these were the people who would blow up the Church of Reconciliation and level it so the Border Guards in the watchtowers would have an unobstructed view of the death strip.

To liberate humanity.

The thought of the Christmas division seems to have kept the stampede moving and it produced one of the most extraordinary escapes.

On an early December evening towards 9.00, eight men, ten women and seven children crossed on a complete train of engine and eight carriages. The driver and fireman hatched the plan in conjunction with someone who threw a switch, diverting the train from the Eastern line to one leading to the West. The train thundered over the barbed wire across the track just beyond Falkensee and came to a halt in a field. Legend insists that while the escapees hugged in delight, some very startled passengers – who had known nothing of the attempt – sat bemused, and the guard, also unaware, marched up and said it was forbidden to stop at anywhere but a station. . . .

<u>9 December 1961</u>   *Dieter Wohlfahrt, a 21-year-old Austrian, and two other Westerners, cut through the wire at Staaken to help a relative get*

*across at 7.15 in the evening. Wohlfahrt was hit by automatic fire and
left for an hour with fatal injuries. The other two regained the West.*

Wohlfahrt, a student at West Berlin's Technical University, had
evidently grown impatient with what was known as the 'tour
system' of escapes. It involved forged passports, go-betweens and
involved many obvious risks. Wohlfahrt decided on a 'commando
raid'[18] instead but was cut down by gunfire as soon as he had cut
the wire. He bled to death.

<u>10 December 1961</u>   *Ingo Krüger, 21, was seen swimming the Spree in
a diving suit and oxygen mask. A police boat tried to haul him up
with grappling hooks and he was taken dead from the water.*

Adam Kellett-Long would remember this Christmas. 'I'd been told
about a terribly moving scene. At one point you could see over the
wall and there were about a couple of hundred East Berliners waving white handkerchiefs to relatives on the other side. By Christmas
that was the only point where people could still see each other.
Shortly after Christmas – I hope not because I wrote about it, but
I'm afraid probably because I did – they heightened the wall so that
that gap was closed.

'Erdmute came in to the office one day and said, "I've got some
oranges!" – a tremendous luxury. What had happened, the tram had
been going along the street and the driver had spotted a shop selling
oranges and stopped the tram. Everybody got off and rushed into the
shop, stormed the shop. Oranges had been brought in to the shops
for Christmas but not too many oranges and long queues formed.'

<u>1 January 1962</u>   *An unknown person died at the wall.*

In January the tunnellers began. In the north, twenty-eight people
aged between 8 and 71 emerged in the West at 2.00 one morning
from a tunnel they had dug themselves.

<u>12 January 1962</u>   *Barbara Hildegard Blass, who had celebrated her
nineteenth birthday on 12 December, died at the wall in unknown
circumstances.*
<u>19 February 1962</u>   *Doris Schmiel, a 20-year-old dressmaker, and
another woman were among five people trying to escape in the north.
Three rounds of machine-gun fire raked them and Schmiel fell, fatally
wounded in the stomach.*

On 22 February Robert Kennedy and his brother Edward visited Berlin. Robert made a short statement in German, 'reading it slowly and with some difficulty',[19] and he reiterated the United States' determination to keep West Berlin free. He went in a motorcade to the wall at Potsdamer Platz and mounted a wooden observation platform to look over. 'It is even more shocking, even more shameful, than I had expected.' Edward was on a private visit and came in by ordinary commercial flight from Paris. It was his thirtieth birthday and city officials gave him a 'tree cake', evidently a Berlin delicacy. Edward visited the East, annoying John F. by showing his passport to an East German. He went walkabout, saw a queue outside a shop and spoke to a middle-aged woman who said she was waiting to get apples. He wondered if she did that every day and she replied, 'No, they don't have apples every day.'

14 March 1962   *Otto Müller, 55, was fatally shot at the Spree, although the circumstances are not clear.*

27 March 1962   *Heinz Jercha, a 28-year-old West Berlin butcher, was shot by a Border Guard while helping people to escape through a tunnel he had dug. He died on the way to hospital from a haemorrhage.*

3 April 1962   *An unnamed Border Guard tried to cross near the Dreilinden checkpoint at 1.45 in the afternoon. A police dog intercepted him and he was shot by automatic fire.*

11 April 1962   *Philipp Held, 20, drowned in the Spree. His mother was informed by the Public Prosecutor in a letter on 30 April, which said only that her son had had 'a fatal accident'. She was told the body would be released for burial and she could make whatever arrangements she wished. A telephone call from the Public Prosecutor the same day, however, said Held had already been cremated.[20]*

18 April 1962   *Klaus Brueske, 23, drove a lorry which broke through the Heinrich-Heine-Strasse checkpoint. Around 20 shots were fired and Brueske was hit in the back of the neck. Two others with him were injured. The lorry got through.*

18 April 1962   *At 7.30, two non-commissioned GDR officers tried to get across in the Potsdam area, taking their rifles and ammunition. One was Peter Böhme, 19. He and a Border Guard, Jörgen Schmidtchen, exchanged fire and both were killed.*

29 April 1962   *Horst Frank, 20, and one other cut through the wire at a railway bridge 15 minutes after midnight. Horst was fatally shot and his body removed by the East Berlin Fire Brigade. The other got across.*

<u>29 April 1962</u>   *Ernest Graupner, 49, died at the wall.*

In May, five women and seven men aged between 19 and 81 emerged in the West from a 40-metre tunnel they had dug. The 81-year-old was called Max Thomas, a gardener who had a plot near the wall. In January, West Berlin officials had formally announced that twenty-eight people had escaped by cutting through the wire but an American news agency talked to them and discovered they'd come out through a tunnel. It ran from a basement in the East to a garden in the Western district of Frohnau. This was the first major escape by tunnel and, as it happened, Thomas had known about it. He lived four doors away from the house whose basement had been used. He'd wanted to go, too, but the organisers told him he and his friends were too old and 'your wives are too fat'.

Thomas resolved to have a tunnel of his own but he was too old to do the necessary digging. He teamed up with a 57-year-old truck driver and two 70-year-olds who moved 4,000 buckets of earth in sixteen days, starting from a small, wooden henhouse. Thomas rigged up an extension cable from his kitchen to light the tunnel and he used that as a warning because whenever a Border Guard patrol came by he switched it off. That alerted the diggers who stopped work until the patrol had gone by. The Thomas tunnel was extremely spacious at 5 feet 6 inches high (1.7metres) because, as he said, 'We wanted to take our wives to freedom in comfort – and upright.'[21]

General Clay was withdrawn that May. Geoffrey McDermott wrote that after Lord Home's visit when Clay might have deliberately gone to Washington, 'from then on, when we met socially he was polite but certainly not warm' towards McDermott and his wife Elizabeth. 'No doubt he had been given a new brief in Washington. I did not let this curious behaviour lessen my respect for him and his work for Berlin; and both Elizabeth and I continued to enjoy the Clays' company.' Of Clay's withdrawal, McDermott added: 'I was told that he received orders to leave Berlin from the President at almost the same moment as his withdrawal was made public in Washington. He was furious. At any rate, he departed without any official Allied farewells. He saved some face with the announcement that he would continue to act as a special adviser to the President on Berlin.'[22]

<u>23 May 1962</u>   *At 5.25 in the afternoon a 'male person' escaped across the Invaliden Cemetery butting on to the Humboldt Canal – one shot*

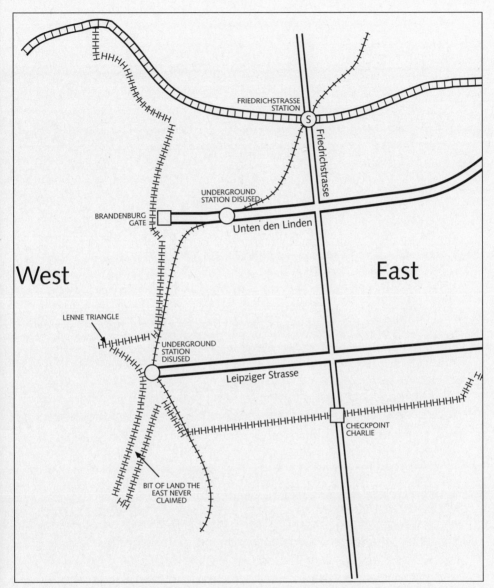

The central drama of Berlin: Checkpoint Charlie and Friedrichstrasse station, conduits between the two halves for 28 years. The station mirrored the drama exactly – the line running underground which Easterners didn't know about and the overground line from the West which terminated at the station. Its continuation was a domestic Eastern line.

*was fired as he neared the wall, another as he clambered over it. He
plunged into the canal beyond the cemetery but other Border Guards
could see him and opened fire. He swam on and reached a 'sort of
platform' leading to stone steps. The Border Guards continued to fire
at him and cut him down. He lay on the platform for some three
minutes while West Berlin policemen fired at the Border Guards to
make them take cover; they hit and killed one of them, a Corporal
Peter Göring. A West Berlin policeman went down the steps with a
ladder to act as a stretcher, secured the 'male person' to it and he was
lifted up.*

The official GDR report, typed out on probably an old typewriter
and dated the same day, is headed REPORT and sub-headed *betr.*,
which is an abbreviation for 'Concerning': Breaking through the
border with use of firearms.

It covers the facts as they are set out above but what it does not
say is far more revealing. Imagine looking up the canal. To the right
was a deep stone embankment which was angled into the water and
above it the old cemetery wall about the height of a man. A further
wall had been built on top of that so that, overall, it would be 18 to
20 feet (6 metres). The 'male person' had somehow to scale that,
scramble down the embankment into the still water and swim some
50 feet (15 metres) to the Western bank. Here the embankment,
made of large stone blocks, was also deep – perhaps 12 feet (3.5
metres) – and vertical. The platform was a tiny 'jetty' with steps up
from it and a metal handrail set into the stone.

This was the view from, and of, the West.[23] 'The 15-year-old
schoolboy T. from Erfurt (Soviet Zone) tried to escape to West
Berlin by swimming through . . . in the Tiergarten district. Soviet
zonal Border Guards shot at him after he had already reached the
Western side of the canal. In order to save the severely wounded
boy, West Berlin police were obliged to return the fire. One Soviet
zonal policeman was fatally hit and another wounded.'

The question of whether Germans would shoot Germans and
Berliners shoot Berliners had now been conclusively answered.

There is something the West Berlin report did not mention. The
border itself was on the *Western* bank so that, in the horror of
Berlin's pedantry, the Border Guards were entitled to fire at the 15-
year-old up to that. The Border Guards' own maps leave no room
for doubt, and neither do anybody else's. It means that the photographer who so assiduously took pictures of where the GDR bullets
chipped the stone blocks by the 'platform' and staircase was not

freezing images of transgression – because that was short of the line.

There is a curious footnote to this, too, but it has been set in its context after another death at the wall three months away.

27 May 1962 *Lutz Haberlandt, 24, was shot dead at 4.40 in the afternoon, trying to cross a bridge beside the Charité Hospital in the city centre.*

5 June 1962 *Axel Hannemann, 17, tried to swim the Spree towards the Reichstag at 5.15 in the afternoon. A Border Guard fired six shots at him from the bank. Hannemann's body was recovered some hours later.*

10 June 1962 *Wolfgang Glöde, 13, died at the wall.*

11 June 1962 *Erna Kelm, 54, drowned trying to swim the River Havel. She had been a nurse and, tucked into a swimming belt, had concealed 'important papers'.*[24]

Two days later a tunnel collapsed and buried an escapee, although by then he had reached West Berlin. Three fellow escapees dug him out with the soup spoons and small shovels they'd used to dig the tunnel.

That same month a West Berliner, Peter Scholz, and friends dug a 60 foot (18metres) tunnel some 9 feet (2.7metres) underground to get his fiancée, her 4-month-old baby and nine others out. The tunnel stretched from a restaurant basement in West Berlin to a house in the East and was narrow (2 feet/0.6metres). 'Progress was painful. Not only was there continual danger of cave-in because of the weight of the earth overhead, but the area was continually patrolled. The slightest noise might have been detected. To keep the infant from crying or being frightened and helplessly betraying them she was given a light sleeping pill, tucked in a metal washbasin and pulled to freedom by rope.'[25] Scholz described this as 'the most difficult part' although, because the tunnel was so cramped, it had all been difficult and crawling it inch by inch took nearly three hours.

18 June 1962 *Reinhold Huhn, a 20-year-old corporal, was shot dead near Checkpoint Charlie.*

In the East, Huhn would be glorified for his sacrifice by having a street named after him, but the contemporary views of the incident from both sides are revealing. To understand them you need to look at the geography and geometry. Checkpoint Charlie was, in fact, on an intersection, with the main thoroughfare, Friedrichstrasse, running through it north to south and a side street, Zimmerstrasse, from east to west. Where Huhn died, Zimmerstrasse consisted of some old buildings which had limped through the bombing in the war, then the road, then the wall. The far side of the wall was the West: a cleared area from Checkpoint Charlie some 150 metres to a skyscraper owned by the publishing house of Axel Springer, a fierce anti-communist who had positioned the building so the Easterners could see both it and the neon news bulletins on a big gantry on it.

At 2.55 in the afternoon in the East, Huhn and another corporal were on duty and noticed two civilians on the roof of the Springer building, watching them. Were they lookouts? Huhn also spotted a couple of workers repairing the roof of a Western barracks but didn't report whether they, too, seemed suspicious. Then a man emerged from one of the old buildings on Zimmerstrasse – No. 56 – and, evidently, walked along to the checkpoint and crossed. He must have been a Westerner. Later 'it was noted that several people came together and were talking', so something was going on. Huhn and his comrade went to investigate but, as they approached, these people quickly dispersed.

At 6.45 that evening the 'same male person' had re-crossed. He, two women and a child were making their way to No. 56. Huhn 'went towards' them and 'asked them to stop. They had to be asked several times before they did. The women and the child were about 10 metres away. The male person put his hand into an inner pocket and soon after a shot was fired. Comrade Huhn went down.' The other Border Guard drew his pistol and fired ten times at the 'male person' but in the confusion he, the women and the child 'disappeared' into the house. A subsequent search of the cellars revealed a tunnel going towards West Berlin. 'Thus it can be assumed that they had gone through it.' Huhn died in hospital.[26]

The 'male person' was called Rudolf Mueller, a young baker who'd gone to the West before the wall was built and spent weeks digging the 24-yard (22-metre) tunnel from under the Springer building in order to get his family out. He told West Berlin police that Huhn asked to see his documents and, as Huhn examined a bag, Mueller hit him so hard that he knocked him down. The other Border Guard fired – but hit Huhn. Mueller and his family then escaped through the tunnel.

At a news conference in the Springer building, however, Mueller was asked how many shots he'd fired (literally, how many times he had pulled the trigger) and reportedly said 'once. The man fell down immediately.' He had surrendered his weapon to the West Berlin police. The official West Berlin position was that Huhn had been shot by the other Guard.

The street was named Reinhold-Huhn-Strasse on 15 July 1966. It would be returned to its original name, Schüzenstrasse, on 1 December 1991. Mueller was tried over Huhn in the normal way – but in December 1998. He was found guilty of manslaughter and given a one-year suspended sentence.

22 June 1962   *An unnamed man was shot down some 20 metres from the wall in the Neukolln district south of West Berlin. He was 'left to lie for about an hour beside the roadway . . . before he was carried away, obviously dead, by the East Berlin Fire Brigade.'*[27]
28 June 1962   *Siegfried Noffke, a 23-year-old painter, was shot at midday at a tunnel he and two others had dug from West Berlin to try and get relatives out. A 23-year-old Eastern mechanic was shot and arrested.*

In fact, the relatives were his wife and child. He selected a place in the Treptow district, where the streets and houses interlocked closely. He and two helpers dug about 30 metres, not knowing that simultaneously another tunnel was being dug two houses away. Together, the digging caused the land to subside and the People's Police waited. Noffke was shot dead and the helpers arrested.

The GDR logic, and self-confidence, reached out to the Church of Reconciliation in Bernauer Strasse in late July. They 'expropriated' the church itself, its property, a training centre for parish sisters and the community centre. Even given that the GDR was officially atheist and had an uneasy relationship with its religious bodies, to seize a church was in itself a statement: we can do whatever we deem necessary and we do not have Western inhibitions about a church being the ultimate untouchable sanctuary. The GDR was breaking Lenin's eggs.

To broaden the context further, the seizure (which likely would have brought a Western government down) was accepted in the East in silence. And the church would eventually be blown up, as we have seen, in order that Border Guards would have an unobstructed view up and down the death strip, the more efficiently to shoot people; and that was the ultimate insult to the ultimate sanctuary. That was also accepted in silence. The distance between East and

West was growing and the Church of Reconciliation silently marked that fact, less than a year after the wall went up.

<u>8 July 1962</u>   *Herbert Mende, 23, died at the wall.*
<u>29 July 1962</u>   *An unnamed man tried to get across the wire to the Western enclave of Eiskeller. He was some 3 metres from the wire when he was fatally shot.*

Checkpoint Charlie remained a macho place where the face-off over Hagen Koch's line was a daily ritual. Bill Bentz, a second lieutenant in an infantry division, was in charge of it on the American side:

It was a very interesting assignment because you had all kinds of orders and instructions to carry out and one of the most interesting was to make sure that several very, very senior Soviet officers were not permitted to enter West Berlin. In the end, in fact, their pictures were posted inside the Checkpoint. I think it's kind of humorous but it also points out the contentious nature of the situation that somewhere in the time-frame before I got there a major incident had taken place where an American official attempted to go over into the Eastern Sector of the city and the Eastern authorities demanded to see this and that identification [Lightner, then the tank confrontation]. This was against the rules, it caused a tremendous problem and thereafter for a long period the instructions to the officer in charge were that if two certain Soviet officers should try to come into West Berlin they were not to be permitted until you had called American HQ and received certain instructions.

OK, that was the cause of that. The way we worked it was, up on the top floor – the very top floor of the building on the left-hand side above the American HQ – there was an observation post where an American military policeman was posted. He watched Friedrichstrasse and the Eastern checkpoint, and he had communications downstairs to our office and out to the hut [in the middle of the road]. If he saw a Soviet car or convoy coming, he'd ring an alarm, I would go out onto the street and the military police would pull a military police vehicle across Friedrichstrasse, blocking the way. It was my duty to observe who was in the car and make sure these two officers weren't. And if they weren't, then we would let the vehicle pass. That was the routine, that was the way it was, because uniformed people had every right to go through without identification. That is what caused this initial problem – the Soviets and East Germans demanded to see the identifications.

Here, too, was an acceptance of normality hewn from anomaly and abnormality. What had been a first step towards the nuclear escalator so few months before had now settled to an awkward but functioning *modus vivendi*. The possibility of friction could itself be hewn, however, from the delicate balance of regulations and understandings at the checkpoint.

Bentz continues:

I was on duty there on May Day, which was the big Soviet day for parades and also a day when they would come over to their War Memorial. Every year at that time they would come across and have their ceremony. This one year the alarm rings and it's the young military policeman upstairs. He says, 'Lieutenant Bentz, there is a 17-vehicle Soviet convoy coming down Friedrichstrasse.' So I go out, we pull the car across, these big limousines are coming down towards us and they're halted. I am checking each of them, I peer into this one car and there was this one guy who really looked like one of the guys in the photographs. I said, 'Just a minute please', actually went back inside, got the photographs and went out again. I looked at the photos and finally decided it was neither of the two officers. I waved them and the whole convoy went through.

It wasn't more than two minutes after that happened that the hot line from the American Headquarters [in Clayallee] rang. It was the senior officer of the Emergency Operations Center and he said, 'Lieutenant, you know that vehicle that you have just let through the Checkpoint?' I thought I'd got it wrong and I was going to have to throw my bars [insignia] down on the table, career over. 'Yes, sir,' I said. 'You know that convoy was observed doing 50 kph in a 30 kph zone,' he said. 'When it comes back through the Checkpoint you are to follow the instructions' – covering such and such. After the ceremony at the War Memorial, of course, they came back, I went out there and we stopped the lead vehicle. In my best English I said, 'You were observed doing 50 *clicks* [kilometres] in a 35 *click* zone – dangerous to the children and residents of West Berlin. Any future violations of this sort would be dealt with in an appropriate manner *di da di da di da*. Do you understand this?' The guy sitting in the back seat said,

'No' in *his* best English. I said, 'All right.' I went and got a Russian interpreter who went through the same thing in Russian. Then we allowed them to pass back into East Berlin.

Such was the delicate balance of regulations and understandings.

Nor was the daily ritual only that. 'I witnessed', Bentz adds, 'several successful and of course unsuccessful escapes across the wall near the Checkpoint. Very nasty business. I was always just amazed by the determination of the East Berliners – I just could not believe it. They'd escape by whatever route was possible, they'd get down off the wall and make a dash across the death strip, try and get up the outer wall against gun fire – across they'd come.'[28]

The first anniversary of the wall provoked angry demonstrations in West Berlin and Soviet vehicles were attacked. Then, four days later . . .

17 August 1962   *Peter Fechter, 18, and a friend hid in one of those limping old buildings on Zimmerstrasse roughly midway between Checkpoint Charlie and the Springer building. From it at 2.15 in the afternoon the teenagers ran across Zimmerstrasse to the wall. The friend got over but Fechter was hit in the lung or pelvis, or both, and fell back onto the Eastern side. It may be he was betrayed before he made his run, was surveyed and simply picked off.*

Perhaps because it happened so close to the checkpoint – 50 metres – that this became a defining moment, captured by camera. Police and photographers and American soldiers were soon at the scene. Motorists who stopped could stand on their bonnets to watch. What they all saw was an image still powerful enough to shock in its brutality. Possibly it was because Fechter took a long time to die, and was doing so both in public and in circumstances which still remain difficult to set down without feeling rage. Maybe it was because he cried out for help and the cries became echoes for a whole city in all its agonies.

The shots came from a window which was an observation post.

Peter Fechter, a slim kid in cheap, dark clothing – his jacket thinly striped – lay with one arm folded under his body like a broken doll, a small pool of blood spreading by his forehead and, minute by minute, bleeding to death nestled against the other side of the breezeblocks. He was left like that from 2.15 to 3.10 p.m.

Dennis L. Bark, a 20-year-old preparing for a career in the theatre at Stanford University in California, was visiting Europe for the first time. He hitch-hiked to Berlin because 'my 18-year-old brother Jared was going to be there. A truck took me into the Kurfürstendamm – a huge German truck – and the guy drove right down the Kurfürstendamm, dropped me and said, "You'll probably be able to find a little place down there that you can afford." And I did. One day my brother and I decided we wanted to go to East Berlin so we went through Checkpoint Charlie and we decided the best way to see that half of the city would be to get on a bus. So we got on an East Berlin bus and we rode to the end of the line. We figured: let's see what that's like.

'It was in the north and we got out. There was nothing there except a few buildings. There was a big empty lot and we started to walk across it to see what was on the other side and all of a sudden out of the ground popped a soldier. He just stood up and we hadn't seen him. He pointed his gun at us and he said, "Halt!" He asked what we were doing and he was speaking German. I didn't speak any German but my brother did. My brother told him what we were doing. The fellow was probably 20 years old himself. He said, "Turn around. You'd better get out of here." It must have been a border area although of course we didn't know it.

'We turned around and went back to the bus stop and waited about 45 minutes for the bus and we finally got on it and made our way back to Checkpoint Charlie. We went through the East Berlin customs house and they looked at our passports. Then you walked out of the door to go towards Checkpoint Charlie and it was a huge area like a football field. They didn't have any barriers then or very few. So you just walked across this area, then across the road and you were at Checkpoint Charlie in the West. You walked diagonally across this area. It was a long walk. We got halfway out there – in the middle – and all of a sudden we heard these loud noises. *Bang-bang-bang-bang*. It didn't occur to us that it was a gun – I had never heard a gun before.'

It was 2.15 p.m.

'We looked up and as we looked up a Border Guard came up to us, pointed his gun at us and said, "Halt!" We looked and saw this body sort of flipping over the wall some distance away – it was so fast I wouldn't have recognised him if I'd seen him again. And then we saw a second man. He may have had his fingers up on top of the wall – I can't remember – but they hit him in the back. He fell down and they didn't go near him.

'There was a lot of hollering and a lot of shots – again I can't remember how many – but a lot, more than two or three. My brother

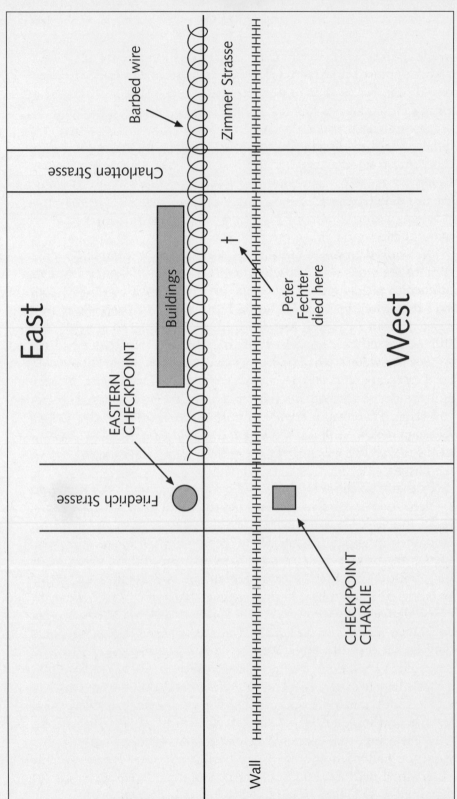

The bitter afternoon. Peter Fechter bleeds to death against the wall and in full view of the world.

in the meantime asked the Guard what was going on and he said, "Nothing, just stay here." He was as scared as we were. He knew they'd fired but he didn't know at what. I was never so frustrated in all my life because I couldn't speak German, and I kept asking my brother questions and asking what the Guard was saying. The Guard didn't say a hell of a lot but he kept us there. We stood for a long time, fifteen minutes maybe, and that is a long time to be standing facing a man with his gun out and pointing at you. We didn't move. We just didn't move. He finally said, "OK, you can go."'

It was about 2.30. Fechter had lain, bleeding, for those 15 minutes and would lie another 30.

'We walked towards Checkpoint Charlie and the white line. We tried to see what was happening but we couldn't because so many uniformed people were down there. I'll never forget putting my foot over that white line because I had a feeling in my stomach of such relief. I mean I can still *see* this feeling [2001], so to speak. I can still see myself as I put that foot over the line. We then asked the American soldiers what had happened and they said, "Somebody tried to escape and they shot him." We walked down the Western side of the wall and by that time some West Berliners were gathering. There was a telephone pole and it had a post about three feet high next to it. I climbed up on that. We were all trying to look over the wall but we couldn't see because he was lying against it on the Eastern side.

'By that time the West Berlin police had come and some American soldiers and the American soldiers threw over, among other things, First Aid kits. I don't remember whether it was West Berlin policemen or American soldiers or both, but they threw over these smoke bombs and some of them were like firecrackers. They made huge noises. The West Berliners got angrier and angrier and started shouting. You could hear Fechter yelling, "Help me, then." What the translation actually means is "Why don't you help me?" My brother could hear it and he translated it. The wall was so tall that you could only see the tops of things. We knew when he was carried away but we couldn't see it done. Nobody could except the photographers who I think had brought ladders with them and that's how they got pictures, but none of the people standing there could see that. And it changed my life, changed my life 100 per cent.'

Al Hemsing 'did, alas, see Peter Fechter. I'd been notified that someone had been shot so I hot-footed it down. I got onto the observation platform and I heard him shouting "Help me!" but not very loudly. As I recall, I had to leave before his actual death.'

The West Berlin police clambered up the crude breeze-block wall and held on to the V-shaped metal rods which secured the strands of barbed wire along the top. A medical kit was thrown over towards where Fechter lay but it broke open and, anyway, he was too weak. All he could do was lie on his back, arms folded across his chest as a priest might have arranged them, then somehow turn onto his side as if trying to regain the foetal position. His left shoe was half off and you could see the white of his ankle.

The crowd chanted 'Murderers!' towards the Border Guards. Finally, four uniformed men, one clearly a People's Policeman, went to Fechter under a protective blanket of ten tear-gas shells. The West Berlin police in turn fired ten tear-gas shells back. The four uniformed men, working in this pall, lifted the body and carried it – limp, sprawled, awkward – across the road to the concrete posts and the wire between them and manoeuvred him over it at a point where the wire was waist high. As they did so, a photographer fixed that image: the men – three helmeted, two with machine-guns – hold Fechter high, and they have his arms splayed, and there is dried blood on his hands and wrists.

Two of these uniformed men trotted away along a connecting street into the East with Fechter hanging between them. Here a crowd had gathered, too, some standing in the long grass of bomb sites, some in a mute cluster further away. Fechter was put into the back of a vehicle and never seen again.

An American lieutenant, who'd been implored to help, replied that there was nothing he could do. His helplessness was governed by the Four Power Agreement, of course, as well as all the practical and logistical difficulties of doing anything, never mind the risk of escalation. His words were evidently translated as 'It's not my problem' which, when taken up by a West Berlin tabloid newspaper, provoked outrage.

The RIAS reporter Peter Schultz was there. 'What can I tell you about that? There was a young man lying on the other side of the wall who was crying out and suddenly he stopped. The police in the West tried to push the people back. The American military police were at the wall but they couldn't do anything and when he was dead a soldier carried him away. I can't answer the question why the Border Guards left him to die. I don't know. I don't know, I don't know. Maybe they were afraid because the distance between them and the US military police would have been 1 metre. There was an American military police officer who came some weeks after, and he said that if it had happened while he was there he would have helped Fechter. Some weeks after that he proved what he said, because there was a wounded person at Checkpoint Charlie and he did help him to the Western side. The man was not as badly wounded as Peter Fechter had been.'

The crowd on the Western side hung around until dusk on this chilled August day and then dispersed.

The GDR Ministry of the Interior's report, compiled the same day, distilled the incident into the language of bureaucracy, but even that could not dehumanise it completely:

On 17 August 1962, at 2.15 p.m., a violation of the border was effected from the capital of the DDR towards West Berlin by a male person at Zimmerstrasse/Charlottenstrasse, section l, 4th company, Guard 3, 4th Border section. In the course of this, a second border violator was taken to the VP [People's Police] hospital, having been seriously injured, where he passed away at around 3. 15 p.m.

At about 2.15 p.m., Sergeant Friedrich and Lance-Corporal Schreiber noticed a male person climbing over the first fence at the corner between Zimmerstrasse and Markgrafenstrasse and making his way in the direction of the wall. At a distance of around 2–3 metres a second male person was following him. Sergeant Friedrich immediately opened fire at the two border violators. The distance between Border Guard to the border violators was about 50 metres. In total, the Sergeant fired 17 times, the guard Corporal 7 times.

At the neighbouring guard tower, Sergeant-Major Schönert and Lance-Corporal Buske heard the shots, and also saw the violators in front of the border protection, and opened fire. Sergeant-Major Schönert and Lance-Corporal Buske fired 11 times in total.

At this time, the lst person had already climbed the wall and was at such an angle to the Border Guards that further shooting would have targeted Western territory. The border violator managed to get over the wall.

The second person was hit and collapsed just in front of the wall. Immediately, Sergeant Friedrich and Lance-Corporal Schreiber took position, observed enemy territory. [Western] police and civilians carried a ladder to the wall to recover the injured border violator, presumably knowing that they would violate DDR territory in the course of their actions.

The report describes police and public gathering on the Western side, and tear-gas shells being thrown 'into DDR territory'. It continues:

In order to recover the injured border violator by our own means, a 'curtain of fog' was laid from the ruined house at Zimmerstrasse 72–74, under the protection of which Staff Sergeant Wursel and Corporal Lindenlaub were able to recover the injured border violator. They handed him over to a police car, which took him away to the VP hospital.

The report recounts 'provocation' from the West, and measures taken against it following the regulations.

After the recovery of the injured border violator, the normal situation was restored, water cannons were removed, special security guards were positioned and a Sergeant (for special observation) called. In addition a patrol to protect the hinterland was established.

Around 3.15 p.m., the Brigade's headquarters was informed that the border violator had passed away at the VP hospital. The identity of the border violator is not known as no papers were found. The police have started an investigation.

The report stated that 'two citizens' who witnessed the incident were arrested. Evidently they had 'identified' one of the Border Guards who fired. 'It was reported that immediately after the event, one young male and one young female stayed at the scene of the crime [the crime, of course, was trying to escape] and that the female made the following remark to the male: "This is the Guard who fired, we have to take photographic evidence." Based on this remark, both people were arrested.

It was noted that a wooden cross was erected in enemy territory, 4 metres away from the wall, opposite the scene of the 'crime', and flowers were laid.

The report came to the following conclusions:

1. The Border Guards' actions were correct, effective and determined. The use of weapons was justified. However, the question remains if the same effect would have been achieved if the Guards had fired single, targeted shots at the border violators.

2. Shots at the 2nd border violator would have been against the regulation/order of the Interior Ministry as they would have hit West Berlin territory around the Springerkonzern [the Axel Springer building].

3. Establishing a 'curtain of fog' was a necessary measure, through which visibility for the enemy was obstructed.

Under 'Measures taken' was written: 'On my order, Sergeant Friedrich and Corporal Schreiber, Major Wursel and Lance-Corporal Buske received an award. . . . The incident won't be mentioned in the report in order to keep the names of the comrades secret.' It was signed by Commander Tschitschke.

Nobody knows who fired the fatal shots but, as it would seem, it was either Friedrich or Schreiber. Neither was responsible for allowing Fechter to bleed to death. Fechter had a sister, Ruth, and Friedrich would make a point of apologising to her – in March 1997.

Hagen Koch, former Stasi employee, now [in 2001] running an archive on the wall, provides a different and slightly conspiratorial context. 'On 23 May 1962 a Border Guard, Peter Göring, was shot by a Western policeman and the GDR made a hero out of Göring. The story is that although the Border Guards were ordered to stop shooting this Peter Göring continued. Only when the West tried to rescue the refugee did they – the West – shoot, and with the intention of rescue. But with Göring still shooting, they shot him.' This seems clear, no mystery at all. However 'all this was a kind of manipulation of what happened. Both sides *had* to have a reason why a Border Guard was shot by a policeman from the West.' Simply put, the East was satisfied that one of their guardians at the frontier had been gunned down by the evil West, and made him into heroic propaganda; the West was satisfied that one of *their* guardians had done his duty under fire. Koch continues:

Göring is declared a hero in the East and a criminal in the West, but an investigation found that Göring had all his ammunition left, and that meant he had refused to fire. That was something to do with his biography: his brother had been in West Germany since 1957, his mother was religious – although she lived in the East she was a member of a church – and Göring himself wanted to go to the West. It means he who was willing to escape was shot by a West German. So both sides lied. There are the two versions and they are not true.

Then on the 18th of June, the Border Guard Reinhold Huhn was shot by a West Berliner, although until 1998 the official version [in the West] was that he had been shot by his comrades. An investigation then found in the GDR archives that the GDR had been correct and he had indeed been shot by a West Berlin citizen. Then on 14 August a Border Guard was shot from the West at the inner-German border (between the two Germanies).

Now Peter Fechter tries to escape at the point where Huhn had been shot and the man who [allegedly] shot Fechter had been a friend of Huhn's. On the West Berlin side, those who shot Huhn and Göring say, 'Look what these Border Guards will do' but they don't say what happened. The conclusion among the Border Guards was that they were afraid they, too, would be shot from the West. 'If I help Fechter they will shoot me.'

The meaning of this is clear. Peter Fechter was not deliberately left to bleed to death but the Border Guards were frightened to go near him, so soldiers were ordered from the barracks at Rummelsburg, the southern suburb, and they took so long to arrive. It was these soldiers and the People's Policeman who bore Fechter away. (The soldier in charge is, says Koch in 2001, 'one of those who still today justify the dead of the wall. He won't talk to anybody.' Koch also points out that to counter the possibility that these soldiers might draw the wrong conclusions about Fechter's death, Ulbricht explained to them 'personally that it was right, because it was an example to others not to try and escape'. Ulbricht presented them with a flag, the only one he ever presented with his own face on it.)

A couple of days later, Dennis Bark left Berlin and prepared to change his life. 'I was the son of a professor of medieval history at Stanford and I was a theatre major at Stanford. I was about to enter my senior and last year and I was getting ready to go to New York. I came home at the end of August 1962 and went to see my father. I told him this young man had died at the wall trying to go from dictatorship to freedom and I didn't know why. I said I had never felt a feeling before in my stomach as I stepped over that line and could I change my major to history? My father said, "Yes, and this is how you're going to do it." So when I graduated in 1964 I graduated with a major in history.'

The delicate balance could so easily be disturbed by something unforeseen like the death of Fechter. John Ausland of the Task Force in Washington said:

We were having a problem after the Peter Fechter case, where the Russians were coming in to their War Memorial in armoured personnel carriers and we couldn't have them running around West Berlin [they were in these armoured vehicles because of the open hostility of West Berliners] 'so we worked out a thing where we would move them from coming through Checkpoint Charlie to an entry near the Brandenburg Gate and therefore near the Memorial.

Frank Cash and I went over with Rusk to see the President and get him to approve our approach to it. As usual he said 'Well, I don't know, I'm going to think about this.' We sat in silence on the way back and then Rusk – it was the only time he did this – invited us in for a drink. He said, 'I know you are very disappointed that the President didn't approve your proposal, and he will, but you've got to remember that whenever he deals with anything concerning the Russians he always has nuclear weapons in the back of his mind.' Now this was on a very minor thing – having them use another entry because the West Berliners were throwing stones at them – but it demonstrated to me, and it's the only one piece of evidence I have from my own experience, the extreme caution regarding nuclear weapons. Looking back, there is no question in my mind that he was right. In our wildest imaginations we couldn't see ourselves living under the Russians but I can imagine people in Western Europe might, especially West Berlin.

23 August 1962 *Hans-Dieter Weser, a 19-year-old policeman, deserted. About 10.13 at night he was seen trying to 'realise his criminal intentions' and was mortally wounded by a burst of eight rifle shots. A Border Guard shot him. Weser, using 'all his remaining strength just managed to reach a few metres inside the westberlin [sic] area'. He was retrieved, taken to hospital and declared dead.*

That month Ausland presented a briefing to Kennedy in the Cabinet Room of the White House. It was based on a National Security Action Memorandum (nicknamed 'Poodle Blanket') which Kennedy had approved in October 1961. Ausland set out four phases if either the Soviet or East German forces interfered with Allied access to West Berlin: *Phase 1*: Small military probes and air force pilots to fly commercial aircraft if the civilian pilots refused. Fighter protection could be deployed; *Phase 2*: If the access denial is complete enough to be 'significant' there would be intense diplomatic activity, a NATO build-up, an airlift, naval countermeasures, economic sanctions and 'covert action designed to encourage passive resistance'. *Phase 3*: If phase 2 doesn't work, the Allies will instigate 'offensive non-nuclear operations' into the GDR; *Phase 4*: If that fails 'there could be a resort to nuclear weapons'. Ausland stressed that this was not an attempt to predict history and 'we have no idea of rushing from one phase to another'.[29]

<u>4 September 1962</u>   *An unknown person died at the wall.*
<u>4 September 1962</u>   *At about 1.45 a.m., Ernst Mund, 41 was seen swimming a canal. A Border Guard approximately 50 metres away fired four shots and Mund could no longer be seen. It was unclear whether he had reached the West and six divers searched for him until 8.00 in the morning.*

Twenty-nine people escaped through Tunnel 29, as it was known, in the Frohnau district of West Berlin. It was dug by students, was 125 metres (413 feet) long and some 6 metres (20 feet) below the wall but had to be abandoned because a broken water pipe flooded it. (In October 2000 the remains of the tunnel were discovered by researchers for a television documentary.)

<u>30 September 1962</u>   *Günter Seling, a junior officer in the People's Army, was fatally shot.*
<u>8 October 1962</u>   *Anton Walzer, 60, tried to swim the Spree at 8.25 in the morning. Two warning shots were fired but he didn't react to them and continued towards the Western bank. A burst of seven shots killed him.*
<u>1 November 1962</u>   *An unknown person died at the wall.*
<u>27 November 1962</u>   *Ottfried Reck, 18. Two 'male civilians' were seen acting suspiciously in a U-bahn station. Two soldiers approached them and they fled, ignoring warnings to halt. Four shots were fired and two hit Reck 'in the top half of the body'. The other man disappeared into the East and a manhunt began. Reck died in hospital at 9.30 that evening.*
<u>Towards the end of November</u>   *An unknown person died at the wall, possibly shot.*
<u>1 December 1962</u>   *Hans-Joachim Nittmeier, 23, nationality unknown, died at the wall.*
<u>5 December 1962</u>   *Two unnamed people were shot at 11.30 p.m. crossing a frozen lake. They fell through the ice and drowned. After the shots were fired there was silence and 'it is assumed this transgression did not succeed'. One of the men may have been called Günter Wiedenhöft, 20, nationality unknown.*
<u>18 December 1962</u>   *Melita Hinz, 50, died at the wall.*
<u>1 January 1963</u>   *Hans Räwel, 21, was seen at 6.15 in the morning 300 metres from a bridge in the Spree swimming West. A Border Guard*

patrol boat gave chase and Guards on it opened fire. The last shot was fired when it was 20 metres from him. He went under and did not resurface. 'It is assumed that the border crosser was mortally wounded.' The boat itself came under fire from the Western side and was hit twice and a Guard slightly injured. 'During this action on our part, the westberlin [sic] territory was not shot at.'[30]

In January 1963 a young Border Guard, Fritz Hanke, was stationed at the Teltow Canal in January. He shot at and killed a man trying to swim through the icy water. 'It was only several weeks later that the bullet-riddled body was recovered. In the meanwhile, however, Hanke had escaped himself, and as a Guard, was naturally subjected to thorough interrogation by the [Western] security authorities. From this it transpired that he had been on duty that fateful night and he was put on trial for participation in a murder. Hanke was duly sentenced to fifteen months in prison, a light punishment but given as a warning to other Guards that they could not escape moral responsibility for their actions.'[31]

<u>15 January 1963</u>   *Horst Kutscher, 32, was shot at 12.10 a.m. Two people were noticed at the wall, a Border Guard called out a warning and then fired a warning shot. The two jumped up onto the wall. The Guard fired two aimed shots and hit Kutscher in his abdomen. The other man was arrested.*
<u>24 January 1963</u>   *Peter Kreitlow, 20, was shot by a Soviet soldier. Five young men tried to cross in the north. Three were from Berlin, one from the small town of Henningsdorf nearby, and the fifth from the northern port of Rostock. They were stopped by a Soviet unit at 1.10 in the morning. They ignored a warning. Kreitlow died, another was injured and the remaining three arrested.*

By now, the logic of the wall was well into working itself out, and the GDR even held exhibitions for Westerners, demonstrating that it was really an 'anti-fascist barrier' after all. That carried an intrinsic risk, because the GDR leadership found it almost impossible to admit they'd been forced to build it to stop thousands of their citizens from defecting. And if the leadership would not tell the truth about this, what would they tell the truth about? This absolute mistrust of the GDR's official pronouncements tracked them down the years, and the internal logic of the GDR itself produced a paranoia where almost *everything* was a state secret. Reputable international financial organisations eventually gave up including the

GDR and the other Eastern bloc countries in their studies because the figures they were given were unverifiable and wildly improbable.

What Ulbricht really understood of all this went to the grave with him but certainly throughout the 1950s he spoke in apocalyptical terms of events in West Germany, and this at a time when West Germany was becoming a stable democracy and the third strongest economy on the planet, with an astonishingly even spread of prosperity.

In 1963, for example, Ulbricht said, 'What we have long predicted is now a fact in West Germany . . . recurring government crises.'[32] The author Carola Stern says: 'We do not know whether Ulbricht believed what he said about the Federal Republic.'

(There's a grotesque irony, too, in the fact that when the GDR finally disintegrated in 1989 its leadership still found it almost impossible to admit that it was being forced into responses to stop thousands of its citizens from leaving. The 'people's state' had no means of communication with its own people and arguably never really had. From 1961 the separation of the two Germanies accurately reflected the separation of Europe into blocs: the GDR felt it couldn't survive if it told the truth about itself, especially *to* itself. West Germany felt it couldn't survive if it did *not* tell the truth about itself, especially to itself.)

<u>Sometime in March 1963</u>　*Wolf-Olaf Muszinski, 16, drowned.*
<u>Sometime during April 1963</u>　*Hedwig Forgert, 44, a female corporal, possibly tried to swim from the Pankow district to West Berlin. 'The reason for this escape has not been concluded yet.' She drowned in the Spree but her body was found and retrieved about 10.35 a.m. It may, however, have been suicide.*
<u>16 April 1963</u>　*Two unknown people drowned.*
<u>26 April 1963</u>　*Peter Mädler, 20, was seen at 4.45 in the morning swimming West in the Teltow Canal. A warning was shouted and then three shots fired. He disappeared under the water and a search for his body was unsuccessful until 4.45 p.m., when it was brought ashore. He had with him a cellophane bag containing all his documents including an army identification and driving licence.*

An Austrian called Hans-Peter Meixner, who was studying in West Berlin, met a pretty Easterner called Margit Tharau at a wedding in East Berlin and soon enough they were in love. They imagined that, having become engaged, she would be entitled to leave as the future wife of a foreigner. Applications were refused and he began to contemplate how he could get her, and her mother, whom she lived with, across. He observed that the horizontal wooden pole at Checkpoint Charlie, which was raised to let each vehicle through, had no vertical struts to it and he noticed, too, one night as he queued to reach the pole, that the driver of a West German sportscar hadn't put his handbrake on. The car rolled towards the pole and part of the bonnet went under it. Interesting . . .

On his next visit Meixner estimated how high the pole came up on his own car, quickly marked that on the flank of the car with his finger and when he measured it later found the clearance was 0.9 metre (3 feet). There was a car hire on the Kurfürstendamm and they had a British sportscar, an Austin Healey Sprite, with a windscreen which could be detached. That took the vehicle just to below 0.9 metre.

The geometry of Checkpoint Charlie then was relatively unsophisticated. From the East a horizontal pole screened the entrance to it and once that had been raised a motorist went to a vehicle and document inspection area. After clearance there he threaded through a 'chicane' of three concrete walls, constructed to make vehicles move slowly and prevent anyone battering their way out in a bus or truck. Beyond that was the second pole, then the line which Hagen Koch had painted, and then the American Sector.

Meixner hired the Sprite and went over to the East quite normally. He would make his run in the early hours. He got Margit to lie across the cramped back seats and put her mother into the boot – she had to curl up to fit. He drove to the checkpoint and the first pole was raised almost on the nod: a glance at his passport, that was all. As he was flagged towards the vehicle inspection area he knew he'd reached the critical instant. The man at the pole might have been uninterested in the car but an inspection would instantly reveal Margit. Meixner hit the accelerator and weaved through the 'chicane', then ducked his head as the car went under the pole: he kept his head raised just enough to see with his left eye where he was going. The Guards, caught completely off-balance, did not even fire a shot.

Two weeks later, an Argentinian who also had a fiancée in the East, hired the same car and did the same thing. Legend insists that one of the Border Guards said 'Isn't that the car we had through the other day?'

Then they put vertical struts on the poles . . .

On 26 June, John Kennedy arrived with his own mythology; came to deepen that. He was on a European tour and West Berlin surrendered to him. During the day an estimated 1.5 of the city's 2.2 million inhabitants came out to cheer him. He was young, very handsome and extremely charismatic, in direct contrast to the 'character' of the wall, and Ulbricht and Khrushchev behind it. Mayor Willy Brandt, who accompanied him, was also charismatic; and Adenauer, who flew in specially, had a certain dignity about him. General Clay was there and would, Kennedy promised, come back if he was ever needed.

The *New York Herald Tribune* wrote of the 'gala mood that had many Berliners smiling, shouting, waving and weeping, sometimes all at the same time. From the moment Mr Kennedy left the plane that brought him from Wiesbaden at 9.45 a.m. it was evident that West Berliners set the highest store by his coming.' At the airport he told a crowd of 5,000 that he had not come to reassure West Berlin because that wasn't necessary. The Allied pledges were 'written on rock', he said. Police had to lock arms to hold back a crowd which stood six-deep at the exit to the airport.

As the motorcade moved away 'some onlookers threw flowers and so many tried to carry bouquets to the President that the escort of 125 white-jacketed motorcycle policemen formed a phalanx that encircled the car. About a dozen flower-carriers got through anyway.'[33]

Outside the city hall, people who had brought their mattresses the night before, and slept on them, in order to reserve a good position for Kennedy's speech, waited.

He went to a specially constructed observation platform at Checkpoint Charlie and he went to the Brandenburg Gate. The gaps between the columns had been draped with banners so that East Germans could not see him. A hoarding had been put against the bases of the columns and positioned so that any photographer taking pictures of Kennedy on the observation platform would inevitably have that as a backdrop. It had a propaganda message printed in English about how the GDR had uprooted German 'militarism and Nazism' and when will pledges like that be fulfilled by West Germany and West Berlin, President Kennedy?

At the city hall, Kennedy stepped onto a broad, deep balcony – large enough to accommodate a couple of dozen dignitaries. 'The roar was deafening when Mr Kennedy came forward to speak. The crowd was in a frantic state, chanting, waving and shouting. Red Cross helpers rushed in all directions to carry away fainting people. The crowd began a chant – Ken-ne-dee – that played counterpoint to the rumbling applause that greeted every sentence of his speech.'[34]

This speech became part of the mythology. He hammered it out: if people think communism is the future, let them come to Berlin. There are those who say we can work with the communists: let them come to Berlin. There are those who say communism is evil but it permits progress: let them come to Berlin – but this last sentence in German. 'Two thousand years ago the proudest boast was '*civis Romanus sum* [I am a Roman citizen]'. Today, in the world of freedom, the proudest boast is Ich bin ein Berliner [I am a Berliner].'[35] There was an immortal simplicity to these few words, whose pronunciation he had rehearsed and rehearsed. Strong men wept and for an unnerving moment it seemed the crowd might lose control of itself.

Dean Rusk, the Secretary of State, had gone to Berlin with Kennedy. 'I looked at the wall and my views were the views of the consensus, of the government. There was a wall, it was put up to keep people in rather than exclude Westerners but it was still a shock to actually see it and a shock to see so many windows boarded up in the houses that fronted onto the wall to block escape routes.

'I was standing next to Konrad Adenauer after the speech was made. I asked him what he thought of the proceedings and, with a very solemn look on his face, he said "I am worried. Does this mean that Germany could have another Hitler?" He said it because of the emotional reaction from the crowd. Afterwards Kennedy thought he had probably overdone it a bit on the emotional side – rousing the emotion of the Berliners. He was concerned about that. I think we'd underestimated the strength of the Berliners' emotions. I was caught by surprise by the strength of it.'

Rusk could, moreover, put the speech into a historical context. 'Well, I had seen a million people at the Templehof airbase [south of the city] at a Hitler rally where you had something like the same thing. It was 1934 and I was a student at Oxford (England). I was studying the political situation in Germany and I went to Berlin. It was a massive city with big avenues, obviously an imposing place but in a Prussian style: not a very attractive city. It was heavy with its own seriousness.

'I stayed with an ordinary family in Babelsberg. The impression Hitler made on me was that he was mesmerising the German people. Of course in 1934 we did not know how much of his book *Mein Kampf* would be carried out and how far he would go. No, he didn't mesmerise me, I never gave a Hitler salute and I never joined in with the chants. I just watched what was happening and I kept my American identity throughout. Berlin was becoming a wildly different city in 1933–34 as Hitler took charge. The Nazis had driven other political parties off the streets and assumed a political monopoly of the demonstrations in the streets. I wouldn't call them happy days, they weren't happy days in Germany while Hitler was coming to power. I'd thought of those days during the cirsis when the wall went up. . . .'

Frank Cash of the State Department's Task Force echoes Rusk. 'The people involved with Berlin were known as the so-called Berlin Mafia.' That was because, Kennedy felt (as we have already seen), once they became involved they identified with the city and lost their judgement. 'But when people got there – and when Kennedy got there – they seemed to change because it was a very striking thing to go and see that this wall actually existed, and that it was built across the centre of a thriving modern city to keep people from coming out. There was nothing like walking up and seeing the wall to get the full impact. Until you confronted it, you could not get this full impact.'

SIX

The Strangeness

The history of Germany is replete with blunders and missed opportunities involving all social and political factions.

Willy Brandt

Kennedy's visit could not mask the truth that the status quo had now been established in Berlin and would endure until the whole political climate of competition and confrontation between the two blocs changed. Nobody had any idea when, or if, that would happen, and each passing day deepened the divide.

By now, the impact of the wall was subtly increasing. As it became more difficult to penetrate, the number of escapes and deaths fell sharply. Statistics, that most inhuman measurement, tell it with their own exactitude. In 1962, thirty people died trying to cross; up to Kennedy's visit in 1963 the number was eight, and there would be another four but not until November and December. The days of impulsive dashes, of vaulting coils of barbed wire, of sneaking through back gardens, were all but over. The noose had finally tightened to the point where human ingenuity would be needed; and, in the sad streets of East Berlin where personal initiative was officially forbidden, there was enough of it – and enough desperation – to create legend.

By now, too, one could feel the two halves of the city moving to their different rhythms, although with its population stabilised the GDR embarked on its own economic miracle. In time it would give its citizens a certain pride in being East German, whatever frustrations they continued to endure. In time, also – the 1970s – the wall would be essentially rebuilt twice, each time making escape more difficult and each time requiring more ingenuity.

That would be accompanied by a constant, if diminishing, tension. John Ausland of the State Department said, 'We had planned if necessary to put fighters into the air corridors and then after Cuba – and people have forgotten this – we had problems with convoys along the autobahn through East Germany in, I think, September 1963. They started to make life difficult and I spent three weeks putting a solution together. I got everyone's approval in Washington, British government, the French government, the West German government. Then I got to the last guy – Kennedy. He said, "Well, do we really want to do that?" The problem in essence was this: I made the mistake of calling a meeting. Tommy Thompson, who was handling Berlin by that time, was out of town. He came back the next day and said, "For God's sake, John, you shouldn't have called a meeting. Come on with me." So we jumped in the car, went over and we caught Kennedy coming out of a meeting. He said, "Mr President, I think you really ought to approve this." Then someone came up, joined in the discussion and said, "Well, Tommy, you really think we ought to do this? Yes?" At that, Kennedy said, "OK, go ahead." It wasn't a big thing: for the first time we did alert our ground troop force and things like that – I don't think anything really awful could have happened. The net result was that we got an implicit agreement with the Soviets on convoy procedures and never had any problems after that.'

In September, the GDR drew up plans for clearing the houses at the border in the first six months of 1964. They did this methodically, setting it all out in nine vertical columns: House number; Map reference; Evacuated; Moved out; Number of families; Number of people; Demolition cost; Overall cost;, Observations. Nos 10a, 12, and 13a Bernauer Strasse were among them. All three were to be evacuated on 28 February: Nos 10a and 13a (three families, fourteen people) to be demolished on 30 April and number 12 (six families, seventeen people) on 15 June. The overall cost for numbers 10a and 13a was 31,200 marks, and number 12 only 14,000. And so it went on, page after page, each line representing someone's home. (The precision of GDR thinking had already been established in these matters. An example of a job specification *c.* 1962 at the wall just along from Checkpoint Charlie shows this: 16 sq m hardboard; 7 kg nails; 30 sq m roofing felt; 1l creosote; 10 sq m glass; 1.5 cu m plants, the work to be completed in sixty hours.)

4 November 1963   *Klaus Schröter, 23, was seen swimming the Spree towards the Western bank at 4.01 a.m. After several warning shots he was fatally hit. His body was found at about 7.45.*

25 November 1963   *Dietmar Schulz, 24, jumped out of a moving S-bahn train at 10.20 at night as it passed close to the border. He suffered head injuries and died in hospital.*

Kurt Behrendt, the resident of Steinstücken, watched the noose and its tightening. 'From the top of my house I had a very good view of the wall. They only began to build it in December 1963. Before that we had a special border, what are called Spanish riders: wooden crosses and barbed wire around them about a metre high – a sportsman could easily have jumped over. To reach Steinstücken you had to come through two controls. The first was from West Berlin – a little hut painted white with a window. It was like a mini-barracks for the Border Guards and had a pole across the way. It was manned by two Border Guards. When they raised the pole you walked about a kilometre along a path to the second control which was similar to the first. After that you were in Steinstücken.

'At first it was a very quiet place, almost lonely, although there were forty houses here. Of course it was a special situation since there were Border Guards all around us. We were the best super-vised place in Berlin and we never needed to use our front doors to lock our houses! You could wander into anyone's living room. Women walked around in complete safety – nobody would harm them. We did, however, used to hear gunfire.'[1]

Because of its location as an enclave butting onto the East, and because an east-west railway line ran through it as well, Stein-stücken became and remained a potential weak link in the wall, and one evening more than a decade hence two lovers and an accomplice would try to exploit that, posing as GDR officers. Ingenuity there certainly was on those sad streets.

13 December 1963   *Dieter Berger, 24, was apprehended after shots were fired at 3.10 in the afternoon and died from his injuries.*

That December, after seven preliminary meetings, a Pass Agreement was reached which enabled West Berliners to visit the East if they could prove they had relatives there. The GDR used the seven meetings in 'fruitlessly attempting extortions and trying to enforce a political recognition of the GDR'.[2] More than 730,000 West Berliners took advantage of this, waiting up to twelve and fifteen hours in snow to go through a special entrance cut into the breeze blocks. They came with parcels and packages; they were of all ages, some children clutching dolls and teddy bears. In a city of so much pathos these humble, private meetings must have been almost unbearable. That was softened because the Pass Agreement was renewed until 1966.

· <u>25 December 1963</u>   *Paul Schultz, 18, got over the wall at 4.30 in the afternoon despite being wounded from 13 shots fired at him. He died immediately afterwards on the Western side. A simple wooden cross would be erected there, his photograph – a young, open face, his hair bushy but neat – in a clear cellophane sachet attached to the cross. Wreaths were laid. His body was taken back to East Berlin in a hearse and there's a fixed image of that as it goes through the checkpoint, Border Guards watching it as if he might have been alive.*

At that other, official level the anomalies reflected the status quo, if sometimes uneasily.

Bill Bentz had 'very interesting times at Checkpoint Charlie. After I completed the assignment as officer in charge down there I went back to my unit for a day or so. I got called by our group HQ and they informed me I was being considered as one of the officers on Flag Patrol. Would I be interested? I said, "What is that?" and they said, "Well, you go over into the Soviet Sector of Berlin in a car with the American flag on the side and drive around the whole of the Soviet Sector."

'The reason they were called Flag Patrols was because essentially they provided visible evidence we had every right to be in the Soviet Sector and we were carrying out that right. It also had various other missions tied to it which I am not going to go into – I will say it involved reporting anything unusual. The British and French had the same thing. The deal was I had a young enlisted man as a driver, I sat in the back seat and we would go over every other day during the day and the night because there were four or five other cars. Mine wasn't the only one for the mission.

'I had been doing this for some time. You know, we would enter at Checkpoint Charlie, they would open the gates and we would drive through because we were in uniform and the car was clearly marked. Then we'd drive around for two or three hours, come back out into the American Sector and write our reports. There were, however, certain areas posted by the Soviets and East Germans as restricted.

'I had been doing this for several weeks – or longer, really – with no problem and this one night was on mission. We went over. We were in an Opel, we carried out the normal mission and returned to pass through the Eastern side of the checkpoint. It was dark. We pulled up to the checkpoint and there were all kinds of Soviet officers around. At that time they basically just had wooden barricades that came down like a railroad crossing and they wouldn't raise it.

'A Soviet officer came over and said, "Get out of the car" and I said, "No, I am not getting out of the car." "Get out of the car!" "No!" So the Soviet officer went around to the back of the car and started jumping on it. I told my driver, "That's it, we're going." He put the car in low gear and we sped on through the wooden barrier with the wood flying, just like a movie. We raced on and got back to HQ where I was usually debriefed. After we drove in there an American Police Captain said, "Well, Lieutenant, you had a little trouble down there." I said, "Yes, sir." Everything was on film: the checkpoint was monitored [by a camera high up in a building and relayed to HQ]. They had seen what had happened. I said, "What's the problem? I have done this mission for a month or so and have never had any problems before." He said, "Come here, I want to show you something." He took me around to another spot and there sat an Opel exactly like mine: painted the same colours, the same numbers as mine and they had manufactured things like a radio cone on top out of tin cans. The only place they messed up was my licence plate' – they'd made a small mistake in the exact wording.

'What happened was that all the time I'd been going over I'd been watched by some East Berliners who wanted to escape. On this mission they rolled their car out with three people in it wearing made-up American uniforms like ours and there were more people in the trunk. They'd waited a couple of hours, which was the sort of time I'd be driving around East Berlin, and then they pulled up at the checkpoint. The barrier was raised and they crossed right over into West Berlin.'[3]

Perhaps the words 'absolute consternation' cover the reaction of the Border Guards when the second Opel came along; a consternation which can only have intensified when they realised Bentz was indeed Bentz; and increased further when their pole was shattered as he, too, was driven away at speed.

Capturing the uneasy status quo are the instructions for the United States military (albeit issued at a later date) to avoid incidents while using their access:

CONTACT WITH COMMUNIST NATIONALS

IMPORTANT
YOU ARE TO READ THE FOLLOWING CAREFULLY

1. WEST BERLIN IS UNIQUE IN THAT IT IS THE ONLY LOCATION WHERE TRAVELLING TO AND FROM THE CITY BY ROAD,

SERVICEMEN AND CIVILIANS HAVE DIRECT CONTACT WITH SOVIET MILITARY PERSONNEL. IT IS THEREFORE VITAL THAT ANY ATTEMPT TO ENGAGE YOU IN CONVERSATION OR THE TRADE/ BARTER OF MILITARY ITEMS BE REPORTED.

2. SHOULD YOU BE SPOKEN TO BY A SOVIET OR EAST GERMAN NATIONAL IN ENGLISH, OR A LANGUAGE YOU BOTH UNDER-STAND, DURING YOUR JOURNEY ON THE CORRIDOR, YOU SHOULD DO THE FOLLOWING:

a. REMEMBER AS MUCH DETAIL ABOUT THE CONVERSATION AS YOU CAN, AS WELL AS THE PHYSICAL DESCRIPTION, DRESS AND RANK OF THE INDIVIDUAL;

b. REMAIN NON-COMMITTAL THROUGHOUT AND DO NOT AGREE TO ANYTHING;

c. DO NOT BECOME OVERLY NERVOUS OR AGGRESSIVE. ONCE IT IS REALISED THAT YOU ARE NOT RESPONDING, YOU WILL BE LEFT ALONE.

REMEMBER, DO NOT ATTRACT ATTENTION TO YOURSELF BY SPEAKING IN RUSSIAN TO THE SOVIET CHECKPOINT PERSONNEL.

3. ON REACHING THE END OF YOUR CORRIDOR JOURNEY, YOU MUST REPORT THE INCIDENT TO THE RMP CHECKPOINT NCO AND COMPLETE THE PROFORMA PROVIDED. BE ASSURED THAT YOUR JOURNEY WILL NOT BE DELAYED, IF IN DOUBT ASK THE RMP CHECKPOINT NCO FOR ASSISTANCE.

HELP US TO HELP YOU

Detentions by GDR police:
  On the prescribed route of travel:
    – Stay in your vehicle with the windows rolled up and the doors locked
    – Do not show travel or identification documents
    – Do not allow your person, your vehicle or your belongings to be searched
    – Use your flashcard to demand your right to proceed
    – If you are not allowed to proceed, use your flashcard to request the presence of a Soviet officer.

  Off the prescribed route of travel – Follow above instructions.
Note: If you are detained by GDR police because you have left the authorized autobahn route, you may expect to be detained for one-

half to four hours. Your vehicle will be physically blocked in and photographed. When GDR police release you, they will indicate the direction you should travel, or they will escort you back to the proper route.

Soviet involvement:
  If Soviet authorities are at the scene of an incident or accident:
    – Exchange military courtesies with them
    – Cooperate with them
    – Show them your travel and identification documents if they request you do so
    – If you are off the prescribed route of travel, do not admit to any wrong doing other than to having made a navigational error.

The precision of these guidelines was important because the Soviet Union and the GDR constantly sought to exploit the autobahn. The petrol and service station at Zeisar, about a third of the way between Dreilinden and Helmstedt, was a haunt of the Stasi, lurking, watching, monitoring. However, I don't intend to give the impression that everything lived in shadowland. Driving the autobahn in 1970, the author overtook a column of Soviet Army trucks with open backs so that the soldiers sitting there could see out. They returned waves enthusiastically and seemed a merry lot – quite different to the GDR military which, like the GDR as a whole, was taking itself very seriously indeed. There's an amusing anecdote[4] about 'a smallish Russian soldier' at one of the autobahn checkpoints who demanded that a United States soldier show his travel papers and the American said, 'Get a taller Russian to see me!'

Long and deliberate delays to transit traffic were engineered whenever the FRG parliament met in West Berlin, bestowing a status on that half of the city which the GDR claimed it did not have. These delays could last up to fifty hours for the military, and civilian queues of 10 kilometres were not unknown.[5]

<u>27 February 1964</u> *Walter Heyn, a 25-year-old divorced farmer, tried to get across at about 10.20 at night. He made his attempt through allotments. Two Border Guards saw him 50 metres away, called a warning and fired a warning shot. He was cut down by a burst of fire and three aimed shots. When he was examined it was found two of the shots had killed him.*
<u>26 March 1963</u> *An unknown person died at the wall.*

<u>5 May 1964</u>   *Adolf Philipp, 20, a West Berliner. At about 1.45 a.m. a Border Guard noticed a man's tracks near the border at an unoccupied bunker. Two Guards went there and were challenged by Philipp, who held a revolver and said 'hands up'. They shot him in the chest. A subsequent investigation showed that he had cut through the barbed wire and walked backwards into the death strip so that anyone coming across his footprints would think he'd been walking Eastwards – and that would throw them off his trail.*

<u>22 June 1964</u>   *Walter Heike, 30, tried to get across at the Invaliden cemetery beside the canal at about 5.40 a.m. He did not react to warning calls or shots. He got over the barbed wire but was wounded by a bullet above his buttock and a Border Guard carried him back from the death strip. Fifteen minutes later he was taken to hospital by ambulance and died there.*

<u>28 July 1964</u>   *Rainer Gneiser, 18, and Norbert Wolscht, 17, may have tried to swim across. Both died, Wolscht of defective diving equipment.*

<u>18 August 1964</u>   *Hildegard Trabant, 37, and Wernhard Mispelhorn, a 20-year-old Berliner, made a joint attempt at 6.53 in the evening. There are no further details.*

On 13 September 1964, Michael Meyer, 21, tried at 5.20 in the morning to cross near Checkpoint Charlie. He ignored warning calls and shots, and the Border Guards opened fire. After having been hit several times Meyer collapsed near the wall and two Border Guards rushed up to where he lay. They aimed their weapons at him.

An American Military Policeman, Hans Werner Puhl, was on the second floor of a house overlooking the incident and headed downstairs to help. By then the Guards were dragging Meyer across the raked sand of the death strip. They noticed two armed West Berlin policemen, let go of Meyer and sprinted off. He tried to reach the wall again and was hit by five shots.

The West Berlin police, in the hall of a house, now sent across warning shots to the Guards who made a second attempt to drag Meyer away. Puhl shouted, 'Let go the boy' and hurled a tear-gas grenade over, forcing them to retreat. Then, aided by some civilians, he clambered over the wall to help.

'In doing so, the American was in breach of the state border', the GDR internal report would point out.

Puhl drew his pistol and pointed it at the two Border Guards while, at the same time, instructing Meyer to lie motionless. Civilians cut the barbed wire on top of the breeze blocks. Puhl came under fire from other Border Guards some 100 metres away but he wasn't hit. When the wire had been cut a rope was thrown over and Meyer was hauled over to the West.

The GDR report said that 'USA officials' had opened fire and 'more than 100 shots were "received"' on the Eastern side.

Later, Willy Brandt officially thanked Puhl.

The most celebrated tunnel rests in legend as 'Tunnel 57' because that was how many people came out through it on the nights of 3, 4 and 5 October 1964, a Saturday, Sunday and Monday. The man behind it, Wolfgang Fuchs, was an adventurer: 'large, generous, warm-hearted and outgoing'.[6] Between 1963 and 1964 he built seven tunnels. Because the GDR had not yet demolished all the houses at the border, comparatively short tunnels could be dug across to them from cellars in the West. As the houses were demolished and the death strip widened, tunnel construction evolved into something approaching an industrial basis with shift work, financial support, electricity, artificial ventilation and ingenious ways of concealing all the soil which had to be removed.

'Tunnel 57' began in a bakery on the Western side of Bernauer Strasse which Fuchs had rented for 100 DM a month. It was known as Operation Tokyo because the 1964 Olympic Games were to be held in that Japanese city in October and digging began in April. The tunnel was to go 145 metres (158 yards) from the bakery, beneath Bernauer Strasse, following a route under the wall itself, the death strip, the inner wall, a Guard hut in one of the side streets and then come up in a ramshackle outdoor toilet in the backyard of a house.

Student volunteers from the Technical University approached the logistical problems of the tunnel in a highly professional way. They had many concerns: a previous tunnel ran nearby but had been discovered and blown up. Probably it was still being monitored. They also knew, because thirty-five people would be doing the digging, that they could not keep going in and out of the bakery. The Border Guards, not far away, would become suspicious. So they stayed there in ten-day shifts. A lookout was positioned on a roof to watch for any sign of the Border Guards using sound detectors.

The diggers sank a shaft 3 metres down from the bakery basement but it struck a well and flooded. When they'd dealt with that they began to dig a narrow passage horizontally out under Bernauer Strasse. The tunnel could only be 70 cm (27½ inches) high because no excavated soil could be taken from the bakery – alerting the Guards – and calculations showed that any more than 70 cm would be too large a quantity to heap into the various rooms of the bakery.

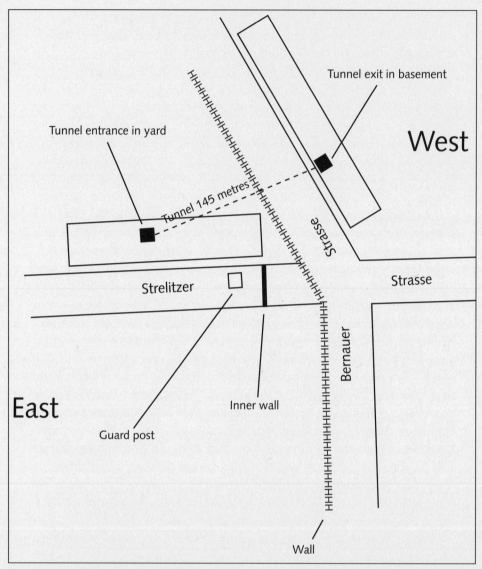

The famous 'Tunnel 57' stretching, from its very secret entrance in an Eastern backyard, out under Bernauer Strasse to its exit – and freedom – in a Western bakery basement.

It meant, however, that only one student could dig at a time. He'd push the soil back to the student immediately behind him who loaded it onto a trolley. It travelled back along the tunnel and was hoisted up into the house, poured into a wheelbarrow and taken away. They needed six months to reach the backyard of No. 55 and by then the disparate group they'd bring across would have been selected and notified; by then, too, the basement and ground floor of the bakery would be completely filled by the soil. Their concern now was what would happen when they came up behind No. 55. Tunnels had been betrayed or discovered before, the Border Guards waiting until people emerged before arresting them. A student was sent to the East and he made his way to the house, positioned himself in the yard and stamped his foot to show the tunnellers where they were. They came up inside the outdoor toilet and had soon enlarged the entrance.

The people who were to cross were contacted by Western couriers and coded telegrams. They made their way at intervals to the house – at least one via Friedrichstrasse station where he stood in front of a timetable. A stranger leaned forward and touched the D of Dresden, where the man had come from. The stranger took him to the house.[7] Fuchs was on a roof with binoculars and a radio transmitter to make sure those arriving were not being followed. When he was satisfied that they weren't, he used the radio to contact the people in the house and they opened the door. The escaper was taken across the yard to the toilet where a wooden crate was pulled away and he (or she) went down into the tunnel. Reports vary between 11 and 30 minutes for the time it took to crawl to the West – at one point water was so deep that breathing was difficult. (A woman escapee was almost too large and got stuck. She began to cry, not least because she feared she'd have to go back. She was pushed through.)

'All the fugitives were shaking with fright. They had been told to cross the yard to the shack one by one, without shoes. One family did not want to be separated at this critical moment. Some walked as if in a trance, they were so afraid.'[8]

Raw emotion consumed the escapers when they emerged in the bakery basement: husband and wife reunited after three years; brothers reunited; a mother crawling past her son in a wide section of the tunnel, realising he had helped dig it to get her out, but they made no sound as she passed because that would have been so dangerous; a child of 3½; a 70-year-old with heart trouble whose lips went blue as, wearing stout gloves and an overcoat, he crawled forward; a 5-year-old lad who'd been told, to calm him, that he was going into a cave as a special treat to see some wild animals and who, when he was hoisted into the bakery, complained there weren't any wild animals down there at all. . . .

On the Saturday, twenty-eight crawled through; on the Sunday, twenty-nine, giving totals of twenty-three men, thirty-one women and three children. And then, in the early hours of Monday morning, it went wrong.

Four students were in the house when two men in plain clothes – Stasi, snooping around, no doubt – came in, one shining a torch. These plain-clothes men did not, of course, know the password ('Tokyo') but looked so terrified that the students naturally assumed they must be escapers. A student said, 'Are you crazy shining the torch? Turn it off and get going.' The plain-clothes men were instructed to remove their shoes so they could cross the courtyard silently, but one of them, thinking fast, said he needed to go and collect a third escaper who was hiding nearby and who'd lost his nerve. The other plain-clothes man said he'd accompany his friend to get him.

The students accepted this, and it was a crucial mistake.

The two plain-clothes men came back after about 15 minutes with a man in uniform although, evidently, the students did not immediately notice him in the darkness. From this moment the chronology is not entirely clear.

The student at the front door was informed he was under arrest. Either just before or just after this, the lookout on the rooftop in the West saw GDR soldiers arriving in a truck and on motorbikes. He shouted into his radio, 'Everybody back now.'

The uniformed man was called Egon Schultz and he was 21. One report says he was unsure of himself but he held a machine pistol and the men in plain clothes told him to release the safety catch: 'Load the pistol.' He went out into the courtyard. A student fired a warning shot. Schultz returned this with a burst from the machine pistol.

By now the soldiers had stormed into the house but, with no time to assess the situation, assumed the escape route must be in the basement and began firing down into it.

In the courtyard, the student fired seven shots towards Schultz aiming, in the darkness, at where the flashes of the machine pistol shots had come from; then all four students fled into the toilet. One, detailed to remain at the entrance guarding it, let the other three go first and followed. Schultz, shot in the chest, lay dying. Whether he'd been hit by the soldiers or the student was unknown.

Although the GDR subsequently shouted, 'Murder' (in their official report they described the death of Schultz as 'murder by

Westberlin terrorists') and demanded the students' extradition; they
didn't, however, produce the fatal bullet or bullets, which they surely
would have done if they had been of Western calibre.

The GDR were clearly concerned about the whole incident. On 30
October an officer called Borning wrote to Erich Mielke, head of the
Stasi since 1957, outlining the situation following the 'assassination
of Sgt. Schultz by Westberlin terrorists'. An investigation uncovered
weaknesses and 'these led to the tragic conclusion of the operation'.
Erich Honecker, the letter said, had already involved himself in the
investigation and the following conclusion and suggestions were
agreed: 'The making sure of the safety of the borders with
Westberlin is to be organised and carried out by one unit only –
organs of the Ministry of State Security [the Stasi].'

By 20 November 1964, proposals had to be made to secure the
border and submitted to Honecker. They must include getting the
various bodies concerned to work together and liaise.

<u>26 November 1964</u>   *Hans-Joachim Wolff, 17, was shot swimming
across a canal at 6.30 p.m.*

In November the GDR government allowed pensioners to go to the
West, to visit or stay. A total of 383,181[9] visited the West from 1961
to 1988, and pensioners formed the bulk of them.

<u>3 December 1964</u>   *Joachim Mehr, 19, tried to get over the wall and
was fatally shot at 2.40 in the morning. He made the attempt with a
23-year-old, Hans-Jürgen Kahl, whose manner of death is unknown.*

During 1964, nine successful escapes were made using an Isetta
bubble car, a vehicle with two seats and a front-opening door which
was so small that the Border Guards scarcely bothered to check if
anyone was concealed in it. However, if the the heater and air filter
were removed, then the petrol tank taken out and replaced with a
small canister, just enough room was created for a person to lie
unseen on the engine and rear wheel. To maintain the Isetta's
equilibrium the suspension had to be strengthened.[10]

<u>1 January 1965</u>   *An unknown person died at the wall.*
<u>19 January 1965</u>   *An unknown man drowned trying to swim across
the Spree. Before he crawled under the barbed wire he left a brown
attaché case which contained a black shirt, a bottle of 'Goldwasser'
alcohol (a liqueur), 12 copies of the periodical* Magazin, *an empty*

fountain pen case, and one sandwich wrapped up in a copy of the
newspaper Freiheit, *dated 21 September 1964. A pair of brown*
leather shoes was found near the water.[11]
<u>3 March 1965</u>   *Ulrich Krzemien, 22, died at the wall.*
<u>4 March 1965</u>   *Christian Buttkus, 21, tried to cross with a female*
companion at 1.30 a.m. Two Border Guards fired 200 shots at them,
killing Buttkus and slightly injuring the woman.

The whole essence of these chapters is one of captivity and trying
to evade it. An Easterner might argue that that's just another biased
(and selective) view from the West. Officially, of course, there was a
view from the East, too, of an embattled, beleaguered sovereign
state prey to gangsters, capitalistic robbers and West German
militarists enticing their people away while they tried to build
socialism. The GDR was meticulous in recording transgressions
against their side of the frontier.

For example, on 1 April 1965, an internal report said a sergeant
of the Royal Green Jackets 43rd and 52nd had been arrested on the
territory of the GDR by a Border Guard. The map reference was
given. 'The person arrested was handed over by the town
commandant of the capital of the GDR, Berlin, Colonel Geier, to a
person authorised by the British town Commander in WestBerlin at
crossing point Staaken.'[12]

But still the escape attempts were made.

The House of Ministries, not far from Checkpoint Charlie, was a
gaunt, stoneblock building five storeys high with its southern façade
forming part of the inner wall itself. The ground-floor windows had
been closed off by metal grilles. The death strip was narrow here:
crude stone blocks cemented together, concrete lintels and barbed
wire on V-shaped metal clasps running along the top. The immediate
area on the West was wasteland – it had been a notorious SS
interrogation centre, now completely levelled to the point where grass
was growing.

A maintenance engineer worked in the building and his job
included checking the lifts. He took his wife and son and they
locked themselves in a toilet until evening, when the building was
closed for the day. In the darkness they emerged and made their way
onto the roof. The man anchored the rope (one report says fishing
line) he'd brought then tied the other end to a hammer and cast it
full across the wall to where Western 'helpers' waited. They had
already secured a steel cable and now attached it to the rope. The
man hauled it back across and in turn secured it at the roof. The

cable now descended, as taut as he could make it, from the roof down over the wall to the grassy area in the West.

He'd made three metal wheels which would run on top of the cable and his wife had sewn three strong body harnesses which were fixed to the wheels. She put hers on and, the wheel running, disappeared into the darkness. She sailed over the wall and hands reached her before she hammered into the ground. The man hooked on the boy and he went too. When he'd landed, the man attached himself to the cable, which by now was so slack that his feet brushed the top of the barbed wire – but he made it.

> **9 June 1965** *An unknown person died at the wall. That same day Dieter Brandes, 19, was shot at the wall.*
> **15 June 1965** *Hermann Döbler, 42, a West Berliner who, with a female companion, was in a paddleboat which strayed across into Eastern waters on the Teltow Canal at 1.55 in the afternoon. They were some 60 metres beyond the line. The Border Guards gave a warning shot and, when that was not heeded, opened fire from a watchtower. Due to the strength of the current the boat drifted back to the Western side and about 2.10 reached the bank. Dobler was dead and the woman critically injured.*
> **Undated 1965** *Divers were carrying out exercises and at 4.05 in the afternoon found parts of a body.*

Kurt Behrendt, who lived in Steinstücken, captures how sudden escape attempts were and how ill-defined. There was no harmony to them, just fear, and perhaps running, and hasty shots, and it all came from nowhere:

Once I saw somebody trying to escape in the night but he was arrested and taken away. I saw it from the roof of my house. I heard gunfire and I saw a man. I couldn't say how old he was because he was so far away. He was standing between the walls and he was almost paralysed because they had already seen him. Some soldiers from the People's Army came and took him to a watchtower and waited with him until a jeep arrived. They put him in the jeep and it went away. I think the gunfire I'd heard was only to warn the man. I don't think he was injured.

This was not the only man who tried to escape. Some reached Steinstücken but the tragic thing was that they were not in West Berlin – on West Berlin soil, yes, but they'd have had to get through the GDR controls where the main street is today and cross from our enclave to West Berlin itself. The American soldiers had a barracks and when somebody managed to get over the wall he was taken to the barracks, which was in a house, and they stayed there until the next helicopter came, after maybe three or four days. The helicopter took them.

Just over there was a street in Babelsberg which used to be called Red Cross Street, and what we supposed was a barracks was in fact the central building of the Red Cross in the eastern district of Brandenberg. It became an office for justice and administration.

This was the point where the whole of the wall round Berlin was narrowest: 5 metres [a corridor covered from both ends by watchtowers between the back gardens of houses]. In a technical sense, people were neighbours but we had no contact at all – that was prohibited to them. Because of the arc-lamps, all was light and very bright. The lights were not a problem because we had thick curtains and blinds. In the summer after dark it was not so bright because the foliage was on the trees but in winter yes, bright! We had our own street lights but we didn't need them. . . .

A man had an idea. He had been married for twenty-five years and he wanted to celebrate it by inviting many, many guests but it was not possible for them to come to Steinstücken because they didn't have residents' permits. He'd have to go to West Berlin to meet them in an hotel or restaurant. Some of those invited came from Western Germany and they'd have to stay the night. He had a big house and he wanted them to celebrate and be able to stay with him. That's normal – but they couldn't. Then he had a spark of an idea: every West German and West Berliner had the same rights he had, so if he went to the local [Western] police they would certainly have nothing against those people having their residence here. He sent these guests to the police and they were given a document, stamped and signed, which said that from a certain day on they had their second home in Steinstücken. It was normal and legal to have a second home.

He'd warned them that there may be some difficulties. The guests arrived at the control. There were two Border Guards on duty and they were very surprised at the documents because they'd never seen anything like them before. People from Steinstücken only had identity cards. The Guards did not know how to handle it. No regulations covered it and they may well have been afraid that something would happen to them if they did *not* let the people through. So they let them through and the celebration took place here, ten or twelve people with children, and some did spend the night. They all got back to West Berlin without any problems.

This was the starting point for many people in Steinstücken to do the same. I did, too, and for most of us it was the first time people could visit us. We did it for some years, but only with friends and relatives, not official people. We had 50 people living here, and after three months we had 1,200 residents! We didn't tell the trick to people we didn't like here.

We could do it like that up to 1967 and nobody did anything to stop it even though this was the time of the cold war. Nobody negotiated on such things: the West Berlin Senate did not negotiate with the GDR and maybe that explains it. We were surprised it wasn't stopped but equally we were aware that one day somebody would come and stop it. In 1967, the GDR authorities announced that from a certain day on – this was the 17th of June – they would not accept secondary residences as a valid reason to cross, but anyone who'd applied before could cross. The decision was not very effective because by that point everybody who wanted one already had one.

The road was built in 1972 and then everybody could get here [the road removed the anomaly because the wall now ran along either side of it (like a neck) and the controls were taken away].[13]

18 August 1965   *Klaus Garten, 24, was shot trying to get over the wall.*
18 October 1965   *Walter Kittel, 23, and an unknown 21-year-old tried to get over the wall near the hamlet of Klein-Machnow. Seventy shots were fired and Kittel died immediately.*
10 November 1965   *Heinz Cyrus, 29, jumped to his death from a window.*
25 November 1965   *Heinz Sokolowski, 47, was shot at 4.58 a.m. It took eight bullets to stop him and he was severely wounded in the lower part of his body. He died at 6.10 in hospital. The official report added that four West Berlin policemen witnessed the incident.*
26 November 1965   *Erich Kuhn, 62, tried to get across allotments at 7.35 in the evening. He was seen crawling about 40 metres from the border by a Guard and did not react to either warning call or shot. He tried to avoid arrest by making off into the allotments but the Guard fired a burst of six shots. He was hit in the stomach.*

The essential problem with telling the story of the Berlin Wall is that it all happened on three levels: the political/nuclear, which is usually the subject of academic study; the silent backdrop of 4 million people finding their everyday normalities and living them, the hardest part to tell because it is so vast, silent and unknown; and those who became – some rainy night with the broken cobblestones glistening behind them and wrecked buildings rising round them – victims and martyrs and brave heroes with *causes*. They stood in their fear reading the shadows and the barbed wire and the distance between here and there. Maybe they heard footfalls. Perhaps the drizzle made the headstones glisten in the cemetery they'd chosen, because tactically the cemetery was a safer route from here to there than open ground or the water.

The most difficult aspect for any historian is holding the right balance between the silent backdrop of the 4 million, and the few who came – for whatever reason – out of the 4 million and chose the shadows and the bullet run. To set down these completed lives in no more than brief paragraphs, often without even the most basic facts, like their names, is a formidable task. It is easy to skim across the paragraphs and, inevitably, many are very similar. And it is easy to forget that each was a human being, loved and missed; not melodrama on black and white newsreels long ago, but real people running as hard as they could towards something or away from something.

<u>26 December 1965</u>   *Heinz Schöneberger, 27, was shot when a group attempted to escape by car. His three companions, a fellow West Berliner and two East Berlin women, were arrested. They were in a Ford Taunus, Schöneberger driving. It came into the checkpoint and at 12.55 a.m. was ordered into the vehicle control area. The second West Berliner was walking next to the car when the Guard at the control ordered Schöneberger to get out. The second West Berliner tried to jump in as the car accelerated away but he was pulled clear by the Guards. The Taunus drove into another West German car at the pole across the road, ramming it, Schöneberger sprang out and ran. Eleven shots were fired at him but he crossed the line into the West, severely wounded. He collapsed. Members of the West Berlin Fire Brigade took him to hospital but he later died of his wounds.*
<u>Sometime in 1965</u>   *an unknown person drowned trying to escape.*

In January 1966, an 18-year-old called Hartmut Richter tried to escape through Czechoslovakia to Austria. Richter's story, woven into the larger story of the wall, remains unusual. He grew up in

Potsdam and was a bright pupil. He was also orthodox: he joined the *Jungpionier* (a children's organisation) because he wanted 'to become like Lenin'. By the next stage, the *Thälmannpionier* (a youth organisation), he had become critical. He was taught that people in the West were enemies but he had relatives over there and couldn't classify them as enemies. He was asked if any pupils in his class preferred watching *Bonanza* on Western television to *Meister Nadeloehr*, a popular children's programme on the GDR channel. He preferred Bonanza. . . .

He did not join the Free German Youth[14] organisation in view of the realities, he states. 'I had lost his faith in babies being found under the gooseberry bush and Santa Claus' – a way of saying he was rejecting 'actually existing socialism', as the GDR described what they had created and were living within. He took the train to Czechoslovakia but was arrested on the way. It took almost a week to transport him back to Potsdam on the *Grotewohlexpress*, a prisoner transport train disguised as a yellow postal wagon. He was held in custody but, shrewdly, wrote to his parents expressing his admiration for 'the heroes of socialism'. While he was in custody, somebody mentioned to him that there were weak points in the wall – at a certain point on the Teltow Canal. Interesting, he thought. He was put on probation in May.

<u>7 February 1966</u> *Willi Block, 32, was hit by two bullets which grazed him and two which struck him 'with full effect' as the official report phrased it. Where this incident happened is not clear.*
<u>14 March 1966</u> *Lothar Schleussner, 23, was fatally shot at the wall.*
<u>15 March 1966</u> *Jörg Hartmann, 21, was fatally shot at the wall.*
<u>19 March 1966</u> *Willi Marzhan, of unknown age, was one of two members of the People's Army who tried to get across at 6.15 in the morning. The Border Guards opened fire on them with pistols and Marzhan, a sergeant, was hit in the head. The other soldier, also a Sergeant, made it to the West. They had been firing with machine pistols at the Border Guards, who were not injured.*
<u>30 March 1966</u> *Eberhard Schulze, 20, was fatally shot at the wall.*

Perhaps this is as good a place as any to examine how the system of manning the border worked. It was, as one might imagine, carefully organised and structured, but not actually as complex as it looks at first glance.

Hagen Koch explains it. The Riot Police, the Border Police, the Border Guards, the Railway Police, the *Vopos* and the People's Police all guarded the border 'because there was what they called the National Border Protection System (*Gesellschaftliches System der Grenzsicherung*). Directly at the border, there were the Border Guards (*Grenztruppen der DDR*), and this existed from 15 September 1961. When the wall went up there were only the People's Police, the Riot Police (*Bereitschaftspolizei*) and the Combat Groups (*Kampfgruppen*). The National People's Army (*Nationale Volksarmee*) were not allowed to come closer to the frontier than 1,000 metres.

'On 15 September 1961, all forces were put under the command of the *Nationale Volksarmee*. Ulbricht said that the border was to defend the GDR – it was a protection against the exterior enemy. At all border crossings, the ministry for State Security, Main Section VI (passport and search section), was present (*Ministerium für Staatssicherheit, HA VI – Hauptabteilung VI – Pass und Fahndung*).

'The correct name of the Railway Police was *Transportpolizei* – Transport Police. Their uniforms were blue. Their task was also to protect transport in West Berlin on the S-bahn and interzonal trains between West Germany and the GDR.

'The Border Police were founded on 1 December 1946 and later became the Border Guards. Their task was, in cooperation with the Soviet Army, to arrest anyone trying to cross the border illegally. Their main focus was the border between the GDR and the FRG from June 1952, when it was closed, but at the same time they had to protect the border around Greater Berlin.

'The Riot Police were units of the People's Police who were quartered in barracks. They continued to exist even after the foundation of the *Nationale Volksarmee* and were under the command of the Ministry of the Interior (*Innenministerium*).

'The official relationship between the Border Guards and the People's Police: there were so-called measures of organization and cooperation (Maßnahmen des OZW – Organisation und Zusammenwirken). The People's Police protected the border installations on the GDR side against the approach of refugees. Controls were coordinated with the Border Guards at both the national and regional levels.

'There were differing numbers of Border Guards round Berlin – governed by the increasing sophistication of the wall. As an example at the end, however, in the section between Pankow and the Brandenburg Gate, the personnel was: on duty per shift – 3 officers, 12 Sergeants, 94 soldiers. Technical equipment – 5 Border Trabants, 5 motorbikes, 10 radio sets, 4 walkie-talkies, 18 radio sets. That means there were about 1,000 Border Guards on duty at any one time. They worked in three shifts so that gives a total of approximately 3,000 Border Guards per day.

'In fact, for a better knowledge of the surroundings the soldiers had to draw sketches of what they could literally see from their viewpoint. They were, however, rotated [among themselves] in the watchtowers. They knew each other but there was no familiarity between them. Two Border Guards manned a normal watchtower (one of them, the *Postenführer*, was in charge). On a *Führungsstelle* – a command post like the one in Treptow – there were additionally drivers, dogs and an arrest group (*Festnahmegruppe*). The Guards worked two different forms of shift: two of twelve hours per day or three of eight hours. The Guards were doing their eighteen-month military service. If they were officers that would be from three to ten years, and at least twenty-five for professional soldiers.'[15]

<u>25 April 1966</u>　*Michael Kollender, 21, was shot as he reached the vehicle trap in the death strip. He dived into the vehicle trap, crawled and was shot again. Kollender was a member of the National People's Army and had had a Kalashnikov with him, containing a magazine with 14 rounds. The safety catch was off and the weapon set for continuous fire. He also had a man's watch, a letter addressed to him, a letter from Oberlungwitz [a small place in the south], a purse with 0.32 Marks in it, one male ring and other small items.*
<u>On this same day</u>　*Peter Petermann, 58, died at the wall.*

Border Guard Rudolf Loschek was 24 in 1966 and, many years later, explained how the system worked:

Every night at nine o'clock the guard changed. We arrived early to receive our weapons. Then we got our daily orders. I can still tell you exactly how it went. 'I order the securing of the border from nine o'clock until you are relieved. Border violators are to be arrested or destroyed.' And then the command to use weapons: 'You must shoot border violators when all means of arrest have been exhausted. You must not shoot at Allied vehicles, diplomatic vehicles, air targets or children.'[16]

It was my last day of service before leaving the army. Well, we'd celebrated, we'd had a few. Suddenly someone called, 'There's someone running over there!' I thought he was having me on. I didn't react. Suddenly I saw two of my men with machine pistols. They were already shooting. They were shooting continuously –

everybody had sixty shots. You couldn't see a thing because of the dust. So I took my machine pistol as well. Suddenly I saw something so I just shot in that direction, without aiming. I was afraid in case they found out I hadn't fired. 'Why didn't you shoot?' It would have been difficult to talk myself out of it. When the shooting stopped you couldn't see anything, only clouds of dust. There was a person lying there, about 2 metres away from the barbed wire, on the control [death] strip. He was still breathing. He was gurgling. Then he was taken away. We didn't know if he was dead.

A day before my discharge we were commended. I got a watch. I can't say I was pleased with the watch. There was no engraving on it and nobody knew what it was. It did not say '*For good service at the border*'.

The postscript to this had to wait until the world had moved and the wall come down.

'We didn't get his wallet or his ring,' Michael Kollender's mother said when, those many years later, she could see the file. For twenty-five years the family had had virtually no information about the manner of his death. 'He was shot many times, many times. It happened early on Monday, between Sunday and Monday. My husband came up and said, "Michael . . ." and I said, "Is he over there?" He said, "It's a lot worse. He's dead." And the world collapsed for me. It was full of Stasi in the mortuary. I'd got some injections beforehand so I was really calm but numb. I pulled the cloth back and saw the shots. On top of his head he had a big bandage. There was blood on the pillow and here [indicating the right eye] a kind of vein was sticking out. It was all burst and bloody. The back of his head was all shot to bits. And I said farewell, and pressed him.

'They didn't let us out of their sight even at the funeral. Some school friends wanted to give flowers, but they were sent back. They went to every garden nursery and forbade them to supply wreaths. No wreath, you see. The one who shot him – I've thought about it so often in secret – could have shot without killing him, even if he was crippled. But not riddle him with holes from head to foot. I couldn't understand that. [Long pause while she composes herself.] Well, at least now we know. Twenty-five years and it seems like yesterday. [Pause, voice lowers.] Twenty-five years.'

29 April 1966　*Paul Stretz, 31, tried to swim across behind a ship at 3.30 in the afternoon. He was shot and went under.*

The official GDR reports record two more incidents on the same day Stretz died. At 10.50 that morning two people, one aged 77 and the other 78, were in a sailing boat some 20 metres from the border line. They were stopped, their papers examined, and they were released. The implication must be that they were a West German couple out enjoying themselves on the water and strayed too close.

Then Stertz made his attempt.

<u>10 June 1966</u>   *Elke Märtens, age unknown, died at the wall.*
<u>26 July 1966</u>   *Eduard Wroblenski, 33, died at the wall.*

Hartmut Richter had now resolved to try and escape again. As mentioned he had heard in prison about a place where potentially the wall was weak: the Teltow Canal, which had attracted many others as it meandered full across the southern part of the city. Richter seems to have reached a point where, although he was only 18, he preferred to risk his life rather than live it in the GDR. Originally he'd considered making the attempt across a lake between his home at Potsdam – he lived with his parents – and the West Berlin district of Wannsee, but other attempts had been successful there and he knew that, after each, the border was tightened. He'd trained and liked swimming but he decided against the lake.

On 26 August he selected a dark shirt and put it on, then put 700 East marks and some documents into a plastic bag and left home. He did not say goodbye to his parents because that would have been a risk for him and a risk for them, too, if they had known. He rode the S-bahn to the stop at Teltow, a village about 2 kilometres from where he wanted to be. He walked to the canal there and slowly followed it towards the border. That meant passing under the main transit autobahn between West Berlin and Helmstedt, near the extensive GDR checkpoint of Dreilinden, on a country lane.

He had had no chance to recce the area. The weak point was where the canal went into the West and, in these comparatively early days, the area was not illuminated as it would have been in Berlin itself. There was the darkness of the wooded countryside on either bank of the canal and he'd picked a largely cloudy night. The geometry of this: an old S-bahn bridge, then about 500 metres (546 yards) on the far side of it, the barbed wire on either bank for another 500 metres, then an obstacle across the canal. Beyond that lay the West. Watchtowers loomed, satanic, threatening shapes but too far apart to illuminate the whole area clearly. In the darkness there were shadowy pools on the water and he would use them. Better, it was drizzling and drizzle could only be extra cover hampering the visibility of the Guards in the watchtowers and anyone patrolling the banks.

He slipped into the water beside the old bridge because it screened him from the watchtowers. He was more anxious than afraid, and the water felt cold. The canal was about 40 metres (43 yards) wide and he intended to go towards the West zigzagging from bank to bank, diving and swimming underwater whenever he could, inhabiting the dark places – the searchlights from the watchtowers really weren't like in Berlin. He swam above water as little as poss- ible because the movement of his arms would make a noise as they disturbed the water. When he reached a bank he paused to recover. Progress was agonisingly slow and he had a watch- tower to get past. He came to the point where the wire stretched along the banks, he zigzagged on and past the watchtower and reached an obstacle stretched across the canal. It was a steel-mesh fence and he summoned the strength to clamber up it – he estimates he had been in the water for four hours. As he slipped down the other side he saw a sign: 'YOU ARE LEAVING THE AMERICAN SECTOR' which, of course, warned people that the American Sector ended here, or in his case began here. He was in the West. He passed out – fainted is his word – and was taken to hospital in Wannsee, from where he sent a postcard to his parents telling them where he was.

His father went to the local police station to report Richter missing 'but they said, "You know what these young people are like. They just go off somewhere and they come back." My father said, "No, no, he's written me a postcard from Wannsee!" The policeman was just baffled.' Harmut Richter would see his parents again, but not until the early 1970s.

<u>29 August 1966</u>   *Heinz Schmidt, a 46-year-old Westerner, evidently jumped into a canal out at Spandau and began swimming East. To prevent this 'provocation' the Border Guards shot at Schmidt and he was hit. He managed to swim back. At this moment 'approximately' ten Western soldiers (unidentified) moved into position and fired at the Border Guards. This involved a total of about 50 people. 'About 4.00 the situation was normal again.'*

<u>6 November 1966</u>   *Gustav Lupke, 86, died at the wall.*

<u>21 November 1966</u>   *Joachim Stephan, 29, died at the wall.*

<u>16 December 1966</u>   *Karl-Heinz Kube, 17, was fatally shot at the wall.*

27 January 1967   *Max Willi Sahmland, 37. At 11.07 p.m. he was shot swimming the Teltow Canal. Despite 53 shots being fired he 'arrived on westberlin [sic] territory without being hit'.*

Were the East Germans wrong and he had been hit?

1 May 1967   *An unknown person died at the wall.*

18 February 1968   *Dieter Weckeiser, 25, was fatally shot at the wall and so was Elke Weckeiser, 22. The National People's Army report says only: 'At 22.50 hours one male and one female, 26 and 22 years old, living in Furstenwalde, were trying to get to the west.'*

6 July 1968   *Siegfried Krug, 29. '01.35 hours. One male person, living in Berlin, was killed trying to escape to the West.'*

15 November 1968   *Horst Körner, 21. At 10.55 at night two Border Guards – one called Rolf Henninger – patrolling in a Trabant jeep out towards Potsdam noticed a policeman hiding behind a tree approximately 10 metres from an old people's home. It was Körner. The jeep stopped and reversed. 'When the Trabant lights shone on the tree' Körner 'came forward with a machine pistol and opened fire. After the first shots', Henninger, hit in the heart and head, was killed. The other Border Guard leapt from the Trabant and shot Körner, who dropped the machine pistol. The Guard assumed that Körner was hit but 'since he did not fall, and since the Guard noted that his driver was dead, opened fire again.' He kept on until Körner went down. Altogether the Guard fired thirty shots. 'A further investigation showed that the culprit had fired fifteen times. Fourteen shots were noted on the Trabant. The culprit still had two full magazines of bullets with him. Due to the angle of the firing, no shots could have reached Westberlin.'*

In February 1969 President Richard Nixon visited Berlin as part of a European tour and for once large crowds were genuinely pleased to see him (his arrival in Rome provoked a riot among 5,000 demonstrators). In Berlin he said, 'Sometimes you must feel that you are very much alone. But always remember, we are with you and always remember that people who are free and who want to be free around the world are with you. In the sense that the people of Berlin stand for freedom and peace, all the people of the world are truly Berliners.' If it was an echo of Kennedy – who had been assassinated in November 1963 – that didn't matter, because it was what they wanted to hear. He visited the wall but at the Heinrich-Heine-Strasse checkpoint where houses from the West directly faced those in the East with only the death strip, narrow here, in between. He looked suitably sombre as he mounted the observation platform. Perhaps someone had told him of Heinz Schöneberger and those awful moments just after midnight three years before, moments enacted just *down there*. Perhaps someone hadn't.

(The geometry of this: Heinrich-Heine-Strasse was a broad avenue running north to south. It had been called Prinzenstrasse and the section in the West was still called that; the section in the East had been renamed after Heine, a poet. A side street bisected the avenue and it was here that the houses faced each other. Those in the West were five storeys and those in the East four storeys, so that all but those residents on the ground floors could see their neighbours clearly across the wall. Beyond the visual they had no relationship. (When it was finally all over, the author tried to interview one of the Eastern residents to hear what it had been like. She was a middle-aged woman who lived on the top floor, so she'd had an excellent view. By her body movements she implied reluctance but, in the Eastern way, was momentarily unsure whether she could refuse an interview. She did, saying, 'I'm very sorry but it's just too traumatic to talk about' and disappeared into the sanctuary of her apartment, taking care not to look back.)

Rudiger Hering, who lived in the East near Falkensee, responded to the question 'Did you ever get used to the wall?' by replying, 'There were three rows of barbed wire and you can never get used to that. It always reminded me of the barbed wire round concentration camps. We had watchtowers, and arc-lamps every few metres which were very bright, totally bright. The wall (as opposed to the barbed wire) came at the end of 1968 and the beginning of 1969. I remember because I had to join the Army in 1968 and I had my first leave in May 1969.'

Bodo Radtke, the East Berlin journalist who was allowed to travel – it was necessary for his job – says that the situation was a psychological one. 'You could live all your days in East Berlin without the West being much of a factor [except TV] and then, when you were going on assignment, you'd take the train from Friedrichstrasse and, as it looped over the death strip and the watchtowers into the West, you'd suddenly think "It simply cannot be, this is not possible in the middle of a city, this is crazy." You'd go and do your work, you'd return to the East and somehow let the craziness drown into your normality – until the next time.'

<u>1 April 1969</u>   *Elmar Scholz, age unknown, was fatally shot at the wall.*
<u>9 April 1969</u>   *Johannes Lange, 29, was fatally shot at the wall.*
<u>13 September 1969</u>   *Klaus-Jürgen Kluge, 21. 'At 20.40 hours, one male person trying to get across the border . . .'*
<u>20 September 1969</u>   *Leo Lis, 45. 'At 20.00 hours a male person, 45 years old, living in Kamenz [a town in the south] was stopped trying to cross the border.'*

In October, Willy Brandt became Chancellor of the Federal Republic. Despite, or perhaps because of, his experiences as Mayor of Berlin he determined to approach relations with the East constructively and realistically. The wall stood, whether anybody liked it or not, and had now for eight years. He'd begin what became known as *Ostpolitik* which, it seemed, marked the end of something and the beginning of something. Nobody knew what exactly, but at least it was a kind of movement across the geometry.

<u>8 October 1969</u>   *Wolfgang Puhlfüss, age unknown, died at the wall.*

The first bitter decade was over.

SEVEN

The Bullet Run

I thought that although all this was only 6 or 7 metres away I would never go there. It would have been easier to go to the moon. The moon was closer.

Roland Egersdörfer,
Border Guard

By now the two halves of the city were moving at different rhythms, obeying different impulses and it struck a visitor with immediate impact. West Berlin had become a bustling place, cosmopolitan, almost glamorous, a cocktail hour of draft-dodgers, revolutionary students and solid citizens making a lot of money; East Berlin had become austere, impersonal, a heavy, brooding place of wide, empty avenues and small, often empty, shops. Author John Ardagh coined a phrase about Dresden in the late 1980s: it still had a 'stunned, walking wounded feel'.[1] In the early 1970s East Berlin had had that.

The wall subconsciously conditioned inhabitants and visitors to the truth that the other side of the city – East or West – was very different. The edifice, itself heavy and brooding, made this statement because, if the other side hadn't been different, the edifice wouldn't have been there. When you crossed, or even gazed at, the web of concrete lintels, tank traps, patrolling jeeps and looming watchtowers manned by Border Guards who really would shoot, you were being subconsciously prepared for the difference. That helped to accommodate the impact, but the impact remained hard enough because you might be on an 'ordinary' city street like Friedrichstrasse on both sides. More than that the division began to be reflected in the people, Westerners fashionably dressed and with a jaunty way of comporting themselves, Easterners in stout clothing, moving ponderously.

<u>1 January 1970</u>   *An unknown person died at the wall.*

The tetchiness – perhaps the extreme sensitivity – in every nuance of the geometry of division remained in full force. A GDR report gives an account of what should have been a trivial incident:

10.06.1970, 17.45 hours, the soldier Peattie, William, Number I/A/SH-2373 0360, born on 21.01.1934 in Glasgow (according to his own words), belonging to the English[2] troops stationed in West Berlin, went over the border of the GDR at Montgomery-Camp pumpstation.

General-Major Poppe, commandant of the capital of the GDR – Berlin – stresses that this is definitely a transgression of the state border made by the English soldier and a serious violation of the sovereignty of the GDR.

The town commandant points out again to the Commander of the troops stationed in West-berlin, General-Major F.C. Boyes Lyon, that the People's Army of the GDR can not permit such transgressions of the border.

For this, the Commander of the English troops stationed in Westberlin [sic] is fully responsible.

Today, the 11.06.1970, at [here there is a gap in the report] hour, the soldier Peattie, William was handed over. His kit and other personal belongings were not taken from him.[3]

<u>19 June 1970</u>   *Heinz Müller, 27. 'At 01.50 hours, one male person got over the wall from WestBerlin to the GDR. . . .' There are no further details of why this particular man was going the other way, or what happened to him except that he died.*

We went to Berlin as a foursome, the Hiltons and the Woodcocks (John and Christine), because we were curious to see what it was like. We drove and, although this book is in no sense a travelogue, getting there is interesting. Across the plain past Hannover to Helmstedt was a straightforward autobahn journey and at Helmstedt – I can see this now, quite passively as I must have recorded it with the shutter open and memory developing it, fixing it – there was the last petrol station in the West then a little further on a hut in the middle of the road. It seemed to be unmanned.

Beyond it you crossed into an open jaw in the wall: watchtowers in the distance, a truck filled with boulders up a ramp (so it could be released and come down to block any escaping vehicle), a machine-gun emplacement behind sandbags in the middle of the road, uniformed men waving you to park the car here, get out and go into that Customs building.

The contrast between the unmanned hut and all this was making a statement no sane person could misinterpret.

We got the visas and stamps and moved along the umbilical cord towards West Berlin. You passed villages and hamlets and fields and never saw anyone. A plague might have been upon the land. Darkness fell and in the East there seemed to be few lights at all, until, all at once, a great saucer of neon – white, and rising into an aura – was making a statement, too. We were approaching West Berlin. It was as you might expect it to be, extensively rebuilt and bustling. It had a sheen, the sense of a frontier town during a goldrush where people were making money.

We went East the next day on foot.

Checkpoint Charlie was like Helmstedt, hitting you hard from nowhere. On the Western side were shops and shoppers who went about their business oblivious of the wall and the watchtowers. The Allied hut was in the middle of the road but you weren't even waved through. If you wanted to go over there you go over there, *buddy*.

You crossed Hagen Koch's line into another jaw in the wall. The Border Guards with their fossilised faces were forbidding and instructed to be like that. The Customs, in a long hut, was deliberately mysterious (they handed your passport back through a hatch so you couldn't see what was happening to it) and equally fossilised. You needed more stamps on your visa and you had to change money in another long hut with queues and forms and receipts and written threats about not trying to take money in or out. The GDR was shaping you to its will and you hadn't even got beyond the checkpoint to find out what the place looked like – but you suspected it was all like this.

At this time Britain did not recognise the GDR and once you crossed the line you were on your own, *buddy*. Amid all these faces and uniforms you didn't forget that. You might not have had rights there and the cavalry certainly weren't coming to the rescue.

Friedrichstrasse on the Eastern side, once you'd left the checkpoint, pleaded with you to remember that before the war it couldn't have looked like this. It was a widowed street in eternal mourning, whole lots empty and overgrown or strewn with rubble, elderly buildings shorn off and patched up: buildings on crutches. The money which made West Berlin bustle *within sight* over there, 50 yards away, was completely absent. You felt in the presence of the bombing raids last night, but they'd ended twenty-five years before.

On one of the sidestreets a small crowd had gathered and we advanced to see what it might be. A British company was shooting an advertisement for Polo mints and they'd hired a beautiful model who stood there wearing a white fur coat as the camera licked over her. The Easterners had gathered opposite her not, we sensed, to ogle but just because something was happening in a city where, clearly, apart from wearing heavy coats and walking with your head down, not much ever happened. We joined the gathering. A young girl – maybe in her late teens – marched up. She wore a plain rain-coat. She scattered words across us like machine-gun fire and gestic-ulated in the way that Germans have. Clearly she was empowered to order us to go. Why? We spoke no German and we couldn't ask. Here, however, was the next statement: our standing there con-stituted in some pathological way a threat to something. She hustled us until we were gone.

We walked to Friedrichstrasse station and had some lunch in a basic café where the locals read the day's newspapers which had been clipped between two wooden sticks (acting as spines) so they would last longer, could be handled easily and passed on to the next customer. We'd seen exactly the same thing in West Berlin cafés. . . .

We walked down Unter den Linden to the square where the old *schloss* stood before they gave it the dynamite. A large number of chairs had been stacked for some imminent parade and a dozen soldiers guarded them. Everything here seemed to be under guard, even chairs; everything here seemed to be suspended animation caught in its own caution and its own exhaustion; and everything here seemed held down under some authority which was nowhere and everywhere. You kept thinking about the dead hand of that reaching out to you, and taking you, and you did have no rights and you did have no representation. You didn't need to have read Kafka to feel Kafka. And it was *real*.

We walked to Alexanderplatz and went into a bookshop (which was still there twenty years later). A jam jar had been placed on a table with a card propped against it asking for donations for North Vietnam – it was 1970. The jam jar already contained coins and crumpled notes lying on them as autumn leaves might have done. It may be that the customers believed, and made their contribution, and were really going to defeat the Yankee imperialists and make the world a better place. It may be that the jam jar was brought out every morning with the same coins and notes in it to appear as if the customers believed and nobody ever put anything in.

Outside, one of those silly things happened. A square-set man with a briefcase was coming towards me and there was a moment where he'd go left or right but he didn't, ploughed on straight at me and I had to side-step him. I thought he'd come *for* me and my nerve went. I said, 'We've got to get out of here.' We walked along Leipziger Strasse to Checkpoint Charlie and went through the wringer of all the controls again. I was ordered, alone, to the currency hut – a bad moment – to settle all our little group's money, however they decreed it must be settled. Then we stepped back across Hagen Koch's line and if we didn't feel as profoundly as Dennis L. Bark had felt at this instant, we did feel a lot better.

In the Allied hut nothing stirred – another statement.

We'd got visas for Poland and went for the day, and thereby hangs a tale, because the lady at the last petrol station in Poland thought we were German because we were in a VW, and filled the tank with diesel in order to demonstrate her dislike of Germans, and the VW struggled back to the GDR border crossing at Frankfurt-Oder and expired with naked flames ebbing from the exhaust pipes. By the time we got back to England we'd missed two night's sleep and had a *lot* of stamps in our passports. We'd devised a system. Woodcock, in the front passenger seat, had a folder with all the documents in and whenever we were challenged (it seemed to happen hourly; even on the umbilical cord back to Helmstedt traffic police flagged you down) he proferred the documents, got them stamped, and we moved on to the next one.

Now, safe across the Channel and motoring through Kent, the garden of England, I needed to fill the car up. I pulled into a petrol station. Woodcock woke from a deep sleep, fingered the folder and murmured, 'What documents do they want?' I mention this because after only a week his subconscious had been altered, so that a forecourt and bright lights must mean an authoritatian inspection or visa stamping or currency exchange or something like that. What if he'd had that not for a week but all his adult life? A week had been enough . . .

<u>18 July 1970</u>   *Klaus Schmock, 19, died at the wall.*

<u>2 August 1970</u>   *Friedhelm Ehrlich, 19, a corporal in the Border Guards, was prevented from escaping while not on duty. He was shot in the lower stomach and died in hospital.*

<u>7 August 1970</u>   *Gerald Thiem, 42, a West Berliner, was fatally shot at the wall.*

On 3 September (1971), what was known as the Quadripartite Agreement on Berlin was signed. *Ostpolitik* was starting to happen although, by definition, the consequences had to be complicated – and were. Author Mick Dennis simplifies this as well as anybody: 'The favourable reception of Bonn's overtures among the GDR's Eastern partners also gave cause for concern. Bonn concluded an accord with the Soviet Union in August 1970 and with Poland three months later. Four-power negotiations on Berlin commenced in May 1970. Brandt made it clear that a settlement on the Berlin issue was necessary to ensure sufficient support in the Bundestag for the ratification of the Moscow and Warsaw treaties. Ulbricht's strategy was to make acceptance of the GDR's full sovereignty a precondition for entering into formal negotiations with Bonn. From Ulbricht's point of view the question of Berlin's status, and the GDR claim to the exclusive right to control the access routes to West Berlin, were intimately concerned with sovereignty. West Berlin should be treated as an autonomous political entity on "GDR sufferance", not on any four-power status.'

The Soviet Union, acting as a global power, had its own interests. As Dennis says, it and Poland 'completed negotiations on their treaties with Bonn without insisting on the prior recognition of the GDR. Ulbricht was also worried about the Soviet Union's concession, in the course of the Four-Power negotiations on Berlin in 1970, that certain economic and political ties existed between West Berlin and the FRG. At the Twenty-Fourth CPSU Congress in March 1971, Brezhnev decoupled agreement on the status of Berlin from the issue of the acceptance of the GDR's full sovereign rights.' It also meant that agreement was reached on the transit routes so that harassment along the autobahn virtually ceased, and, tying up one loose end, a road to the Steinstücken enclave was agreed. The problem of the other enclave, Eiskeller, was solved in 1972.

Dennis concludes that 'Ulbricht's determined opposition to Four-Power responsibility for West Berlin, and his obduracy on the transit routes, threatened not only a speedy settlement to the negotiations on Berlin but, because of Bonn's coupling of a Berlin agreement with the ratification of the Moscow and Warsaw treaties and the calling of a European Security Conference, also jeopardized Brezhnev's policy on détente. When, on 3 May, Ulbricht announced his retirement as First Secretary of the SED, most observers assumed that the Soviet Union had been instrumental in his removal.'[4] Within three years, sixty-eight countries would recognise the GDR as a sovereign

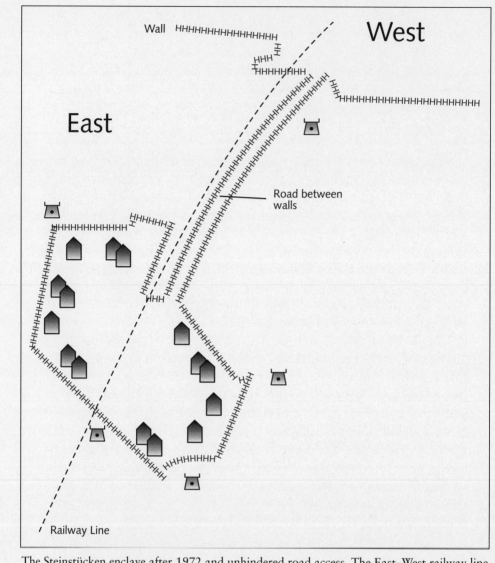

The Steinstücken enclave after 1972 and unhindered road access. The East–West railway line was a potentially weak point in the wall.

country (the Federal Republic not among them) and it would be admitted to the United Nations in 1973.

<u>25 December 1970</u> *Christian-Peter Friese, 21. 'At 00.03 hours, one male person, 22 years old, from Naumburg [a town in the middle of the country] trying to cross from the GDR to WestBerlin . . .'*
<u>7 January 1971</u> *Rolf-Dieter Kabelitz, 20, was fatally shot at the wall.*

In late January 1971 telephone links were restored between the two Berlins. They had been cut in 1952 and few lines had remained before 1971: the Western Allies' headquarters and the Soviet Embassy was one, the Western and Eastern airports – Templehof and Schönefeld – another. The GDR needed to contact S-bahn stations in the West because they ran the service. Evidently the two police forces had a teleprinter link and, among other things, it was used to try and identify bodies found at the wall. Initially ten lines were restored (there had been 4,000 in 1952) and from July were charged at the same rate as foreign calls.

Telephone links remained problematical between the two Germanies, however, and an anecdote illustrates that. A farm was bisected by the frontier and the two brothers running it decided that one would stay in the East, the other taking their mother to the West. The frontier cut the land into two distinct farms and the brothers farmed them, often doing the same tasks on the same days within sight of each other. The Eastern brother had children, and presents were always sent from the West on their birthdays, but phone calls could take up to nine hours to cover the 200 metres between the two farmhouses. The calls had to be booked and went on a circuitous route down to Bavaria, across and back up the other side.

In May, as has been seen, Ulbricht was replaced by Honecker.

<u>15 July 1971</u> *Wolfgang Hoffmann, 29, died at the wall, possibly shot.*
<u>24 July 1971</u> *Werner Kühl, 22. At 10.45 p.m. a Border Guard in Britzer Allee, a wooded area in Treptow, noticed two people sprinting. They were 100 metres away and heading for a ditch before they reached the wall. The Guard opened fire, killing one and injuring the other in the left forearm. He was taken to hospital. 'The injured person was a Westberlin citizen, aged 22. An investigation is continuing. Further information is not available.'*

On 3 September the Quadripartite Agreement was formally signed.

2 December 1971 *Dieter Beilig, 30, a West Berliner was arrested,
possibly at a checkpoint, but escaped from where he was being
detained and was fatally shot.*
1 January 1972 *Horst Kullack, 23, was fatally shot at the wall.*
13 January 1972 *Günter Semmler, 15, was fatally shot while trying to
climb the wall.*

The division did not spare friends and relatives. Klaus-Peter
Grohmann, the man who on Saturday 12 August 1961 had yawned
in an effort to make his mother-in-law go home, lived in the south of
West Berlin not far from Potsdam. He'd understood 'only a few days
afterwards, when they started to build the wall properly, that it was
going to be permanent. Of course I had friends and relatives in the
East, in Potsdam, but telephones were cut, everything was cut and
you couldn't communicate with anybody over there. The next time I
went to Potsdam was 1972 when the new contract was made
between the East Germans and the West. I went to see my relatives
there and in Dresden.

'I said to my wife that evening, "Tomorrow morning we're going,
please take the music cassettes out of the car" – it was forbidden to
take them into the East – and she put them in her handbag. In the
morning I said, "Come on, let's go, we've got to be early at the
border because it could take a long time to cross." We got to the
border and they asked the usual questions: "Do you have weapons?
Do you have cassettes?" I said no. They told my wife to open the
handbag and there they were – she'd forgotten to take them out. But
who the hell thinks like that, who the hell thinks about cassettes? It
cost us three hours, by the way.

'The visit was a pretty tearful affair and at the beginning it was
only for one day. You had to apply for a permit, you had to pay an
"entrance" fee and, as I've said, when you reached the border you
were heavily searched. Whenever we left West Berlin by car after the
wall was built to go to West Germany [the transit route] it could
take three hours at the Dreilinden checkpoint, two hours to drive to
Helmstedt and then sometimes three or four hours at the Helmstedt
checkpoint: they'd put a rod into the petrol tank, they'd look
underneath the car . . .

'I went back to East Berlin in 1989 though, of course, I'd been to
Potsdam that time. We'd drifted apart and, anyway, they weren't
that close relatives. I don't know. People became different and we've
only really been able to talk since reunification. I mean, we talked
then as well but we tried to be careful with politics, and there was

the question of getting them into trouble. That's why we didn't actually visit them for so long.

'I love soccer, I really love soccer and when the East Germans played and I heard the commentary I started to hate the team and in that team there were Berliners. If, for example, France won against the GDR I said to myself, "Great, that's the way I want it." This is how bad it got, and the same applied to the people across there.'[5]

14 February 1972   *Manfred Weylandt, 30. At Rummelsburg, an area in Treptow, about 11.30 p.m. a Border Guard at the Schilling Bridge noticed a person trying to swim across the Spree to West Berlin. He was shot and, in the official report, probably killed. The use of the weapon was 'parallel' to the border, meaning no shots entered West Berlin.*

The division did not spare even the dead.

The Invaliden cemetery, perhaps the most famous in Berlin, was in the East beside a canal, and the canal was the border. The cemetery was subdivided into what have been termed 'burial fields' and three of these lay in what was now the death strip. Another three lay within the area designated as forbidden to ordinary Easterners because it was so close to the border.

One official publication subsequently said the cemetery was 'full of traditions and contradictions'. It had been neglected after the war and the GDR would have levelled it except that it contained the graves of General von Scharnhorst, a famous nineteenth-century military figure who created the Prussian General Staff, as well as other notables. They were considered too important and too emotive to permit the complete levelling. (The cemetery also contained the graves of General Werner von Fritsch, accused under Hitler of homosexuality and killed on active service in Poland; and a war minister whose headstone was riddled with machine-gun fire from 1945.) These, including the imposing Scharnhorst monument, designed by the famous Berlin architect Schinkel and regarded as classical, were only open to the public from a distance and then only twice a week. However, step by step, in 1962 and 1966, then between 1972 and 1975, about half of the 6.2 acres were cleared, until only 230 of 3,000 graves remained.

7 March 1972   *Klaus Schulze, 19, was killed at 9.45 p.m. 400 to 500 metres from some dwellings at Falkenhoh, a village in the countryside to the east of West Berlin. A second person escaped in the direction of*

Gross Kuhlake, a very small Western enclave. At 11.25 two West Berlin policewomen were between 400 and 1,000 metres away but the official Eastern report said that they did not involve themselves.

<u>30 December 1972</u>   *Cengiz Koc, a 5-year-old Turkish child living in West Berlin, drowned.*

<u>23 January 1973</u>   *Peter Kreitloff, 30. Shot. No further details are known.*

<u>15 March 1973</u>   *Horst Einsiedel, 33, was fatally shot at the wall.*

<u>27 April 1973</u>   *Manfred Gertzki, 30, made his attempt near the Reichstag at about 5.45 p.m. The Border Guard immediately shouted 'halt' and fired warning shots but he ignored them. 'Aimed fire' opened up, he was hit and fell into the Spree. The Border Guards set off by boat – for a moment Gertzki resurfaced – but the current was too strong. After other boats and several divers joined the search the People's Police retrieved the body around 6.30. Some hundred West Berliners had gathered and, by the time the body was brought out, twenty of them were still there. Several took photographs.*

<u>14 May 1973</u>   *Siegfried Krobot, a 5-year-old West Berliner, drowned.*

<u>20 July 1973</u>   *Klaus Gomert, 18, died at the wall.*

On 2 November, Roland Egersdörfer began his three-year National Service. It would take him into the Border Guards and I propose to give an extended portrait of him because Border Guards, those ominous figures with the binoculars in the watchtowers, were as human as anybody else. Egersdörfer was from Frankfurt Oder on the Polish border 100 kilometres from East Berlin, and a letter came telling him he had been called up and where he should report – Perleberg, a town in the north – for his six months of basic training. 'After these six months you did not know where [on the border] they would send you. The first day you'd get your equipment and uniform then you'd go to your room and arrange your things. Then you started training, quite normal training, although every second day it was political: one day you spent eight hours in the field – maybe marching 15 kilometres – next day you had lessons in Marx and Lenin and so on.'

<u>In November or December</u> *Anna Kirste, a 78-year-old West Berliner, drowned.*

<u>5 January 1974</u>   *Burkhard Niering, 23-year-old reserve policeman, had a machine pistol and made his attempt at Checkpoint Charlie about 7.35 p.m. He took one of the men working in Passport Control hostage after firing two bursts and tried to make this man run with*

him as cover. The alarm sounded. Two other men from Passport Control shot Niering in the stomach and in the wrist. The incident lasted three minutes and he died in hospital at 9.05. During the incident there were approximately twelve cars, one an American military vehicle, inside the checkpoint and the checkpoint itself was closed from 7.35 to 7.45 – a serious contravention of the Four Power Agreement, of course.

On 12 April, Egersdörfer's training finished and he was a sergeant. 'I had ten days holiday, came back and they told me I was going to Berlin. They said the second company of Border Regiment 33. I didn't know what that meant.' He soon would. With his equipment he went by train via Potsdam to Köpenick 'and that was our destination. Everyone got out and our names were called. There were several lorries and when your name was called you were told which one to get into. You were driven to the barracks. The main building was of red brick and had a fence round it. Although it was only about 300 metres from the border, this was not the section we were to guard. During the first days I didn't think much about guarding the border because I was very happy to be in Berlin, not somewhere out in the country. In order to get to know our section of the border, I accompanied patrols for more than a week.'

Egersdörfer's section was 23.8 kilometres, and each company comprised seventy men. They had to man between thirty and forty control points – the watchtowers and underground stations where the Western trains never stopped. Intriguingly, Egersdörfer reveals that not all watchtowers were always manned. If there were three close together, like the three at Bernauer Strasse forming 'a relatively small section', one might be unmanned. 'The watchtowers in the 1970s were a bit different to those we knew later and in the daytime you couldn't really see if they were manned.'

A precise ritual had to be enacted before each shift. 'There was always a specific time when we were told we could get our weapons and then we gathered outside. We had a kind of rucksack but its contents were controlled. You could take food and a thermos flask but no bottles [which could be broken and used as a weapon] or cameras. If you were on the early shift you'd be given breakfast at the barracks. The *Postenführer* [man in charge] had binoculars and a Very light pistol. The leader of the first group would say, "We are all present and we are prepared", then the leader of the second group would say that, too. The company Commander or sometimes his deputy would address us. Only then were we told where we had to go and with whom.' There were two Guards to a watchtower.

'The Commander had a piece of paper and he'd read out who was the *Postenführer* of each watchtower and who was his companion, an ordinary Guard. During the first year the watchtowers had names but after that they were given numbers, so Ackerstrasse [at Bernauer Strasse] was 25. We received the "watch tower table" which was four pages full of technical instructions. For example, which order you should fire the Very lights, which colours, who should respond to them and so on. These were changed every four weeks. When you were in the watchtower and wanted to signal an escape you had a button, but if you happened to be patrolling between watchtowers you fired the Very light to signal it.

'The Commander might speak about the previous day, evaluating any incidents. Then the pairs of Border Guards stepped forward and were given a special order. "Border break-outs are to be avoided. People who try to damage the border are to be arrested or destroyed." There was no specific shoot-to-kill order written down – the order was always given orally.'

The Border Guards were required (in theory, certainly) to give a warning shot and if an escaper ignored that, to shoot to wound. 'Everybody knew that it is very difficult to target, say, someone's arm at a distance and we had Russian machine pistols, 30 bullets in the magazine and 30 in your pocket [and firing in bursts threatened precision].'

They were taken to their watchtowers by lorry, the pairs dropped off along the way. There was a metal gate at the inner wall and the *Postenführer* opened it with a key, and locked it after they had gone through (but 'sometimes they forgot to lock it again and if the Commander came past and noticed, they were in trouble'). They walked to the watchtower and the handover required its own special ritual because at no moment must security be off-balance. They positioned themselves at each side of the watchtower ('one to secure this direction, one to secure that direction') while the ordinary Guard came down and replaced the *Postenführer* who went up and had the watchtower formally handed over to him. The departing *Postenführer* came down and replaced the newly arrived ordinary Guard, who went up inside the watchtower. The replaced pair walked to the gate, went through, locked it and waited for the bus to come back from its dropping-off points. 'It was said that if all four of them had been in the watchtower at the same time for the handover they'd talk to each other and not be so attentive' – being in fact, off balance, and any escaper watching diligently over days or weeks would observe that.

Once settled, the two Guards faced the eight hours. There was nothing to do except watch and talk. 'After some time you'd know each of the seventy people in the group and their lives. You'd also talk about possible situations and what you'd do. "What if an escaper came from just *there*?" I don't know of any Border Guard who said "I won't shoot" although I am sure some of them thought that.'

These strange, forced relationships had, of necessity, an undercurrent running through. Would any Guard broach the subject of escaping themselves? I asked Egersdörfer if, during these long hours of talking, he felt the Guard with him was looking for his reaction, probing a little. He only had that feeling once, he said, and then of course there was always the risk that they'd been put up to it by the Stasi to gauge *his* reaction. It happened on patrol in Bernauer Strasse and the other Guard asked 'What would you do if I was going to escape?' Egersdörfer replied 'Rubbish. You couldn't get over the wall – it's 3 metres high.' Egersdörfer, who cut the conversation with the Guard at that point, is still not sure whether he was serious or not. Border Guards were known to kid each other about these matters, and sometimes even pretend they were going to make a run for it, but these were visible games and definitely not serious; they passed the time.

'Each group had a Stasi officer and he rated Guards for reliability. They always paired one who was reliable and the other who was not so reliable. If the Stasi officer noticed that one particular pair got on well together they were kept apart. The watchtowers didn't all have the same status – some were more important than others. They were termed "confirmed" and "unconfirmed".'

There was also the matter of communicating with headquarters, other watchtowers and signalling an escape attempt. 'We had three buttons you could push: one [the middle button] to talk to the section leader, one to talk to another watchtower and a third so you could listen to what everybody was saying. You could not speak to another watchtower without everyone hearing – although we did say funny things sometimes and make jokes. After two years, you could see on a board which watchtower was speaking. This was only within a section. If something had to be reported, it would go to headquarters who would contact the other sections.

'We had heating but it was cold in the winter. The heating was the same as in the old overground trains, metal heaters they put under the seats and which people took for their summer houses. They were quite good!'

The watchtowers had no toilets and the bodily functions might themselves have pitched security off-balance so a ritual for this had to be enacted, too. 'If someone wanted to relieve themselves, they called for the patrolling jeep. You had to wait for this to arrive. One Guard would go upstairs to replace the man who needed to go, he went down and did it against the inner wall. Then he went back up, replaced the replacement, and the patrol jeep went on its way.

'In my time, you had windows consisting of three panes of glass and the middle pane could be opened but if the situation was urgent and you didn't have time, you shot through the glass. In fact, in my time not all watchtowers had windows which could be opened.' This meant, of course, that the glass was not bulletproof, making the Border Guards themselves targets for any sniper in the West. 'When you are in a watchtower for eight hours, you think about these things. In a sense, you were a prisoner of the wall. And it was very hard at New Year because if you were patrolling they'd throw fireworks at you.

'When your shift was over, your feelings were always the same: "Thank God I didn't have to shoot." Another feeling was always the same, too, for all the Guards: "If you shoot, you may kill somebody and if you don't shoot you will be punished." Everybody hoped it wouldn't happen in their section on their shift.'

(As it happened, Egersdörfer never did have to shoot in his three years. He was asked at an interview in January 2001 if he would have done. 'I have thought about this a lot and today it is easy to say, "No, I wouldn't" but at that time I think I would. That was because of our education and our political training. We were told that everyone who tried to escape was a criminal and we were told this in a way which we really believed.')

'One of my first periods of duty as *Postenführer* was during the night of 11/12 June on the watchtower *Humboldthafen*. It stood about 10 metres from the railway viaduct where trains and the S-bahn came from Friedrichstrasse station and went over to the Lehrter station in the West. At about 22.00 we replaced the other pair of Border Guards. On a watchtower, there are always two directions that have to be guarded: always the main direction (areas with obstructions to a clear line of sight, difficult to overlook, with buildings on them, etc.) and this is always the direction for which the *Postenführer* is responsible. In contravention of the regulations, I let the other Guard persuade me that he could do my job and he took the main direction, which was to the left. This section included the railway viaduct and the unlighted railway line which you could see at an angle of 20 degrees. I secured the direction to the right, a section of about 200 metres up to the checkpoint at Invalidenstrasse. No incidents happened during that night.

'The morning shift arrived at 6.00. While we were cleaning our weapons at about 7.30 in the barracks we were called to the company Commander. We were asked who was in charge and whether we had noticed anything. We said no. What could it have been? The Commander said that a ladder had been discovered leaning against the railway viaduct. He asked us again but we said we had not noticed anything and we were allowed to leave.

'What if a person really had escaped along the viaduct and my Guard hadn't noticed it? The most impossible thoughts went through my head. I was in charge, I was responsible. The punishment could easily be prison and for days I could hardly sleep – there was this permanent uncertainty – but we continued our guard duties.'

17 June 1974 *Guiseppe Savoca, believed to be a 6-year-old Italian living in West Berlin, drowned.*
21 June 1974 *A man, possibly a Border Guard and between 30 and 40, was fatally shot at the wall.*

'One afternoon, which must have been around 30 June,' Egersdörfer says, 'myself and the other Guard, plus the political education officer responsible for our company, were summoned to the Commander. Two civilians were present. We were asked again whether we had noticed something unusual that night of 11/12. He informed us that between 02.00 and 03.00, the night-time break when the S-bahn wasn't operating, a male person had crawled under the railway lines in the direction of the Lehrter station. The incident became known because the person returned to the Chauseestrasse checkpoint on 15 June without having given himself over to any West Berlin authority.[6] We were told to leave.

'Some days later, the incident was evaluated in front of the whole company and the company Commander was very upset that such a thing had happend in his company. From that time on, he would remind me of it at any opportunity he got.'

In May, Brandt resigned as Chancellor of West Germany, brought down after a GDR spy was discovered in his office. Paradoxically, by now the GDR was an accepted member of the international community, and the international community itself – or rather thirty-five European countries plus the United States and Canada – prepared to regulate its affairs. The postwar boundaries were recognised and human rights (including the free movement of people and ideas across frontiers) were agreed. It was known as the Helsinki Agreement and it was signed in August 1975.

The importance of this in the East remains problematical but there can be no doubt it generated hope and a subsequent disillusion when little or nothing changed. Frank Eigenfeld, an Eastern biologist, has said that 'during the seventies, hope blossomed again because of the Warsaw Pact treaties with the Federal Republic, and when those did not end up changing much, we began to hope again during the so-called Helsinki process.'[7]

On 25 August, with the episode of the viaduct escape still unresolved, Egersdörfer got five days' detention and, 'to be honest, I was happy not to have experienced something worse'.

The paranoia pervaded everything. Egersdörfer records this:

In the summer of 1974 Guards were in a street in the area of Bernauer Strasse, near the house that formed the inner wall.[8] A woman of about 35 approached our Trabant Kübel[9] and said, 'I do not know whether you are the right people to speak to but I live in this house and every evening – and during the night – I can hear knocking and scratching noises from the basement nearest to the border. It's the basement of a man who was in prison once for trying to escape. Maybe he is digging a tunnel to West Berlin[10] because such things are said to have happened in the past.' Then she said goodbye and went away. I reported the incident and we were told to go back in one hour. When we got there a man in civilian clothing was waiting for us and he introduced himself as an employee of the Ministry of State Security. He asked us about the incident and showed the strongest interest in the woman who'd talked to me. I couldn't give him her name because we hadn't thought of asking her for it so a description was all I could do. I don't know if anything came of the incident.

Egersdörfer remembers something else:

Twice a year, our company was deployed in the section of area 35, which went from the bank of the Spree at the Reichstag via the Brandenburg Gate to the south – every six months every company had to go to a field camp for training [and therefore had to be replaced]. I was on the night shift in the section from the

Brandenburg Gate to the checkpoint at Friedrich-Zimmer Strasse [Checkpoint Charlie]. I was patrolling on a motorbike. At about 8.30 in the evening it was already dark and the watchtower at the Brandenburg Gate informed us that 'a male person' stood at the inner wall. I was ordered to check this person. We went there and saw him. I opened the gate through the inner wall so that my driver could take the motorbike out. I approached the person and asked him for his identity card. There was no permission in the document for him to be in the border area and it gave Guben [on the Polish border] as his place of residence. He was dressed very normally, an anorak, jeans. I asked him what he was doing and he answered, 'I want to go over there!' I asked him, 'What do you mean by over there?' He said, 'Well, over there!' and he pointed towards West Berlin. I asked, 'Where is the other one?', on the assumption that there would generally be two making an escape attempt. 'I am alone!' I said, 'You are now under arrest. If you try to escape I will use my pistol.' He nodded – that was all. I checked him over and then fired my Very light – one green star. Shortly after, the company Commander came, questioned him once again and took him in a Trabant Kübel to a police station. I learned later that the man wanted to go to West Berlin because of family difficulties.

In 1975 Pastor Manfred Fischer, a Westerner and a Lutheran, assumed his duties in his parish on Bernauer Strasse. The church he ought to have taken over – the Church of Reconciliation – was on the Eastern side, actually within the death strip, and closed. The two cemeteries were on the Eastern side, also: the inner wall ran along the cemetery borders but the exclusion zone – beyond which people were forbidden to go without permission, as a way of further minimising escapes – ran through the cemeteries. To visit a grave, you had to apply for a special permit – a *Grabkarte*: 'Permission to go to the exclusion zone between the GDR and Westberlin [sic].'

Each card, coloured green, was numbered and stated which cemetery could be visited. It carried full details of the applicant – name, age, where born, present address. It stated that the card was only valid in connection with a *Deutscher-Personalausweis-Nummer* (identity card number). A Roman IV on it meant the card-holder was male, a V meant female. It was issued by the cemetery management and the card bore the formidable official designation of I/16.01 F250/67 KB 2070.

(There was also a border pass: 'Permission to enter the exclusion zone at the state border of the GDR and Westberlin.' For this the applicant had to provide a photograph as well as give personal details. There was also a *Passierschein*, which allowed someone, for a limited period of time, to enter the exclusion zone at the state border of the GDR and West Berlin for either private or official reasons. People who were to spend longer than twelve hours within this exclusion zone had to report that. The *Passierschein* was valid only with the person's identity card. Either 'private' or 'official' could be typed over using the traditional row of capital Xs.)

By 1975 a new church had been built on the Western side and that is where Pastor Fischer took up his duties. He had never met nor knew anything about the part of his congregation in the East, and had not, of course, been able to pay even a visit to the church.

Fischer understood the extraordinary history of Bernauer Strasse where, 'if the residents on the Eastern side leant out of their windows before 13 August 1961 they were in the West. Before that, for these people it was not a dramatic thing. They opened their front doors and stepped across without thinking about it.

'When I came the wall was up, but not the final kind of wall which the world remembers from 1989. It was being renewed and reconstructed all the time. The parish borders in Berlin are not accurate, if I can put it like that. There was a little bit of my parish in the district of Mitte [East] but most of it was in Wedding [West]. When Wedding was built up – and became a new district made up of three former districts – the parish boundary remained the same. I didn't know how many members of my parish were on the Eastern side and I didn't know their names. I had no information.

'We'd had the biggest urban renewal project in Europe so everything was torn down and rebuilt. In this way I was really used to seeing things blown up! The more modern wall was built in 1980 and from sometime in 1983 we got to know that the Church of Reconciliation would be blown up. The problem was that the explosion would break windows in the houses on the Western side and people could be injured by flying glass. These people would have to know when they should open their windows to prevent that.'

Talks began in East Berlin between the government and the religious leaders there, and then with politicians and the police in the West. 'They said the church would be blown up but I didn't know when. That was the situation in 1985.

'The Eastern government was a very, very accurate bureaucratic government. They did nothing until it was planned, permission sought, paper, paper, permission, planned, re-planned, paper, paper, permission. They told the West Berlin police of the whole operation so that the windows would be opened.

'I had a sabbatical and in January I was invited to the United States. I was in New York staying in a church apartment and I happened to be watching television. In the United States there is very little information about other countries, so I could not be forewarned. It was three o'clock. I watched the church being blown. In one sense I was not surprised because I knew it was going to happen at some time, but I was very surprised to see it on the television. This was my church although I had never been in it.

'Your feelings change between when something happens and when you become fully aware it has happened: these are two separate moments even when you see something and you are involved in it. It's the same when someone dies: the full impact is not always immediate. I needed one year to really get this mixture of feelings resolved. How do you call it when you say goodbye to someone who dies? A funeral. I tried to make a funeral sermon – a memorial service – for this church and I thought for a year how best to do it and first I asked a lot of people for their feelings.

'We did it one year later, in May, and it lasted three days. One man composed music for us and we had an open-air choir. There was a girl who organised dancing and she danced against the wall – which was not allowed. When we were going to do this I had to talk to the police and ask them not to notice! Every event which took place near the wall on the Western side was accompanied by the West Berlin police: you were not even allowed to touch the wall because it belonged to the East and was on Eastern land – when they wanted to work on it they built a wire pen on our side for their workers to come through into. Thinking about this sort of thing will last thirty years at least.'[12]

The division, this unkindest cut, was merciless on families. Brigitta Schimke, who lived in the city centre facing the twin curved roads and the sunken garden – which had now become the wall – still had a sister and brother on the other side in the West:

In general, living in front of the wall one became accustomed to it because the view you had of it was an everyday view. My brother Dieter was an engineer and when foreign businessmen visited his factory he showed them round West Berlin, including the wall. Opposite our apartment was an observation platform in the West and he made sure to take them there. If he knew a delegation was coming he'd write to me – we didn't have a telephone – saying which day and at what time he would be there. I'd stand on our little balcony and look at him while he told the delegation he had a sister over there. They couldn't really believe it. When I saw him I turned away from the watchtower in the death strip so I couldn't be observed, and I gave him tight little waves.

Very bright neon lights came on every night and if it was foggy or rainy they put them on during the day, too. The Border Guards patrolled outside on foot all day and night on the street outside my apartment which was in front of the inner wall. We gave them warm drinks when it was cold or it was Christmas. They were not supposed to go into the houses although they did when it was cold. They were never from Berlin, a deliberate tactic because then you wouldn't have Berliners shooting at Berliners, and also if they were Berliners people might know them.

One day a man made a run across the death strip and managed to reach the far wall but the roll-bar on top of it there stopped him. They shot him although I think he only had a slight injury to his knee. A very brave doctor from the hospital round the corner – a woman – rushed to the scene and demanded the Border Guards brought the man to her so she could treat him.

We did have problems living facing the wall. They installed lamps in the cellar so they could see if anybody was tunnelling there and they closed the attic – because we were so close, it might have been possible to string a rope across somehow. My husband had a 17-year-old cousin from Rostock who came to visit us and he was interrogated by the Border Guards because they thought it suspicious that someone would come from Rostock to so close to the wall. He had to tell them he was just on a visit.'[12]

The way the world is, and will always be, there was humour at the wall as well as grief. Egersdörfer recounts how, being so close to the West, with binoculars he could see across in the most vivid detail. I mention that I'd been told the Guards had a method of spreading the news if a pretty girl was undressing on the other side so they could have a look. 'Yes, and there were some girls who knew what they were doing because they would do it all the time. We could even see their buttons!' Were the women exercising power over the Guards, who could do nothing except watch? 'But we had to watch them! It was our task and our duty! There was one particular girl and she'd been given a nickname, *Long Tooth*, although I don't know why. In German it's not actually a nice name – you'd call somebody you didn't like *Long Tooth*. I can't say whether she was attractive or not because if you've been in a watchtower for hours any woman might be. *Long Tooth* was so popular that sometimes she was even mentioned in the Commander's briefing before our shifts. He'd say she'd been seen at such-and-such a time. Some people assumed she might have been paid to do it because she did it so regularly and professionally. There was a file on her.'

In the paranoia, this assumption was no light thing. If *Long Tooth* turned her light on, drew her curtains back and began stripping, of course the Guards would watch – and be off-balance in their attention to duty. 'The Commanders were always afraid of such incidents.'

Egersdörfer could also see pedestrians in the West, and cars, and into a Western corner supermarket. He could even read the prices on the items. 'I knew the people were quite well off. I thought that although all this was only 6 or 7 metres away I would never go to it. In a way that was depressing. It would have been easier to go to the moon than cross the 6 or 7 metres. The moon was closer. But you had your family and your home and a good many people still work on the assumption of "Why didn't you come?" I can only speak for myself, and though I thought about it I never wanted to escape. And you must remember that we knew so little of what we know now. We knew there had been some resolutions in Helsinki [the Agreement on rights of travel] but we didn't really know what was in the texts because they were published only once in *Neues Deutschland* and then taken out immediately.'

Hartmut Richter, then a resident of West Berlin for almost ten years, had been able to return to East Germany because, from 1972 when Honecker replaced Ulbricht and applied for United Nations recognition, people who had escaped before 1971 were pardoned and could make visits. Richter became involved in helping people escape but, in March 1975, was caught attempting to get his 21-year-old sister Elke to West Berlin in the boot of his car. He was held for a year in Stasi custody then sentenced to the maximum fifteen years in prison for 'trafficking in human beings'. He was transferred from one prison to another because he exercised a bad influence on his fellow inmates.

3 April 1975 *Norbert Halli, 22, was fatally shot – he may have been trying to get past Border Guards in disguise.*
5 May 1975 *Mert Cetin, a 5-year-old Turk living in West Berlin, drowned.*

'Although people had generally got used to the wall,' Thomas Flemming would record in *The Berlin Wall*, 'there were still events which caused the West Berliners' emotions to rise. One such instance was when 5-year-old Cetin from Kreuzberg fell into the Spree when he was playing. Some West Berlin divers arrived within a few minutes but were not allowed into the water and had to watch helplessly as the boy drowned, because at this point the whole breadth of the Spree belonged to East Berlin. A GDR border boat arrived too late at the scene of the accident and could only recover the Turkish boy's body from the water.

'This incident released a storm of anger and indignation. Hundreds of people gathered on the Kreuzberg bank of the Spree and held up banners accusing the SED regime of "Child murder" and "Inhumanity". These kinds of events, which brought the Wall sharply into the public consciousness, did not fit into the GDR's plans. After the boy's death East and West came to an agreement about "unbureaucratic" emergency help with "accidents at the border".'[13]

The RIAS radio reporter Peter Schultz covered the wall going up and he, like Brigitta Schimke, explains the pain of division as it unfolded over the years. In August 1961 his wife Astrid had been pregnant:

Her parents lived in the GDR 50 kilometres from Berlin and it was a great shock for her when our daughter Martina was born two weeks later and she couldn't see her parents and they could not see their grandchild. We sent photographs but there was no other form of contact – no telephones – although we received letters from them and so we knew that they knew they were grandparents. The next time we saw them was Christmas 1963 when, for the first time, West Berliners got permits to cross.

We all crossed to East Berlin and then they could see Martina. We met at a bar which was run by my uncle in Senefelderplatz, near the U-bahn station. It was very emotional. I had had no contact with my uncle except letters, but that was a normal situation after 1961. I can't imagine how it was normal – impossible. On one side we were so happy to see each other but on the other side we knew that we would part again: we were only allowed to stay that one day and you had to be back at midnight. We were there from nine in the morning until six or seven in the evening.

The next time we saw them was one year later. Every time we had Christmas or Easter you could get the permits. The bar at

Senefelderplatz closed but my uncle still lived there. In 1965 my wife's parents got to West Berlin – it was what they called a gathering of families (they were pensioners) and you could apply for that, bring your furniture. Of course they had to leave their house and the ground it stood on. These were expropriated and the house had a new owner.

My uncle is dead. He died in 1966 – we heard by letter – and, no, I couldn't go to his funeral. I'd have been allowed to go if it had been my father or mother but it wasn't a first degree relative. All that . . . it's over now, thank God.

Because of my profession at RIAS, I've seen the whole world, the USA, Asia, Japan but not Potsdam where I studied. I saw American presidents here and in America but not my neighbours, not Potsdam. What is the feeling? I don't know. It's crazy. I've been back to Potsdam, I've friends there – colleagues from the school – and we met. I think [spring 1991] it will need a long time to get used to it mentally, to rediscover ourselves.'[14]

<u>17 May 1975</u>   *Henry Weise, 23, died at the wall.*
<u>4 November 1975</u>   *Lothar Hennig, 23, died at the wall.*

The man who fled with his family, and who would only give the name Mateus ('that should be enough'), remembers 'my aunt's son worked for the Stasi. I only saw him when I went back to the East for my grandmother's funeral and he spoke no word. That was German family life for you. Pretty unbelievable.'

The division did not even spare those who worked for international companies.

Erdmute Greis-Behrendt of Reuters describes in a telling phrase that 'then came a very different time – I went back to West Berlin in 1976'. She had not been there, of course, since 13 August 1961 when she'd travelled home quite normally on the U-bahn and noticed nothing unusual. Now 'it was the year after the Helsinki Agreement and the Reuters bureau chief in East Berlin applied for me to go to London for some training. It was turned down flatly. Since 1972 we had had to pay our salaries into a government department account and then we would get it back. It was for people working for foreigners or foreign companies. These were now the people who would issue the passports and they said, "No way." The correspondent said, "Right, I will raise this matter at the Helsinki follow-up conference in Vienna"' which was due imminently. 'He was really very good at it! A couple of days after that, the department phoned me up very excited and said, "Come to our office immediately and bring your nicest passport photo."'

Erdmute couldn't believe what she was hearing. To get the passport 'took a little while – but a couple of weeks later I held it. I had a small son, 6 months old, and we were sitting in our flat, my husband and I, wondering whether I should use that visa to go and stay in the West. I said I just couldn't, the baby was too small and I just couldn't.

'I hadn't been to West Berlin since 1961. It was absolutely . . . amazing, although of course I had known it before. West Berlin was brighter and it was louder and there was more traffic but it hadn't really changed. I crossed at Friedrichstrasse – I took the S-bahn and got off at Savigny Platz because that was where the [Western] Reuters office used to be. I knew what the office looked like because before the wall I used to go over there. I wanted to try a trip across first. I went over secretly, so to speak, and thought, "Good God, I can!" I just had to sneak over and see some people and get the feeling, you know. I went back to East Berlin and told everybody I had been in the West and people just looked at me.

'Then, when the day really came for my flight to London, it was the correspondent who took me to Tegel. And then whoosh . . . London, which was lovely! I had never been before. When I was in London there were so many new impressions coming towards me but I never for a minute thought it was necessary to stay. Somehow, suddenly everything looked so normal and the East German problems were so far away. I phoned my husband every now and then and asked how my son was, and how things were going, and it didn't seem necessary to do anything drastic. It was only after I came back that it struck me it was a chance I hadn't used.'[15]

There was a fundamental misconception in the West that Eastern countries, having signed the Helsinki Agreement, would honour it however reluctantly. They were wrong. In 1976 the GDR started to build their Mark 111 wall, the most sophisticated of all. It replaced the old horizontal lintels laid one on top of another between vertical posts, with self-standing L-shaped slabs which could be joined to form a continuous, smooth surface. These were topped by a concrete cylinder so that anyone leaping up could gain no handhold because their hands would slip back over the cylinder. (The wall round the Brandenburg Gate was constructed in a different way, broader and lower, as an anti-tank barrier.) The slabs were 3.6 metres (11.81 feet) high minus the cylinder, 1.2 metres (3.9 feet) wide and weighed 2,750 kilograms (6,062 pounds). Each segment cost 359 Ostmarks and about 45,000 were put in place.

Erdmute Greis-Behrendt's father had remarried and reached retirement age. 'You could just apply to go to the West and he was permitted to do that. It was difficult because he asked each of us, his three children, whether we agreed to this or if we had any objection. I said, "Of course not. Why should I? It is your decision and you are old enough to make your own decisions. You don't have to ask me." He said he needed it in writing and we all wrote little letters saying, "I have no objection to my father moving to West Berlin." I couldn't go, of course not, but he could have come back to visit at any time. He came back but he didn't really visit us. It was his second wife. She didn't like his children.

'I didn't have relatives in the West but I did have lots of friends – I'd gone to school in West Berlin. When I got my first passport to go to England in 1976 – the invitation to do some advanced schooling was actually just a pretence for getting me out – I visited them all.'

Greis-Behrendt was in an almost unique position in that she was working for an international news agency and the only one which had offices in both parts. Yet, before that day in 1976 when she sneaked across, she couldn't go to the other one. *How did she cope?*

'We were so absolutely busy I hardly had a moment's time to consider it. Of course I noticed it when there was a free moment and I reflected on things. I knew that it was dreadful and of course I had so many friends in West Berlin.'

But you were in daily contact with the forbidden West.

'Of course, but it was a nice contact.'

It was also a constant reminder, and most people in the East didn't by definition have that.

Incidentally, Reuters correspondents were changed every eighteen months because, in Greis-Behrendt's words, 'East Germany was regarded as a hardship country.' That meant a procession of corres-pondents came and each brought their 'new library of books and I read through them'.

It remains astonishing how well she took it all.

'Well, what else was there to do?'

Go crazy?

'But I didn't want to go crazy! I was quite young when the wall went up, 23, 24, and I thought, "It can't be the end of the world, it can't be the end of my life, it won't last that long."'

But it did, and, the way the world is, abnormality becomes normal given a decade or two.

<u>16 February 1977</u> *Dietmar Schwietzer, 19, tried to get across from some allotments at 7.07 a.m. The Border Guard noticed him after he had clambered over the inner wall but triggered the alarm – in some places the border had acoustic and electric alarm systems. After a warning shot he was hit and died being transported to hospital.*

The division between East and West Berlin did not spare the railway system, originally designed and built to service a whole city.

To see in one's mind's eye the geometry of Friedrichstrasse station is not at all easy, because here absurdity piled upon absurdity. Friedrichstrasse housed both a proper overground railway and an underground line, and was itself divided by internal walls. The underground line ran from the south of West Berlin under East Berlin, through disused stations bearing spidering pre-war gothic platform signs. These stations were guarded by GDR soldiers and the trains never stopped except at Friedrichstrasse, where only Westerners could board or alight if they had the right papers. The underground then continued under East Berlin until it surfaced in the north of West Berlin. Every day on this line commuters passed under the wall while they read their newspapers, barely noticing the ghost stations along the way, and re-emerged still reading them.

The railway station at Friedrichstrasse served as a terminal and a connection, and internal walls, partitions, separated these. The terminal was for domestic Eastern travellers: they arrived, got off and went down stairways into East Berlin. The connection was for international travellers coming in from, or going to, West Berlin and beyond to western Europe.

As at the other checkpoints, Border Guards controlled it and the Stasi were the customs, checking and examining and stamping papers. If you were a Westerner or you were an Easterner with a *Visum* you could pass through the checkpoint, rise to the international platform and take a most normal train ride through the wall. A few minutes later you were at the Lehrter station in West Berlin – which Lutz Stolz had been due to go to on 13 August 1961 to meet the other members of his football team.

Friedrichstrasse had a tall room, coated in something not dissimilar to lavatory tiles, where Easterners waited for friends, lovers and relatives from the west to come through a big metal door from the international platform. Beside this same door they bade farewell when visits were over. The room was known as the Hall of Tears.

The underground, a potential escape route to West Berlin, was so prohibited to Easterners that it did not appear on their city maps and anyone born after 13 August 1961 had no idea it existed. Many of these young people who often frequented the terminal above it were openly shocked when, after 9 November 1989, they learned that the underground ran there, and had always run there.

Peter Dick was a Canadian who went to live in West Berlin and became fascinated by the absurdities:

> I started to picture these dilapidated subway stops that had not been used since before the wall but nothing prepared me for the experience of riding through them. You emerged from a dark tunnel into a station/platform and the train slowed to a crawl as you went through (without stopping, of course). Unlike all the other stops on the western side, or the Freidrichstrasse 'official' stop, these unused stations were dimly lit, crusty and rough-finished in concrete. In some places light bulbs hung from the ceiling on their wires.
>
> At either end of the platform stood a lone guard with rifle on shoulder. A friend informed me that these stations had to be guarded from potential Eastern citizens who might try to sneak into the station and somehow hop aboard a moving train. The guards were there to prevent any possible escape via the subway or unused stations. I looked at some of these stations and realised that at one time, when the city had been whole, they had been some of the busiest stations in Berlin, people flowing through them. I had dreams about this for months. Riding a different line one day – the S-bahn line – there was an underground section where we went through the Unter den Linden station, which again must have been the heartbeat of Berlin before the wall and it, too, was now derelict.'[16]

The division did not spare those who, by geographical chance, lived in the historical enclaves like Steinstücken, and Eiskeller further north. In fact there was a sort of enclave in the city centre, the Lenne Triangle, too. This was a wedge of land butting onto Potsdamer Platz; it was technically in the Soviet Sector, but when the wall was built the GDR felt it would be easier to abandon it, and did. The triangle was allowed to grow wild until the West Berlin Senate bought it in 1988. Before 1988, it had never been checked for unexploded wartime bombs because the West wasn't allowed to go there and the East showed no interest in the place at all.

The division did spare Steinstücken, at least partially. Kurt Behrendt, the amateur radio operator who'd moved there in 1957, says that 'in 1971 there was a conference of the four Allies and they made the Berlin Agreement. They decided that since Steinstücken was the only enclave where people lived out of a total sum of ten enclaves [well, nearly], it should belong to West Berlin and should be given free access. A road had to connect it with West Berlin and was built in a relatively short period of time after the two German sides had decided exactly where it should go. They agreed that the strip should be 20 metres wide, plus a 6-metre path for bicycles and pedestrians, and that it should be incorporated into the district of Zehlendorf.'[17]

Eiskeller had one resident family, the Schabes. The father, Martin, says:

'Steinstücken was an enclosure, and Eiskeller – ice cellar, because there was one which kept the ice for Falkensee – was an enclosure. We had a normal way to go out, well, simply a path, no tarmac. There are photographs of my son Erwin cycling to school being escorted by a British armoured car. The Russians cut the road from here to Spandau and we couldn't cross but the British Army came and said 'please remove that'. Erwin's school was in Spandau and he was talked to several times by Soviet and GDR military. Sometimes he didn't want to go to school and pretended they'd been talking to him as an excuse! We always had to report the incidents to the British because it was their sector and they patrolled here. Sometimes the Soviets and East Germans wouldn't allow Erwin through so we decided to call for an escort. We even had a British military helicopter which was only removed in 1990 when the wall went.

I was born in Caputh, which is near Potsdam. My father was a gardener at the Sans Souci palace but in 1926 he went to the eastern side of the Oder, which is today Poland. I was a soldier for five years during the Hitler war and, from the beginning up to the end, I was in Russia. I was taken prisoner in 1945 – I was captured near Frankfurt-an-der-Oder and taken to Kiev by train.

I was a prisoner for three years and was one of the first to be released from the camps because I'd struck up a friendship with a Russian doctor. In this area they said *Schabe* for Sunday and I was called Schabe so it was a kind of sympathy. I had to repair fences and we all ate out of one pot. We worked in the forest cutting trees – we had to cut a certain amount of trees at a certain length. We were allowed to collect mushrooms and I've never eaten so many in my life! During my time in the camp, I experienced that the ordinary Russian people were very friendly. They gave us bread.

When I was released I went to my parents, who lived in the
district of Frankfurt-Oder. They didn't know I was alive. Then I
came to Berlin and it was *kaput, kaput, alles kaput*. I didn't
recognise Berlin. Terrible.

Then I came here and built it all by myself. In 1948 you didn't
see that it was virtually surrounded by the Soviet Zone. That
started in 1953 with the controls. Before 1953 it was just an
ordinary fence. In fact, when I first moved here there was
nothing, just the farm and fields. In a sense, Eiskeller belonged
politically to the east, to the district of Nauen, although in reality
[on the maps] only the woodland in the middle actually belonged
to the east. We'd go into the woods to gather mushrooms and it
wasn't a problem. You only needed a piece of paper and nobody
really cared.

After 1953 I helped a lot of people to escape – a young couple,
who were engaged, got here. They asked me if they could get to
West Berlin and I said, 'You certainly can't but the East German
military know me and I will help you to do it.' I had a horse and
cart. I put them on the cart, covered them with straw and got
them through. There were no British soldiers yet.

The nearest shop we had to go to Spandau in the West – up to
1953 we went shopping in Falkensee in the Soviet Zone but after
1953 we couldn't even go to Schönwalde [a hamlet just up the
road]. They built a fence, and they built it very quickly. Later they
reinforced it with metal supports. Some people tried to escape
over it and we'd hear shooting. We saw the Russians on patrol.
[Ultimately, when the last generation of the wall was in place] at
night you could read the newspapers by the light from the arc-
lamps.'[18]

The people who watched over this division – the Border Guards –
were charged with sparing no one and ultimately would not be
spared themselves. That ought to have included Honecker who, as
head of the GDR, bore ultimate responsibility for the shoot-to-kill
policy, but a court case against him collapsed on the grounds of ill-
health. This is how Honecker thought.[19]

The regulations for securing the border are established in the
border law. Fatal shots as occurred in the FRG have never been
introduced in this country.
Was it a shot with prior warning or what was it?
You have to enquire about the rules on the use of firearms.

They are the same in the FRG as in the GDR, and are as the present rules for the police.

Haven't you talked about it with West German politicians again and again?

I had several talks about it, among others with Strauss [Franz Josef Strauss, Minister-President of Bavaria and an opponent of Ostpolitik] and also with Social Democratic ministers. I asked them, 'Tell me, what about your rules on the use of firearms?' They said that suspects are required to stop. If these persons flee, there is a warning: 'Stop!' And if the person has not stopped by then, there is a warning shot. It was the same with our police in the GDR.

In connection with the development of the relations between the GDR and the FRG, I also endeavoured, as far as it was possible, to humanize the relations in this field. It took many years to reach a situation in which it was recommended to Border Guards not to make use of their firearms unless they had to defend their own lives – in other words, if they had to claim the right to self-defence. This was in 1986 and 1987.

It was also planned that warning shots should not be fired any more so that the other side could not launch campaigns in the media on the continued existence of the so-called shoot-to-kill command. This had been our policy from 1986/1987 onwards. We did not want to have ourselves 'disturbed' by shooting at the border. Therefore the then defence minister declared that a shoot-to-kill order did not exist at all.

Don't you feel sorry for about 200 people killed at the wall?

I feel sorry for our twenty-five comrades who have been treacherously murdered at the border. Our requests to the government of the Federal Republic to hand over these people were rejected.

Did you know that many people saw the wall as a declaration of the moral bankruptcy of socialism because it could not make people stay in the country?

What do you mean by 'many people'? The construction of the frontier had been a necessity in times of cold war. Thus we were able to stop the bleeding white of the GDR. You really have to stick to the decision taken by the members of the Warsaw Pact. It was done in order to safeguard peace and to secure the socialist society's construction.

These were not the words of a leader about to implement the Helsinki Agreement, or who had ever even considered implementing it, and the East made no attempt to disguise the fact that people were still trying to escape, with all the potential for tragedy that that carried. In July 1977, an attempt along the autobahn from Berlin to Helmstedt went horribly wrong. (The autobahn had become a favoured route to escape down because, since the transit agreement, fewer cars were searched.) A couple and their 6-month-old son were in the boot of an Opel, driven by a man hired for 3,000 DM. The car broke down and he spent a long time trying to flag down help before he got a tow to the checkpoint. By then the baby, who'd been tranquillised, had suffocated in the heat and lack of air. Discovered, a GDR court sentenced the driver to eight years in prison and the parents five years each.

<u>12 October 1977</u>   *Frank Neitzke, 19, died at the wall.*
<u>22 December 1977</u>   *Gerd-Michael Frenk, 31, died at the wall.*
<u>Around 2 April 1978</u>   *Hans-Joachim Manowski, a 34-year-old West German, died at the wall.*

Some of the Border Guards found themselves caught out by an anomaly, because when the wall finally fell they sought rehabilitation for deliberately shooting to miss. Peter Kull was a case in point.[20] He was posted to Berlin in October 1961, when he was 19, as a Guard. In February 1962 'I saw a man running across the death strip. As I outranked the soldier I was on duty with that day, I ordered that we go in the opposite direction the escapee was going. After I knew the man was through, I gave the alarm signal.'

Kull claimed that if he was being observed by other officers he 'simply aimed so that I would miss' the escapers and, once, fired at the wall rather than a man riding a bike across the death strip. He only just managed to explain that away. He was betrayed when he tried to help three people to get across, and was imprisoned and abused – nine months of solitary confinement when he had to stand facing a wall without moving for long periods. The abuse included being beaten unconscious. 'When I came to in my cell, I had a terrible pain between my legs. I thought they had only kicked me, but the nightmare was that there were burns all over my genitals. I guess they did it with a cigarette lighter.'

Kull, who kept as much documentation as he could, said 'I suffered and went to prison because I helped people try to flee a communist dictatorship. Afterwards everybody treated me like a criminal but my father told me, "Don't worry, Peter, some day people will look at you and say something different."' (After the wall fell Kull hoped 'this time had finally come'.)

None of this – the escapes, the failed escapes and the full apparatus to prevent the escapes – covers the breed of people everyone hated: those who pre-sold escapes and disappeared with the money. Wolf Quasner, a noted escape organiser has called them the 'rogues'. They came from the shadows, preyed on the yearnings of the vulnerable and merged back into the shadows. Quasner began organising escapes because he saw the misery the rogues were causing. Who they were, how many they were, how much they made and what devastation they wreaked cannot be quantified because the details still lurk in the shadows.

By 1978, one estimate suggested that more than 500 Western hire cars had been used to make escape attempts in the East. Karl Schwarz, speaking for the car rental industry in Düsseldorf, said: 'These escape operators never tell the car hire firm they are taking the vehicle into East Germany, let alone that they plan to use it to bring out refugees.'[21]

One case seems to encapsulate everything. West Berliner, Horst Poser, did a job for a celebrated escape organiser. He was smuggling a refugee family out through Czechoslovakia – the wall in Berlin and the German–German frontier were now as near impregnable as human planning could make them – and was caught. He was imprisoned in the GDR. He claimed he had been given amateurishly forged documents and sued the escape organiser for the 606 days he spent in prison. The Stasi supported Poser, as a ploy to get at – and destroy – the escape organiser. They cut his prison sentence and advanced him money towards paying his legal costs.[22]

The Western court, trapped in a truly desperate morass of the moral, the ethical and the legal, retreated to the only place which remained to it: the pragmatism of compromise. They awarded Poser damages, *small* damages.

Far away from all this, a simplistic man was preparing to confront the world by making no compromises. He was an old man and one who saw the world in black and white, not colour. The fact that he was neither tactician nor theoretician, neither academic nor sophisticate wouldn't have mattered except that, as President of the United States, he would be the most powerful man in the world. He called the Soviet Union the 'evil empire' and didn't intend to coexist with communism, but defeat it.

Whatever, the second bitter decade was over.

EIGHT

Thaw

I spent three wonderful weeks in Paris. As a result of all this, it became clear to me what an incredible crime the state had committed against us by never letting us travel. I stood in the cathedral at Notre Dame with tears in my eyes and could hardly believe that I was actually seeing such beauty.

Ursula Sydow,
East German Publishing Editor

Nobody knew. Nobody suspected. Nobody foresaw. The 1980s began with the GDR looking settled and relatively prosperous, and the FRG looking a model democracy and extremely prosperous. Neither country seemed to be living behind a façade. Both were welded into opposites: the GDR to the Soviet bloc, the Warsaw Pact and the COMECON trade organisation; West Germany to NATO and the European Union. More than that, each day which passed solidified this. West Germany's claim to be the only legitimate German state was demonstrably fiction and, although Western opinion polls suggested a certain reluctance to abandon the belief in eventual reunion, each passing day made that more remote, too. Nobody knew that the Soviet Union, for decades a secretive monolith, would begin to crack. Nobody suspected a thing.

In 1980, Ronald Reagan defeated Jimmy Carter for the American Presidency and the man of simple vision assumed the power. He understood, as so many Americans do, about winning and losing, and he mirrored America: he was a winner. He set about rearming to the point where, as someone observed, the United States could fight three major wars simultaneously.

Exact date unknown *A Border Guard called Walther was, it seems, a victim of an escape attempt.*

On 2 October 1980, the West German government bought Hartmut Richter out of prison (or exchanged him). He went to West Berlin where, he insists, the Stasi constantly tried to smear and destroy him. 'I only have a victim's [Stasi] file, not an offender's file,' he says. He claims that Stasi agents in the West bugged his apartment and tried to penetrate his circle of friends.

> 4 November 1980   *Ulrich Steinhauer, a 24-year-old corporal, was shot through the heart by the Border Guard with him out in the country to the east of West Berlin. The bullet struck him in the back and went through him. It happened at 4.35 p.m. and therefore in the darkness of late afternoon. As it would seem, the other Border Guard wanted to desert and Steinhauer had been trying to prevent him – five shots were fired at him.*

The GDR report of this incident lives on as a testament to a mindset which insisted on detailing everything, however meaningless. Apart from the fatal shot, Steinhauer had also been struck a glancing blow but the investigators were unable to 'ascertain whether this happened before or after death. Furthermore, neither the direction nor the precise circumstances' could be 'ascertained by turning the body.' Five shots were missing from the weapon and five shells were found. 'It is not known yet whether this was in individual shots or in quick succession. On the corpse there are no signs of hitting or strangling.'

> 22 November 1980   *Marietta Jirkowski, 18. Three people tried to get across at 3.40 a.m. Each had a ladder and they selected a spot out in the country to the east of West Berlin. Jirkowski was accompanied by two men. They got into the death strip but that triggered the automatic alarm. After a warning was shouted and fired, she was hit in the abdomen. She died of the injuries at 11.30 that night. One of the men got back and disappeared into the Eastern hinterland. An investigation did not locate the other man or resolve whether he reached the West.*

This book is not about the implosion of the GDR economy, or how fragile and trapped in a time warp that economy had really been, although the implosion would have a direct bearing on the wall. And if nobody knew, here are a couple of tantalising clues. A news item on a Western radio programme, broadcast as the 1980s began to unfold, said that one of the GDR's profitable exports to the

West had been cheap and reliable washing machines. Now, however, Western markets were demanding more sophisticated machines and the GDR seemed unable to regenerate and re-tool their manufacture. If they couldn't do that for something which earned priceless hard currency, what state was the rest of their industry in? The second clue was provided by a GDR radio presenter. I asked him when he realised it was going wrong. Although he couldn't remember the year he did remember the moment. He'd been driving to work and saw a queue outside a food shop and he hadn't seen that for many, many years.

16 March 1981   *Dr. Johannes Muschol, mid-20s, was in the death strip at 11.07 a.m. and ignored both a shout to stop and a single warning shot. As he reached the wall itself the Guard opened fire and killed him. His body was transported to the nearest Guard tower and then taken away.*

On 13 August 1981, the twentieth anniversary of the building of the wall, Hartmut Richter and some friends tried to put a wall round the *Aeroflot* offices in West Berlin.

The distance between here and there – between the two ends of Friedrichstrasse, if you like – and the cumulative effect which each passing day had had since 13 August 1961, is beautifully explored and defined by a piece written by author Irene Böhme.[1] It is about a Westerner visiting family or a friend in the East and if it is couched in general terms it gains from that. This scene was replicated a thousand times:

For the West German, work is something you do with zip and verve. Work is the source of one's success and money supply, not a subject for social occasions. At most you make a passing remark about a successful deal, or a coup that came off. If you've got problems at work, you maybe admit it to your spouse but hardly to your best friends. If you didn't take early retirement entirely voluntarily, you keep that inside the immediate family circle.

Western man is programmed for success, he must always appear fighting fit and hide his weak points. If he then encounters someone who positively savours the opportunity to expound the problems he has at work, he is shaken and horrified. The only explanation he can think of is that in the GDR people are totally destroyed by the state. If he says as much, his host suddenly becomes a passionate defender of the system. He had been talking about how he was feeling, his low spirits, the way in which, deep within himself, he enjoyed conflict, he had wanted to show how the pleasure he took in fatalism was an optimistic attitude to life, he had uncovered the complexities of his self-image. His guest can't have been listening if he now talks about the state and tries to force a political interpretation on personal feelings.

Our tragic search for what we have in common obliges us to play down this situation too. Conversation is diverted to other areas, preferably to cars: that's something you can always agree about. But the West German will be unable to forget that he has had to look into the soul of a broken man, and how abruptly this downtrodden creature began defending the state. And the East German will not be able to forget that he has bared his soul to a philistine, and tried to discuss the meaning of life with someone who is unwilling to give it a moment's thought. Both repress how uncomfortable they feel.

Again it is the impression of similarity that prevails, as though the discrepancies between them came from outside and arose purely by chance. The one is unaware just how much the Slav has already entered into his character. The other is unaware of just how much, in certain matters, he thinks and feels like an American. Both have a sense of something alien, and brush it aside, without thinking or speaking about it. Each regards his behaviour as normal, and it doesn't occur to him that he is different because for thirty-five years he has been living a different everyday life in a different Germany.

Us and them: there shouldn't be this distinction. They cling desperately to each other, so restricting each other's normal range of movements, and the fraternal embrace threatens to suffocate them.

Astonished at what he has seen, the West German returns home, satisfied with his good deed. He never said that he found the streets stank, he turned a blind eye to dirt and disorder, he enjoyed the countryside, and the art and architecture of the past. If he was perturbed, he kept the feeling under control, adopting a mien of provincial imperturbability. He has been a good guest, though it was a strain on his nerves and his purse. He decides to visit the GDR again, because he has come to understand how important his visit is for his compatriots. He has shaken off a few prejudices, but his opinion of the country has been confirmed. He shudders when he recalls how careful he had to be in his dealings with people, how much he could not say openly, how alien everything was to him. He now knows, with greater certainty, that he prefers his own cares and worries, and that not just his standard of living, but his way of living is better. He crosses the frontier, takes a deep breath, he's home again. He's carrying no objects of value in his suitcase but a sense of value has stirred within him.

The Easterner waves goodbye to the parting visitor, contentedly feeling that he's been a good host, that he's offered something that cannot be found elsewhere. It has been a strain on his nerves and his purse. He has shaken off a few prejudices, his opinion of these Westerners has been confirmed, you can't speak freely and openly with them. After this visit he knows with greater certainty that although he is poorer, his way of living is better. He takes a deep breath, he is home again. He sees these wall-skimmers on their way, as the farmer does the migrant birds. They come once a year, pecking and chirping, and then fly on.

4 June 1982   *Lothar Fritz Freie, a 27-year-old West German, was shot in the left hip and left upper leg at 11.20 p.m. on a bridge opposite the Wedding district. He was given first aid and, at 12.03, was taken to hospital. From 11.30 to 11.50, ten West Berlin policemen observed the incident.*

Dennis L. Bark had not only changed to studying history at Stanford, he had studied in Berlin and come to be fascinated by the city. A group of historians from all over the world, dedicated to private enterprise, met every two years and in 1982 held their gathering in Berlin. Bark says, 'I wanted to lay a wreath at the Fechter memorial and probably about 35 of them came. Important people were among them and it was a heavy deal. Afterwards Axel Springer gave a reception for all these people. It was quite something. I had been back to the spot many times and what I felt was, well, I'll tell you: 1982 I was forty and I thought, "Dennis, you are old enough to order your own wreath, to afford it, to decide what words you want to put on it and to get all these people to come. It's nice that you can do that."'

In October, Helmet Kohl became Chancellor of the Federal Republic, defeating Helmut Schmidt, who'd taken over when Willy Brandt resigned in 1974. Leonid Brezhnev died on 10 November at the age of 75, to be succeeded by Yuri Andropov, long-serving head of the KGB, who was 61. Andropov was ill with a kidney disease and, at the end, would exercise his power from a hospital bed.

Cumulatively, it was the beginning of a decisive shift in generations and thinking, but nobody knew, nobody suspected, nobody foresaw the consequences.

> <u>April 1983</u>   *Rudolf Burkert, a West German of unknown age, died at the wall.*
>
> <u>25 December 1983</u>   *Silvio Proksch, 20, climbed over the inner wall from a narrow side street in Pankow just before 7.30 p.m. and sprinted towards the outer wall. After two warning shouts and one warning shot, he came under 'aimed fire' and was hit. He was arrested about 30 metres from the outer wall, given first aid and taken to hospital. He died from his injuries at 8.46. The official report added that the weapon was only used parallel to the West Berlin border.*

Andropov died in February 1984, to be succeeded by Konstantin Chernenko, 72, a grey acolyte of Brezhnev and now the oldest man to become Soviet leader. Like Andropov he was ill. There is a union here, centred around a bitter sort of joke, between the fates of Freie and Proksch – both anonymous except in the instant of their deaths – and Brezhnev, Andropov and Chernenko with their special hospitals and teams of doctors and, if necessary, Western medical technology to keep them alive. The union is that the three Soviet leaders ruled half a world, and had to take responsibility for it. That included the wall and its victims. The bitter joke was that, because Soviet leaders didn't retire and the medicine kept them alive so long, 70 was only middle age in the Kremlin.

> <u>2 July 1984</u>   *Unknown person. At 3.35 p.m. a male, between 60 and 70 years of age, was noticed lying on the ground about 250 metres north of a bridge over the Teltow Canal. He was 6 metres inside GDR territory. An investigation at 4.10 showed that he was dead. His body was passed to a Special Commission at 8.07 and taken to a medical centre for a post-mortem. The man was wearing a shirt and long trousers but no identification papers were found. The official report said that on the other side West Berlin policemen and firemen 'as well as one US Army person' were observing. This US Army person infringed the GDR territory by approximately 2 metres.*

Just 2 metres? The pedantry of the geometry had become a yardstick for the moral questions of right and wrong.

Whether attempts to cross the wall had diminished because, by now, the wall itself was an awesome thing, or whether it was because life was more tolerable in the East, or whether a whole generation had grown up knowing nothing but the normality of the wall, nobody can say – but ordinary people kept nursing their reasons for trying, and they kept coming.

Peter Meyer, an East Berliner who worked on the railways, was one such person. Evidently he saw Westbound trains every day with Western passengers free to go where they wished, while his wife Hanni watched Western television and wanted the good life portrayed there. They had a son of four called Markus and no doubt they wanted the good life for him, too. It was spring 1984.

Meyer's mother knew a pensioner who had the right to travel to the West (as all pensioners did[2]) and asked him if, when he was over there, he could find somebody to help.[3] He found an Arab who said he could get them out but wanted money in advance. Meyer raised that, the pensioner returned to the West and paid it. The Meyers were told to go to Prague and wait by a statue where they would be contacted – but nobody came. In a bar Meyer met a Westerner, a journalist, who knew Wolf Quasner, the escape organiser. The journalist rang Quasner who could, and did, get Meyer's wife and son out easily enough. Meyer was more of a problem and he stayed in Prague.

Quasner decided that Meyer needed a double who would donate his genuine passport, and found one – a Ghanian. That was intriguing because a black man was much less likely to be challenged. He dispatched a couple who were expert in make-up and they transformed Meyer into a Ghanian, cutting his hair and making it into African stubble. His face was covered in black dye and his nostrils enlarged. He was introduced to another Ghanian and together they flew to East Berlin then crossed by S-bahn from Friedrichstrasse station.

<u>1 November 1984</u>   *Peter Böcker (or Boecker), 24, was fatally shot at the wall.*

Yet still they came, or tried to come.

<u>1 December 1984</u>   *Michael Schmidt, 20, was fired at and injured by the Border Guards at 3.18 a.m. at Wollankstrasse. He'd scaled the inner wall on a wooden ladder and, using a second ladder, moved forward and over the alarm system – but he activated it. He kept going towards the wall but he'd been seen from a watchtower about 200 metres away as he climbed the inner wall. He was given a warning shout and warning shot but ran faster. Aimed shots brought*

him down. After he'd been given first aid he was taken to hospital at
4.11. From 3.40, a West Berlin police patrol, a Customs patrol and
two French soldiers witnessed this; Wollankstrasse was opposite the
French Sector.[4]

The Associated Press covered this death although, of course, the
reporter had no way of knowing the name of the victim. The report
said that 'a person trying to flee across the Berlin Wall early
Saturday apparently was killed in a hail of bullets fired by East
German guards. The shooting drew sharp protests from West
German officials. West Berlin police, quoting residents of the
Wedding district, said 20 to 30 shots were fired at 3:15 a.m. and
then East German Border Guards searched an area near the wall for
about 55 minutes before finding a body.

'The guards placed the body in a military vehicle, covered it with
a tarpaulin and drove away in the pre-dawn darkness, according to
the witnesses. Police said it was not known if the victim was a male
or female.

'West Berlin Mayor Eberhard Diepgen said the shots "that
apparently killed a person have once again revealed the inhumanity
of the wall". West German government spokesman Peter Boenisch
demanded that East Germany "once and for all stop using firearms
against those who just want to exercise their human right of free
movement".

'Gen. Olivier de Gabory, head of the French mission in West
Berlin and speaking also for the U. S. and British allies in the divided
city, accused the East Germans of "brutal force" and demanded they
cease "this inhuman practice".

'The latest shooting came just one day after East Germany
dismantled the last of some 55,000 automatic shrapnel-shooting
guns along the border with West Germany, 110 miles or more to the
west of Berlin. The guns, which were triggered by vibrations from
anyone trying to climb border fences, were not deployed along the
Berlin Wall.'

This report, couched in the vivid reportage demanded by the
Western media, stands in direct contrast to the dry GDR report, of
course, but more than that it captures the barbarism of still
behaving like this in a European capital towards the end of the
second Christian millennium. In its misguided way, the GDR report
(and all their similar reports since 1961) reflected a whole way of
thinking. It was not just that no human touch, however small and

however fleeting, was permitted; it was bleaker than even that. The fallen might as well have been skittles.

<u>10 December 1984</u> *Alice Paula Olga Gadegart, 70, died at the wall.*

The pathological insecurity of the GDR leadership remained undiluted, and they were still prepared to kill for it. That touched on a question which has been already posed – if they were able to lie over why the wall was built, what would they tell the truth about? – and in these hard days, with the killing still going on and the wall frozen into permanence, who could know, or suspect, or foresee that the answer was coming before the end of the decade. When it did come, the answer to what they'd tell the truth about was: very little.

And still the escapees came, or tried to come.

Marina Brath and her husband Peter had to live through the abnormality of normality. Marina was born in Prenzlau, a town north of East Berlin towards the Polish border:

I decided to leave for the West in 1983–84. We made the decision together. We lived in an apartment in the Lichtenberg district, on the second floor of a small building. It's a long story, OK? My husband was hindered in his job – he worked in an hotel. Some office people said to him, 'If you don't join the Party you'll work as gardener or work as just anything.' We tried to get a visa for the West at the Office for Inner Relations in East Berlin. We didn't get a form: you only wrote a simple letter stating why you wanted to go, that's all, and you left the letter at this Office. That was rejected. We had to go back and they told us we couldn't leave. We complained in a letter to Honecker and three or four Ministries but nothing happened.

We knew it was a big risk but we also knew we had no future. That I would never see my parents again was a small risk because I thought my own life was more important than the relationship between my parents and me.

We'd been to the West German Consulate in East Berlin, to the American office and we tried to register ourselves as political prisoners. Anyway, there was no answer from our State so we surrendered our passports and declared ourselves stateless. Then we waited in our apartment because we knew there would be an official reaction. A few hours later the Stasi came in two cars, one of them a Trabant. They were not in uniform. There was a knock on the door and one of them said, 'Please come with us, we want to clear up some difficulties.' They showed us no identification. I went in one car and my husband in the other. I sat in the front seat and two men were in the back seat. I couldn't see my husband because the distance between the two cars was too great.

My car went to Keibelstrasse near the Alexanderplatz. I was taken to an office – a Stasi office but normal looking – and my husband was already there. They didn't say anything, they only asked questions. 'Why do you try and get out of Berlin? Why did you declare yourselves stateless?' Then they did say things, about our private lives but five or six years out of date. I don't know how they knew. I remember questions, questions and I was very frightened. I was questioned the whole night and I had no sleep. My husband had been taken away and the same man questioned me the whole night.

Then I was taken to a prison – not exactly a prison, because it's not clear yet whether you are guilty or not. It's a pre-prison and it was in the district of Pankow. I was put in a cell and I spent twelve weeks there. I was given old work clothes to wear. During that time I was able to communicate with my husband once. The same man who'd asked the questions came and we were brought together so we saw each other again – my husband was in the same pre-prison. No touches but we could speak.

Eventually we were tried and declared guilty. The trial was in a court nearby – a little room, one judge, one prosecutor and one defender – and the charge was Hindering State Offices. It was like a show. I could have spoken but I felt so pressured that there was no point. In reality the situation was that I could have spoken but they would not have *heard* the words I was speaking.

'The man 'defending' me was private and I could choose him, the state didn't give him to me. He had arranged some business between prisoners and the West German government, I think for money – the deal was the better the prisoner the higher the price. We never spoke of this. Everybody who wanted to go to the West knew this defender. He wasn't sympathetic, just a dealer in the East. He advised me to plead guilty because then it might not be so hard to get to West Germany eventually.

Before it started they all spoke together and it was decided I was guilty so the actual trial was like a show. My husband had been put under pressure. They told him that if he said anything wrong I'd be sent to a psychiatric ward – so they *assaulted* him by suggesting they would hurt me. The trial lasted half an hour. It wasn't only like a show, it was a sort of joke thing. The judge said, 'You are guilty and you go to prison, you are not a good citizen.'

I was sentenced to one year and four months and my husband one year and eight months. We received the judgment together and then we were separated again. We couldn't say goodbye. He was taken through one door and I was taken through another directly to prison – Stollberg (in the south of the GDR). The building had three floors, beds and only cold water. All the other prisoners were political.

I sewed pillows to be sold to the West – you couldn't buy them in the East. I didn't know the time, the day, the hour, anything, but I'd been there eleven months. One day someone knocked on the door, came in and said, 'You, you and you, come!' We were taken in a van to another prison in Chemnitz[5] and there we had to declare why we wanted to leave. We had to fill out some forms, then we got our private things. In the courtyard there was a bus from the West and at this point my husband and I saw each other for the first time – in front of the bus. We sat together on the bus and at the moment we crossed the border I felt *angst* and at the same time happiness. There was no freedom to travel in the Eastern bloc. The bus went to Giessen [a reception centre for refugees] near Frankfurt without stopping and from there we could decide which town we wanted to go and live in. We got tickets and went to West Berlin. We flew to Tegel because we didn't want to travel across the GDR again.

My first impression of West Berlin? Astonished, shocked, yes. I was still in my own city but the difference was like day and night. I still [1990] don't regard West Berlin as normal. I like to buy strawberries in winter; I am *still* astonished that you can buy strawberries in winter.

Husband Peter was then working in computers.[6]

In March 1985 Chernenko died and Mikhail Gorbachev came to power at the age of 54. The dinosaurs in the Soviet Union were either extinct, or soon to be, even if across the bloc as a whole they lumbered on. Nor is the analogy lightly chosen: dinosaurs possessed large bodies and were unable to survive a sudden climate change. Honecker's thinking had been shaped an aeon before and he was simply old – born in 1912, five years before the October Revolution brought communism to Soviet Russia. Gustav Husak, the Czechoslovakian leader, was born in 1913; Janos Kardar (Hungary) 1912; Nicolae Ceauşescu (Romania) 1918; and Todor Zhivkov (Bulgaria),

1911. Moreover, writing an introduction to a book on the devout communist and spy Kim Philby (born, incidentally, 1912)[7] John le Carré penned this phrase about the formation of Philby's beliefs: 'all Kim's life was early'. It was true of Honecker, true of all of them.[8]

22 August 1985   *Wolfgang Behnke, 46, died at the wall.*

Gorbachev took power with few of the inhibitions which held his predecessors so tightly. He knew change was essential for survival and new words drifted into the international language: *glasnost* (more open government) and *perestroika* (reform). To the dinosaurs this was worse than incomprehensible, it was heresy, and events at the wall in 1986 showed the distance between *glasnost, perestroika* and the pre-war people running the GDR.

And still they came, or tried to come.

On 26 June the Associated Press reported that 'an East German soldier apparently trying to escape to the West was sent sprawling by gunfire just short of the Berlin Wall and carried away in a truck by other border guards, witnesses said.

'West Berlin police spokesman Hans-Heiner Salbrecht said witnesses in the Frohnau neighbourhood, in the northern part of the partitioned city, heard a volley of shots Wednesday evening and saw a uniformed soldier sprawled on the ground near the wall in communist East Berlin. They told police the man "was still making movements" when East German guards loaded him into a truck that took him away, Salbrecht said.

'Another police spokesman, Klaus Roennebeck, said the soldier was still alive when Guards took him to the truck. Roennebeck said police had nothing beyond the witness reports because East German authorities provide no information on incidents at the wall. At least 73 people have been killed trying to cross the wall, but more than 4,900 have succeeded in escaping, according to West Berlin police figures.'

In August, two Border Guards – a 21-year-old private and a 24-year-old corporal – escaped by abandoning the watchtower they were in and scaling the wall. Reportedly they threw their guns back over and walked to the nearest inn (The Wallflower) where locals bought them a beer. As has been seen, such escapes were extremely uncommon because the Border Guards worked in twos but were rotated so that they did not know each other, making raising the topic of escape extremely dangerous.

To emphasise this point – and echoing Roland Egersdörfer – Jens Bernhardt, a Guard who did escape, reflected, 'There were always two Guards but your partner and the tower you served in were changed regularly so you didn't get to know each other well enough to build up trust.'

<u>3 September 1986</u> *Rainer Liebke, 35, died at the wall.*

Two men successfully crossed on 12 November despite being shot at; eight days later a 33-year-old used what appeared to be a home-made ladder and clambered to the top of the wall at Bernauer Strasse. At least seven shots were fired at him, hitting him in both legs, and he fell forward into the West and was taken to hospital. Protests were lodged with the GDR government.

<u>21 November 1986</u> *Rene Gross, 21, and Manfred Mader, 38, made their attempt in Treptow at 5.04 a.m. The official report said 'it was noticed that somebody was trying to get through the border using force'. They approached in a lorry along a side street which ran straight to the wall. The plan was evidently to ram their way through the gate the Border Guards used, to get to the death strip, which they succeeded in doing. But the Border Guards fired forty-nine shots and both were hit. The lorry was, the report added, '50 centimetres from the wall' when it was stopped. They were given first aid, but died on the way to hospital. The lorry was driven away at 5.58.*
<u>24 November 1986</u> *Michael Bittner, 25, was arrested at 1.19 a.m. to the east of West Berlin. He'd approached the inner wall with a 3-metre high ladder and clambered over it, then faced the alarm system. He scaled that but triggered it and was shot. At 2.15 people on the Western side were observing.*

The Associated Press covered Bittner's death.

East German border guards today shot a man who climbed to the top of the Berlin Wall from the Communist-ruled Eastern Sector, officials said. The Intra-German Relations Ministry in Bonn said the would-be escapee was a man and that he probably was dead.

Police in West Berlin said a witness reported hearing shouts of "Halt, stand still!" from the East side of the Berlin Wall at about 1:30 a.m., followed by 30 to 50 shots. A person on top of the 14-foot-high wall who apparently was trying to escape to the West fell back into East German territory, police quoted the witness as saying.

According to the police account, the witness peered through a break in the wall in West Berlin's Frohnau district and saw what was "apparently a man", sprawled on the ground covered with blood.

The witness heard an East German Guard say to the person, 'I got you, you pig', then heard another Guard complain loudly. The complaining Guard, who threw his hat on the ground, was disarmed by colleagues and escorted away. The person who was shot was covered with a tarpaulin and carried off. Police did not explain what the Guard complained about or why.

The witness saw a ladder on the ground near where the person lay, police said. Police said they had no other witnesses to the incident. In Bonn, chief West German government spokesman Friedhelm Ost said it was the fourth time in 12 days that East German Guards shot at people trying to escape. Some of the escapes were successful.

The escape brought to ten the number of East Germans who crossed the border – to West Berlin or West Germany – within seventeen days.

Michael 'Micha' Bittner's mother, Irmgard, a woman with a strong, open, almost plain face, came home from work that morning and listened for his alarm clock to ring. She heard it every morning. For some reason, she felt she needed to hear it now – and she didn't. She made her way up to the little balcony of their apartment to water the flowers and noticed that Micha wasn't there. She was confused and searched for any note he might have left explaining where he'd gone. She found nothing.

A Western witness to where Micha had been, Wolfgang Vogt, would come forward and say these words: 'I saw somebody trying to get over to our side, over the wall. I saw a hand, and a head, and then he fell back. I wanted to get over but more shots were fired. It was a salvo of shots from a machine gun. It sounded like *drrrr*. Then I heard someone coming from the watchtower. He was shouting very loudly, "I got the bastard! I got him!" He was murdered. And with malice, because he had already been shot when he fell back. So why were more shots fired? They shot him again. He must have been full of holes. The amount of bullets must have left him unrecognisable.'

Irmgard Bittner waited for three and a half years to discover Micha's fate. 'I had to guess where my son was.' With each day that passed, whatever hopes she had diminished because, as a mother, she knew her son would have contacted her somehow, wherever he'd gone. To herself, she could not accept that he had died and even as hope faded, it somehow remained. 'That's why for three and a half years he died a little bit at a time.' As she spoke those words, two years after she found out the truth (1991) she was holding herself hard from breaking up. '*They* [the State]' – the functionaries in the monolith, the Kafka people – 'didn't admit they'd killed him,' she said.

When asked who was responsible for his death, she seemed suddenly emptied of emotion, her blue eyes gazing down; then her whole face twisted in exhaustion. 'A good question,' she said, softly. Then, from a deep place: 'All of them.'

A wooden cross was placed in front of a single section of the wall out at Frohnau on the Western side, in commemoration. There was a metal plaque in the tall upright and it bore the simplest of inscriptions.

'I've often dreamt of Micha – of his death – and that ugly old cross there in Frohnau. That cross scares me somehow. I go there because I haven't got a grave, because I can put a few flowers there. But I don't feel closer to my son because I know he isn't there. I just don't know where he is. I'm sure they have burnt him.'

12 February 1987 *Lutz Schmidt, 28, made his attempt at 11.34 p.m. in Treptow. 'A male person was arrested after a weapon had been used.' The man did not have personal documentation but was 'probably' Schmidt. Although the visibility was 50 metres – mist or fog or lashing rain, perhaps – he was seen and warned. He didn't react. Then they fired and he was hit. After first aid he was taken to hospital and handed over to the 'appropriate authorities'.*

There is the chill of authoritarian anonymity to that phrase, and when set into a historical Germanic context it becomes very frightening indeed; this was 1987, not 1937.

Reagan visited Berlin in mid-June 1987 and stepped onto a platform in front of the Brandenburg Gate. Unlike Kennedy, who walked wreathed within a certain mystique, Reagan walked outside it. He was slightly stilted in presence and delivery, a man with the common touch at one remove from common people. It was not as if he was playing the role of President, more that the role was playing him. This audience had been carefully selected but reacted quietly to what were described in the Western media as the provocative parts of his speech. He said the wall was 'a gash of barbed wire, concrete, dog runs and guard towers', as if nobody except his speech writers had noticed, but in a stirring call he added, voice amplified: 'Mr Gorbachev, open this gate. Mr Gorbachev, tear down this wall.' These words are remembered, and they take their place as an attempt at an update of *Ich bin ein Berliner*. The words with which he ended the speech, however, have been largely forgotten. 'This wall will fall. It cannot withstand faith. It cannot withstand truth. The wall cannot withstand freedom.' They might have sounded glib political rhetoric, even to the speech writers who actually wrote it, especially after the wall had withstood everything fot the last twenty-six years, but there can be no doubt that Reagan believed them; and no doubt, now, that the stilted man from the black-and-white age was right, and was going to win.

<u>18 August 1987</u>   *An unknown man died at the wall.*
<u>29 September 1987</u>   *Falk Schröder, 25 – a West Berliner or a West German – committed suicide in circumstances which are unclear at the wall.*
<u>18 November 1987</u>   *The body of Peter Urban, 29, a West Berliner, was found. He was estimated to have been dead for between four and five weeks.*

Nobody knew. Nobody suspected. Nobody foresaw. Between 1987 and 1989, however, 'as the Moscow–East Berlin conflict steadily grew in intensity, East German dissidents and reformers within the Communist party gained confidence'.[10]

At least in June 1988, Honecker confirmed that the shoot-to-kill order at the wall had been rescinded, although that would be tested in the most direct way eight months later when a waiter from the East felt he wished to open a restaurant in the West and went across the death strip to try it.

There had been, too, an increase in the number of Easterners who were given permission to go across on visits. Lutz Stolz, the trainee engineer who'd been going to play football in the West on 13 August 1961, had 'an aunt in West Berlin whom I was allowed to visit between Christmas and New Year's Eve in 1988. I had not seen her for twenty-eight years and she was very ill so I couldn't stay with her. I had to stay with one of my friends.'

His wife Uta says:

He had to be back in the East at midnight of December 31. At 11.30 I got a call from him telling me that he was going to finish his cognac and come back. I went by S-bahn to Friedrichstrasse station, I sat on a bench and waited all alone. The station was deathly silent. There were two Border Guards scrutinising me constantly while I scrutinised the iron door' – from which Lutz would emerge.

At 12 o'clock on the dot the door opened and I saw my husband with a special kind of hat on his head that he had always wanted to buy for himself. I had organised a taxi and we hurried out of the station. He'd been liberated by the cognac and wanted to express all his impressions immediately. 'This visit has opened my eyes to see what is wrong in the East,' he said.

I had seen the West before, in March 1987 and March 1988, when I was allowed to visit an aunt who actually was the wife of my blood-related uncle. Then my uncle died and, according to the Eastern police, she wasn't my aunt any more. So I simply made a unmarried sister of my mother's out of my aunt! She had the same name, so things worked out: they let me visit her. I came back with a lot of luggage and struggled through this damned iron door that only had a handle on the inside. After that second visit, they fired my husband as trainer of the regional soccer league 'because his wife had Western contacts'.

Lutz continues:

We had heard of the development in the West, we knew that they were getting on much faster, but as things [propaganda] were really rammed into our heads all these years we did not really believe it. For me it was worse when I came back from my journey in 1988. From that time on I did not believe in anything I heard or read in the Eastern media. They told us that, in the West, people would only stay outside the shops and look at the window displays because they could not afford things, they told us look at the growing unemployment rate . . .

I experienced something very different. I went through the big department stores, I saw the big purchasing power and their *will* to buy things. The department stores were sometimes so crowded that they almost tore the buttons off your coat. And among the 8 or 10 per cent unemployed were 4 or 5 per cent who did not want to work, who were satisfied with their unemployment. They were unskilled, they were lazy and lived on their unemployment money – which was more than somebody in the East who worked all day long would ever earn.

This is why I was in such a rage when I came back, it wasn't only the alcohol I had consumed in West Berlin that day. When I came out of the 'hatch' at Friedrichstrasse [the iron door] to see all the grey I was furious. It felt like going to Poland from East

Germany. Measured by all the glitter in West Berlin . . . until this point I had always believed somehow. . . .[11]

This should be contrasted with the recollections of Birgit Kubisch.

I was born in [East] Berlin in 1969, so eight years after the wall was built. My parents worked in North Africa – the GDR embassy in Algeria – for four years. My sister and I went with them. I think I had seen almost all the Socialist countries except Albania and Cuba and North Korea. Of West Berlin I had seen what the TV showed us, because we had the Western TV. What do you see then? You see shops. I had never been to the end of Unter den Linden, actually not until I was eighteen or nineteen. [It faces the Brandenburg Gate and, of course, the West]. Strange. I don't know why, I can't tell you why.

You know, you have a certain sort of education and until you are maybe fourteen, fifteen you don't doubt much about what you have learned. Only at a certain age do you begin to think about some of the facts, to question. I always had one problem, in that I could not believe the wall was the solution to having a capitalist town in a socialist country.

I only saw the wall when I was visiting friends who lived near it. From certain places in East Berlin you could see some of the West – if you went, for instance, by S-bahn near the district of Köpenick. I saw houses. I had an image. Maybe I had a different sort of image to other people because my parents worked in foreign countries and we knew people who lived in other countries. Maybe I had a more realistic picture, not sort of black and white between the East and the West.[12]

The GDR was her whole world and the West held no particular interest for her. After all, why should it? But now normality itself was uncertain, something which had not happened since 13 August 1961. Gorbachev had made it clear to his satellites that the Soviet Union would not interfere in their internal affairs.

Still the escape attempts were made. In March 1988 three men in a truck drove through the barriers across the Glienicker Bridge just before dawn. Reportedly, they had loaded the 7.5-ton vehicle with empty propane gas tanks and calculated that the Border Guards, not knowing they were empty, wouldn't shoot and risk an immense explosion. The three men guessed correctly. The truck battered a path through two steel gates and an electrified fence on the Eastern side, and continued across the bridge, smashing through the West Berlin control. (The bridge had long been used to swap spies, among them American pilot Gary Powers in 1962 and Soviet dissident Anatole Sharansky in 1986.)

> **5 February 1989**   *Chris Gueffroy, 20. Gueffroy, the waiter who wanted to open a restaurant in the West, made a night-time attempt with Christian Gaudian, 21, in Treptow. The two men, without what was described as 'special help' – ladders, presumably – got over the inner wall. At 11.39 the alarm sounded when they were about 5 metres from the outer wall. The Border Guards reacted immediately. Gueffroy was shot through the heart and died. Gaudian was shot through the foot.*

These two young men were the last victims of bullets at the wall, although Gueffroy was not the last to die because of it. Like the first victim – Rudolf Urban in 1961 – it is neither simple nor straightforward. Urban, remember, made his attempt on 19 August but died later, so he was and was not the first. The last named escaper to die would make a balloon and try to cross in it. The last one of all would have no name and no details, a horribly apt epitaph for the wall.

The death of Gueffroy provoked international outrage but, in small and almost subtle ways, it demonstrated that the winds of change had begun to whisper. The Gueffroy family were allowed to place a death notice in the GDR press, something which had not happened before. It listed family and friends and announced that the funeral would be on 23 February. Some 120 people attended, young faces expressing grief in public, and a photograph of the image of that would appear in the Western media. Gaudian was subsequently tried and sentenced to three years in prison but West Germany bought him out.

3 March 1989   *Winfried Freundenberg, 33.*

At 1.50 a.m. on 3 March 1989, the Ministry of the Interior was informed by a man that he had seen somebody in the gasworks in the district of Weisensee filling a balloon. The man said that he had seen this at 1.35 as he was riding past on a bus. Immediately, a car was dispatched to the gasworks. At 2.10 a balloon of approximately 5 metres in diameter was seen rising with one person in it. The balloon hit a power cable of 380 volts which plunged the area into darkness. Due to this, it could not be ascertained in which direction the balloon was flying. When investigating the situation at the gasworks, a plastic tube was found, connected to the gas supply, and it had obviously been used to fill the balloon; the gas was still escaping from it.

The person was Winfried Freudenberg. When his wife was arrested she confirmed that her husband had committed this crime. She had helped him to make and fill the balloon. It had been planned for a long time and to achieve it Freudenberg got a job at the gasworks. Both of them were due to go in the balloon but a car had passed close to the gasworks, frightening them as they filled the balloon. The woman abandoned any idea of going and Freudenberg immediately started to ascend as fast as he could.

Futher investigations were carried out in the areas of Frankfurt-Oder and Potsdam because they didn't know where the balloon had gone. At 9.15 Freudenberg's car, a Trabant, was discovered and impounded. According to the weather station at Schönefeld airport, when the balloon ascended a north-east wind was blowing. As soon as it was daylight the search was resumed by helicopter.

But they were searching in the wrong place. Freudenberg reached the Western district of Zehlendorf, but the balloon fell from what police described as a great height, killing him.

On 8 April, two youths tried to escape through the Chaussee-strasse checkpoint but were halted by a warning shot. This was the last shot fired at the wall.[13]

<u>16 April 1989</u>　　*An unknown man, about 18, drowned.*

Nobody knew that that was it, the last of them, even though another seven months would pass during which, at any moment day and night, someone might have died because, for whatever reason, they wished to be free to go wherever they wanted and the journey to that began only on the other side of the wall. This book is the people's story, often told in the vividness of memory, but the italic paragraphs marking each death are dotted through like tombstones in their silence: each death, however shorn of detail, has not been a person's story. None spoke except perhaps, like Peter Fechter, to cry out in their fear and their agony. Each death has been another sort of story: of how anonymous we are, and sometimes how brave and how cruel and how obedient; of unimaginable circumstances leading ordinary people to the sprint into arc-lamps and watchtowers and gunfire; and of those ordinary people suddenly cast up upon a deadly stage. I wish I could give you a definitive list of every name and, perhaps, a little human anecdote for each but the italic paragraphs are all I can do. It remains the ultimate violation of these ordinary people that many have no tombstones of their own, because they were buried or cremated in official anonymity. So the paragraphs in italics here will have to serve.

In May, Hungary dismantled its wire border with Austria, and Hungary was a favoured holiday destination for East Germans, who drove down through Czechoslovakia towing their little caravans to camp round Lake Balaton. All they had to do now was go to the Hungarian border instead, select a quiet stretch of woodland and walk across. Once in Austria they could continue to West Germany where they would automatically, and instantly, become West German citizens. Nobody knew, but some did foresee it: this was the beginning of the final steps of the logic. By 1 October 30,000 had gone.

The rest was a straightforward end game played out to its own logic which intensified week by week into day by day and then, like the last convulsive spasm of its existence, into moment by moment. The actual process of this would run full across the fortieth anniversary celebrations of the GDR's founding, due at the beginning of October.

Bernie Godek, a 36-year-old major from Huntington, New York, was assigned to Headquarters Company, United States Command Berlin 'in July 1989 – I can remember it was the fourth of July. I had been stationed in West Germany before that and never visited Berlin. Some people did. They used to travel the autobahn from Helmstedt to Dreilinden but many of us perceived that it was just too difficult a thing to do – the processing of paperwork and getting permission. We were down in Bamberg and we enjoyed it there – in fact we loved it down there. We didn't have much interest to go to Berlin at the time.' By 'we', Godek means himself, his wife Donna, daughter Jennifer, who'd celebrate her twelfth birthday in late October, and son Christopher, who'd celebrate his ninth on 9 November.

Of course when in the army you go where they decide you'll go, and the Godeks moved into a detached house which was technically 'just in the British Sector. The houses were intermingled with some of the local German homes.' It was in the Dahlem district.

Godek's duties would be at Checkpoint Charlie but 'as a matter of fact, before I actually went up to visit the Checkpoint for the first time I had received briefings from several different individuals within the command. The most trivial thing there could suddenly become enormous and people wanted me to be sure that I didn't do anything wrong when I did go up there and that I was familiar with the procedures of everything. There were a number of dos and don'ts and I needed to be familiar with those.

'Having never seen it before, my first impression was surprise at how simple our checkpoint looked. I think I'd expected to see something a little bit bigger, something a little bit more elaborate on our side. There was nothing except a little metal building [the hut] and that was it. But on their side I was simply amazed – amazed at the contrast between the simplicity of Checkpoint Charlie and that metal building and the complexity of the crossing point on the East Berlin side. A monstrous complex. In general things were still very rigid.' All unknowing, Godek's posting would do more than introduce him to this rigidity which now spanned generations – much more.

On 8 August the FRG Consulate in East Berlin closed because it was swamped by refugees, and five days later the Consulate in Budapest closed for the same reason. Six days after that a symbolic Pan-European Picnic was held on the Austro-Hungarian border and 900 East Germans went over.

Godek remembers that 'once the official announcement had been made that Gorbachev was coming to East Berlin for the anniversary celebrations, several nights before he was due to arrive I received a call at home late in the evening, maybe about midnight, from the checkpoint. The Military Policeman on duty said, "Sir, you need to come out here right away. There is something going on." I asked him what and he said, "Well, there appears to be some engineering vehicles mustering on the opposite side of the checkpoint." We knew that because we had cameras positioned so that we could see over the checkpoint [into the East].'

From three storeys up on the side of a building a camera captured every movement beyond the white line and relayed the pictures to a screen in the hut and an observation office on the floor above the Café Adler. The office was named after General John Mitchell, the US commander in the city for four years, and a brass plate on the door announced that: the Mitchell Suite.

The Military Policeman added that, 'There seem to be some Border troops there, too.'

Godek said, 'OK, I'll be right there.' He called 'my driver, Sergeant Yount – my assistant – and he picked me up at home.' Michael Yount was an acting NCO. Godek recounts:

We went to the checkpoint. Sure enough, I looked at the camera and after that I went up into the Mitchell Suite with a pair of binoculars. I observed a collection of engineering vehicles – there were fork lifts, a mini crane of some type, some dump trucks and a couple of trucks of the Border Guards. We really didn't know what to expect because we hadn't seen anything like this before. I started to notify people within the Command as to what was going on. There were procedures set up where I would make notifications to certain individuals based on what activities I was observing, especially if strange things were happening – and this was very strange. Very, very strange.

I would say that after about an hour of observing them, they proceeded through their checkpoint and started progressing towards Checkpoint Charlie. We watched and we watched and we watched, and they stopped at the end of the roadway: they stopped about 5 metres before the demarcation line [Hagen Koch's line]. Remember the wall never sat on that line, it was always back from it. Then they walked up very close, probably within a metre of the line and they were talking and looking. They appeared to be officers from both the Border Guards and the engineering unit that was there.

Sgt Yount was fluent in German so he went outside and I walked up to within a metre of the line. I was very close and I was watching everything they were doing, which made them a little nervous. I tried to mirror their activity. According to what they were talking about, Sgt Yount said, 'It appears as if they are going to come up and extend the wall to the demarcation line.' That surprised me. After a period of time they started bringing up some of the engineering vehicles and, along with that, we noticed construction material in the back of some of their trucks. There was wood, there was some cement and blocks, things of that nature.

As they came forward with their equipment, I instructed the Military Policeman at the checkpoint to get out the movie camera so we could start videotaping this. This he did. Again this made the East Germans there a little nervous and after about fifteen minutes of us being out there with a video camera they then produced a soldier with a video camera who started videotaping us videotaping them . . .

They started bringing up the materials and they started extending the wall from its current location using this wood and cement blocks. They extended it right up to the demarcation line and they continued to do this. They took this new wall straight across the front of Checkpoint Charlie leaving just enough room for two lanes [so cars could enter and exit at the same time]. They knew that we would demand our right to access into the Soviet Sector. As the construction went on we were still trying to figure out what it was, what they were up to, and they fortified it pretty well. The cements blocks they were putting down were in fact more than that, they were cement slabs. They produced a formidable barricade. They didn't leave a lot of room for people. They'd have to go into the vehicle lanes.

This is now about two o'clock in the morning. We're starting to gain a little bit of media attention and of course your late-night pubs in West Berlin are clearing out – and this was the place to go. Next thing you know, we had a crowd of West Berliners gathering at the checkpoint, yelling at the Guards, yelling at the construction workers. So now we have a little bit of a commotion going on.

The really interesting thing was, and as far as I can tell this had never occurred before, their senior officer in charge walked down to within inches of the demarcation line. He was inspecting the construction work. I was walking the line – even – with him, and I was within inches of it. Of course I didn't go over it although I was authorised to do so – he wasn't. At one point I let him go ahead. I stopped. Then he turned around and came back. As he came back and he was shoulder to shoulder with me he leaned out and he bumped me rather hard, which surprised me and surprised Sgt Yount. He said, 'I can't believe he just did that to you.' I said, 'I can't believe it either.' So I walked back, caught up with him and from my side of the line I bumped him. At that point he walked away from the line. Sgt Yount said, 'You do realise that we have just had a serious international incident' and I said, 'Yes, but let's keep it between ourselves!' I walked away.

Normally an East German would have kept away from anything like that, and that's what was so unusual about it. He made an attempt to have physical contact with the American officer in charge of Checkpoint Charlie and, I repeat, I don't think it had ever occurred before. It seemed pointless, and not a word was spoken, but I assume he was trying to tell me that he was very annoyed that I was out there and watching so closely what they were doing. That was his way of telling me that 'You're really annoying me. I've got to get this job done and you're out here scrutinising me.' That was the message I got.

We figured out why they put the new wall up. In fact I think it was explained to us through official channels afterwards, and the reasoning was twofold. The main reason was that they expected riots and demonstrations on the West Berlin side against Gorbachev's presence in East Berlin and that turned out to be true. We had some very terrible demonstrations, and some very physical demonstrations the day after that wall was put up.

Secondly it was another means of protection at a point where the wall was open, at Checkpoint Charlie. I think not only were they trying to prohibit the West Berliners from getting over that demarcation line and demonstrating inside their checkpoint but using a bit of precaution on *their* side against East Berliners. It was one more barrier that Easterners would have had to go through: they had Guards positioned at those little vehicle lanes, armed Guards. They were there for the entire time that Gorbachev visited.'

By now opposition groups were forming within the GDR, demonstrations were taking place in Leipzig and the FRG Embassy in Prague was itself swamped by refugees. They were allowed to emigrate but, to save face, the trains had to pass through the GDR to the West. In Dresden some 5,000 people gathered to try and board them. A day later the GDR closed the border with Czechoslovakia and had now cut itself off from the twentieth century.

A day after that Honecker was at Schönefeld airport to greet Gorbachev, guest of honour at the fortieth anniversary celebrations. Honecker, hands deep in the pockets of his dark coat but looking somehow neat and dapper, walked across to where a bank of the media hovered. He was asked how he felt. 'Those who are condemned live a long time,' he replied – the notion made him smile – and added that on such a morning he felt like a Berliner. A group of senior politicians stood around him and one, Egon Krenz, stood behind him, hands in coat pockets, too. His smile was drawn between obligation and genuine amusement. Honecker was asked what he'd be saying to Gorbachev; he turned and said, 'Wouldn't you like to know!' That made everybody laugh.

Moments later the big white and blue Aeroflot jet landed and taxied towards where the group waited for it. A dutiful crowd waved GDR flags as Gorbachev, overcoat unbuttoned, came down the gangway with his wife Raisa beside him. Honecker advanced and they shook hands, then Gorbachev, himself smiling, bent forward and the two men embraced, kissed three times on the cheeks in the Russian way. GDR television described this as 'hearty greetings between two men who know each other well'.

The Gorbachev visit became a juxtaposition, with demonstrators on the streets of East Berlin calling, 'Gorby, help us! Gorby, help us!' It was utterly unthinkable even five years earlier for any Eastern bloc population to plead genuinely with a Soviet leader to liberate them.

Perhaps it can be explained in this way. Stalin had tried to shape the twentieth century and had been responsible for the deaths of uncounted millions. Gorbachev was allowing it to reshape itself without killing anyone at all. The transition between the two mentalities, from the Middle Ages to Enlightenment, was fundamental and it had happened.

At Checkpoint Charlie the mood was different. Godek resumes the story: 'As I've said, the demonstrations that went on from the West Berliners were just terrible. I couldn't help but feel a little compassion for the Border Guards, the armed Guards that they'd positioned at the new wall. They had quite a number of them there, had them in depth. The West Berliners were throwing beer bottles and eggs and anything they could get their hands on across that wall, that temporary partition, to hit those Guards who were there. I specifically remember the Commander – he was a little guy, really short, which surprised me a little bit. . . .'

He was called Günter Moll. 'He got pelted with eggs at one point but he stood there firm even though the egg yolk was pouring down from his hat and his shoulder and his chest where he'd been hit with the eggs. He didn't flinch in front of his troops. He eventually did, trying not to make too much motion, wipe some of it away so it wouldn't fall on his face too much. He wasn't the one who bumped into me. The individual who did that was a rather robust guy.'

Gorbachev met the GDR Politburo on 7 October and listened to Honecker extol the virtues of the country without even mentioning the refugees. Gorbachev rolled his eyes as if to say 'OK, Comrades, that's it, what are you going to do about it?' It meant: 'The Soviet Union will not interfere in you regulating your own affairs.' There must have been an unsuspected beauty about the moment: the wall which was so solid and so lethal would be destroyed by a minimal gesture – the eyes of the man.

As it happened, the new wall at Checkpoint Charlie was dismantled when Gorbachev had gone, but that must have been pre-planned and seemed to presage nothing.

Krenz and Berlin Party secretary Günter Schabowski overcame what has been described as their mutual mistrust and sounded out as discreetly and delicately as they could, other Politburo members. On 18 October the Central Committee met. At 9.59 a.m. Honecker entered the room as usual and shook hands with all twenty-six members. He was just about to read out the first point on the agenda when Willy Stoph, the Prime Minister, said, 'Erich, allow me.'

Honecker, taken by surprise, said, 'Well, yes.'

'I propose that Comrade Honecker abdicates his function as General Secretary.' Stoph added that two other comrades should go, one of them being Günter Mittag, the economics supremo.

Honecker, obviously stunned, made a fleeting attempt to return to the agenda. That was protested. 'All right then, let's discuss it.' He searched the room among the most sympathetic of these old comrades for allies, and found none. In accordance with communist practice all decisions had to be unanimous, obliging Honecker to vote against himself to maintain that. Ultimately, the logic was as unforgiving as that.

Krenz took over a country breaking up, technically bankrupt and deep in an identity crisis, something it was unlikely to survive given its history and especially with Big Brother the other end of Friedrichstrasse waiting to help. Krenz tried to buy time and bought less than two weeks of it.

It had reached the day-by-day stage.

Demonstrations increased, the Politburo met the opposition and announced that from 1 November every East German could travel to the West for thirty days, but these were gestures, holding measures, concessions from the planned place which had no plans. And everybody saw, and knew. The monolith could neither disintegrate nor adapt to changing climates, and certainly not at this pace. On 1 November Krenz met Gorbachev in Moscow and said that demolishing the wall was 'unrealistic', a statement which itself would become *unreal* inside eight days.

The FRG Embassy in Prague was swamped again and a million people demonstrated in East Berlin. On 8 November the Politburo resigned (some members were re-elected but the currency for those things was long exhausted). Krenz was clinging on and the logic was preparing to consume him.

Next morning, Commander Günter Moll got in his Skoda and drove from his apartment in the suburbs to the checkpoint where he'd enact the usual rituals of control. It was Thursday and, he assumed, just another day of clockwork within the unchanging geometry.

At 9.00 that morning four men met at the Ministry of the Interior in Mauerstrasse behind Checkpoint Charlie, two of them Stasi. The Politburo wanted new travel regulations to solve the 'Czech problem' because the Czechs were unhappy that Prague, flooded with refugees, was still a staging post to the West. The four men decided to tackle the problem 'head on'[14] by recommending that Easterners should be allowed to travel, although with the understanding there would be procedures for obtaining visas. At 12.00 the proposal was given to

Krenz in a Politburo meeting. It was approved at 12.30 and passed on to the Council of Ministers (a symbolic body). At 3.00 work was going on to resolve the details of how the new regulations would function and at 3.30 the proposal came back from the Council of Ministers, rubber-stamped. Although the regulations constituted another concession the intention was to control the process.

Krenz read the regulations again. 'Whatever we do in this situation we're bound to make a mistake but it's the only solution that spares us the problem of dealing with this through third countries, which harms the international image of the GDR.' Schabowski wasn't in the room at this moment. As the government's press spokesman he was constantly being called away to talk to journalists: not that that could have mattered. Could it?

Checkpoint Charlie from the air and from the East, *c*. 1985. Note the vehicle lanes and, at top, the Allied hut in the middle of the road. *(Photo: Berliner Mauer-Archiv)*

Left: East (right) meets West, law meets law. *(Photo: Kazuhito Yamada) Below:* The Brandenburg Gate on the Western side two days after the opening of the wall. The police vans are to maintain law and order. *(Photo: Kazuhito Yamada)*

Above: The (very former) Invalidenstrasse Checkpoint and this is where Birgit Kubisch crossed to the West in November 1989 for the first time in her life. The exact line is marked vertically and across the road – all that remains a decade later. Here she is posing at either side. Which is East and which is West? Doesn't matter now . . . *(Photos: author)*

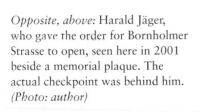

Opposite, above: Harald Jäger, who gave the order for Bornholmer Strasse to open, seen here in 2001 beside a memorial plaque. The actual checkpoint was behind him. *(Photo: author)*

Right: Bornholmer Strasse – and this is precisely what thousands of Easterners first saw of the West. The checkpoint and watchtowers are on the other side of the bridge. Normally at night it was like this but on 9 November 1989, as the teeming thousands came through, it almost choked on its own emotion. *(Photo: Kazuhito Yamada)*

The Café Adler. The wall and the Eastern checkpoint were to the right and Hagen Koch's white line between where the two cars are. The entrance to the Café, where the first Easterner burst in to get his hand stamped, is under the C of Café (left). *(Photo: Birgit Kubisch)*

An apartment in a block in East Berlin. In this study and the corridor outside is more material on the wall than anywhere else in the world. Hagen Koch of the Berliner Museum-Archiv (right) and author. *(Photo: Birgit Kubisch)*

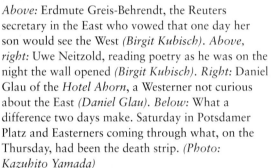

Above: Erdmute Greis-Behrendt, the Reuters secretary in the East who vowed that one day her son would see the West *(Birgit Kubisch)*. *Above, right:* Uwe Neitzold, reading poetry as he was on the night the wall opened *(Birgit Kubisch)*. *Right:* Daniel Glau of the *Hotel Ahorn*, a Westerner not curious about the East *(Daniel Glau)*. *Below:* What a difference two days make. Saturday in Potsdamer Platz and Easterners coming through what, on the Thursday, had been the death strip. *(Photo: Kazuhito Yamada)*

The bridge near
Friedrichstrasse Station
and, by chance, old
friends from East and
West meet. In this one
instant, twenty-eight
years of abnormality have
returned to the normal.
(Photo: *Kazuhito
Yamada*)

The orderly column of ordinary people at Friedrichstrasse Station waiting to cross to the West by train, November 1989. Every one would have a story to tell. *(Photo: Kazuhito Yamada)*

NINE

A Quiet Night Like This

The wall will still be standing in 50 or 100 years if the reasons for its
existence are not removed.

Erich Honecker,
January 1989

Beyond the barricade Günter Moll could see Hagen Koch's faded,
hand-painted white line bisecting Friedrichstrasse and still
marking where the tectonic plates met. Beyond that he could see the
West clearly, the alien place, the hostile land which was known to
him only by reputation and image. Under no circumstances would
he step across the white line.

Beyond the line Moll could see the big roadside board informing
travellers that they were leaving the American Sector and the Allied
hut in the middle of Friedrichstrasse, long and creamy in colour,
decorated with the Stars and Stripes, and the Union Jack and
Tricolour: the British and French had offices there, too. He could see
the window in the hut from where American Military Police
watched the three watchtowers across the line and the Border
Guards in the watchtowers gazed back. They were forty paces apart.

Beside the hut Moll could see a corner café and, further away, a
shop but not the bank because the angle from his office was wrong.

Often enough from the turret of the watchtower on the right, its
roofing like a pelmet, binoculars lingered on a 29-year-old waitress in
the Café Adler on the corner just the other side of the line. She was
financing her studies to become an art teacher. Every evening she saw
the binoculars sweeping her through the tall window of the café and
she wondered what the Guards thought. She did not regard them as
remote, only as people of her own age – and probably younger – who
she could not reach. She was called Astrid Benner.

They surveyed her ferrying coffee and beer and schnapps – korn
in the dialect – and sometimes she felt sorry for them. 'We'd have

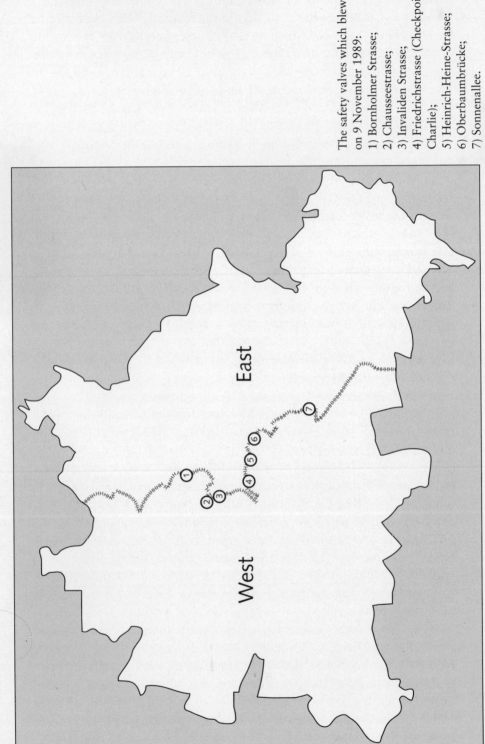

The safety valves which blew open on 9 November 1989:
1) Bornholmer Strasse;
2) Chausseestrasse;
3) Invaliden Strasse;
4) Friedrichstrasse (Checkpoint Charlie);
5) Heinrich-Heine-Strasse;
6) Oberbaumbrücke;
7) Sonnenallee.

parties, it was colourful, it was fun and over there it was so sad. I sensed the Guards in the tower were interested and I would like to have made contact with them but, of course, I couldn't.'[1] If any one of these Guards tried to come to her he'd risk being shot, and she couldn't go to them because nobody ever approached a watchtower. You risked being shot yourself and, even if you weren't, you'd certainly be hauled away; and who knew what would happen to you then?

Astrid Benner worked within hailing distance of Moll but she knew nothing of him. The line held their worlds apart, too.

As Moll drove off she had already been serving for an hour. She'd taken the underground from her university class and emerged at the station beside the café as the day ebbed into darkness. No doubt the Guards swept her as she went into the café. They watched everything, especially a pretty girl. It helped pass the time. They'd evolved the system about that. Any chance of using the binoculars to watch a girl undressing in a bedroom on the Western side, like *Long Tooth*, and the word went from watchtower to watchtower like an electric current – but she was only serving the way she did each evening.

Moll took his Skoda round the gentle curve of buildings flanking the checkpoint's rear, some sharply modern, some riddled with staccato bullet marks from 1945. Any journey into the East was always movement through time and you could read the story of the city through its buildings and its streets renamed across the years to commemorate heroes of socialism.

Moll reached traffic lights with red figurines on their stems, arms outstretched to hold pedestrians from crossing, and green figurines who made walking motions to release them. This was the pre-determined civilian clockwork. He was already deep into the East now and out of sight of the checkpoint. At these traffic lights a postal museum stood, a brooding, sombre stone edifice. The stone wasn't merely chipped by the rifle fire of '45 but gouged deep, each mark so vivid that the mortar shells might have burst only a few moments before.

When the lights changed he turned into Leipziger Strasse. Before the war it had been a shopping promenade but the Allied bombing broke it and no doubt the street fighting finished it off. So little usable survived that the whole lot was demolished to make a broad avenue lined by workers' apartments, each a cliff-face of socialist reality. Their balconies, small as birdcage perches, rose in vertical ranks floor by floor.

As Moll drove, a cluster of little Trabant cars putt-putted like lawn-mowers around him, square Wartburg saloons hiccoughed forward and an occasional pug-nosed lorry lumbered under the weight of its load. He was in the evening rush hour going home, same as every evening.

Far down Leipziger Strasse he passed the twin spires of the Nikolai Church, the oldest church in the city and, restored from the bombing, beautiful in its simplicity. The church was drawn in great contrast to the cliff-faces around it. Then he passed the rear of the SED's headquarters building, where Krenz and the Central Committee were meeting, discussing economics. He drove towards the park dominated by the Soviet war memorial, turned towards the suburb of Treptow. He'd be home nicely in time for dinner.

At 5.30 p.m., Chris Toft, a 36-year-old British Military Police sergeant, lined his duty men up in the barracks near the Olympic Stadium far to the Western side and gave them a normal briefing, then issued them with pistols as he did each evening. 'We went to the loading bay and I supervised the loading of the pistols. The bay was surrounded by sandbags and they pointed the pistols at them while they were loading in case one went off by accident. They got into our white Volkswagen Combi with Military Police written on the side and drove off.'[2] They headed across the city towards a small control room near the wall in the British Sector where they'd take over patrolling from the day shift while, at 5.45, Toft settled in the main control room at the barracks. Desks were arranged in a square and each had a little bank of a switchboard. Another evening, that was all. Toft had the usual personnel around him, a desk NCO, an interpreter, a German liaison officer from the city's riot squad. At night there might be trouble, likely as not involving drunks, and a liaison officer was always present to help coordinate action between the civilian authorities and the British military.

Some time around 5.30 Schabowski spoke to Krenz about a press conference scheduled for 6.00 which he – Schabowski – would give. Krenz handed him the piece of paper which had the new law on it. 'Announce this,' Krenz said. 'It will be a bombshell.' Schabowski did not read what was written on the paper.

In the Café Adler, a place of wooden chairs and tables and a semi-circular bar nestling around one corner, Astrid Benner put a cassette into the tape recorder on a shelf. It was music to take the dull edge off the place, music to soothe the boredom. 'Because of its situation the café was not very popular after nightfall and I was working alone the whole evening, only me. One person was enough. In the daytime the café was popular with tourists looking at the checkpoint but in the evenings not many people came, never more than twenty. It wasn't very interesting to be there then.'

Moll reached his apartment, small and cosy, parked the Skoda and settled in front of the television. His wife Inge began to prepare the meal.

At 5.45 Bernie Godek left his 'very simple office, beige walls with a drab green carpet and a military couch covered with artificial leather look-alike' at a barracks not far from the Olympic Stadium and drove the ten minutes to his four-bedroomed house in the wooded suburb of Dahlem. It was son Christopher's ninth birthday and they were having a party. Every year Godek tried to be home for that, wherever his duties took him.[3]

He knew Commander Moll, although by sight, not by name. In a sense, Moll did not exist because if any incident developed, Godek would demand the presence of a Soviet officer.

The party was going well. Godek took off his uniform shirt but 'I still had my fatigue pants on and my boots and a green tee-shirt. My wife asked me if I'd go ahead and cook up some hot dogs in the microwave for the kids so I started heating them and putting them in buns.' Ordinarily he might have switched the TV on, but not now.

Godek bore the responsibility of his life calmly although at moments he found ensuring Allied access at Checkpoint Charlie 'a hell of a thing'. While, of course, the checkpoint lay within the American Sector it was an official crossing place for all the Allies, hence the presence of the British and French in the hut. Allied military vehicles still went daily trawling in the East as they were entitled to do, just as Soviet vehicles could – and did – still enter the West.

The party was due to go on for another hour or so and Godek was good at serving hot dogs, the way dads are.

At 5.50, Schabowski travelled the hundred yards or so to the International Press Centre where he would give the press conference. He had a heavy face, nearly Slavonic, all cheeks and jowls. It was about to become extremely famous. He wore a light but formal suit in soft tartan, a white shirt, a dark blue tie with a pattern angled down it. The press conference room was full: maybe a hundred journalists.

At 6.00, the British Military Police Volkswagen arrived at the small control room near the wall – it was about a mile from Checkpoint Charlie. The men in the Volkswagen duly relieved the dayshift, clambered into their vehicles and began to patrol the wall in this, the British Sector. The Volkswagen continued on to Checkpoint Charlie to also relieve the dayshift in the hut before it headed back to the barracks.

At 6.00, Schabowski entered the press conference, a tall room of polished wooden walls and rows of red seats, and walked ponderously towards the platform at the far end where he'd sit behind a long desk. Television cameras probed at him – GDR television was covering the event live. He sat and began talking about the day's developments.

They were all in place now, or nearly in place. Godek sliced more buns and Toft waited by his little switchboard for the first radio reports – routine traffic, as it would surely be – to come in. Astrid Benner listened to the taped music and flitted to and fro serving seven customers.

Maybe the Border Guards observed her, maybe they didn't.

Moll watched television, and there was Schabowski wandering along a great verbal path which probably wouldn't lead anywhere.

Far up Friedrichstrasse on the Eastern side a dark-haired student of journalism made her way to an evening class. In her twenty-one years Brita Segger had never been to the other end of Friedrichstrasse nor imagined she ever would. She could go to Vietnam because that was approved, but not the Café Adler. Even geographically the Café Adler just down the road lay much further away than Hanoi, or the moon.

She worked on a people's factory newspaper as an apprentice and the evening classes were to teach her the art of writing. She needed to pass her *abitur*, the examination which would take her to university and an assured future for the rest of her life. All she'd have to do was write the Party line for ever and ever and ever. She walked the few minutes to her class.

Inge Moll flitted out from the kitchen to catch moments of the television. Günter watched with interest but no particular sense of anticipation. He was 47 and far too old for speculating, because his domain was one of certainties.

Schabowski had seven microphones in a thicket before him. He'd put on his half-lens spectacles and they gave him the air of a schoolmaster. He dipped his head and droned on. At no moment did he raise his voice to generate anything but a monologue in monotone.

At 6.53 an Italian journalist sitting on the rim of the platform, microphone in hand, broached the subject of travel. Schabowski announced that 'today' new regulations had been drawn up to allow East Germans to travel. 'Private trips abroad can be applied for without questions, and applications will be dealt with at high speed.

The People's Police have been instructed to hand out long-term exit visas without delay, and the conditions which have applied up until now are redundant.'

That brought a sharper question from the floor: 'When? Immediately?'

Schabowski stroked his chin with his right hand, a contemplative gesture, and peered over the half-lenses towards the questioner. He reached down and turned the paper he had been reading from, searching for something and, as he searched, he murmured, 'As far as I know immediately, without delay.' Twice, three times he turned the piece of paper, abandoned the search. He pursed his lips. He had not, after all, read it when Krenz gave it to him.

It was 6.57.

Now the questioning moved to West Berlin and if East Germans could go there – an obviously, and perhaps profoundly, delicate thing. Schabowski wondered if anybody had told the Soviet Union about the new rules. It was too late for that now. He consulted the paper and found what he needed: crossing was permitted to West Germany and West Berlin.

Only once, and then only slightly, did he raise his voice. He might have been working through a litany about tractor factory production or announcing a friendship visit by the fraternal comrades of the People's Republic of Mongolia. Schabowski was unaccustomed to altering the tonality of his voice, no doubt because that had never been necessary. In an authoritarian state, when people in authority spoke others just listened.

It was 54 seconds after 7.00 p.m.

The timetable which had begun by being measured in months, taking as its starting point 2 May when Hungary opened its borders and the East German exodus began, and then in weeks since the fortieth anniversary of the GDR on 6 October, had now descended to hours; and not many hours remained – about four and a half.

Within four minutes, the news agencies – Reuters, DPA and Associated Press – were sending newsflashes. In the confusion, Reuters and the DPA concentrated on the fact that there would be new travel arrangements but Associated Press went hard that the borders were going to open.

Erdmute Greis-Behrendt 'was in the office, actually. The Press Conference was in the building where our office was – the International Press Centre – and we didn't know what to expect. Some Reuters people had gone down to it but I watched on television. Schabowski used to come over for Press Conferences and they were always held at the Centre. The Conference was on the ground floor in a huge big room.

'We had no warning of what he was going to say although we thought something might happen. We had a little argument after he said, "As far as I know immediately." There was a bit of confusion about what it meant and nobody seemed to be sure. However, we made up our minds that we had understood it correctly and that he just opened the wall: we replayed a video of it to make sure we weren't getting it wrong. And then, of course, everybody was very busy writing and writing and writing.'[4]

Greis-Behrendt remembers a certain confusion over whether people would need identity cards or visas and it transpired they'd need visas, which would be issued by travel offices. She was dispatched into East Berlin to visit these travel offices to see what was happening there – all else aside, it would give confirmation of whether the wall was really opening if visas were being issued. They were closed, 'all dark', in her phrase.

TREPTOW, EAST BERLIN, 7.00 P.M.

Moll heard what Schabowski said but felt no sense of urgency, even at the word *immediately* 'because things had always been the way they were and there would have to be a process for any change to be made, it would all have to be worked out legally. Perhaps the following day, perhaps the day after that, I would get some instructions but probably they'd take longer. I didn't think about it any more.'[5] Still Inge flitted, dipping in and out of the news.

BORNHOLMER STRASSE CHECKPOINT, 7.00 P.M.

It was a deep place, slightly sloping up towards an old bridge. It was an extensive place, too, with a wide awning under which vehicles were checked before they could continue to the bridge. The West began on the other side. The man in charge of the Border Guards, Manfred Sens, watched the Schabowski press conference on television and made his way to the opening in the inner wall. He wanted to warn the Guards there that people might come and ask if they could cross but by the time he arrived a few people had already gathered.

The man in charge of the passport control, Harald Jäger, watched the Schabowski press conference, too. They were working 24-hour shifts and he'd begun at 6.00 that morning. He was eating his supper in the canteen – bread and sausages – and saw the conference on the black and white television set there, but when Schabowski said, 'As far as I am aware, immediately', he stopped eating because he almost choked. Rubbish! he thought instantly. What does this Schabowski mean by immediately? He's had a moment of verbal diarrhoea! Immediately – that is simply not possible.

This division between Border Guards and passport control must be examined because, as the hours tightened into minutes, it assumed particular importance. The Border Guards, by definition, secured the border, including the seven checkpoints – here at Bornholmer Strasse, Chausseestrasse, Invalidenstrasse, Checkpoint Charlie, Heinrich-Heine-Strasse, Oberbaumbrücke and Sonnenalle. The passport controls were part of the state security service, the Stasi, and there was no doubt in Jäger's mind that he was effectively in overall charge of Bornholmer Strasse. He was 48, had been in passport control for twenty-eight years and knew the form. For the twenty-eight years all checkpoints had functioned normally although this was disturbed by the weight of traffic at holidays when they had 'a lot of trouble'.

Jäger describes the relationship between passport control and the Border Guards as 'a division of tasks. Everything which happened within the checkpoint – citizens coming in, citizens going out – was our responsibility. The Border Guards were responsible for the outer security, which meant regulating who could get in to the checkpoint.' Jäger entertained no doubts about his position or responsibilities because these things were 'regulated, fixed in writing'.

In the canteen were others, but chatting to each other, not really listening. When they saw Jäger's reaction they asked him what his problem was. He thought he'd better go and telephone headquarters and find out what was going on. He left his supper and walked to his office, which, because of the size of the checkpoint, took a few minutes. He got there at about 7.15 and already by then the number of people who'd gathered had risen to about ten.

He rang his headquarters to speak to his boss 'who was responsible for all the controls within the capital [East Berlin] and he was informed of everything that happened at the checkpoints. I wanted to know if it was right that GDR citizens were allowed to travel abroad, because it was clear that Schabowski could not just give such an order. There was a chain of command, measures that would have to be prepared and of course we would need enough extra personnel at the checkpoint to cope with such a measure: stamps, technical equipment, everything. There would have to be a regulation about which document they were allowed to travel abroad with. We didn't know which document we would have to ask citizens to present.'

At 7.17 the West German television channel ZDF's programme *heute* (*Today*) carried the news, but as their sixth item. Reflecting the confusion, they spoke only of new travel arrangements. At 7.30, the GDR news programme *Aktuelle Kamera* carried the news as their second item.

Jäger rang his boss, who had seen the press conference. 'I have never heard such rubbish in my life,' his boss said. 'Did you hear that rubbish, too?'

'Yes.'

The boss asked how many people had gathered, and Jäger phoned what was called the *Vorkontrolle*, the point where people entered the checkpoint. Between ten and twenty people, he was told. He reported that to his boss, who said, 'You must wait: sit and wait.'

Jäger made his way to the *Vorkontrolle*, where Sens was. That was about 7.30, and even as he walked there the pace quickened. He estimated there were some fifty to a hundred people there now 'and they were asking if they could travel. They had seen the Press Conference and come to see if it was true. I told them it was not possible because according to our regulations they needed a passport and visa and without them they couldn't go' – you had, of course, to apply for a visa and ordinarily if you wanted to go to the West you wouldn't get one, you'd get trouble instead. 'I told them to come back the following day and some of them went away. There was a fence to which they could go, a little fence, and only those with a passport and visa could go beyond it – it was like a little dead area. It belonged to the Border area: they were already on the area of the checkpoint but not in the checkpoint itself, so now they stood on an area which was normally prohibited.'

DAHLEM DISTRICT, WEST BERLIN

The telephone rang at Godek's home and he heard a voice he knew well, Sergeant Nathaniel (Nate to his friends) Brown, the American duty man in the Allied hut. Brown told Godek he had 'an indication that something was going on because local news media were starting to show up. They said there was talk of the wall opening but, being the kind of guy he was, Sergeant Brown doubted it at first. Then he got a call from one of the local media asking him if he knew anything about it. He decided it was time to ring me to let me know what he had been hearing. I told my wife that based on that I needed to go to the checkpoint right away. I never really told her why, I never shared that information with her and that's the way she probably preferred it. Her attitude was 'as long as you have something important to do you just go do it'. I felt a bit sad because I always enjoyed doing the hot-dogs.'

Godek called Sergeant Yount and relayed what Brown had told him. Godek asked Yount to 'meet me at my office. Our Military Police vehicle was parked there so we used that as a central point.' When Godek arrived he called Colonel John Greathouse, a political military adviser who was working late. Greathouse asked Godek to '"Come by and pick me up." He'd like to go there with us.'

Brita Segger continued to learn the art of writing.

CHECKPOINT CHARLIE, BETWEEN 7.30 AND 8.00 P.M.

Of Astrid Benner's seven customers five were women who worked on a newspaper round the corner. They used the Café Adler as a haunt because it was conveniently close to mull over the doings of the day. They were talking about the woman's page. A photographer came in and said that 'in the next hour something will happen here'.

Astrid Benner wondered what he was talking about.

'Don't you know? They will open the border.'

The women didn't know either because the taped music had insulated them. One said 'Can you believe it? Let's listen to the radio.' Benner flipped the tape out, turned on the big box radio with its strong speakers and everyone heard it together, a recording of the laden voice of Schabowski seemingly coming at them from wherever Benner twisted the dial. All channels were carrying it and trying to wring a meaning from those final words about the lifting of travel restrictions.

The women, according to Benner, 'got excited and said, "We'd better get back to the office" and they started to run. I thought to myself, "What will I do now? I am by myself here." I called my boss, the owner of the café, at his home. "Hell," I said, "you have to get here because I am totally alone and thousands of people may be coming at any moment. This is the first place they'll reach. . . ."'

The owner, Albrecht Raw, made it inside 15 minutes with his wife Nellie.

Outside, Benner saw 'a few people beginning to arrive from our side, the Western side. They stood round and some came into the café for a drink. A feeling grew like it was New Year's Eve, a sort of mounting excitement but nothing happened. We were listening to the radio, commentators were talking and talking but nothing happened. We felt it had to, and now, but it didn't.'

Across the line the checkpoint ticked evenly. The white light fell on its carpet, the binoculars tracked from the watchtowers. There was minimal movement under the Customs awning. The checkpoint presented itself as it had always done, set in its terrible permanence.

'When my boss and his wife arrived we wanted to drink champagne,' Astrid Benner says. 'Then I had an idea. *It's not just we who ought to be celebrating. The Border Guards should be celebrating, too. Let's give them some champagne.* My boss thought it was a good idea. I got a tray out and set about twenty glasses on it, he opened two bottles.'

Benner and Raw came down the three shallow steps of the café and turned towards the white line. An hour before this would have been unthinkable and extremely dangerous: the Guards in the tower lurked

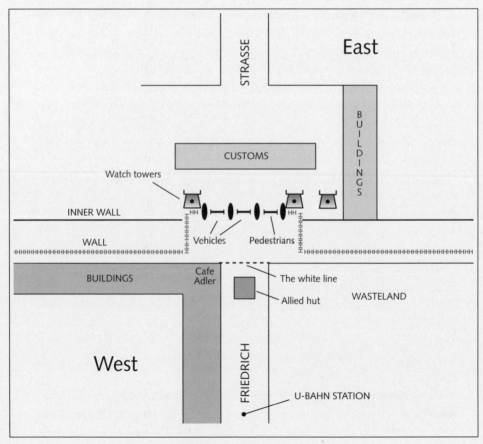

Checkpoint Charlie (not to scale).

like menacing presences behind the windows, trained to shoot. Benner and Raw crossed the white line, walking at a stately pace towards the watchtower. Benner didn't 'think of the possibility the Guards would shoot us because we were making such a friendly, open action and everybody could see it was not dangerous'. Something fundamental, she felt, had altered. As they walked, two Guards emerged from the watchtower and advanced urgently towards them. 'They wore grey uniforms. One stood in the background and the other came directly to us – always two Guards, one covering the other.'

The first intercepted Benner and Raw midway between the line and the tower. Astrid offered him champagne.

'Go back,' he said.

'But we have to celebrate this exciting day, don't you want to celebrate with us?'

'No, no, we don't want that, please go back again.'

'If you don't want to drink now take this bottle. You can drink it later.'

The Guard, Benner would remember, was 'severe just like the Border Guards were but I could sense he didn't know what to do. I assumed he had heard the news from the Press Conference but of course he might not. When it was obvious he wasn't going to accept any champagne we re-crossed the line and drank with the people standing there. By now, slowly, more and more people had gathered. Then we returned to the café and began to prepare for a big party. We went into the cellar to get glasses and telephoned anybody who might be able to lend a hand but either they didn't have time or they weren't at home. My boss's wife had never worked in this line of business but she said, "OK, I'll help." The Guards were back in their tower watching us through their binoculars.'

After this innocent little flurry the checkpoint re-set itself in concrete.

Moll's telephone rang. Simon informed him that 'a waitress and a man from the Café Adler had come across the line and wanted the Border Guards to drink with them. The Guards had told them they were on duty and not allowed to drink, the waitress and the man had returned to the café. I told Major Simon it didn't seem a serious situation but to keep his eyes open and watch everything. If it did become serious he should call again.'

Far to the other side of the city Godek picked up Greathouse who told him about the press conference. It was a lengthy drive. They reached the checkpoint and 'there were just a few people in the area, as a matter of fact. It really didn't look much different to the way it looked on any evening. A few tourists always milled around. Some media personnel were there, some people were just lingering. We walked to the hut and spoke to Sgt Brown. The *imbiss* [the snack bar beside the Allied hut] was open and one or two people stood eating. Nothing unusual.'

Godek had those unseen eyes, the camera up on the side of the building above the café relaying every movement on the Eastern side to a screen in the hut as well as the Mitchell Suite. 'Colonel Greathouse asked me to take him up there because he wanted to use the telephone. I unlocked the door and let him in so he could make some calls. I went back down to the checkpoint to monitor and sense what was going on. More and more people started showing up, more media started showing up.'

They were selling champagne by the bottle in the Café Adler now.

Sergeant Michael Raferty was on a couple of days leave and during the afternoon he'd picked up his wife and daughter from the airport. They were returning from a trip to the States. Raferty sat watching the news in his pleasant flat near where Godek lived. He was due to take over from Brown in the hut the following morning, 5.30 sharp, but when he heard Schabowski's voice chewing through the statement, heard the question and answer he rang the checkpoint. Brown said, 'Nothing was going on. That kind of shook my head because of what had been on the news. I thought I must be blowing this out of proportion.' Raferty woke his wife and said East Germans were being given the right to travel. From deep within her jet-lag she said gently, 'That's nice' and drifted back to sleep. He decided to get a good night's sleep himself. He was due, after all, to start at 5.30.[6]

At 7.42 p.m. one of the telephones in front of Toft rang. Major Watson, his commanding officer, at home, had heard from someone that 'the BBC World Service stated the border would be opening and did I know anything about it. I said no, I didn't. He said, "Can you find out?" I asked the interpreter and he said he knew nothing, he phoned the police and they didn't know, either, then he phoned the city's customs service and they did know. They said, "Yes, it's opening at midnight."' In a very British way Toft said to the interpreter, 'Oh, thank you very much' and phoned Watson, who said he'd be there at eleven. Toft had a ruled piece of paper in front of him which he used as an incident sheet. On it in careful handwriting he set down at the top of the page using military time: '1942 hrs. Telephone message from Maj. Watson stating BBC World Service had reported East Germany has lifted all travel restrictions to West Germany. All Royal Military Police informed.'

Silent as thieves, cautioned by great fear, lured by the press conference and a fascination they could no longer resist, people started to come from the dark and ghostly side streets of the East, each footfall a trepidation. They came to these side streets from Leipziger Strasse and hesitated. From their side the checkpoint looked more forbidding still, a crossing point for foreigners. No East German without a visa on his passport – vetted by the secret police, the Stasi, and rarely granted – ventured near any of the city's checkpoints but especially not this one. It was a criminal offence – 'unwarranted intrusion into a border area'. That was not a nicety. Something very nasty would happen to you, probably three years in jail, and GDR jails were not necessarily places you wanted to go.

In the twenty-eight years of the wall and the checkpoints, so many had died and the communal, unstated memory of that lingered. But now they began to come and not one of them knew if the press conference was a confidence trick, an attempt to buy breathing space. Every one of them knew the word 'immediately' might mean now, tomorrow, a week, a month, a year. Every one of them knew about the shoot-to-kill policy.

BORNHOLMER STRASSE CHECKPOINT, 8.00 P.M.

The fifty to a hundred had grown to several hundred. Jäger had rung headquarters again to describe the situation but his boss repeated that there were no new instructions and he should 'send these people back'. Jäger began, however, to form an impression that something was going to have to give.

At 8.00, the West German television channel ARD's programme *Tagesschau* – a daily review watched by many Easterners – led with 'GDR opens border' and this can only have increased the curiosity of thousands upon thousands of East Berliners to go and see if it was true. There were even rumours that Bornholmer Strasse had actually opened. However, whether you went to a checkpoint to try your luck, disbelieved the whole thing, or simply continued with your life regardless, seems to have been a matter of chance as well as choice: where you were, what you heard, what you didn't hear.

FRIEDRICHSHAIN DISTRICT, EAST BERLIN, 8.00 P.M.

Uwe Nietzold was 'a student and I had never been to West Berlin. I'd seen it from the S-bahn and from gliders, because I had tried that. You could approach the border line up to 5 kilometres and the allowed height was 2,500 metres, and that means you can see a lot. So I'd seen the wall, and forests and houses in the south of West Berlin.

'That night I went to a poetry reading with my club, a culture club but everybody wrote their own thing and read it out to the others. They discussed their writing. It was in the building of *Neues Deutschland* because the printing department had financed it. They tried to encourage young people to write. It was usual that every factory and enterprise had a cultural department. This meeting was in a little canteen and began at 6.00.

'I read a short story about a little boy with a ball which he'd discarded – he was sitting in a playground alone playing games on a little computer. The moral was that children weren't playing with other children and conventional toys any more, they play alone with computers.

'At 8.00 somebody came in – a member of the club, but late – who'd seen the press conference. They said, "If you can believe what was said, we can go to West Berlin and everywhere else tomorrow morning." I didn't believe it. I thought it must have been a mistake. Some people thought it would happen but not tomorrow morning. The meeting continued and we didn't take it seriously. . . .'

CHECKPOINT CHARLIE, 8.00–8.30 P.M.

There was an inherent sense of theatre about this place and always had been. Since August 1961, it resembled a stage in the structure of its background, its foreground and its personnel who, in a sense, were actors moving in their allocated parts across it, never deviating from the script. This night the last act was being played out, obeying the formalised structure in which it was set.

By 8.00 only a few were congregating on the Eastern side of the checkpoint, but along the street at the rear of it because fear kept them from approaching. By 8.30, several hundred people had gathered on the Western side.

Elsewhere, as this was happening, the night began to touch people at random, and in differing ways.

Ernest Steinke was chief editor of RIAS 1, the broadcasting station founded in 1946, but since 1968 a German and American broadcasting station. 'I worked in the Eastern section of this station and I saw the press conference on TV. I went to the studio afterwards to tell the people there what had happened. Somebody had asked Schabowski when people could go over to the Western side and he said, "We have a new law, it's OK." Someone asked, "What time?" and he said, "I don't know but I think the law is ready and they can go now." He also said they had to have a passport and a visa. I went up two flights of stairs to the studio and people asked me what had happened. I said the people could come over and someone said, "There will be thousands coming, a hundred thousand." I pointed out that they had to have a visa, had to go to the police for a stamp and "the police will open tomorrow morning at eight o'clock, maybe, and there will be a lot of people going there. I guess about ten o'clock they'll start coming." Then I went home and went to bed to go back to RIAS early next morning. . . .'

RIAS radio reporter Peter Schultz felt 'the impression it made on me was even stronger than the night it had gone up – throughout the years, we had seen people dying at the wall, we'd seen people jumping out of the windows at Bernauer Strasse; I'd covered Peter Fechter. After twenty-eight years of these experiences, there was nobody in Berlin who believed that the wall could come down again after a sudden and comparatively short period: no journalist, no politician, *nobody*. When it happened it was – again – like a shock, but this time a positive shock. When I saw the press conference on TV I had an idea something would happen but I thought it would be the next morning. A football match was being televised [on Western television] and there was a flash that the wall was open and thousands of people were marching in the direction of the checkpoints. So I went to the radio station. . . .'

KÖPENICK DISTRICT, EAST BERLIN, 8.30 P.M.

On the other side of this wall, Lutz Stolz and his wife Uta watched the match, too. 'I am a great sports fan', says Lutz, 'and we were watching the quarter final in the Stuttgart Necker-stadium on TV. There wasn't just anybody playing but Bayern Munich which has been our top team since the war.[7] It was during half-time that they announced that something very surprising had happened in Berlin, that presumably they had opened the wall. We switched over to the East channel at once and it was broadcasting [a recording of] Schabowski's Press Conference. He did not seem to be very convinced of what he was saying.'

Uta continues: 'He acted as if it was only an error, as if it was not a fact. We did not take it as an absolute truth because there were so many things happening those days – every day something different. Schabowski had the sheet of paper, and he read it as if out of context. Actually it was not completely clear what was meant and, in fact, he did not say clearly that the borders were open: from that moment on, travel permits would be issued without applying in advance – which didn't really mean that you could simply go to the wall and cross, something not possible for nearly thirty years. And it took twenty to thirty minutes to understand. We switched over to the West channel to see what was happening. People simply wanted to understand, and when they did they rushed off. . . .

'We had had some cherry brandy while we watched the soccer game because my husband was enjoying the game so much. When we switched over again to watch the second half we drank a lot because of the message. And when the game was over, they confirmed the message. I remember it very well. I took my Persian cat in my arms and went down to the courtyard[8] where, also because of the cherry brandy of course, I wanted to sing – any song that came to mind. I don't know why, but I remembered one from school, *Bruder, zur Sonne, zur Freiheit,* but I did not remember much of it.[9] I was swaying from side to side with the cat in my arms.'

Lutz adds: 'Standing in the courtyard, I shouted, "We are free, we are free." Of course, we had drunk a lot. We went to bed at about half past eleven, inebriated (and, as usual, I got up at 5 o'clock and went to work at 6.00–6.30). . . .'

TEMPLEHOF, WEST BERLIN, 8.30 P.M.

Daniel Glau worked in his father's hotel, the Ahorn, just off the Ku-damm. He manned the switchboard in the office on the first floor and dealt with whatever problems arose. He lived in his own apartment in the district of Templehof and was there now. He had no relatives in the East, something he did not think unusual. 'As time went on, people died so the number of people with relatives went down. I had never been to East Berlin. I'd seen the wall but it was not interesting for me. Sometimes I looked over it, yes, it was very depressing to see the same people as here, in the same town but we had much money, we had everything we liked to have and they had nothing. I could tell that just by looking. I was at home. I heard it on the radio, they said only the wall falls and I didn't believe it because I had lived here twenty-four years and I had known the wall for twenty-four years. I didn't know how it was before the wall. I know thousands in the East made for the wall but my reaction was *keep cool.* It didn't affect me so much.'

He was the same age as Uwe Nietzold.

BORNHOLMER STRASSE CHECKPOINT, 8.30 P.M.

The hundreds gathering had grown into thousands. This was unlike Checkpoint Charlie because it was within easy walking distance of a vast residential area. Some of the tall apartment buildings actually overlooked the checkpoint. Cars were drawing up in numbers now, too, blocking the long, wide, straight avenue towards the checkpoint. 'The police came,' Jäger says, 'and demanded that the citizens leave the area. They were told to go to the police stations and ask for papers to travel abroad. Some left and did that but the police stations didn't know anything about it and the citizens came back angry because they felt betrayed – and they thought it had all come from the checkpoint.'

At some undefined moment the mood began to change in the dead area: this corridor flanked on the left by the side of a building and to the right by head-high metal railings. The corridor led to the little fence (actually of wire mesh and about 10 feet high, but little in the sense that it was not really designed to withstand assault). The corridor was wide enough to allow about ten people to stand shoulder to shoulder. It was full, all the way back. The mood – impossible to quantify with any precision – changed slowly from the habitual subservience before uniformed men to insisting on the rights Schabowski had said they now possessed. Jäger caught that mood.

Street lights fell on the columns of waiting cars, shimmered on the moist cobblestones of the road. Drivers got out, chatted, and one held a map towards a television camera. He laughed in embarrassment that he might ever be able to use it *da drüben* – over there – in the impossibly distant West, which lay up the slope and across the steel-spanned bridge. A pretty girl in a short coat got out of a Trabant and loosened up by wandering into the lamplight. And everybody wondered.

Jäger was now ringing headquarters every twenty minutes with situation reports and always his boss said the same thing: no new instructions, sit it out.

CHECKPOINT CHARLIE, 8.30–9.00 P.M.

In the Mitchell Suite, Yount and Greathouse watched. Yount phoned Godek in the hut and reported that he had noticed 'some vehicles coming into an open cement area at the back of the checkpoint and it looked as if they might be carrying East German soldiers. The vehicle movement brought about a lot of concern because the last time we had seen that they'd built the extension to the front of the check-point. We saw Guards coming out and although we really didn't know what to expect we figured it might turn into a nasty situation.'

They were Guards not soldiers. Moll had sensed days before that, with the government truly floundering and demonstrations on the streets, he might need reinforcements and had requested sixty of them. They were armed.

BORNHOLMER STRASSE CHECKPOINT, 9.00 P.M.

The few thousands had become many thousands. The waiting cars now stretched back to Schönhauser Allee, a main road several hundred metres away. They choked the side streets all the way back to Schönhauser Allee, too. Jäger surveyed the men he had available, sixteen or eighteen, and knew how hopelessly inadequate that was. He telephoned for reinforcements and about fifty were dispatched to 'protect the checkpoint'.

Major Sens had telephoned *his* headquarters to ask for instructions but no orders had reached them and so they could give him none.

In the corridor people shuffled to and fro and, through the wire mesh, watched the normal passport control going on. The lights were bright there, almost a glare.

At 9.00, Jäger rang headquarters again, the press of people mounting and growing. He gave a situation report and his boss said that what Jäger and his men must do was to pick out the most 'aggressive' among the people waiting and let them through. That would calm things, take some of the pressure off. These 'aggressive' people were, unknown to them, to be punished, because the photographs in their identity cards were to be stamped *on the photograph*. Anyone trying to return with a stamp like that would be refused re-entry. Without being told, they were being deprived of their citizenship, and the decisions would have to be made by the passport controllers on sight. Jäger was ordered to keep a list of those allowed through – their identity card number, their date of birth and so on. He was also ordered to pick out a few non-aggressive people and let them through, so the waiting mass wouldn't realise that aggression was the way to get through.

It was the bureaucracy of madness.

If Harald Jäger could see full down to Schönhauser Allee he'd be looking at 20,000 people, with more coming.

He ordered three passport huts to be opened and at 9.20 the people they picked out were filtered through them. Jäger estimates the number as between 200 and 250; some got the stamp over their photographs and some didn't. And they came through, in single file, emerged from the huts and – some dancing, some scurrying, some close to tears, some shaking their heads in disbelief – they went past the final watchtower and over the bridge to dreamland.

CHECKPOINT CHARLIE, 9.30 P.M.

Moll's deputy rang again and said about a hundred people, some foreigners, had gathered on the other side of the line and were imploring the Guards to please let the people from the East come through. 'I told him to make sure that everything remained quiet, that law and order was maintained. I told him it was his duty to ensure that normal traffic – the cars and buses – should continue to cross as usual. I added, "I will be there as soon as possible . . ."' Within a few minutes Moll got into his Skoda and set off on the journey back.

Brita Segger finished her evening class and was very tired. She walked to Marx-Engels-Platz and waited for the train to the suburb where she lived. Somewhere, as the old train rattled through the seven stations to it on the elevated rail, Moll in the Skoda passed her going the other way. He was driving quickly. On that journey Moll made a decision: no Tiananmen Square, no raking gunfire across civilians, no single death, never mind a massacre.

BORNHOLMER STRASSE CHECKPOINT, 9.30–10.00 P.M.

Jäger had the flow of people more or less under control while, in the corridor, so many waited as they had done for so many years, for so many things. There was an honesty about them, and their stout leather jackets and tartan shirts and heavy shoes, working men's honesty, but they wanted their rights and they would wait for them, too. They had time. They had the rest of their lives. They were noisy, but mostly football crowd noises, good-natured, semi-banter, some jokes; but the fact they were making the noises at all suggested that the fear of men in uniform was, perhaps for the first time in their lives, going away.

At some unremembered moment the tone of Jäger's conversations with headquarters itself began to change from situation reports to a request to let everybody go through. During one conversation he found his boss in the midst of talking to the general responsible for all security in Berlin. Jäger was allowed to eavesdrop and he heard the to and fro although he was forbidden to say anything himself.

His boss: 'The situation is exceptional.'

General: 'Is this correct? Jäger: has he panicked or has he given a real description of the situation?'

Boss: 'I have known Comrade Jäger for many years and if he says it is like that, it is like that. Rely on it.'

General: 'I have my doubts . . .'

At this point, Jäger could stand no more. He shouted into the phone, 'If you don't believe me, I'll hold the receiver out of the window and you can hear it for yourselves.'

The line went dead.

Of equally immediate concern, letting the more aggressive people through had not really calmed the situation. Relentlessly, by weight of numbers and weight of expectation, the pressure kept increasing.

CHECKPOINT CHARLIE, 10.00 P.M.

Moll turned off Leipziger Strasse past the postal museum and was astonished to find the street leading to the checkpoint choked with Trabants and Wartburgs. He had to park where he could, some distance away. As he walked people noticed his uniform and asked 'How do we get through, how do we get through?' He couldn't tell them because he had no idea himself and, anyway, his sworn duty was to stop them using whatever force necessary. He had a lot of that. Only he knew he wouldn't use it.

Greathouse asked Godek if he'd mind taking him through the checkpoint 'for a feeling of what was going on over there'. It was a way of maintaining access to the East and also a way of keeping himself informed. Godek decided he'd be better monitoring from the hut but told Yount to drive Greathouse. They went on a routine sweep which lasted thirty minutes.

Moll arrived – perhaps he glimpsed Yount and Greathouse going by, perhaps not – and 'informed myself about the situation. There must have been about two hundred and fifty people on the western side and they wanted to cross. I decided to go and speak to these people. I did not go alone, I had three or four Border Guards with me. The Guards in the watchtowers wouldn't shoot me, I was in charge, it was my area, my men wouldn't think I was trying to get across.

'I talked to the crowd and I explained that there were no new regulations yet. I went to a watchtower and called my superiors at the Border Force's Headquarters.' This was a plain and typical barracks off a long, straight street near Treptow, a horizontal steel pole blocking the entrance, a reception hut with shifty Guards of its own, a parade area, basic buildings – their corridors laid with cheap linoleum which creaked underfoot – taut military offices, phones, in-trays, out-trays, and an occasional potted plant to soften the impact. Khaki vehicles stood parked in clearings, ready. The headquarters ticked to the same rhythm as the Border Guards at the checkpoint who it ultimately controlled.

Moll asked about the new regulations. No new regulations. Law and order should be maintained. 'More and more people came from the underground station on the other side. I deployed my reinforcements in a line to hold these people back.' This deployment was behind the forward barrier and Godek watched it, a soldier monitoring the formation of other soldiers, watched the Guards being arranged, their boots stroking the concrete quietly as they made the line, parade-ground power tight as a Roman phalanx and governed by the same ethos: order, stand, obey, be prepared to fight. The Guards had revolvers but no machine-guns.[10]

Greathouse and Yount returned from their sweep in the East where they'd seen movement but nothing really unusual. Still the crowd grew all around the hut, the *imbiss* and the Café Adler.

Brita Segger reached her 'little flat' far away in the East and turned the radio on. She wandered into the bathroom to clean her teeth and distantly heard from the radio a voice saying the border was opening. She thought, 'No, no, that's a joke.' She emerged from the bathroom, switched it off, went to bed and fell asleep immediately.

The single phone in the American part of the hut came alive. 'We started getting calls from different radio and TV stations in the United States. They could call directly to the hut because it was an unclassified number; it was published in our telephone directory,' Godek says. He found himself 'on line with a radio station in New York City, there was another call from a radio station in San Francisco and Colonel Greathouse did an interview. I took a call from Sydney, Australia asking us if we would mind confirming what they had just heard, then we got a call from Canada. The thing they were interested in was, "Tell us what you see outside." They weren't so concerned about what we had heard or what we thought was going to happen, but, "Tell us what you can actually see out of the window." We were getting so many calls Colonel Greathouse told me to deal with them. He had notifications to make and because our phone was constantly ringing he went up to the Mitchell Suite to do that. The phone there was not a published line. Before he went he said, "This is what you can talk about and these are the things you are not prepared to talk about." It was clearly understood we must not speculate.'

Below the Mitchell Suite, in the Café Adler, the little team of three worked hard serving but braced themselves for a total onslaught, the place overrun from the East. Perhaps it would come in a moment, perhaps it would never come.

Godek studied Moll's reinforcements. 'They were acting as they normally would. They stood back from the white line in a typical formation, very cold faces, stone faces. They seemed almost not to be bothered about what was going on in front of them. We had seen all that before but again we were really concerned about potential developments because we didn't know what they were going to try.

'Rumours started heating up about the checkpoint opening, mostly coming from the press. I would walk around outside still trying to get a sense of developments. People asked me if I knew when the checkpoint was opening and I'd tell them I didn't, I'd tell them I hadn't heard anything. I had two concerns. The first: was the scene going to turn ugly, would there be physical altercations between the Border Guards and the crowd on our side? The second: were the Border Guards going to try and seal the checkpoint in case a crowd did try to cross from East to West?'

Any sealing, even momentarily, would, of course, be a direct violation of the Four Power Agreement and news of it would travel fast to Washington and London and Paris and Moscow, while Godek requested the presence of a Soviet officer, as he had to do in case of incidents. If a Third World War ever did start it would probably start like this, with the sealing of the checkpoint, and escalate all the way up.

At around 10.00 p.m., some sixty to seventy Westerners crossed the white line in front of the checkpoint so that technically they were on East German territory.

At the same time Godek estimated the total number of people in the West as 2,000 and 'in a narrow street like the one where the hut was that really packs them in. We were still able to maintain our movement – our movement being Allies wanting to go over for dinner or returning from a day of shopping or whatever in the East. There were Allied people coming through, some on foot, mostly by that time in vehicles. These were either military or military-related personnel and they registered with us before they went so we knew who was over there. By 10.30 the large majority were back.'

At 10.35 some 100 people had crossed the white line, but the Border Guards pushed them back. Moll monitored the crowd on the Eastern side and estimated it at between 70 and 100. He monitored the crowd on the Western side and 'there were hundreds, maybe thousands. We had had these problems every seventeenth of June on the anniversary of the "revolt" in 1953 [the workers' uprising put down by Soviet tanks at the end of Leipziger Strasse beyond the postal museum] and in most cases the people who came to the white line were our former citizens who had fled. They were very aggressive. This evening I looked into the faces of the crowd and they were somehow peaceful. They were normal people, not people who wanted to provoke anything. They were drinking champagne and what they wanted was the checkpoint opened. They were polite to the Border Guards. I called my superiors again and there were no new regulations.'

MITTE DISTRICT, EAST BERLIN, 10.30 P.M.

At 10.30, Erdmute Greis-Behrendt 'phoned my husband at home and said, "I'm checking that you're still there" and he said, "What do you mean?"' She was in the Reuters office and had been watching television, if only to get confirmation from their news bulletins that Reuters had interpreted the press conference correctly. She asked him if he'd been watching because 'the border's going to be open tonight'.

He replied, 'Yes, I've been watching television but I really haven't been able to put it into perspective.'

'Where is our son?'

The son, Maximilian, had just gone to bed.

'Get him out of it and go in the Trabbie to the first Western transit point and you cross over. It's the night of nights *tonight*.'

'Do you think that?'

'Of course. You must be there. Go, go, go!'

CHECKPOINT CHARLIE, 10.30

Greathouse asked Godek if 'we would be willing to venture through the crowds with our vehicle to exercise our right of free access because by then it was essentially a mass of people out in front of the hut. Sgt Yount and someone else attempted to go through but they had to stop. The crowd was solid. Not far behind Yount was a Soviet vehicle with four uniformed soldiers in it – they had been over in the West for whatever reason – and they were trapped maybe four, maybe five vehicles behind ours. Finally this Soviet vehicle caught the attention of some of the crowd who started rocking it, which to us seemed rather unusual because they didn't show that reaction to Sgt Yount in ours.'

Inside the Café Adler, Astrid Benner heard 'screaming begin, just screaming. I couldn't tell what they were screaming.' It was the crowd, and the screaming actually a chant deep from the pits of many stomachs.

Moll moved to the front of the checkpoint and tried to calm the 2,000, 3,000. A flashbulb burst nearby and the moment was captured for the morning newspaper. 'Already I had a feeling that this could not go on. Something had to happen. I knew my men would not be able to hold them back, it was not possible, so they withdrew behind the wall.'

This 'totally surprised' Godek. Border Guards did not withdraw in the face of a crowd. Quite the opposite, they fronted it out.

By 10.45, ZDF and ARD were broadcasting that the checkpoints at Bornholmer Strasse, Sonnenallee and Invalidenstrasse would open. What was happening at Bornholmer Strasse and Checkpoint Charlie was being duplicated at each of the other checkpoints; and at each, as the structures of obedience broke down, Border Guards and passport controls were facing extraordinary decisions unaided. Their predicament was not helped by the singular fact that they had spent their careers *not* really making any decisions at all, never mind anything like this.

A photographer at Checkpoint Charlie noted that 'by now the Guards didn't look aggressive and they had not a clue what was going on. You could see that on their faces. They didn't pull back behind the wall in formation. They looked very undecided among themselves. First one or two pulled back, then a few more, then a few more . . .'

They vacated the wedge of road between the white line and the wall itself. In a few moments around ten Westerners moved across the white line through the barricade and up to the wall. Within seconds thirty or forty more followed and then, in a vast slow-rippling wave, more followed.

Moll walked briskly to the watchtower and telephoned headquarters a third time. No new regulations. At this instant, with so many people so near and more and more arriving, Commander Günter Moll was the loneliest of men. He did not know that what was happening here was happening at the six other checkpoints simultaneously, that a great current flowed through the city. The checkpoints had no direct communication with each other for security reasons, so that no one could coordinate a mass exodus or indeed coordinate anything at all. He gave the order to close the small pedestrian gate. Sealing the vehicle gate would have represented violation of the Four Power Agreement and risked escalation of the situation.

Sergeant Yount struggled through the crowd and moved past the line of Border Guards, crossed the checkpoint, followed by the Soviet vehicle, returned after what seemed a long time and reported that yes, a crowd had gathered in the East, they were very quiet but he sensed anticipation.

Obedience had been studiously bred into them, waiting was what they did, mute and uncomplaining. It was never wise to complain. None of them put a foot inside the checkpoint, none made an intrusion.

In the hut Greathouse took a decision and informed Godek of it. 'He decided that we did not need to be accessed. We accepted a point in time where our access would be completely blocked – by ordinary people. I was with the Colonel when he made the decision and it was based on two factors: the emotions of the people on our side and the reactions of the Border Guards. Their conduct changed shortly after 11.00. The crowd started crossing the line in a mass from our side, something completely unheard of before. People meandered over, people tried to climb up onto the wall. The first couple were initially asked by the Guards to "please come off it" but there was no physical contact at all, they weren't dragged off. Eventually enough people were up on the wall that the Guards just let them sit there.'

The current had reached here, unspoken, unregulated, spontaneous – but here. These people on the wall sat with their legs draped down, almost lolled, casual as you like.

Godek continues: 'Just in front of one of the watchtowers, the one to the left as we looked at it, there was a little grassy area and the crowd started milling on that and the Guards let them sit there. Then people sat on the wall next to the watchtower actually looking in at the Guards, something else completely unheard of. The mood was jovial, almost carnival. When Sgt Yount came back from his last sweep Colonel Greathouse said, "We don't need to press our rights, we need to just let this happen. This is a moment for the German people."'

The current caught the Guards and embraced them: a lover's embrace.

'Some of the Guards took their hats off and threw them into the crowd. I couldn't believe it. People were talking with them, they

were talking with the people which they had always been prohibited
from doing. We saw smiles on their faces.' Major Godek was a calm
and conscientious man. He read the implications of these little
gestures perfectly. He knew.

One of the Westerners grabbed the cap of a Guards officer, put it
on and stood laughing. The officer said, 'Please may I have it back, I
need it or I'll be in trouble.' The cap was returned. At this instant, the
wedge of road was a solid sea of Westerners, the full 2,000, and they
pressed against the low wall, although gently, no push and shove,
almost no jostling. Behind it the Guards – nearly all capless – stood
milling. Hands reached across to try and shake theirs. This low wall
was of wood and three Guards pressed their hands against it to stop
the pressure of the 2,000 from tipping it over. Someone wearing
trainers and an anorak clambered onto it from the West and stood
precariously beside the pedestrian gate, turned back to the West and,
arms outstretched, gestured as if to say 'Well, what are you waiting
for?' That was greeted by reverberating laughter among the 2,000.

Two stout supports flanked the pedestrian gate and Moll – he had
his cap, he still looked as if his uniform had been moulded to him –
clambered onto one of them, surveyed the sea which had flowed to
just in front of him. His arms were slack at his sides. As he surveyed,
he knew. Nearby a photographer asked a Guard to haul him up
onto the wall so he could take pictures from both sides and was
deeply astonished that the Guard did.

BORNHOLMER STRASSE CHECKPOINT, 11.00 P.M.

The crowd in the corridor were waving their arms and they could
see the ones who'd been picked move into the entrance to a passport
control hut. A gate in the fence had been opened to let them
through. Many people – waiting or going through – joked self-
consciously. People tried to ebb into a gateway for vehicles. Five
passport officers tried to make sure they didn't because, like a dam,
once a crack appeared the whole edifice would be swept away by a
tremendous torrent.

'Although I was their superior,' Jäger says, 'the people I was
working with that night were experiencing what I was. They kept
demanding that I do something but I was not sure what to do. So I
kept asking them, "What shall I do? Order you to shoot?"' It was a
rhetorical question, of course, but born because he had neither the
rank nor the authority to order the checkpoint opened, but there
seemed no alternative.[11] The thousands were not going to go away.

At 11.15, Rudower Chaussee in the extreme south became the first checkpoint to open.

'We kept discussing what to do,' Jäger says, 'discussing what to do, discussing what to do.' The geometry still held: to one side of the fence the thousands herded like so many cattle, growing increasingly restless; to the other side were empty tarmac lanes, marked by red and white plastic cones, leading up to the inspection awning. The tarmac glistened as the cobblestones did. Here, uniformed men moved through their motions but it was evident that they were now moving faster. The crowd began to remonstrate with anybody in uniform they could reach. 'We're coming back,' they kept mouthing. 'We're coming back.' It deepened into a chant. Someone slapped a customs officer on the shoulder, said 'Stop being so silly' and everyone smiled.

Someone else said, 'There aren't any more cars coming' – so why can't we go through the car lane? Hands were hoisted with fingers splayed in the inverted V for victory. The chant became 'Open it! Open it!' and those in the middle of the crowd began waving their arms aloft. The chant deepened to an insistence – 'Open it! Open it! Open it!' – and continued rhythmically. A bearded man at the very front tried to reason with four or five customs officers. The chant melted into the crowd and died there, was renewed at the same rhythm as 'We're coming back! We're coming back! We're coming back!' Someone pushed at a customs officer, who reacted by pushing him back with both hands and those around shouted, 'No violence, no violence.'

Beyond the fence was a pole across the road and Jäger 'had been standing there all the time. I could telephone from a little hut. The situation was now so hot that we'd reached a point where we could go no further. All I was thinking about now was to avoid bloodshed. There were so many people and they didn't have the space to move. If a panic developed, people would have been crushed.' He was thinking something else: if any of the uniformed men, armed with pistols, fired – for whatever reason, and who could know what reasons there might be? – anything, *anything*, could be unleashed. 'I just did not want anybody to die. We had the pistols, there were instructions not to use them but what if any of the men had lost his nerve? Even if he had shot into the air I cannot imagine what reaction that might have provoked.' He called headquarters again and 'I said, "We will have to let all of them out." The boss replied, "You know your instructions and you must do only what they say."'

The decision was passed deftly back to Jäger.

He said, 'It cannot be held any longer. We have to open the checkpoint. I will discontinue the checks and let the people out.'

He went from the telephone, and might have surveyed the entrances and exits of this checkpoint – the entry to the huts, the coned-off lanes, the gate in the fence, the vehicle gate, the pole across the road. He said, 'Open them all.' He had a feeling something important, perhaps profound, was at hand and, although he didn't exactly know what, he sensed that 'something very bad would happen to the GDR'. Later, when it was being talked over, someone said to Jäger, 'That's it, that's the end of the GDR', but now he had time only for something approaching a gut reaction to his own action.

He was at the pole, 'eight to ten' fellow officers beside him against 'hundreds of people just in front of us; no, thousands'. These officers turned from the pole but the press of the people forced it back; and they came, 20,000 strong, came in a torrent, came with no violence, came stepping sprightly. A young man in a jerkin engulfed in the torrent, clenched his fists as he moved past. A young woman danced herself clean off the ground, her hands clapping above her head. An inscrutable man with his hands in his pockets might have been going for a stroll.[12] A child rose above the torrent on father's shoulders.

For a moment Jäger turned and faced them and was suddenly lost among them. Instinctively he directed a man over there: that's the way across. For another moment, when he emerged, he stood alone, surveying his creation, this mighty mosaic of movement.

And the 20,000 denied people went up the incline past the final watchtower, where a stone-faced Border Guard watched them impotently, and crossed the bridge to dreamland.

The checkpoint was a natural funnel but even so they were through in 45 minutes.

Jäger felt 'my knees begin to tremble and I had a very bad feeling in my stomach. I went to the telephone and rang headquarters. I said, "Comrade *Oberst* [the boss's rank], I opened the border. I couldn't hold it any longer. I let them all out." He said, "It's OK, *junge*"' [it's OK, guy].

With hindsight, the opening seems natural and inevitable and sanitised by the fact that it did not go wrong: no shot was fired anywhere. Harald Jäger could not know that, and what he had done might have put him in jail for the rest of his life and brought lasting official vengeance on his family. That's why his knees trembled and his stomach turned over. 'Normally, you'd expect something to happen to you. I had refused to carry out – well, implement – the orders.' The fact that he had done this because he needed new orders and didn't get them might not have been any defence at all. Nor did he know, because each checkpoint was isolated from the rest, that mighty torrents were flowing there, too, and the same decisions were being reached.

Jäger phoned his wife when he had a minute. She'd been at work all day and partially isolated from events. 'I won't be home at 6.00 a.m.,' he told her, 'I've opened the checkpoint.'

'You're kidding,' she said, and made fun of him.

In the control room at the Olympic Stadium, Toft heard voices from the patrol jeeps 'starting to get excited'. He felt that himself. The radio crackled in front of him, a report from the British section of the hut. He wrote: '2325 [11.25] hours. Large crowd of East Germans at checkpoint on East German side. Crowd building up on western side.'

At 11.35, the Heinrich-Heine-Strasse checkpoint opened.

CHECKPOINT CHARLIE, TOWARDS MIDNIGHT

The impression that 'something had to happen' was growing stronger and stronger on Moll. 'The crowd were calling to each other, "Let us go! Let us go!"' He was under an arch of sound, a chant rising from the West – 'Come! Come! Come!' – and echoing back from the East – 'We're coming! We're coming! We're coming!' He made a fourth and final call.

In the hut Godek watched. Greathouse departed to see developments elsewhere in the city but, before he did, he said the word was that the checkpoint would open, sometime. 'He also informed us that we had been receiving reports of crowds forming at some of the other crossing points. My British counterpart, Major Ross Mackay, stopped by. He'd been to the Brandenburg Gate – which was in the British Sector – and some of his crossing points and he reported the same kind of atmosphere.

'If anything impressed me it was the completely different attitude of the Guards, their change in behaviour. It was the fact that they tossed their hats into the crowd, these same Guards I had seen during previous demonstrations with their stone faces. They were being offered champagne, they were being offered beer. They didn't accept anything but they were laughing. One Guard had his hat removed by someone sitting on the wall and didn't make any attempt to get it back.'

The current exposed the Border Guards for what they were: people.

In the Café Adler Astrid Benner heard 'the noise grow and grow. We could see the Guards in the watchtower still using their binoculars but you knew they didn't know what to do except keep doing that.'

Brita Segger slept on.

Sergeant Michael Raferty slept on.

They were still precisely a world apart.

At 11.40, the Oberbaumbrücke and Chausseestrasse checkpoints opened.

Moll made his call. No new regulations. 'I felt pressure from the people calling to each other but I also felt pressure from history.' He had an immediate problem, itself one of geometry. Nominally he commanded the whole of the checkpoint including the area under the awning where (as we have seen) the Stasi manned the customs, but this had never been tested. The Stasi, that state within a state, wielded stark and immense power even at this minute to midnight. They employed more than 30,000 people; they had more than 250,000 agents and informers in every nook and cranny of the land; they had compiled at least 6 million excruciatingly detailed files on their own citizens, one for every three of the population, sometimes right down to how many times a grandmother telephoned her granddaughter. It was not unknown for fathers to inform on sons and sons on fathers. Love affairs were particularly charted, the where and the when of them. Any political deviation provoked their wrath. The Stasi were the custodians of the revolution and the guardians of it. Their armaments were second only to those of the GDR Army, their power used to strike at any enemy of the state real or imagined. They could take a life, keep anyone in their own prisons, destroy a career, extend their retribution to relatives of the guilty, and there was no law, no legal process to prevent any of this except the most vague. The very existence of the Stasi covered only two paragraphs of the Constitution and the paragraphs were deliberately ambiguous, granting them autonomy and no accountability. The Stasi were feared, and rightly so.

Moll walked briskly from the watchtower to the Customs and spoke to the most senior officer. Moll knew nothing of this officer, not even his name. Moll risked his career and quite possibly his life when he said, 'I am opening the border.' He could not do it without the Stasi. What might happen if he said the people could

GOSEN, OUTSIDE EAST BERLIN, MIDNIGHT

Uwe Neitzold had listened to the readings at the culture club at *Neues Deutschland*; about 10.15 a newspaper worker had come in and said that people were at the border. 'We wanted to see it – eight or nine from the poetry group – and we went to Friedrichstrasse on the S-bahn.' At the station he noticed the underground. 'We didn't even know that the underground went under our own city. How could I know? I was 25 and nobody had told us. If you went to Friedrichstrasse you only saw the S-bahn station and only the Berliners who had lived there before 1961 knew – my family came to the area in 1965. Anyway, Friedrichstrasse was totally crowded so we walked to the Invalidenstrasse checkpoint, we stood and we looked because we couldn't make up our minds. There were at least 2,000 people in the street and we couldn't *see* the checkpoint! I suppose we were 200 metres away and all we *could* see was the checkpoint lights. We couldn't *see* that people were actually crossing. We still didn't believe it was open. We thought they'd keep the border closed. We stood there for around twenty minutes, the time was late and we agreed to go home. We thought it was all a demonstration like so many in the past few days.

'I lived with my parents on the outskirts of Berlin – a village called Gosen – and if I missed the last bus I'd have had to wait until five or six in the morning for another one. I got home at midnight.'

Gosen was a small, quiet place, a slumbering Eastern village and the house where Nietzold lived had been built by his father with his own hands: someone with the intrinsic dignity of a working man. Gosen was silent, as it was every night, and Nietzold was very tired. Apart from the illusion at Invalidenstrasse, it was all much ado about nothing. His parents were asleep. He went to sleep, too.

TEN

Dawn

They built the wall to keep people in and they took it down to keep people in.

American joke

Some 5 minutes ticked by, 10, 15 and no person emerged from the Customs at Checkpoint Charlie. The Stasi were in unknown territory. The people before them and those stretching back had driving licences or indentity cards or passports; navy blue passports bearing the title of the German Democratic Republic and valid only for travel to 'friendly' countries – Cuba, Vietnam, Mongolia, North Korea, Eastern Europe. No person had authorisation to be granted a visa to the West; but the current had flowed under the awning.

Checkpoint Charlie did not fall to an assault from American tanks; no bomb tumbled into its heart from a dark-laden sky; no shooting rang out across the concourse; not even a punch was thrown. Checkpoint Charlie fell into the valley of emotion, as did both halves of Berlin. At 2 minutes past midnight the Eastern police announced that all checkpoints were open and the biggest party in the history of Germany was under way.

At Checkpoint Charlie the Stasi began stamping. They stamped anything, possibly even the driving licences. The current was travelling too fast for pedantry, too fast to be stopped in any way including, perhaps, by armed intervention. Everything got a plump, sharp *Visum* on it, thump, next please.

Godek saw a group emerge from the Customs under the awning, saw them being directed diagonally across the concourse away from the pedestrian gate to the vehicle exit. By stringing them out there would be no rush, no crush, no stampede. Order was being maintained full up to the white line. In a certain sense this was one of the last authoritarian gestures of the cold war.

Moll watched 'the people pass through the Customs and hesitate at the vehicle exit leading to the white line because they did not know how to react. They saw the Guards there and the Guards waved that they could go through.'

Godek said to Sergeant Yount, 'This is it. There's no stopping them. There's no turning back.' Godeck (continuing): 'I'll be very honest, we knew what our mission was and that was to be a symbol of freedom. We tried not to get wrapped up in the emotion but we looked at each other and as two grown men we had a tear in our eye.'

A group came through, maybe 150 strong, maybe 200. Cautiously, sheepishly, they reached the line and kept on coming. In the end, after the twenty-eight years of fear at and around this forbidding place, it was the simplest thing in the world.

Toft's radio crackled and he wrote, '0028 hours. East Germans now crossing to West'.

Perhaps that was the moment which can be, and ought to be, developed, fixed.

In Bernauer Strasse there was no checkpoint, just the wall. However, Pastor Manfred Fischer 'was coming back from visiting a friend at about midnight and I passed Chausseestrasse', where there was a checkpoint, two streets away from Bernauer Strasse. 'I saw a crowd of what looked like families and I thought, "What's this?" People were lying face down and, although I didn't know what had happened, it seemed there had been an accident. I reasoned that I wasn't needed because there were so many people there. When I got home the phone rang immediately and people from the parish said, "Have you heard?" I said, "No, I haven't heard anything." They said, "We want to go to Chausseestrasse. Do you want to come with us?" I said I'd just passed it and thought there had been an accident. So I went back and the people lying face down were Easterners and they were looking at a map of West Berlin which they'd spread out! All they'd had was an image in their minds, they didn't know where things were exactly. It was as if they'd dug a tunnel and emerged on the other side. . . .'[1]

In the Café Adler, Astrid Benner was very busy and suddenly a man exploded into the place He was a little bit fat, around fifty, small, a typical worker wearing a typical worker's cap. He shouted, 'I am the first! I am the first!' The whole café burst into applause. He ran to the bar and said, 'Give me a stamp of the café – otherwise nobody will believe I was here.' Benner stooped, brought out the inky pad in a tin and pressed the tiny wooden handle of the stamp onto it. These stamps were – and are – used on bills all over Germany to signify they've been paid: cafés and bars each have their own stamp. The man held his hand out rigid and she stamped the back of it.

CAFÉ ADLER
Friedrichstraße 206
1000 Berlin 61
Tel.: 030/251 89 65

He had proof he'd been, because being there was the only way he could have got the stamp.

Says Astrid, 'His eyes were wide open, he thought it was all a mistake, all a kind of dream and at any moment he would wake. I gave him a glass of beer and he drank. We gave free beer to the first twenty, thirty who came in but then it was too much to know what we were doing. After ten minutes the café was completely full. People were calling out "I'm from the East and I'm really here" and people were crying . . .'[2]

Godek watched professionally. 'After the first group, for some reason it stopped and nobody came for five or ten minutes, then another group of about the same size, and it all happened again like that a third time. After that it was a continuous flow.'

Moll had the most vivid impression of 'people . . . people . . . people'.

Godek felt the full current. 'These people were received like long-lost family members, patted on the back, embraced, given glasses of champagne, given flowers. It was fascinating to see their reaction to our military presence in the middle of the roadway. Initially it seemed to be to ignore that. They were very cautious of glancing at us or making any reaction to us. We smiled, we waved, we stuck our heads out of the window, we said hello. They'd glance at us but keep on going. They were very hesitant to make any contact although they were obviously curious. I got the impression they were asking themselves, "Are these friendly men, are these not friendly men?"'

The Easterners had spent all the twenty-eight years being taught that anyone in an American uniform must be an imperialist warmonger who was trying to smash their socialist homeland and enslave the globe; they had lived within seconds of an American nuclear first strike; and they'd spent all twenty-eight years being very circumspect about anyone in uniform, even their own kind.

A humble, almost private moment among all this was when a young woman came through the checkpoint, preceded by a friend. Of necessity she moved diagonally behind Moll's reinforcements; her face was full of incredulity. As she reached the exit she looked ahead for the reassurance of her friend and, all in the moment, gave a subtle yet profound sideways glance towards the very last Border Guard, bespectacled, his arms limp at his side. Then her face craned up, grinning wildly, as if she was beseeching, 'Can I really, can I truly?', and then was over the white line into the melee – the patting and the tears and the phosphorescent flashbulbs of the cameras stabbing at the darkness – to find the rest of her life which would never be the same again now.

The 'siege' inside the Café Adler held fast. 'A friend of mine had arrived and I asked if he could take care of the entrance because too many people wanted to enter and there was no room for any more, none, so when some left he let exactly that number in. The chief editor of a newspaper arrived and he started to serve.' Astrid Benner felt her certainties breaking up.

Godek watched the crowds at the checkpoint. 'When they reached the line they stopped then they took a step over it. People cheered for them as they made that step over, a deliberate step over.'

And still they came.

Toft's radio cracked and he wrote, '0050 hours. No vehicles allowed across Checkpoint Charlie'. It meant no vehicles could *get* across Checkpoint Charlie.

The 'siege' outside the Café Adler held fast. Something approaching delirium danced in the faces and the eyes of the people; complete strangers embraced and any bottle was a bottle to drink from. It didn't matter whose hand held it. A morass of ordinary folk jostled shoulder to shoulder, and somewhere in the middle of this, just by the Allied hut, a live bear, red muzzle over its nose, stood on its hind legs looking benign and bemused. The official symbol of Berlin was a bear and the owner of a children's circus had brought it: the perfect gesture. Someone put a Guard's hat on its head and that got a reverberating cheer of its own. At 0135 Toft recorded people 'chipping away at wall with hammers'.

In the growing confusion the British thought they still had one of their vehicles out in the East where it had been all night. It ought to have re-crossed at Checkpoint Charlie but could get nowhere near. Toft recorded the message from the British section of the hut: '0149 hours. Possible military vehicle now moved to a southern crossing.'

Some 11 minutes later – at 2.00 a.m. – deep from within her slumber Brita Segger heard her doorbell shrill. She wondered who it was at such an hour. The bell rang and rang. 'I got up and went to the door and it was my boyfriend Mehmet, a Kurd living in the West. He said, "I've been waiting at the checkpoint for you for hours." I wondered what he was talking about. He said, "The border's open. I've been waiting but you didn't come." He assumed I'd seen it on TV and assumed I'd be coming', and Checkpoint Charlie, because that was where foreigners crossed, where she'd have deduced that Mehmet would be waiting for her.

Mehmet: 'Get dressed, we're going to the West.'

Brita: 'It's the middle of the night, I've got to work early in the morning and I'm very tired. No.'[3]

Mehmet: 'You have to come.'

She gave in, dressed and they went in his car, a new Audi 80. To someone from the two-stroke Trabant culture this was luxury itself. They drove from the sombre suburbs of the East down a long highway which thrust towards the city centre like a rod. Just before it ended, they passed a complex of square and oblong buildings with antennae and aerials, a giant grouping stretching a long way back resembling a web: the headquarters of the Stasi. No doubt a telephone had rung there from the Customs at Checkpoint Charlie reporting the opening and getting the reply 'No new regulations.'

The highway became Karl-Marx-Allee, its architecture on such a scale that people were incidental to it; and the road itself had been Stalin Allee before the dictator's disgrace, before the timeless safety of renaming it Karl-Marx-Allee. If Mehmet and Brita looked over to the right they'd have seen the statue of Lenin in an oval-shaped platz; Lenin, the foreigner who was prophet and architect to their own country, up there on a big plinth in his waistcoat and suit, arm outstretched, beckoning and guiding. A minute before midnight he had still been that, prophet and guide. Not now, not as Mehmet and Brita passed him. If they looked over to the left, at the apartment block just before a square, protruding building called the Café Moscou, they'd have seen a darkened ground-floor window. Birgit Kubisch, having dismissed the BBC World Service news bulletin as relaying just another rumour, was sound asleep there.

They might have seen, also, the twin spires of the Nikolai Church which had outlasted Lenin and all his successors, but by then they were into Leipziger Strasse and wondering about the checkpoint. Mehmet parked the Audi 50 metres away – like Moll the nearest he could get – and, like Moll, they walked the rest of the way. Brita Segger would gain no precise impression of the geometry because 'there were so many people, I remember a lot of lights and it looked to me like a very big party going on'.

Brita and Mehmet moved into the Customs area but the stamping had evidently been abandoned, the Customs overrun, just like the Café Adler, now so near. Brita clutched her passport but found it irrelevant. In her twenty-one years that was as astonishing as anything she had ever known. 'We went across and a couple of girls came through at the same time and they were very happy. At this moment I didn't understand what I was doing. Without thinking I was in my boyfriend's arms. We danced for a little but in the road and people were shouting, "Hello, how are you?" People were drinking champagne and wine and singing and crying.'

Brita stood only a few paces on the Western side of the white line and amid the delirium began to think. She hadn't heard Schabowski's press conference about exit and re-entry visas because she'd been at evening class, hadn't heard the analyses of that because, cleaning her teeth, she knew perfectly well it was a joke, and she'd gone to sleep instead. Now here she was beyond the line of no return. 'I thought, "I can't get back. They're allowing people to leave but they won't allow them to re-cross." I could not comprehend that it was possible to cross the border normally in both directions.' Her complete possessions might well prove to be what she stood up in, and if she couldn't go back she was cut adrift from all she knew, her flat, her family, her career. She would be a penniless orphan in this alien land where, apart from curiosity and affairs of the heart, she had no great wish to be. If the checkpoint re-set itself in concrete and she did go back, she'd be regarded as having fled the state, a serious criminal offence.

She reasoned that 'if I went further up the street away from the border that would somehow mean I'd gone fully into the West and I really wouldn't be able to get back.' She and Mehmet lurked in the crowd, but near the line so that she could skip across it. 'I wanted to have a look at the West but not live there, I wanted to look and go home. We met three West boys and they said, "Come on, we've a car, we're going to the Ku-damm."' Brita and Mehmet decided it was a nice offer but, Mehmet said, their car was only just over there and why not take that?

'No, no, don't go back,' Brita said.

Mehmet pointed out that, while these boys were offering a lift, once he had the Audi over here they'd be free to go to the Ku-damm, to the Brandenburg Gate or wherever else they wanted. Something else had become true, too. With all the borders open in Berlin *and* between East and West Germany, the car represented freedom to go anywhere else, Stockholm or Madrid, Paris or

Istanbul, Rome or Amsterdam and all places in between; but so far
Brita had remained near the line.

Then she said, 'Ok', the way people do, and Mehmet set off into
the bowels of Checkpoint Charlie to fetch the Audi. When he'd gone
she did move away from the line, to a point facing the underground
station. She stood outside the bank and 'many people spoke to me'.
The current made strangers curious about strangers, made strangers
want to clasp hands and – perhaps – become family again. '"What
are you doing?" they asked and I said I was waiting and that I
hoped my boyfriend would be able to manage it with the car. He
arrived after about twenty minutes. He'd come through another
checkpoint although I don't know which because I didn't ask. We
drove to a little restaurant and ate a Turkish meal. It was the first
time I had eaten Turkish food and it was very good. We drank a
little bit of champagne and I smoked Western cigarettes. Now it was
nearly three in the morning and we took the car to the Ku-damm.'

Toft wrote, '0225 hours. No vehicles crossing but people allowed
to cross'. Eleven minutes later the radio crackled again: '0236 hours.
250+ people on the Western side right up to the barrier, no vehicles
allowed through, crowd still in good mood'.

Brita had images of the Ku-damm in her mind already, as so many
Easterners must have done because they'd all seen Western television
for years. The Ku-damm represented capitalist realism overlaid by a
multicoloured neon backdrop of galactic proportions.

The opulence of the shops cascaded over the eye in a caress:
mannequins in designer creations, caves of jewellery, luxury car
showrooms, porno kinos, perfumeries, chic restaurants – French,
Italian, Chinese, Greek, an Argentine steak house – international
bookshops, fast-food places and slow-food places, stores specialising
in delicacies, whole windows heavy with chocolates; and, further up,
curious glass display squares mounted in rows on the pavement
containing more jewellery, leather handbags and shoes and gloves
and Parisian silk scarves; and so it went, on and on.

In the early hours of this morning the Ku-damm presented a freak
spectacle: it was completely overrun. You could pick out the
Easterners by their hardy jerkins and coats, their stout shoes made
to endure, their old-style caps and hats that Westerners hadn't worn
for years, their eyes darting in curiosity and wonder.

'The clothes in the shops were not so important to me, it was
interesting to look, yes, but that was all,' Brita Segger says. 'For me,
it was important I was there, there with my boyfriend, and I could
go on the same streets as he went on, see the same buildings he saw

every day. We went to a restaurant on a corner – the Café Kranzler – and people were dancing and drinking and we had another glass of champagne. Outside there was a flower shop which was open and the man in it gave me a present, a black rose with a long stem.'

Erdmute Greis-Behrendt says her husband Thomas and son had gone to the wall straightaway after she'd rung home at 10.30 p.m. Thomas 'phoned me at the office about half past three in the morning. My son said, "Mummy, we have just come back from West Berlin. It's really absolutely super. I'm going to bed now because I'm dead tired." This was so touching to me because he had never been before, of course. They'd driven towards the Invaliden-strasse checkpoint in our Trabbie to cross there and when they couldn't go any further they'd parked the car and walked. They were pushed through the checkpoint with thousands of other people and they found themselves on the other side. They took a taxi to the Ku-damm, and that's what they did. As my son told me how wonderful it had been I was trying not to cry because there are so many moments in your life when you should be with your child and this thing happened and I wasn't.'

Toft wrote, '0346 hours. Checkpoint Charlie reports lost military vehicle still on east side. . . . 0405 hours. East German authorities starting to clear Checkpoint Charlie by moving them into the West. East German authorities not wearing hats.'

The Café Adler closed some little time later. Since 4.00 a.m. people had been drifting away and in any case 'we had no more to sell. The wine and champagne and beer was all gone – well, we had just a little bit of beer left. It had been so crazy we were exhausted. We had to close. My friend who had been on the door drove me home.' Astrid Benner couldn't sleep. The excitement had been so strong that as she lay she could feel her heart beating.

The Easterners were re-crossing and that posed a particular problem for Harald Jäger at Bornholmer Strasse, if they had the stamp over the photographs in their identity cards. He points out that Bornholmer Strasse was the only checkpoint which had oper-ated that policy because 'there was no other checkpoint where so many GDR citizens had gathered'. And now here they were, unaware that they were no longer citizens. He remembers a couple who must have been about 35 and they had the fatal stamps. The woman started to cry: she had left her children sleeping in their apartment nearby while she and her husband had a sneak look at dreamland. Jäger made the only decision a good, honest man can make. He waved them back through. (Others, turned away, no doubt discovered that the various checkpoints hadn't been operating this system and re-crossed there; and, anyway, the days of such bureaucratic madness were to end soon enough.) Jäger also points out that Easterners discovered the other checkpoints had been opened because, fanning out into West Berlin, they would re-cross at them. Jäger himself, isolated and working so hard, only discovered this on the Friday afternoon.

Toft wrote, '0458 hours. Three missing soldiers plus missing vehicle have returned to West Berlin . . . 0503 hours. Guardroom informed of soldiers' return . . . 0507 hours. Checkpoint Charlie. East Germans slowly crossing border on foot from East. East German vehicles returning to east. Four East German Border Guards on border line sending back West Berlin citizens from barrier.'

They were trying, perhaps, to re-set it in concrete, but they had come far too late to change history. From this moment on, a measure of crowd control would be exercised but the right of any Eastern citizen to cross and re-cross would never again be seriously challenged.

Raferty had woken in the most blissful ignorance and called a Military Police patrol to take him to the checkpoint. During the journey, they told him of the night's events. The vehicle couldn't get near the checkpoint itself and had to drop Raferty way down Friedrichstrasse because the street was still blocked solidly with Trabants, Wartburgs, Western cars, people . . . people . . . people. When Raferty reached the checkpoint it resembled a 'madhouse. I had to elbow my way to the hut. Most of the people were Westerners coming to have a look, crowding around just looking.'

Mehmet and Brita drove to the Brandenburg Gate shortly after 5.00 a.m. The old stone charioteer still rode the stone horses up on top of colonnades that still bore the chipped marks of fire and counter fire from 1945, but here the wall was so broad that Border Guards could stroll two abreast on its curved circumference as it looped round the front of the Gate. Not this night. The top of the wall presented a fresh spectacle of its own. Some 200 or 300 young Westerners had taken possession and stood or sat or danced.

Many times Brita had seen the Gate and the wall from her side although no close approach could be made. You had to stand 100 yards away behind a metal fence and gaze. Now she was curious to see quite what it looked like from the other perspective. On this Western side an observation platform of tubular scaffolding had stood for many years and it was much favoured by tourists because they could peak through the Iron Curtain from a safe distance.

To this place Kennedy had come and two decades later Reagan. On 10 November 1989 they were succeeded by many ordinary folk, among them the 21-year-old trainee journalist holding a black rose. She looked across at her own half of the city, looked at this wall which cut through with the brutality of a plough and she expressed in a single word what millions of other ordinary people felt: *Madness*.

Those on the platform naturally assumed she was a Westerner. 'No,' she said, 'I'm from the East.' Persistently they asked her if she wanted to go back and she said, 'Yes, of course.' They said if they were her they'd stay, they couldn't understand why she wanted to go back; and that was the real division of their city and hers, not this wall but the distance between the ordinary people of East and West understanding each other.

Brita kept looking at her watch. Dawn was creeping in from the East. Those around her, still incredulous that any sophisticated young woman would voluntarily re-cross, were informed that she had to go to work and that was where she was going.

She and Mehmet drove to Checkpoint Charlie and got out of the car. Raferty or Godek might have glimpsed them but we'll never know because there'd been people . . . people . . . people. Brita said a little nervously and a little mischievously to Mehmet, 'I'll see you later on this afternoon – in the West.' Mehmet had been her boyfriend for two years but she had never, of course, visited his apartment. 'I kissed him good-bye politely because we were in public. I said, "See you."' During the night she'd been 'losing my fear of whether I'd be allowed back across but it was still there. I took my passport out and stood in a queue with some workmen. They had their helmets and overalls on and I stayed with them. We chatted a bit while we waited. We went into the room where the Customs officers were and the workmen said they had to go to work. I said that, too. Then we just walked through.'

RIAS reporter Peter Schultz says, 'We made a programme with a lot of colleagues and then I went to Invalidenstrasse [where Uwe Nietzold had tried to cross the day before] at four or five in the morning when a colleague relieved me. There were thousands and thousands of people and Trabbies were coming. People were embracing each other, drinking champagne and knocking on the cars. My first daughter was born 29 August 1961 and my second in 1965 so the whole of their lives the wall had been up. I went to the Brandenburg Gate, that was my Gate, *my* Gate. I saw people dancing on the wall and the soldiers with water cannon . . .'.[4]

Toft wrote, '0632 hours. Checkpoint Charlie: East German vehicles going East to West and vice versa. About twenty people milling around checkpoint area. Four East German Border Guards on border line.'

Brita Seggar worked 'about ten minutes away and when I reached my office I put the black rose in a jar of water'. Her colleagues wondered where she'd got it. She told them, the Ku-damm, you know.

Astrid Benner woke after three hours' sleep. Normally a couple of waitresses could handle the daytime in the café but not this Friday and anyway 'I wanted to be there.' The Café Adler had run out of bread as well as everything else and she went to the shop and bought some, then took the underground and started work again. Albrecht Raw had already re-stocked the café with wine, champagne and beer. 'People,' as Benner says, 'are very quick.'

That Friday itself fell into a valley of emotion.

The Trabants putt-putted in an endless column past Raferty in the hut and Astrid sensed it as it happened: 'The traffic in the whole area suddenly broke down.'

Raferty had much else on his mind. 'You've got to remember the Friday was also an American holiday (Veterans Day, for Federal employees including the military) and a lot of our travellers showed up to go over. We processed hundreds and hundreds and at least three hundred and fifty vehicles, too. Sgt Brown ended up staying over.' By 1.00 p.m. the street was so full that Raferty had to 'climb through the window of the hut because I couldn't get in the door. A Military Policeman was standing there, I asked him to cup his hands and I used that as a step-ladder.'[5]

Raferty noted what Godek had noted. 'You'd see the people from the East pause and take a deep breath before they crossed the white line because they understood what it meant. Almost everybody did and immediately they were cheered.'

During the afternoon Brita Segger returned, although through the Invalidenstrasse checkpoint in the north – where Germans ought to have gone, not Checkpoint Charlie. This time she went to Mehmet's apartment.

Between 3.00 and 4.00 Godek surveyed a 'tremendous line of pedestrians and vehicles waiting to get back over [to the East]. Half the pedestrians had shopping bags or plastic bags with oranges, bananas, all sorts of things.'

For the twenty-eight years the people of East Berlin had known only the most minimal consumerism. The whole shift of the society had gone the other way, towards subsidised rents and basic food which everyone could afford and which never rose in price, free medicine, a massive university programme on an absolutely egalitarian principle. The cost was to the consumer because the money the government had available remained finite. To get a telephone might involve a wait of eleven years; a Trabant (amazingly made of compressed brown paper) as much as fifteen; a colour television took a year's wages to buy; and, while the staples of life were often abundant, much of East Berlin still looked threadbare and meagre and morose, almost brooding on the old wounds, when it was measured against the West, as it now was by the line of pedestrians.

They carried what they had never touched before: exotic fruits – a woman brandished aubergines – and 200 packs of Marlboro cigarettes and electrical playthings; and often, with a terrible tenderness, nothing but presents for their children, the pocket-calculator games you could hold in the palm of your hand, Snoopy versus the Red Baron, whatever that might be.

These people, if one may risk a generalisation, had suspected they were relatively impoverished before they crossed and saw for themselves, but that only sharpened the depth of irony. They or their parents just happened to be on the wrong side of the road on 13 August 1961.

Some went the whole way and nursed ghetto blasters and video recorders in the cardboard boxes stamped Tokyo, Japan; held them with the same tenderness that they held new-born babies, in both hands.

None of these people resembled refugees. They were what they had become, strong and solid and privately not *un*proud of what they had collectively hewn with their bare hands across all these hard years from *Year Zero* in 1945; but now here they were in dreamland and they were humping and heaving as much of its luxuries home as they decently could. Most were joyous, intoxicated, held by feelings of release, some were humbled and baffled by the choice available, ten different brands of everything. Some were frankly ashamed it had come to this but had to go and look all the same. Some wondered about the human condition which could still be bought so easily. Some already wondered about the future because, in the political sense, there could be no going back.

At 4.00 on that Friday afteroon, Birgit Wuthe, like Astrid Benner a part-time waitress, arrived at the Café Adler. She was 22, a student of politics and the Border Guards in the tower must have enjoyed sweeping her with their binoculars because she liked France and had acquired the Parisian way of moving her tight *derrière*, which oscillated as she flitted from table to table:

I'd been working at the café for five months but I wasn't there on the Thursday night. I was sleeping at home in my apartment in Wedding and I heard the news at seven o'clock in the morning. My father telephoned and said 'Turn on the TV!' I did and I was quite surprised. They were showing pictures from the night: lots of people crying and shouting and jumping, beating the roofs of the cars.

That morning, the Friday, I had an appointment with a girlfriend – she was moving and I said that I would help her. I jumped into my car and tried to get to her where she lived in Templehof but that was difficult because the streets were full. I still didn't realise the full extent of the situation. And my friend wasn't very interested in this whole thing because she was so busy with the move. After I'd helped her I went to the café by tube. That was in the afternoon and when I went up the steps from the U-bahn station just before 4.00 it was too much. Checkpoint Charlie was only for diplomats and foreigners – I wasn't allowed to cross there, for instance – but I realised very quickly that *masses* of people were crossing it. The checkpoint was *full* of people. Zimmerstrasse was packed with people and they wanted to hear the sound of the wall peckers [people chipping off bits of the wall as souvenirs]. Cars couldn't get through the crowds easily.

I started working at 4.00 and this was the day [Chancellor] Kohl was in front of the café and there were *so* many people I couldn't get out to see what was happening in front of it! One of the owners served for the first time. A girl and a boy asked if they could help and we said, 'Well, it would be nice.' We were charging for drinks – that was possible – and most of the people drank beer. We were open until four o'clock in the morning and we only closed because the glasses ran out, not the beer. Customers took the glasses outside [to watch] and left them. There were *millions* of bottles.

Those drinking the beer were at last drawing it from the same well.[6]

Late in the afternoon Godek and Yount were standing outside the *imbiss*. A man from the East approached and 'just kind of stared at me. Sgt Yount, was fluent in German, and when the man spoke and I asked what he'd said. "He's saying hello to us, that's all."'

Yount mused 'Isn't this a great day?' and the man said yes, then put his arm around Yount who said, 'We are very happy for you.' The Easterner offered Godek and Yount a drink from the bottle of beer he was carrying. There were at this moment ½ a million Soviet soldiers in the GDR, officially there as liberators and guardians against the Yankee peril. What courage did it take for an Easterner to approach two American servicemen in public and offer them a drink?

In the early evening Raferty himself crossed the line. 'We had a bus full of travellers over there, we had heard there was a problem and I wanted to make sure everything was OK. Usually there was not a soul at that time but now I had to dodge people who were coming my way. When I wanted to re-cross, the Border Guards tried to get me in back of this line full of East Germans waiting to cross. They were checking passports and stamping them. I said, "No way" and I walked back right down the middle of the checkpoint. I told Major Godek when I got back and he just laughed.'

What would have been one of those potentially serious incidents at this time the day before was now so trivial you truly could laugh about it. The Border Guards had abandoned any pretence at protocol and were simply trying to keep thousands of people on the move.

The world had gone sane.

'To be honest,' Raferty says, 'the Border Guards and the Customs were dumbfounded. They didn't know what to do. One day they're guarding the checkpoint real tight, the next day they're just looking at passports and stamping them.'

Raferty finished his shift some time around 8.00 that evening.

I had to ride the subway because no vehicle could come to get to me. I had a 104-degree temperature. It was such a long day compounded with all the travellers we'd had to look after and the Trabants coming through right by the hut. We'd had the window open so I'd been breathing the fumes from their exhausts. I got a real bad fever. I had to wait for like three or four trains at the underground station before I could finally squeeze into one. By the time I changed lines heading for home I was real sick, I thought I was going to throw up. I looked over and there was this little girl and a man. I speak a bit of German and I asked him where he was from. He said from the East, from Potsdam and this was his first time in the West. I was just trying to keep the conversation going. The girl was his daughter and it was her first time, too. I took my Berlin Brigade badge off my sweater and pinned it on her scarf. Her father started crying and all I wanted to say was 'Get me off this thing, I feel sick!' When I did get off, everyone was waving at me. All night I dreamed about Trabants . . . Trabants . . . Trabants.

And that was the Friday, or at least fragments from it. Many are the tales told: at least 4 million, because that was the combined population of Berlin.

Godek worked thirty-six hours straight, full on into Saturday morning, and he didn't feel tired because adrenalin took care of that. He was reluctant to leave but he had an eye appointment.

Astrid Benner received a telegram from a friend, Harriet, who lived in Dresden in deepest GDR and to whom Vietnam and the moon had been closer than the Café Adler. The telegram said she was coming to East Berlin and would be at the Friedrichstrasse station far up the street in the East.

This station had, as has been seen, its own geography and geometry. The underground was so prohibited to Easterners – because it was a potential conduit to West Berlin – that it did not appear on their city maps. Young people, many regularly using the domestic mainline station immediately above it, were openly shocked – like Uwe Nietzold and Birgit Kubisch – when they learned after 9 November that an underground line ran there and had always run there, north–south and linking one part of West Berlin with another.

That Saturday, Harriet arrived at the mainline station and Benner was there to meet her but 'we had a problem finding each other because we were both in streams of people. You had to go up some steps to the checkpoint and the Border Guards were still there. Harriet hadn't been able to find her identity card, she only had one from when she'd been a child and she thought she wouldn't be able to come over with it but the Guards didn't care: they took a quick look and we were through. We got on the underground' – the north-south line. They caught a southbound train through the empty stations which had been blocked off for the twenty-eight years – Französischestrasse, Stadtmitte – and, passing directly under Checkpoint Charlie, reached the underground station by the café. Harriet knew she'd reached the West because this station sign was not in old gothic, it was new. Unconsciously she was reflecting her expectations of the West.

Benner says, 'Harriet hadn't much money so I said she would be able to work in the café to earn some. She spent her first day in the West making sandwiches and looking at Checkpoint Charlie from the Western side.'

This was the new normality and Harriet, making the sandwiches for a little pocket money, had found a measure of it already. People, as Astrid Benner has said, are quick.

ELEVEN

Pieces

When I went to a home appliance store in the West for the first time,
I walked through the aisles and just mumbled to myself like a senile
old man, 'This can't be true, this is unbelievable, I must be dreaming.'

Bernd K, skilled worker
quoted in *We Were The People*

The day after the wall fell there was a private moment at Checkpoint Charlie, and in a way it was more touching and more
profound because nothing happened, nothing at all.

For years a man called Helmut came daily to the checkpoint and
everyone remembers Helmut – Godek, Raferty, Yount, Brown, the
British. Helmut was a legend and the legend grew as it was handed
carefully down from one generation of soldiers to the next in the
Allied hut.

This is how it was described to Raferty: 'Helmut was from the
East but worked in the West and one day he walked across to go to
work' – it can only have been Saturday 12 August 1961. 'When he
tried to get back to where he lived in the East they wouldn't let him
so he decided to relocate himself in the West. His family were on the
other side. As he got older he had a couple of strokes and he was in
a home somewhere near the Checkpoint but he came every day.'[1]

Raferty handed the legend on to Godek and this is how he describes it:

Helmut was a very old man, probably in his early eighties. He
would come religiously and stand maybe two or three feet short
of the white line and look through the Checkpoint. He would
watch and he would watch and he would watch. After he was
done, he would stop in at the little sliding window on the side of
the Hut and, in German – he never spoke a whiff of English – talk
with the American soldiers. One day Sgt. Raferty asked him why

he always came. Helmut relayed the story that he worked in a little factory in the West and when the wall went up he was never permitted to return to the East.

So every day for years and years Helmut came. He wore the same dark blue suit, brown shoes, white shirt, a tie canted over to the side a little bit. We would give him badges, we would give him ranks and his whole lapel on his left side was like a decorated war hero. He was so proud of that stuff. The first time I went to Checkpoint Charlie he was talking to Sgt Raferty and I was introduced. The next time I saw him I took the little Major's oak leaf off my hat because he didn't have one and pinned it on his chest and he wore that proudly, too.

Well, I guess it was the day after the night the wall opened up that Helmut came as usual and I assume he did his usual thing, walked near the line, started over towards us when he'd done that. He came to the sliding window and he talked briefly and he took off. We didn't see Helmut again for a month. As a matter of fact we had such a relationship with him that we became a little bit worried about him. A month later he returned but this time we didn't notice him go look. He just walked up to the window and we asked him if he'd been sick. He said no. We said, 'But we haven't seen you up here – what's the matter?' He said, 'There is no reason to come.' We asked if he had been over to the East and he said, 'No, there's no reason to do that either *because I can.*' It brought tears to our eyes.[2]

Helmut took off and never did come back to the place which, soon now, would no longer exist.

Maybe, in the seething multitudes who bodily seized dreamland – overrunning and overwhelming the transport system, packing the bars, blocking the roads with their put-put Trabants, dancing along the Ku-damm, drinking a lot of their own beer and a lot of other people's – every moment was somehow private. In the first weekend after the fall, 4.3 million Easterners got exit stamps. In round figures, 2 million visited West Germany (and caused a 60-kilometre traffic jam at Helmstedt), and 2 million visited West Berlin. You could pick any of these people to understand what that privacy mean. Take a 22-year-old student, Katrin Mongau, who was studying languages at the Humboldt University, the country's best. She had never been to West Berlin 'although every day when I took the train from the city centre to Köpenick where I lived I could see it: new blocks of flats'.

I had relatives and acquaintances in the West and I always thought it was one town, Berlin. When I looked across I thought I wanted to visit that part, too, visit my relatives. My grandmother, who was born in 1910 and died three years before the opening, could [as a pensioner] and I know she was very sorry for us. As a young girl, my mother always went to the cinema in West Berlin. She was studying in Dresden when the wall was built and it was a horror for her.

I heard the news on Friday morning. I came home very late on the Thursday because I was with friends. My mother had been watching the Schabowski press conference on TV but it was too boring for her and she switched it off [before he said the fateful words]. I don't even know that if she had heard the news she would have believed it.

So I got home, we didn't know anything about it and we only found out next morning on the radio. We heard that last night the wall was open and thousands of people went to West Berlin. We also heard that you could only go to West Berlin until eight o'clock this Friday morning – they'd try to close the wall again to have everything back under control. I called my friend – I had a date with him – and he said, 'OK, it doesn't matter that the wall is open.' We could not really believe it, you see. He had to go to work and I had to go to the University so we couldn't get to a crossing point before 8.00. I thought I'd go to the University and see what could happen next, because if they had opened the wall I didn't think it would be possible for them to close it again.

At 12.00, I went from the University to the S-bahn at Friedrichstrasse Station on foot with a girlfriend and there were not so many people at the checkpoint there. Before this, to take a train to the West you had to go out of Friedrichstrasse and under the bridge, go through a control, a body search and then you went up into another S-bahn platform [the one forbidden to ordinary Easterners]. I asked two building workers, 'How does it work with the documents?' and one said, 'It's not very difficult. You only get a stamp and you can travel to West Berlin for three days.' I had my identity card with me and it was stamped each time you crossed – although sometimes the place was so crammed full that they stopped stamping the cards and just let the people through.

I stood on the platform with my girlfriend and the S-bahn arrived in the station. Masses got out and by now there were masses on the platform, too. We were among the first to get on and we got a seat. The train was so crowded that we didn't see the wall as we went across it. We were busy with ourselves. We were talking to other people because everybody was happy and everybody was talking to each other – but we did see the Reichstag. We got off at the Zoo station and we changed trains: we went on the U-bahn to Nollendorfplatz because a friend of ours had left East Berlin shortly before and I thought I'd never see him again. He wasn't allowed to come back, even for a visit.

We couldn't find the place where he lived, although I'd looked at the city map, and we hadn't so much time because we had to be back at seven o'clock in the evening. It was the time of carnival and we had to dance. We decided to go to the bank [to get the 100 DM welcome money offered to every Easterner] and we waited ten minutes, then we took the underground to Wittenberg-platz to look at the KDW [the famous luxury food emporium]. It was the first department store of this kind I had seen and it was, I thought, very dear so I didn't buy anything. I only looked at everything to get the whole impression.'

Katrin was looking, for the first time in her life, at the pleasure of plenty – something normal and unremarkable in the West for going on three decades. She can have had little true comprehension as she stood there of what it took to create the plenty, which was approaching life from a completely different direction. The Westerners had little understanding of her and hers, either, assuming that they would surrender everything before the altar of this plenty they'd coveted. The reality was always going to be a messy balance between these two extremes, this gain and loss – for the West, too.

Then already we had to return to East Berlin. I called the cousin of an acquaintance of my mother who lived in the West and she said, 'Where are you? When are you coming' I had to tell her I was sorry but I had to dance that evening. I said we'd come the following day.

I went back [to East Berlin] and danced, then after the show I went with my friend to Eberswalder Strasse, which is near Bernauer Strasse, because we had heard on the radio that they were breaking down the wall there to make a checkpoint. There were very many people, and also television and radio. Some building workers were breaking the wall down very slowly and a lot of Army officers watched. That must have been ten or eleven in the evening and the people who were standing had hammers and they began battering the wall down. They found a big piece of steel, shaped like a pole but big and heavy, and five of them – ordinary people – used it as a battering ram. They broke down the wall with it. My friend helped. I couldn't – it was too heavy for a woman, I think. The people watching counted out 'One . . . Two . . . Three' and the five hit the wall with the pole. Their hands were already bloody so others took over. I gave an interview in French to a French TV station. Afterwards, when we left, we took a piece of the wall with us from the East, which was very nice because it was totally white.'[3]

The graffiti, the clever slogans, the adolescent messages, the artwork had all been on the Western side. No East German had ever done anything like that because you were shot if you tried.

In the morning Birgit Kubisch 'went to university and had the feeling that people were very excited. We were sitting in the canteen discussing it and somebody said, "I can't believe it but it's true, the wall has come down." I still didn't believe that one could simply go through without showing one's passport. Then a girl said, "You know, I've been to West Berlin. I've been there. I've been to the Ku-damm." People made plans to drop their lessons or go after their lessons. I thought how strange it all was because the whole street was covered with people rushing, the buses were crammed full.'

So far away on the other side, and now so physically near, Daniel Glau went to work at the Hotel Ahorn. 'Of course the Ku-damm was full of people and very under pressure. You could tell the people from the East because of the way they dressed, their shoes, their behaviour. They were very . . . I will not say unfriendly, but it was very hard for them: another culture, forty years of looking over their shoulders. I had no experience of anything like that. I left earlier for work because I knew I'd need more time to get there.'[4]

Uwe Nietzold 'slept late. I got up at eight o'clock. I should have been up at five to get to my lectures and now it was half past seven. I had to hurry to get the bus so I didn't hear the radio or watch any TV. When I reached Friedrichstrasse it seemed quite normal. I walked to Humboldt University and there should have been a lecture on the sixth floor about the penal code, starting at 9.15. I got there at 9.30 and the University was empty, no people. For the lecture not even the professor was there and I couldn't get into the lecture room. I saw some people standing outside it and they were very excited, speaking, talking, shouting. I spoke to somebody who said I could go to West Berlin without any problems. I couldn't say a

word. I was speechless. Then some of the department staff came and
said that every lecture was cancelled because nobody was there.

'A friend came and said, "I don't believe it but let's go." We went
to Friedrichstrasse station and joined the queue but it was so
crowded we decided to go to Invalidenstrasse. There we saw the
queue – a tremendously long queue – and joined the end of it. It was
so long we were just about to turn away when a West German car
came – a Ford – with a woman driving and it was moving very
slowly. She brushed against my friend, got out and said she was very
sorry. She'd hit his leg. She apologised a thousand times and asked
how badly he was hurt. He said, "You could do us a favour and
take us to West Berlin." We got into the car in the back seat – we
didn't know whether it would work to go in a West Berlin car with a
GDR identification pass and no visa. We came slowly to the control
because there was also a queue of cars. We gave the officer our
identification from the window, waited five minutes, got the papers
back and we could go through.

'She drove to Wedding because she lived there and we went to the
nearest bank. We were almost the first so we didn't have to join a
queue for our 100 DM [welcome money]. To be *given* money was a
bit embarrassing. The big impression came in the late afternoon
when they switched on the lights – everywhere neon adverts. I'd seen
something like it once when I'd been in Vietnam. Before, I'd been
free to go there but not the Ku-damm. That's a paradox. I didn't go
into the shops. I was afraid. There were too many people, too many
goods and I didn't know how to move. I looked around and then
I saw a man selling watches for 50 DM and I saw one I liked very
much and I bought it. I didn't know what else to buy! I didn't feel
I was still in Germany, I knew it, but it was in my head not in my
heart because it was so different. I re-crossed at about six o'clock
because there was a big demonstration in front of the Old Museum
in East Berlin and I was interested in it.'5

The parents of Marina Brath, the girl who'd been bought out of the
GDR prison, came to see her in West Berlin 'one day after the wall
came down' – this Friday. 'They didn't telephone first because they
didn't have one. They came to the hotel where I worked but I wasn't
there, I was at home. They went to my flat, I opened the door and
there they were. I was really shocked: my brother Alexander, who'd
been eleven when I left, was now 18 and a young man! My mother
cried a little. They weren't interested in the shops, only in seeing me.

'Mother hadn't believed it the night the wall came down when
she watched it on television. I made a meal and we talked the whole

time. My mother saw the apartment and said wow! My brother only looked at me and he said, "Oh Marina, my sister." I don't know what they thought of me leaving. My mother was in the Party and she believed in the good things of the system because she was a child of the war. That's the difference between the generations.

'I went over to see them after four weeks. I felt angry and frightened. I felt strange. I felt like a stranger. I felt an inner pressure and I wasn't really relaxed – no, I wasn't actually frightened but *different*. I still feel it [1990]. After that I had my first dream about the prison – no, nightmares about the prison. I went to see a doctor and he said the feeling will stay with me for a minimum of between ten and twenty years and, if I'm unlucky, maybe forever.' (To the author: 'Feel my hands. They're cold when I talk about it, that's the problem.') [6]

Brigitta Schimke, the former Westerner who'd married an Easterner – Erhard – and lived in the apartment overlooking the wall, and what had been the sunken gardens, 'saw Schabowski on television and we heard the famous sentence. We managed to get the telephone from the people on the first floor. We had a plug. My brother [who she'd waved to so discreetly from her little balcony while he stood on the observation platform over there in the West] had already called and asked when we were coming and said the champagne was on ice. My youngest son was at home. I said he should go on his motorbike and visit my brother who lived in the district of Rudow (in the south-east of West Berlin). I went across the next day' – on the Friday.

Erhard 'didn't really dare to cross. I could not really believe we could, but I did cross. We drank champagne and it was very touching, people were giving roses and beer to the Border Guards. People were walking in the death strip, East people, West people, everybody together.'

(In 1992 Brigitta crossed what was now a green strip 'every day to get to the bus to work. I am very happy but it's not yet a normal feeling.' Brigitta met someone who, 'we found out later', had been in the same church congregation in the West 'and we both realised we were Protestant and we'd been confirmed there. The church was called the South Star but the wall divided the parish and afterwards we'd had no contact.')[7]

The British Army caught the mood of this Friday perfectly and if there is a slight schoolmasterish feel to what they set down afterwards, in their *Berlin Bulletin* publication, then never mind.

It is not every day that you find yourself standing in the midst of history as it unfolds around you. The staff at the Havel School felt that the event . . . presented too good an opportunity to miss and were determined that they would do whatever possible to ensure that the children would always remember they were among those fortunate few who were in Berlin when 'The Wall' was breached.

Following a couple of telephone calls we were grateful that 62 Transport and Movement Squadron RCT [Royal Corps of Transport] could provide us with a coach for the morning without our normal prior booking procedures.

Parties of our youngest pupils, this year called Year 5 under the National Curriculum Council's recommendations, eagerly boarded the bus. In total, over 130 children were to have an experience of a lifetime.

Pausing only to buy flowers at the Garden Centre, where a further 50 were donated to our cause by a tearful sales assistant, we were off to the Staaken Crossing Point between the GDR and West Berlin. When they arrived, their teachers described the background and set the scene. The plan was that each child would have the opportunity to present a flower of greeting to a person coming across what had been until fifteen hours earlier a closed border.

The reality proved to provide an even more moving experience. We were privileged to witness many scenes of tremendous joy and beauty as visitors streamed across the once-daunting boundary. One man stopped his car in the car park just behind where we stood – the first place he could legally stop after crossing the line. Once our children had overcome their initial reticence, he found himself swamped with flowers. And all the while he stood staring at his bleak surroundings as if he were in the finest palace saying over and over again – 'This is my first time!'

Another Trabant responded to our waves and stopped beside us and as the children joyously gave their flowers, the moment proved too much for the young couple in the car, and they both wept openly.

Later we went right down to the actual crossing point and joined in the celebrations with the many Berliners who had come to meet friends and relations as they poured through.

Meanwhile, a very small number of senior pupils were taken by private car to the area near the Brandenburg Gate. Here they witnessed similar scenes of joy. We have precious memories which we will never forget.[8]

Katrin Mongau, the language student who'd promised to go to the West again on the Saturday morning to see the 'cousin of an acquaintance of my mother', did go, 'together with my mother, and this was the greatest thing for me: the first time my mother had been because on the Friday she was working and didn't feel like going to West Berlin alone. My parents are divorced.

'We left at six in the morning. The acquaintance was not very far away [as the crow flies] – we lived *here* and she lived *there*. Today it takes us fifteen minutes by car but then you had to go all the way round on the S-bahn and U-bahn and it took an hour and a half. We had to change on the U-bahn several times but we had a map so we knew where. She was a distant cousin and I'd seen her only once or twice in my life when she'd come to East Berlin. So I knew her although there had not been very much contact. We have no telephone and I couldn't get letters from Western countries because it was not allowed.

'She lived in an apartment, we arrived, we had breakfast and it was impossible for us to think! We were so happy. I was crying, not too much I think, and my mother was crying too. It was too great for us. After breakfast we went to her daughter and we spent the whole day together. Later we walked a lot. In the evening it was the same for me: I had to return for dancing, there was a show and people had bought the tickets in advance. At the checkpoint I thought, "What if I can't return?" But I could because when the show was over I returned and we spent the night there.'[9]

Rudiger Hering, who lived in the East near Falkensee, 'didn't have television or the radio on so we didn't really notice what was happening' on the Thursday. On the Friday, 'I had to start work at 5.30 in the morning – I worked in an agricultural machine factory in Falkensee. I went there and at the entrance to the factory the woman on the gate asked me where I was going.'

Bemused, Hering said he'd come to work, of course.

'What?!' she said.

It begs the question of how many of the factory workforce were now in the West or at home with hangovers from the West. The night shift had left at 10.00 the previous night and, evidently, not been told what had happened, but they'd have heard soon enough and you could walk to the checkpoint at Staaken.

Hering's wife Ingelore telephoned. 'Everybody would need a visa stamp and she had already been to Staaken to get hers. I worked until four, then I went home and picked up my identity card and driving licence. My son [14-year-old Marko] came from school and we went to Staaken together. They charged me 15 marks to stamp the visa!'

Everything was now in order and, on the Saturday, the family went to Spandau to see Hering's uncle, taking an overnight bag. Hering's wife and son did not know Spandau at all. It had always been a kilometre away, but the wrong kilometre.[10]

Birgit Kubisch, another language student,[11] contemplated crossing on the Friday but found the crowds too claustrophobic and waited twenty-four hours until Saturday:

It was a very strange feeling. We went at nine in the morning – my step-sister Connie and her husband Manfred, who were on an ordinary visit from Dresden and now absolutely wanted to see West Berlin. We took the S-bahn to Friedrichstrasse and we wanted to cross there but we saw all the people so we decided to go to Invalidenstrasse where, actually, there were fewer people – a lot, but not so many. They didn't control the passports any longer. The Border Guards were drinking champagne and some of the people crossing had little bottles and gave them to them. The Guards said, 'Thank you very much' and drank. There were so many people I couldn't see the checkpoint itself. A Guard was standing, a chair was 5 metres away from him and we went straight between them. It took us maybe a quarter of an hour.

The first impression was the Guards with their bottles of champagne not controlling the passports, and the people very excited, some of them laughing but others being very quiet, silent. They were just looking and I can't say what they were thinking, but not everybody was loud and funny.

If you are there for the first time you want to see. I sort of looked into myself. It may be strange but I was somehow sad because even today [1990] I still cannot understand that it had lasted so long. I can understand that somebody wants to build a society which is an alternative to capitalism, but the more you think of it the more you think you can't build such a society by putting a wall round it.

I was shocked by the amount of traffic in the West – so many cars. We went to the Ku-damm because my sister and her husband wanted to buy a radio for their car. First they wanted to get their money because every GDR citizen got 100 Deutschmarks [the welcome money]. I got mine only later, in December or January, because I felt ashamed. I did not want charity. I felt like a beggar. Anyway, this first time the queue to the bank was 500 metres and

I was walking along this queue, looking at the people there and I felt shocked. No, ashamed. And what shamed me even more was people from the West distributing cakes as if the Easterners were so poor they didn't have the money to buy cakes themselves. Maybe it was not meant as a humiliation. Somebody offered me one of these cakes and I said, 'No, thank you.'

But you know what was even more humiliating? The people from the East humiliated themselves. They were so greedy they took three of the cakes – they held two in one hand while they were eating the third. Maybe I was too proud. I had 30 Deutschmarks which I'd collected. Relatives had sent it and I got some from my grandmother.

I didn't like the Ku-damm because I do not like advertising and anyway you couldn't enter the shops because they were so crowded. Even my sister and her husband said 'oh no' but they absolutely wanted to have this radio. We found an electrical shop which was also very crowded but we went in and they bought the radio for 59 marks. We had some french fries and Coca-cola in the street because you couldn't get into a café.

On the Saturday Lutz and Uta Stolz went over, crossing at 11.11 in the morning (people remember important moments like that). 'I did not intend to go immediately,' Lutz says, 'because I needed some time to digest it, to realize the new and different situation. We crossed at the Warschauer Bridge and when we arrived at the border there we met a friend who'd queued for four hours to get his Welcome Money. I noticed how friendly the Border Guards suddenly were. We weren't sure how all these new regulations would work.'

'I thought somehow they would manage to control it again,' Uta adds, 'and that all this was a wonderful ghost story which wouldn't last for long, I did not really believe that something would develop from that.'

The Stolzes didn't go to get the welcome money. 'We wanted to visit some friends who helped me a lot when I studied medicine at the Charité [East Berlin's leading hospital],' Uta continues. 'This was in the 1950s and I studied medicine for two and a half years. I lived in a furnished room. My grant was 95 Marks, 35 of which I had to pay for the room. These friends helped me with money and food, and I spent many weekends with them. We went to visit them – I hadn't seen them for twenty-eight years. They could not remember my name but when they saw me they recognized me.'

'We also went to the sports grounds where I had played soccer when I was a child,' Lutz says. 'All the changes in West Berlin were somehow frightening for us because of course we hadn't seen them over the years. Take for instance the *Stadtautobahn* [the dual carriageway which is an inner ring road]. It has facilitated the traffic but it has also led to the destruction of many buildings. We tried to find old buildings and places we remembered. Before the wall went up, about 80 per cent of the members of my soccer club went to the Western part of the city to play so I was always going there. I knew West Berlin almost better than East Berlin. I had many friends there and I spent most of my spare time there. We went looking for that.'

'This was', Uta states, 'our first day in West Berlin. It ended with a surprise at home. I had forgotten to turn the washing machine off. Chaos. The wallpaper came off the walls. And that was it, our first contact with freedom.'

'When,' Lutz remarks, 'we went for the first time by car we visited my cousin who lived in Rudow [a district in the south of West Berlin], although we had seen her several times through these years. The worst was for people who went to the West in the 1950s and had no contact at all after that.'

'The fact that the gap between East and West became bigger and bigger was due in part to the way in which West Berlin and West German people were treated by the Border Guards,' Uta says. 'This is one of the reasons why they said they did not want to have anything to do with the East anymore.'

Lutz reflects that 'my wife and I have remained the people we were and we are happy that we can go wherever we want. I keep saying that the freedom we have obtained is the greatest thing. But you can only judge what this freedom means if you were not free before. Nobody else can. What can a Westerner know or tell anybody about freedom? He cannot judge this. In the East we were stultified and spied on and these were the classic characteristics of an Easterner, the characteristics that we got from our government. This is the conclusion I have drawn.'

The RIAS radio reporter Peter Schultz covered the opening of a section of the wall at Bernauer Strasse on the Monday. 'There were a lot of press people, media people. Professionally it was a good job, not easy but a very good job. Highly emotional? Tears? Yes – there were three walls, an older one and another two. It was a cloudy day but there were masses of people, like an avalanche, and it became one street again. And the people who went over were from the

because I didn't have money and I knew there were so many people in the department stores – more people than goods. You had to join the queues at the banks for more than two hours to get your Welcome Money and while I understood why people wanted to have the money I personally thought it was primitive to stand there.

It was a beautiful museum in a palace and I spent two hours looking at it. Then I walked to Checkpoint Charlie, because I knew a bit how the streets were. I'd an old map – 1951 – with the whole of Berlin on it [Eastern maps only showed West Berlin as a blank space, remember] and I had studied it before I went. I wanted to see this Checkpoint Charlie, the most famous in Berlin.

The next time I crossed I went to other museums like Spandau. There was a plan in East Berlin to knock down the 100–150-year-old buildings from Alexanderplatz to Friedrichstrasse but since we had no money to build modern buildings it didn't happen, so in one way it was good not to have had the money.

It was not really policy, more a fact that after the war people liked to throw everything old away and wanted to have something modern, something new. For example, a very beautiful old wooden table would be thrown out in order to have a plastic table. Then there were plastic lamps, too, trashy things. . . .[15]

There are two ironies in these words. The first is that a museum director would have, and need, a 1951 map to find his way to another museum within the same city. The second is that soon enough East Germans would be throwing so much of what they had into heaps in the streets and replacing them, yet again fifty-four years later, with things modern and things new.

Erdmute Greis-Behrendt had already been to the West with her husband. 'When the people started getting out through Hungary [in summer 1989] my husband and I got permission because it was my father's eightieth birthday. However, we couldn't get permission to take our son. In the West we read the newspapers and saw the news about events in Hungary. We bought a lot of very nice presents for our son and after we came back home he was sitting in our garden. He said, "Thank you for the presents but I think I will have to be 65 before I can go and see it myself", and I said, "Never! I swear to you that you will not have to wait until you are 65." The flight through Hungary had started and I knew it couldn't be stopped.'

She crossed again 'about three weeks after the wall opened because I was working the whole time. I had been very close to it once before, about a week after the opening. The East Berlin entry visa of one of our visiting correspondents had expired and he needed to go across the border to the West and return: as he returned they'd give him a new one. We drove to Checkpoint Charlie and they said, "Oh, if that's all you need, just drive round one of the huts, get out and we'll give you a visa." That's what we did – so I didn't [actually] get to West Berlin, only the other side of the Checkpoint . . . then we had an evening free and I went across with my family and that was very touching.'[16]

Erkhard Gurtz was serving in the GDR Army and, born in East Berlin, had never been to the West although 'we all watched Western TV and we saw another life, a better life'.[17]

The night the wall fell, Gurtz, then 20, 'was in woods on the border line in the south of the GDR and I had a little walkie-talkie. The operator said, "A lot of people are on the wall, there are demonstrations and they want to pull it down." There must have been some sort of live communication because I heard a voice saying, "Let the wall be pulled down." Two hours later I heard that the government had ordered the Border Guards in Berlin to open all checkpoints [which they hadn't]. It was crazy. Then a jeep came up to the other side and the soldiers in it looked out of their windows. They spoke to us across the border. They shouted, "The wall has fallen, you are free. We are a united Germany – Come, Come, Come." It was very difficult for us. We had standing orders not to speak to the Western Army and it was very dangerous to speak. So we stayed in the woods and we did not speak.

'My mother wrote me letters about the situation in Berlin and my heart was beating. Everybody could cross the border in Berlin except the military, who were not allowed to. It was three weeks before I could get leave. I went on the train from Meiningen [the nearest town to where he was serving: it was in the south of East Germany] to Berlin and the people looked down on me because I was wearing my Border Guard uniform. They said to me, "Go home, go home", and I said, "I am going home!"

'They had a strong look in their eyes. Some people were happy and friendly to me but a lot of others were very angry. We went to the U-bahn and people started to shout at us. We tried to hide ourselves. Someone asked me, "What will you do now? The army's finished for you" and I said, "It's not finished. I have one week's leave and then I have to go back."

'When I got home my mother repeated that the border was open but "you can't cross". I was very angry. The order from the Army chief was "you don't cross the border". People could cross with ordinary passports but I had a military passport. However, I had an idea: *my brother Uwe looks like me and maybe I can go across using his passport.* Uwe was 28, but he had an old picture in his passport. He came to mother's apartment to visit and we had a conversation there. He said, "Everybody can cross, but what about you?" I *was* very angry. I explained what I had in mind and he said, "It's dangerous for you, but it's your decision." I said, "Yes, it's my decision and my problem." He said, "Here, you can have the passport. If I'm asked, I'll say I've lost it."

'I went towards Checkpoint Charlie, my heart was beating and I was sweating a hundred metres before I reached it. I thought, *it's too dangerous for me, too dangerous.* If this went wrong it would have been big trouble – I had disobeyed orders and I would have gone to prison for a long time. I waited until a lot of people were crossing together, I went to a Customs officer checking the passports and I showed him my brother's quickly. I went past him and suddenly I was in West Berlin. I went to the first shop which was selling souvenirs about the wall [the 'Museum at Checkpoint Charlie', a collection of memorabilia about the wall and escapes]. I looked at them but I didn't buy any – I'd just come from the wall! The question I started to ask myself was, what happens when I try and re-cross to go home?

'I had no money but I wanted to see the Kurfürstendamm. That was my ambition. I asked people directions and they told me bus number so and so. I got on the bus and you didn't need to pay, you only had to show the GDR passport. I got out at Kurfürstendamm and I walked, just walked – just walked in streets I had never been in before, walked for seven hours. When I got back to Checkpoint Charlie it was very dark. The Border Guards there had by now a very good life – the right mentality for controlling people! There was a queue, a lot of people, and I could feel my heart beating again as I waited. I was sweating again. It was the first time in my life I had the feeling of fear – I never had this feeling before.'

Gurtz moved past the Border Guards to Passport Control and two officers stood there. 'One waved his finger and I showed the passport and he said, "Go!" and I walked through again. I hadn't told my mother – maybe it could have been dangerous for her, too, if I'd been found out – and my brother hadn't told her anything either. My brother could have been in trouble. I got home and said, "I have been in West Berlin" and my mother said, "You're mad!" It was a beautiful thing my brother did. I think about it all the time.'[18]

Klaus-Peter Grohmann, who'd visited Potsdam and Dresden in 1972, ruminates on his feelings when he returned to East Berlin in 1989 for the first time since 1961:

I thought *my goodness*! I was so happy to be there again and I thought, *this is part of my town as well*. Actually it was a fantastic feeling to see the Dom [cathedral] and be able to walk down Unter den Linden again, but somehow it didn't seem to have that much to offer. And it's strange. We still [early 1990s] travel around in circles and they are still the Western circles, just as in the East they travel in Eastern circles. I'd had friends in the East – everybody had – but after that length of time there was no more contact, no more writing. People started to get married and have children. People built up new lives on both sides and the distance between us got worse.

We have to get over this, we have to start enjoying common things again and learn to be the same. It's difficult. In the East they missed forty years of evolution and I'll give you a practical example of that. I've bought a farmhouse in the East, at Leitzkau near Magdeburg. There, the walls are still painted with chalk and I recall that the last time I had to wash a wall was at the age of 23 [in 1959!] when I had my first flat, but even then we had powder to which you just added water and you didn't need to wash the wall again. So that's a small example of what they missed.'[19]

Pastor Manfred Fischer, who had inherited the Church of Reconciliation and never put foot inside it before it was blown up all those years ago, now faced reuniting his congregation on both sides of Bernauer Strasse:

It was different from East to West. We had a religious town initiative with people from Mitte and Prenzlauer Berg in the East, Wedding and Tiergarten in the West. We talked about it. Let me give you an example of the differences: one of our members lived in the East and he could look onto Bernauer Strasse but he needed months to take it all in. First he went to the wall, then he went through it but only a little bit, then he went past the [deserted] watchtower. He did all this slowly – *until psychologically he occupied this area*.

There is the word Zone and it is a political word in our German language but it also carries very, very different meanings between the East and West: same word but altered by context. In the West, nobody talked about the American, British and French Zones but they did use it for the GDR, calling it the Occupied Zone, the Russian Zone.

To writers and artists and philosophers, zone means a forbidden area where you cannot go and the man really had that feeling: *this is a zone – you can never even touch this*. He was a normal man and I want to describe how it wasn't an easy thing for him to go through an open street after twenty-eight years. It was *not* just going through.

Now look at the Western people. They'd shrug and go straight through. But me, too, I had troubles going over this border because we lived here [and saw it every day]. I couldn't cross here, I couldn't.

I can't describe how these people from the East came to this church step by step. It was a very, very unique situation and it changed day by day. The Chausseestrasse checkpoint [south of Bernauer Strasse] was 'opened' on the night of 9 November. Here [Bernauer Strasse] the wall itself was opened on 18 June 1990. These were the steps: first on 9 November all the checkpoints were open but they were still checkpoints. Then new checkpoints were to be added. Two months later the first was built at the end of Bernauer Strasse, but still controlled.

The next step was a checkpoint in Bernauer Strasse but only occasionally controlled. Then the U-bahn station which was exactly on the wall was opened in the summer – a completely new step, because you couldn't go there before. The first opening of a street without any controls was Ackerstrasse [a side street] – no controls, no police, nothing. On 30 June they stopped the controls all over Berlin, because by then it made no sense to control the other crossing points. People don't remember this. A year later, they'd arrive and ask, 'Where was it? Where was the wall?'

Slowly people came to us. I recognised them because somehow you know your own people. You'd say, 'Hello, what's your name?' We are very open. We had a coffee bar every Sunday and we invited people and we offered them a cup of coffee. We discussed. They'd say, 'Yes, I'm from this house over there, I've come to look' and so on. It wasn't a lot of people from the other side of the parish because there were not many members there any more: first only very few houses are left, then the percentage of Christians was very low and the percentage of Lutherans even lower.

However, people came from other churches – the Elizabeth-kirche, the Sophienkirche, all these churches over there. And before, my people couldn't be buried in the cemetery and couldn't even visit it. Well, they could visit but they had to obtain permission weeks ahead and then go to the right checkpoint. It was half a day to get to the other side from here. It was also very difficult for the old people – for someone in a wheelchair, say, who wanted to see the grave of their husband. One of these old ladies told me, 'I came to this house to be nearer to the cemetery where my husband is buried' but she could hardly go.

After the church was blown up, people who'd moved away would come back and say, 'Where is Ackerstrasse?' [you couldn't see over the wall]. They came to a very strange, unknown place and they had no point of reference. I tried to maintain links because otherwise it's like a balloon which has burst and nothing is left. Always you make the past nicer than it was and that is why I fought to keep the section of the wall here standing as a reminder of what the past really was.[20]

Come together; that was the slogan of the moment. Only gradually did people from both sides fully begin to understand how far apart they still were and how, as Pastor Fischer says, even physically it had to be done step by step.

Kurt Behrendt, so long a resident of the Steinstücken enclave, says:

When the wall came down nobody knew what was going on. Even before the road was built in the 1970s there had been two factions. One said it was good we were enclosed because it was so quiet. The other said, 'OK, but we can't see our families.' When it was obvious the wall was coming down the situation was the same, two factions. Then the wall peckers came, too!

The wall came down in the spring and summer of 1990. It had been opened at some places in order to combine the streets from here to Babelsberg. I could walk across the strip and meet my neighbours and it was a very good feeling. I was always in favour of the wall being opened. It was also a very strange feeling, and many of the people sort of hesitated but – since I had my camera and I was so curious to see and take pictures of everything taking place – I was not so hesitant. I took my camera and observed the people.

Walking along the streets over there I didn't know where I was. There were two phases: first we could go to Babelsberg but we were hesitant, unsure at the moment we stepped onto the death strip. It *was* a very strange feeling because the border authorities were still in power and, although they let the people through, you were afraid they'd suddenly come and say, 'It's over, you can't go there.' That's why they were hesitant.

I was very sad when I saw Babelsberg. I knew some places in the GDR and East Berlin and I had assumed that there would be lots of buildings which were very well maintained. At first glance everything looked very good in Babelsberg but when I looked closer I saw many of the buildings were rotten. This does not refer to the people. On the contrary, I felt a kind of admiration for them because they were able to live with what they had – the few things they had. When I saw Babelsberg I realised what it meant for the people to have lived there. The general feeling was that they were sad. And when they demolished the watchtowers and removed the wall my general feeling was that people in the East did not really know what would happen.[21]

A reminder of how strange, perhaps sinister, this past had been, is given by Birgit Wuthe, who worked at the Café Adler, had a boyfriend in the East and went to visit him so regularly – two or three times a week – that she was well known to the Border Guards at Friedrichstrasse railway station:

Lots of things happened at the checkpoint. One day they stole my passport – I turned my back and it was gone. I don't know who stole it and a week later a woman called me. She worked in a government office in West Berlin and she said, 'I found your passport in my bag. Could you please pick it up?' I went to her office and I thought, 'Well, this wasn't an accident, I don't believe this.' I mean, I'm not stupid.

In May 1991 my boyfriend's parents [the father was a diplomat] had moved to Guatemala and their flat was empty. My boyfriend wanted to see how the flat was and he went there. He still had the key. He opened the door, went in and telephoned his mother in Guatemala. He spoke to her for one and a half minutes. He said, 'I'm now in our flat and it's nice that, for the first time, I can use the telephone and the Stasi are not listening.' At this moment the line was cut. That's really strange. . . .'[22]

Gerda Stern, the lady who'd joined the Communist Party in 1932, watched the opening of the wall on television from her East Berlin apartment:

I felt it was right because I thought that the idea that people can travel is itself right. When I saw the thousands of people crossing I thought it was the end of everything I had worked for in my life, yes, of course. It was very hard. I am still a communist [1990], and socialism is not dead. We won't be dead!

I am very glad that many intelligent people, having been members of the Party, think the same – even Christians. It was not communism, anyway, it was not even a good socialism: but the overall idea of socialism I believe in. Why was I a communist? Because I wanted everybody to live a good life. There shouldn't be some very rich people and others who are hungry. The world can't always be like that.

I went to West Berlin after the wall came down. I was of course interested because I was born there and spent my youth there. I wanted to see some of these places but I didn't find them – they weren't there any more. I went by car with a friend, not even a whole day, just a trip over. I went to see where my parents had lived in Wilmersdorf. They'd had a little villa but it wasn't there any more, either. I didn't like West Berlin – it's a different town.'23

The problems of growing together had barely surfaced and when they did the distance asserted itself again. Lutz Stolz's wife Uta says that 'after the change [the *wende*, which is how East Germans summed up the events of 1989–90] many of the old friends from childhood wanted me to come to West Berlin, and they invited us several times, but when this first euphoria was over, relations with many of them became much cooler. Actually there are only two left with whom I have regular contact and who did not regard us as mentally less gifted, as stupid Easterners. One has,' she states, referring to herself but speaking for many Easterners, 'a certain pride, of course.'24

Rainer Hildebrandt opened the Museum at Checkpoint Charlie in the 1960s. It commemorated, and still commemorates, those who escaped but has a wider feeling about what it wants to say: all abuse of human rights is unacceptable. Hildebrandt was awarded Germany's highest civilian honour, the Federal Merit Cross, when he was almost 80. A perceptive man – the first time we met he said, 'I can read you straight away, I know you, you are a dreamer!' – he used to tell the tale of an East German who was arrested for distributing unauthorised leaflets and taken to the police station. The leaflets were blank and when the police asked him what was going on he replied, 'Anything I would write on a protest leaflet, everyone already knows.' He had to be released, as he knew he would have to be, but he had made his point: protest is always possible.

When the Stasi files were eventually opened, and so-far unknown deaths at the frontier were revealed, Hildebrandt said, 'We have to find ways to find the truth. Then those who are guilty can grapple with their responsibility and those who are not guilty can grapple with the task of forgiveness.' As a philosophical statement, it beats the hell out of watchtowers, Border Guards and shots in the night.

In 1990 the GDR government, now non-communist, gave a watchtower from Checkpoint Charlie to Hildebrandt's museum and, for good measure, gave him another from Stallschreiberstrasse, a street near the Heinrich-Heine-Strasse checkpoint. Hildebrandt said in 1993 that 'there's no real interest in Germany' in such things any more. 'It's a form of repression. For some, it's because they suffered too much under the old regime. For others, it's because they did nothing against it.' He offered to give the towers to anyone who could find a good home for them. In December 2000 one tower remained and it was demolished 'under cover of darkness.'[25] A story of capitalism triumphant, evidently: the person who owned the land it stood on wanted to build offices there and was uninterested in having a watchtower instead.

Dennis L. Bark went back to Berlin in January 1990 and went to the place where Peter Fechter died. He hammered a chunk out of the wall, took it back to California and 'had a case made for it. It's in my office.'

During the Second World War, Leningrad withstood a ferocious and prolonged Nazi siege, during which the population was decimated by starvation; but somehow it clung on and survived. In a Leningrad cemetery there's an inscription: *Nobody is forgotten, nothing is forgotten*

There should be one in Berlin, too, where Fechter lay calling out, '*Help me, help me*', but – post the wall – they put up a building where his simple wooden cross used to stand and where, invariably, people had come to lay fresh flowers any day one went to it. Although they did construct a monument round the corner, it is not the same thing and never will be.

The two Germanies were reunited on 3 October 1990.

Checkpoint Charlie has gone now, gone as if it had never been, although for years after 1989 the bullet marks of 1945 remained scattered across the flanks of buildings and gouged deep into the dark stone blocks of the postal museum, also gone.

For the tourists going to it after the wall fell, the watchtower still stood beside a small segment of the wall. The watchtower's door was padlocked against vandals, and the padlock made in West Germany. The awning, the Customs offices, the lanes for traffic and the path for pedestrians were taken down and taken away. Checkpoint Charlie was so emptied that almost no sense of poigancy and no sense of its passing lingered. Checkpoint Charlie became a car park. Then, of course, they erected buildings on it so that, with a breathtaking narrowness, one of the most famous and emotive places on earth became just another construction or two.

The statue of Lenin was taken from Leninplatz, the broad area surrounded by apartments off Karl-Marx-Allee. As it was being taken down it was cordoned off so people couldn't get to it, which provoked some wry Berliner comment about the purpose of walls.

It frightens many, including Germans, that the places of their past and the people of their past can be taken away so easily.

At Checkpoint Charlie, *c.* 1990, Turkish and Polish vendors sold medals, caps, insignia, Soviet generals' hats and any other Eastern memorabilia they could lay hands on; sold them as vendors do, from trestle tables and car boots or they arranged them on the concrete where Moll's men had stood. A nation was for sale and they were selling it. They did brisk trade in chippings from the wall encased in polythene with an authenticity certificate for good measure, and charged more for bits which had been daubed with graffitti, especially anything multicoloured.

The tourists, disgorging from buses, would gather round their guides and hear, in summary, tales that are told: of the shoot-to-kill orders *just about here where you're standing*; of the wooden platform *just over there*, built to give JFK his feel of the forbidden East; of Peter Fechter being left to bleed to death *just over there, a bit further on*. You could read on the faces of these tourists, wherever in the world they'd journeyed from, a question: Can it all have been true? Did it all really happen?

Bernie Godek remembers that some time after the wall fell there was a celebration at Checkpoint Charlie; a mass of people, and Commander Moll was 'doing his best to try and keep it open for vehicles. A marching band came and I was about 5 metres away from him. He looked at me and I looked at him and we both smiled and kind of shrugged our shoulders as if to say, "Well, what are we going to do? Let it happen." He actually smiled and he was a completely different person to that night when the wall came down.'

On 22 June 1990 a crane lifted the Allied hut clean away while bands played and the Foreign Ministers of the United States, France and Great Britain made speeches. Douglas Hurd remembers 'this ceremony was essentially devised by my American colleague Jim Baker. The hut was lifted away by crane after the ceremony of closure. We all made speeches. Jim Baker acknowledged that mine contained the neatest phrase ("Charlie has come in from the cold"). Then we went on to a more serious negotiating meeting of the 2 plus 4 Group of Foreign Ministers. The Soviet Foreign Minister Shevardnadze made some proposals which I described in my diary as "ridiculous" for imposing conditions on the Germans after unification. It seemed to me then, and is certain now, that he did not expect these proposals to be accepted, but made them in order to placate his critics at home in Moscow. Indeed at lunch that day, attended only by Ministers, he told us that he had stayed awake all night because of the criticisms made of him by a particular Russian General and the applause which they received.

'It has always seemed to me that the main point about the Wall was its brutal ugliness. It is nothing like the other great walls of history – the Chinese or Hadrian's. It was essentially cheap and insignificant, which characterises the nature of the regime which it protected. I am glad that bits of it are being preserved, so that its real character will not be forgotten.'[26]

But there was no plaque to mark the position the hut occupied, in the road or in the world. Raferty was pretty sure the hut was stored somewhere and, when he returned to the States years ago, said he'd be upset if he discovered that it wasn't. That hut, he insisted, was 'my second home'.

This has been a story about people caught within the logic of the wall.

In the early 1990s I went over into the countryside west of West Berlin exploring where the wall had run, trying to follow its course. It was surprisingly difficult in places now that the actual wall, the watchtowers, the tank traps and the dog runs had all gone, and the swathe of no man's land between, where inner and outer walls stood, were being reclaimed by long grass. From a distance the cleared strip blended into the countryside.

The main road in one hamlet ran to where the inner wall bisected it. Old, detached houses lingered on either side of the road, and they'd been improved by improvisation: building materials were scarce. The houses were substantial and sombre. Little Trabants stood under home-made lean-to garages, gardens had been tended but, somehow, not landscaped in any way. Trees overhung the street, keeping the daylight away. A *bier haus*, very near the wall, provided something to do in the empty afternoons: the menfolk, now unemployed, smoked and drank and played cards and made earthy jokes.

I sat down next to a swarthy man nursing his beer. He had eyes which did not look into yours but always towards the bar, the card school, the window, somewhere else. Sure he remembered the night the wall went up and the days which followed. There used to be two houses over there at the end of the street but they fell on the other side, so one dawn trucks came and the families were moved out. It wasn't very nice to see and you don't forget that, especially the children. We never saw them again and the houses were torn down to make the death-strip. He put a paw of a hand round the beer and drank, now looking straight ahead past me.

Escapes?

I don't know. It was quiet around here. You'd hear shots from time to time, always at night and over by the woods, but you never found out what happened. That was the same with everything: you didn't find out.

Big changes now?

He gripped his beer again and he was looking full at me, a deep and sudden anger alive in his eyes sweeping my question aside.

You know what I want? Twenty-eight years of my life back.

He was called Rudiger Hering and he has been quoted several times already, but that last sentence seemed to say what so many would have said, a whole generation of them.[27]

Later that afternoon I drove further north because, judging by the map, another hamlet had been reconnected with the West. I found where the wall had bisected it here and, as luck would have it, the old patrol road in the death strip was intact. It meandered away into the distance, following the contours of what was now returning to the green and pleasant meadowland. A new sign said 'Cycling Only', but I ignored that and set off. A family of three came cycling along the strip towards me, obviously West Berliners by the cut of their clothes and the quality of their bikes, and they flagged me down. They saw the car had British registration plates and the man said in English, and in that impossibly prissy Germanic way, 'It is forbidden to drive here!'

'Listen,' I said, 'this is the last place on mother earth where anybody can forbid anybody anything now. Haven't you heard?'

He wasn't looking for twenty-eight years you see, just a cycle ride cocooned in law and order.

That was the difference, and it wouldn't be going away for another generation, maybe two. And anyway, after what Hering had said, I felt better.

A gentler example or two of such things. Each visit I made I stayed at a small hotel – the Ahorn – on Schlutter Strasse, one of the streets off the Ku-Damm, and the proprietor's son, Daniel Glau (who's been quoted already) played an active part in running the place. He was 24. I was curious about his reactions to the East because he had grown up with the wall. (It was, people would tell you, like living at the seaside and the wall was the sea: always there, nothing you could do about it. What lay on the other side was lost in the darkness of the deep.) Says Glau:

> The first time I decided to go over was in spring 1990. I was not curious before that. I didn't feel it was my town. My parents have a different relationship with this town. My relationship was with West Berlin and West people. East Germany was not Germany for me, it was like Czechoslovakia, Hungary, Bulgaria, so to say. Because I have lived twenty-four years with this I didn't say, 'I am going to another area of Berlin.' I'd say, 'I go to East Berlin' in the same way I'd have said, 'I'm going to Prague or Budapest.'
>
> I crossed at the Gleineker Bridge and I went to Oranienburg and Potsdam by car. As I drove across I thought I liked the bridge very much. I stopped and looked across the water to the other side. I went just because I thought I'd like the park near the bridge. I had a strong feeling, an unusual feeling: It didn't look like West Berlin and the people were not the same.
>
> In one way there's more culture than we have here, more friendly feelings between the people, but in another way the people are very hard and very different. It was depressing, yes. I had a feeling this was not a free place.
>
> On the first visit I was only looking for the green places, for the surroundings of the town, not for the town itself – because I had never seen the surroundings of Berlin, the parks and the lakes. I think the surroundings are very nice and I thought this is where my parents would have gone on a hot summer's day.[28]

A young journalist from Munich came along one day, doing work experience, interviewing onto a big tape recorder she had slung over her shoulder, and I ran her around in the car a bit. We were out on the road by Potsdam, a rutted road, patched and cobbled and sinking, the grass verges gouged where lorries had parked and mud gathered in the tyre tracks. The buildings to either side had that uncoordinated 'we survived' feel to them, a bleakness, a paucity wrapping round them.

This is your country now, I said.

No, no, she said. *This is Romania.*

Yes, a generation away, maybe two.

Conrad Schumann, who'd jumped the wire on Bernauer Strasse at 4.00 on the Tuesday after the wall went up, became symbolically famous round the world because in Christopher Isherwood's words a camera recorded it – Schumann fixed forever in mid-air over the barbed wire – and it was developed, carefully printed, fixed.

Schumann was, of course, a simple, ordinary man: taken from the scene in a police van to be debriefed. All he'd wanted was a sandwich.

After that it was a story of alcohol, modest jobs and a confusion about the strange fame which one moment had given him. That brought a truly terrible irony of its own because Schumann had escaped communism, the GDR and the wall, but he could never escape the image of him escaping.

When the wall came down he made guest appearances at the Museum at Checkpoint Charlie but 'he was no longer recognisable from the photo: now he was a podgy middle-aged man with tattoos on both arms'. He'd lived in Bavaria for years, working on Audi's assembly line. In June 1998, after a family argument, his wife found him hanging from a tree.[29]

Roland Egersdörfer went to the West, but the corner supermarket he had gazed into so intimately with his binoculars had gone so he never did get inside.

They carried the body of Chris Gueffroy away that February midnight in 1989, but they could not carry Chris Gueffroy away. He'd keep coming back long after they – the pall-bearers – had gone from the place.

His mother Karin, a woman with an open, saddened face and soft, sympathetic eyes, would recount how the Public Prosecutor came and told her that her son was dead. She would say that publicly there was a policy of official denial about death at the wall but, with condemnation ringing round the world, this route had been blocked to them. Denial was an obscenity too far. That was only a technical aspect, though. The simple truth was that, as a mother, she had nothing left to lose and consequently that liberated her to seek justice. She told the Stasi that, some day, she would see them charged with the murder of her son and they laughed in her face.

That 'some day' turned out to be a September day in 1991 when four former Border Guards were charged with killing Gueffroy. In court they were frightened, avoided eye contact and wept often. They pleaded the only sane defence available – *obeying orders* – although those grounds had been dismissed at the Nuremburg trials after the Second World War when *obeying orders* had been rejected absolutely. The simple charge of *crimes against humanity* overrode everything.

According to one witness, the four accused 'mumbled' answers to questions in Eastern accents so heavy that the Western judges couldn't always understand them. And in a corner Karin Gueffroy watched – relentlessly, as someone noted.

The man who fired the deadly shot, Ingo Heinrich, was sentenced to three and a half years and his comrade, Andreas Kühnpast, two years suspended. Two years later, Heinrich's sentence was reduced to two years on probation. Heinrich, who in civilian clothing became a most ordinary clean-cut young man, subsequently took part in a British television documentary where he explained the context of what had happened. He acted within the GDR's laws and, at the time of the shooting, could not imagine ever being tried for acting *legally*.

The interviewer, Joan Bakewell, wondered if he felt 'trapped by history'.

He said: 'As you grew up from kindergarten it was driven in to you what you had to do. The West was always condemned right from kindergarten and that carried on through school and into the army. And somehow at that point in time you believed that the West wasn't the true way: that the Eastern socialism, or more specifically communism, was going to be the future.' He'd add that if you refused to fire you faced court martial and military prison.

Karin Gueffroy demanded that anyone who picks up a gun accept the consequences of that and, if they fire it, they look deep into their conscience to see what is there.

The logic of the wall, which began so long, long before, was almost played out but sharp fragments remained. The men who gave the orders to shoot were acquitted at the Gueffroy trial, and there was an extreme sense of unease that – higher up still – those who introduced the shoot-to-kill policy, and demanded under harsh penalty that it be carried out, were absent from the courts and courtrooms as justice was meted out to the hapless footsoldiers. There were other senses of unease. Westerners were doling it out to

Easterners – victor's justice – and these were Westerners who had never known the grip of totalitarianism on the whole of your life. To the GDR citizens, the GDR was not a freak show run by criminals, it was *life*. Worse, since the West had recognised the GDR as a sovereign state, those who acted within its laws were answerable only to it, weren't they? It was murky territory and only dimly through it could you glimpse a 20-year-old running hard, hard, hard across a death strip at 11.39 one night because he wanted to open a restaurant, and going down, shot through the heart.

But he was there.

Egon Krenz was sentenced to six and a half years in prison in 1997 – Schabowski got three – because, a judge ruled, 'the Politburo was responsible for border security. The Guards were in fact given an ideological order to shoot.'

They carried the body of Peter Fechter away that August afternoon in 1962, but they could not carry Peter Fechter away. He'd keep coming back long after the pall-bearers had gone.

On the thirtieth anniversary of the wall going up there was a ceremony where the simple wooden cross to Fechter's memory stood. The German Interior Minister attended, as did the Mayor, and Fechter's sister Gisela Geue. (Fechter had two sisters. The other was called Ruth.) 'He was the only son, the darling of the family,' Geue said. She explained that the Stasi had 'hounded' the family. Her parents had been hauled from their apartment to identify their son, and the Stasi searched it, looking for anything suggesting his 'political crimes'. They found nothing. 'After that, for the whole week up to the burial, we were practically besieged and watched,' she said. 'They didn't even stop at the cemetery. They took the flowers away.'

She was crying. 'Now anyone can go through, and our brother, our Peter, he was shot only because he wanted to go from Germany to Germany, and then these inhuman people did not help him.'

Her parents became 'miserable mental cases'. Her father died, brokenhearted, in 1968 and her mother in February 1991. 'She did not really understand the opening of the wall.'[30]

Still Peter Fechter would not go away. In August 1997 a Berlin court convicted two former Border Guards of manslaughter, although the judge, Hans-Juergen Schaal, explained that the trial hadn't found which of them shot him. Both were given suspended sentences: Rolf Friedrich, aged 61, twenty-one months and Erich Schreiber twenty.

'Joint manslaughter was committed here,' Schaal said, 'because neither of you consciously tried to miss the target.' He stressed that neither Guard had been responsible for allowing Fechter to bleed to death but also stressed that the fact it happened was not acceptable.

Friedrich said afterwards 'I am sorry and would like to apologise to his sister.'[31]

The wooden cross was taken into the Museum at Checkpoint Charlie to accommodate (I've used this word very deliberately) the new building going up where it stood. The new monument round the corner is circular and quietly dignified. There is no sense of drama about it, no striving to stir your emotions, no gesturing to personalise the past. It stands to record a fact, and it records it. The cross, painted a reddish colour which resembles dried blood, is quite different.

Hartmut Richter lived on Bernauer Strasse, so that he could see the wall every day. These days he works at the Church of Reconciliation, a new structure which has been built where the old one stood in the death strip. It's circular and the exterior is of wood. It has clean lines and a great timeless dignity in a modernistic way. Beside it there's a statue of a couple clasping each other, donated by Sir Richard Branson, three enormous bells rescued from the original church and what seems, from a distance, to be an anchor. In fact it's the ironwork from the top of the original spire. When the church was blown up the spire fell and was spread over some 60 or 70 metres – the ironwork fell into the adjacent graveyard and workers there hid it, kept it safe for the day which surely would never come, but did.

Richter is not the sort of man you'd expect to deal in irony, yet he does. He feels that those Stasi members who dealt with him up to 1989 as a 'hostile' entity owe him, and others like him, a real debt. As he says, the Stasi earned a lot of money in their jobs, more than normal workers did, and get high pensions now.

Harald Jäger owns a newsagent's shop in the old East, and thereby hangs a tale. Birgit Kubisch and I tracked him to there, but when we visited the shop his son-in-law, serving, said Jäger was away for the weekend and didn't give interviews. 'He's had some bad experiences.' That I believed. Ex-Stasi don't, as a rule, like the light of day anyway and they have their reasons. We said we'd come back on the Monday and if Jäger refused, he refused. We went back. He is a tall man carrying, as befits one of his size and age, a comfortable semi-paunch. He has, though, a certain presence about him: not respectability but something more. It is the same presence as Günter Moll.

The geometry has been reduced, here, to a neighbourhood community centre (which is what any self-respecting newsagent's really is): cigarettes and tobacco, sweets, magazines, newspapers. One customer can't, for some reason, pay for his morning paper and gets it on tick. Of course. Much laughter about that. You know, the way it goes in your local corner shop, too.

So I make my pitch and yes, he's had bad experiences, been *turned over*, as we say in the media. That story only emerges later: a female Wessie who wrote that by the tone of his voice she could hear a Stasi hissing diabolical orders. He was so angry that he faxed off a challenge to her facts, refuting them, and, most unforgivable sin of the media and *our* power without responsibility, she did not even reply.

He doesn't exactly say he doesn't give interviews, but he isn't giving any today. Tomorrow? But I'm leaving early tomorrow. All right, he says, this afternoon; 2.00 p.m. at the checkpoint, that OK? A particular man: he says there's a monument there with a metal plaque and he gives quasi-military directions with the requisite points of reference so we can't miss it, and we don't. He poses before the monument and we walk down the incline past the domain where, during those brief, teeming hours on Thursday 9 November 1989, he held great power over 20,000 people. It's a car sales area now, the models arranged in rows where the awning used to be and, on lines stretched between poles, small plastic triangular flags – part decoration, part advertising – hang limp. There's no breeze today.

I expect whoever owns it has a deal for you. But I bet he doesn't have the deal that Harald Jäger had on 9 November 1989.

We find a café, a couple of youngish men playing snooker, a prim madame supervising the whole thing, the slot machine silent, a sense of mid-afternoon emptiness hanging over it. We sit and he tells the tale. When he's done I'm curious because Ulbricht and Honecker and Krenz went looking for the power and the fame and found it but, as the logic of 1945 finally played itself out so deep into Bornholmer Strasse, all this devolved onto Jäger, who hadn't sought anything, really. He seemed ambivalent about that, didn't care one way or the other. What happened happened.

I'm still curious about how, on a whim and just over there where the cars are arranged, he could have stamped a human being's identity card and potentially changed their lives forever by whether he chose to stamp over the photograph or not.

'Now I am on the good side because it turned out to be good for me but I often think about what might have happened if it hadn't happened like that.'

Like Moll, at decisive moments in a dialogue he swivels his eyes towards yours. You have the recurring thought, within those eyes, about the Tiananmen Square option which was theoretically open to both but which neither considered. That, unstated, is in the eyes, also. These two men were never going to do anything like that.

'I am getting sick of thinking about this, I am still afraid today because I would have been the one responsible. . . .'

Just for a moment, in memory and imagination, the car park is cleared and it is all going on again, the awning, the excluded area, the uniformed officers striding the glistening tarmac like emperors, everything regulated and controlled, and dreamland too far away to be even seen over the metal-spanned bridge. Ordinary traffic is passing across it today because it's just an ordinary road.

Nothing else.

In January 2001 I asked Birgit Kubisch to read again the interview she had given ten years before and reflect – as she wished – on what she had said.

'I want to comment on two things. Crossing for the first time is exactly the way I remember it although there are some things I'd forgotten, like the bottle of champagne and the Border Guards. One of the reasons I hadn't crossed earlier than I did was my fear of the crowds but the other reason was that I just wasn't sure whether I should go or not.' That would mean confronting actually existing capitalism, which might well destroy a great deal of what she believed in and had worked towards.

As I've already mentioned, deep misgivings jostled silently with the jubilation and the momentary triumphalism.

'I think that what I thought then was quite realistic. Somehow it *was* not just a cheering moment, it was also a moment of contemplation. I was thinking what the future would be – the immediate future. Obviously I couldn't predict what would happen in ten years. I could understand somebody wanting to build a society which is an alternative to capitalism – capitalisim as I knew it then.'

What do you think now of this capitalisim you do know?

'Well, I still think that in the beginning the GDR really had been an attempt to do something different and I still believe it.'

Is an alternative possible, a viable alternative that gives you all this? (Ms Kubisch has a modernised apartment within walking distance of the East Berlin city centre, has a computer – which she complains is too slow – and email and a mobile phone. She likes

Indian food. This is a complete culture away from waiting fifteen years for a Trabant.)

'You could write a different book on that.'

I repeat, you have lived in both systems. Is there any alternative that could give you all this?

'Not at this time. And the more I think of it the more I think you could not have built an alternative by putting a wall around it. That hasn't changed at all. But I also happen to think that you have to understand historically why they built this wall and ask if they thought about how long it would last. I don't think they did. I think they were reacting.'

If you are going to build an alternative, people have to want that alternative, and then you don't need a wall – but people here had no choice.

'But you know it was an immediate consequence of the war.'

What do you miss?

'I miss the things that everyone would miss in their lives, not so much to do with the GDR but with my childhood. I don't really miss anything else because I always followed events and thought about why they were happening. I might miss a kind of certain security, you know, for planning your career but then, on the other side, there are so many things I could not have done if it hadn't happened. I am very split.'

What I meant was that when East Germany existed there was a communal feeling of everybody doing something together. They had to do it and they were all in it whether they wanted to be or not and it created a sense of community.

'I have worked in some schools and I miss the way children were treated in schools: everything was prepared. I miss this sense of group feeling and maybe I miss it now because everything is so much more individual.'

Precisely the opposite of before.

'But what strikes me most is that there are still huge differences in the mentality of people in the East and West after ten years. In one way they have to do with really technical things – salaries, finance, economy – but in another way they have to do with your history and in the way in which the reunification took place.'

Henrietta, your sister's baby girl, won't know any of these differences as she grows up.

'She won't. We can tell her but will she be interested? We talk about things very freely, we don't close our eyes to what was wrong and right before, but she will lead her life quite normally and if it is anything to her it will be just history.'

*Take countries like Britain, America, France. There is a continuity
– however strained – between successive generations.*

'What we have here is a generation in the East which feels a
stranger in two distinct ways. One is that they have lost their home
country – whatever the GDR might have been, it gave a sense to
their lives. The other is that they won't have the understanding of
the next generations because those generations simply won't be able
to understand what happened. So they feel a stranger in the two
distinct ways.'

This is made more poignant because, on a damp, grey, soulless
Saturday afternoon we all go – myself, Birgit, her sister and husband
and Henrietta – in search of a remaining watchtower in the Treptow
district. The watchtower stands in a broad triangle of grass – the
death strip, now a park – *but* there are tall trees, obviously older
than ten years, near it and wouldn't they have been cut down
because they afforded cover? We fall to discussing whether the
watchtower has been moved from somewhere else and placed here
and we can't say. (It hadn't.)

Little Henrietta is being pushed along in her buggy, chewing
biscuits and sweets.

We search for where the wall went but what with the grass
growing and roads resurfaced and bushes planted and buildings
built and rebuilt we can't tell that, either. What will be left for the
Henriettas to find, twenty years on?

Virtually nothing.

When I drove to Berlin in 1991, Ms Kubisch liked my Ford Sierra
but wondered how a company as big as Ford could make a car
without handles to wind the windows up and down. I introduced
her to the electronic buttons – as a child of the Trabant culture, she
had never seen them before. She was delighted and spent the rest of
the day working them. I hired a VW Lupo on my last visit in 2001
and she exclaimed: 'They've got handles. You wouldn't think anybody made cars like that any more!' Both moments were innocent in
their way, and of no consequence when they are set against the
weight of the tectonic plates, the enormity of the wall or the fate of
such as Peter Fechter, but they do measure the subconscious movement from one normality towards another.

The world had moved all right although you were constantly
forced to ask yourself a question: moved where?

That's another story altogether.

Notes

By definition, Berlin is a convoluted and complicated subject. For reasons of simplicity, I give West Berlin and West Germany always with a capital W, and East Berlin and East Germany always with a capital E, except when I'm making general references to east and west. Officially East Germany called itself the Deutsche Demokratische Republic (DDR) – the German Democratic Republic (GDR) – and I have used this abbreviation more or less throughout. West Germany called itself the Bundesrepublik Deutschland (BRD) – the Federal Republic of Germany (FRG). The status of Berlin remained disputed throughout but, in practical terms, East Berlin was regarded by the GDR as its capital, and referred to only as Berlin; West Berlin was regarded by West Germany as a part of itself but not as a capital. Bonn was that.

The East Germans were dismissive of West Berlin when they were obliged to mention it and referred to it as Westberlin or Berlin (West).

There was widespread misuse (and perhaps misunderstanding) in the whole western world about the Soviet Union, which constituted a group of republics – for example, Georgia and the Ukraine. [The USSR = Union of Soviet Socialist Republics.] Russia was the largest and dominated. Frequently in this book, people say Russia and the Russians when they mean the Soviet Union. By a happy coincidence, the USSR existed throughout the period this book covers and so whenever anyone speaks of the Russians it always means the Soviets – I have not felt free to alter direct quotations from the people I interviewed, so when they say Russian you will know what they (really) mean. . . .

(I got the dirtiest look of my life when, in a Moscow park in the early 1970s, a charming couple took the chance to practise their English on me and I complimented them on the Russian educational system. 'Russian? We're Georgian,' they said with obvious annoyance, and walked away.)

Quotation on p. ii: *Demian*, Hermann Hesse (Panther Books Ltd, London, 1969).

Chapter One

1. Hitler evidently disliked the city because of the Berliners' irreverence, indiscipline and delight in all carnal (and carnivorous) pleasures. Their wit was fast-moving and waspish, as befits any capital. Two examples:

     The first: I met a single and independent woman who danced on the wall the night it came down even though she was pregnant. When she moved apartments, the concierge said – eyeing her enlarged stomach – 'But where is your man?' 'Man?' she replied, 'I'm the Virgin Mary.' And that, she reported to me, shut him up, all right.

     The second: When Erich Honecker was ruling the GDR, he watched the sun rise in the East and asked it why it was smiling; and the sun said 'Because I'm going to the West . . .'
2. Quoted in *The Berlin Bunker*, James P. O'Donnell (Arrow Books, London, 1979).
3. *Child of the Revolution*, Wolfgang Leonhard (Collins, London, 1957).
4. Interview with author.
5. *Eastern Europe in the Twentieth Century*, R.J. Crampton (Routledge, London and New York, 1994).
6. *Berlin Twilight*, Lieutenant-Colonel W. Byford-Jones (Hutchinson & Co., undated).
7. Interview with author.
8. *German Democratic Republic*, Mike Dennis (Pinter, London and New York, 1989).
9. Interview with author. The first time I went to Berlin to begin researching this book I travelled by train and, leaving on the way back, I sat next to a man in late middle age. We chatted and like all people touched by Berlin he had a tale to tell. He looked at me very hard, however, when my tape recorder came out. He said he'd call himself Mateus, and nothing more.
10. Interview with author.
11. Friedrichstrasse station will be fully examined later in the book, not least because in a city laden with symbolism it became, like Checkpoint Charlie, an almost *exquisite* symbol, and in several different dimensions simultaneously. We shall see.
12. *Khrushchev and the Berlin Crisis (1959–1961)*, Vladislav M. Zubok, Working Paper No. 6, Cold War International History Project (Woodrow Wilson Center, Washington, DC, 1993). The

joke may have been the very idea of a pompous and portly bureaucrat like Ulbricht, who seems to have been one of the twentieth century's great bores, having a mistress at all.

13. *The Wall and How it Fell*, Special Edition for the 5th Anniversary of the Fall of the Wall (Press and Information Office of the Land of Berlin, 1994).
14. Interview with author.
15. Interview with author.
16. *Ulbricht and the Concrete 'Rose': New Archival Evidence of the Dynamics of Soviet–East German Relations and the Berlin Crisis*, Hope M. Harrison, Working Paper No. 5, Cold War International History Project (Woodrow Wilson Center, Washington, DC, 1993).
17. Ibid.
18. Ibid.
19. Ibid.
20. *The Berlin Wall*, Norman Gelb (Michael Joseph, London, 1986).
21. Harrison, op. cit.
22. *Germans: Biography of an Obsession*, George Bailey (Free Press, New York, 1991).
23. Harrison, op. cit.
24. Ibid.
25. *New York Herald Tribune*, 4 August 1961.
26. Interview with author.
27. Gelb, op. cit.

Chapter Two

Quotation at head of chapter: a chance remark to the author about how much work would have to be done after the fall of the wall to rebuild East Berlin.

1. Interview with author.
2. The Factory Fighting Groups, formed in 1953 as 'Factory Combat Groups' were designed as Communist Party troops in the event of civil war (*The East German Army*, Thomas M. Forster (George Allen & Unwin, London, 1980)). They became a sort of territorial army, had a membership of 500,000 and were, as their name implies, based at, and drawn from, their workplaces.
3. Interview with author.
4. The CIA interviews with Morris and Polgar I recorded from a television programme on video. Unfortunately I didn't get the beginning or end of the programme and so I have no idea who broadcast it or when. What they had to say seemed so important

historically that I have included it anyway. If I have tiptoed across somebody's copyright, sorry.

5. Ibid.

6. *Willy Brandt: Portrait of a Statesman*, Terence Prittie (Weidenfeld & Nicolson, London, 1974).

7. *Man without a Face*, Markus Wolf (Jonathan Cape, London, 1997). I have not, incidentally, dwelt on the role of spies for three reasons. First, it has already been covered, notably in George Bailey's extensive *Battleground Berlin*, and *Stasi: The Untold Story of the East German Secret Police*, John O. Koehler (Westview Press, Boulder, Colorado); second, to get at the truth is by definition extremely elusive in the espionage shadowland; and third because I wanted ordinary people's memories. With all possible respect, spies are not that. Let me just say that all these spies *on both sides* put together did not know the wall was going up (even taking into consideration Gehlen's claim – see below) and they did not know it was coming down. Apart from that, I assume, they were gimlet-eyed on every nuance of everything. . . .

8. *The Gehlen Memoirs*, General Reinhard Gehlen (Collins, London, 1972).

9. The Kurfürstendamm was, and is, a huge avenue stretching across West Berlin. It was famed for cafés, smart boutiques, salesrooms, restaurants and hotels. (The quality of the prostitutes who lined a certain section of it like sentries, equidistant and selecting their prey with subliminal accuracy, was famous; and by a law nobody understood, they became more beautiful – girl by girl – until you reached the intersection with Schluter Strasse, when they ceased altogether.) The avenue was frequently abbreviated to the Ku-damm and it was to this, on the night the wall fell, that the Easterners swarmed. *Everybody* had heard of it.

10. Official GDR document, courtesy of Hagen Koch's archive.

11. Interview with Birgit Kubisch.

12. Interview with author.

Chapter Three

Quotation at head of chapter: *Goodbye to Berlin*, Christopher Isherwood (Hogarth Press, 1939, rep. Minerva, London, 1989).

1. Interview with author.

2. Interview with author.

3. Interview with author.

4. Interview with author.

5. Interview with author.

6. Mary Kellett-Long's diary. She was kind enough to give me all the entries I wanted, but more than that she had a way of seeing the essentials and expressing them in vivid yet straightforward language.

7. Interview with author.

8. *Berlin: Success of a Mission?*, Geoffrey McDermott (André Deutsch, London, 1963). (The title is a play on a book *Failure of a Mission* written by Neville Henderson, about the British in Berlin up to and at the outbreak of the Second World War.)

9. Interview with author.

10. Interview with author.

11. *The Ides of August*, Curtis Cate (Weidenfeld & Nicolson, London, 1978).

12. Bailey, op. cit.

13. Interview with Birgit Kubisch.

14. Interview with author.

15. Interview with author.

16. Interview with author.

17. *Willy Brandt, Portrait and Self-Portrait*, Klaus Harpprecht (Abelard-Schuman, London, 1972).

18. The time gap from Berlin to Washington is today [December 2000] six hours but was it that in August 1961? Various books written subsequently are not unanimous. Some say five. I am indebted to Edith Kohagen of the *Presse und Informationsamt* of the Landes Berlin. I asked her if she could find out and she replied: 'I called the *Physikalisch-technische Bundesanstalt* in Braunsweig to get the solution. The Federal Institute is responsible for the time in Germany. They told me the time difference must have been six hours (I repeat: six hours) because we had no summer time. Between 1950 and 1980, in fact, there was no summer time in Germany.'

19. Interview with author.

20. McDermott, op. cit.

21. Interview with author.

22. McDermott, op. cit.

23. Harpprecht, op. cit.

24. McDermott, op. cit.

25. Interview with author.

26. Interview with author.

27. *Washington Post*, 14 August 1961.

28. Interview with author.

29. Interview with author.

30. Interview with author.

31. The East Berlin journalist Bodo Radtke had, of course, the

opportunity to travel. His family were originally from that part
of Germany now become Poland, and he happened to be
reporting a cycle race whose route passed near the village which
had been home for generations. He found the street and,
oh yes, people remembered the Radtkes. The race concluded,
he got back to East Berlin and told his father the tale, and asked
his father if he wasn't sad that he'd been driven from his home,
it was in a foreign country and – Poland under Lech Walesa's
counter-revolution now out of bounds – he could no longer go
back even to have a look. 'Yes', his father said, 'yes, of course
but if this is the price of peace, let's pay it.' I am persuaded that
those who have known war, and where the logics of war go,
all feel the same and if they don't they are very dangerous
people.
32. And I am writing these words as a Westerner.

Chapter Four

1. Peter Johnson's diary.
2. *United Press International* report.
3. Interview with author.
4. One of the lessons of studying the wall is that, even if you think
   you are open-minded and have breadth of vision, at some stage
   you'll probably discover you haven't. You'll be betrayed by your
   subconscious, just as I was in the paragraph about each American
   President since 1949 being constricted by the risk of nuclear war. It
   wasn't until I reflected, that I realised how instinctively and
   hopelessly Western the perspective was. After all, every Soviet
   leader has felt exactly the same constriction.
      You can fall into this trap in other ways. In the early 1990s
   I was at a party in Marzhan, the new town on the edge of East
   Berlin, and a young woman was recounting her trip to Paris – still,
   then, a wondrous adventure for anyone who'd spent their lives
   behind the wall. I ventured that the trip must have been even
   better because, the currency union completed, she'd been able to
   take the mighty Deutschmark. She looked at me and said, 'Typical
   Westerner, seeing everything in terms of money.'
5. *Berlin: Von der Frontstadt zur Brücke Europas*, Rainer
   Hildebrandt (Verlag Haus am Checkpoint Charlie, 1984).
6. Interview with author.
7. Interview with author.
8. *Violations of human rights, illegal acts and incidents at the sector
   border in Berlin since the building of the wall (13 August 1961–15
   August 1962)*, published on behalf of the government of the

Federal Republic of Germany by the Federal Ministry for All-German Questions, Bonn and Berlin, August 1962.

9. McDermott, op. cit.
10. GDR document, courtesy of the Hagen Koch archive.
11. Gelb, op. cit.
12. Interview with author.
13. Interview with author.
14. Interview with author.
15. Interview with author.
16. *The Fall*, Reinhold Andert and Wolfgang Herzberg (Aufbau-Verlag, Berlin and Weimar).
17. Honecker was being naturally protective of the GDR and thus trying to equate what happened at the wall in Berlin, and the inter-German border, as something quite normal in international terms. His words must be restricted to that context, not reality. The direction the European Union was taking was utterly different: the abolition of border controls altogether.
18. Happrecht, op. cit.
19. McDermott, op. cit.
20. Interview with author.
21. Interview with author.
22. Interview with author.
23. Interview with author.
24. McDermott, op. cit.
25. The number of people killed at the wall may never be definitively known.
    I have leaned heavily on *Opfer der Mauer* [Victim of the Wall] by Werner Filmer and Heribert Schwan (C. Bertelsmann Verlag GmbH, Munich, 1991). It is a thoroughly researched book using official (but previously highly secret) GDR reports of the incidents. Yet even here the record is incomplete and you come across entries like 'Unknown person, deceased 4.9.1962' because that is all the authors have been able to discover. Other published sources give victims which Filmer and Schwan don't, and vice versa. This leads me to think that, across the twenty-eight years that the wall stood, there may well have been fatal attempts at escape which were unreported in the West and for which no documentation survives in the East – or people who just drowned in their lonely anonymity. Nobody knew they were swimming for it and nobody ever came across their bodies. Hagen Koch, whose Berlin Wall archive is a treasure-trove of primary documentation, has compiled a list of 172 fatalities (not all attempting to escape: children playing and falling into the water by the wall then drowning. An explanation for this is in the text.). Koch's list begins with an

unnamed East German Border Guard who died in an accident with a gun sometime after 13 August 1961. Koch also records someone unknown on 13 August itself but has no further details of any kind; and lists an unnamed 18-year-old who drowned on 16 April 1989 – making him the final victim. That the first and last victims are likely to be held forever in *their* anonymity seems to reflect how the wall literally dehumanised.

26. Peter Johnson's diary.

Chapter Five

1. Interview with author.
2. *Violations*, op. cit.
3. Gelb, op. cit.
4. She is generally referred to as Schulze, without a first name, presumably because she survived and therefore does not appear (as far as I'm aware) in official records or lists. That is bizarre, because newsreel of her escape is so standard that it's almost impossible to find a documentary film on Berlin which does not contain at least some of it. Hagen Koch is fairly sure she was called Frieda and I've gone along with him.
5. *The Berlin Wall*, Deane and David Heller.
6. I have taken certain liberties in re-creating this. The participants told me their tales, often repeating verbatim what people had said to them. As a result, they were themselves quoting others.
   I have lifted these verbatim quotes out and used them as if spoken by the people themselves. The result, I feel, is still as authentic as you can get over dialogue four decades before, and much easier to understand.
7. Gelb, op. cit.
8. *Battleground Berlin, CIA vs KGB in the Cold War*, David E. Murphy, Sergei A. Kondrashev and George Bailey (Yale University Press, New Haven and London, 1997).
9. Interview with author.
10. *Violations*, op. cit.
11. Interview with author.
12. *The Berlin Crisis* (National Security Archive, Washington).
13. This was a little joke at my expense, an American gently teasing a Brit by suggesting that the British were responsible for Joe Kennedy discovering sex – in London. I suspect that the Kennedys discovered it for themselves, and most Americans, too, which is why there are 260 million of them. (Not all can have journeyed to London for lessons.) And that's my little joke in riposte.
14. Interview with author.

15. McDermott, op. cit.
16. Interview with author.
17. *Violations*, op. cit.
18. Heller, op. cit.
19. *New York Herald Tribune*, 23 February 1962.
20. *Violations*, op. cit..
21. *The Ugly Frontier*, David Shears (Chatto & Windus, London, 1970).
22. McDermott, op. cit.
23. *Violations*, op. cit.
24. Ibid.
25. Heller, op. cit.
26. GDR Interior Ministry document.
27. *Violations*, op. cit.
28. Interview with author.
29. Department of State document drafted by John Ausland on 20 July 1961 circulated to the US Ambassadors in London, Paris and Moscow, and to US offices in Berlin and the UN. Reproduced by kind permission.
30. GDR Ministry for National Defence document.
31. *Escape from Berlin*, Anthony Kemp (Boxtree Limited, 1987).
32. *Ulbricht*, Carola Stern (Pall Mall Press, London, 1965).
33. *New York Herald Tribune*, 27 June 1963.
34. Ibid.
35. Kennedy's speech appears in full at The History Place, webmaster@historyplace.com and I am grateful to them for letting me have it. They also say 'Did you know the JFK Library has a big site with that speech and others?' Well, I know now – and so do you. It's http://www.ca.umb.edu/ jfklibrary/main.html. Here is the speech:

I am proud to come to this city as the guest of your distinguished Mayor, who has symbolized throughout the world the fighting spirit of West Berlin. And I am proud to visit the Federal Republic with your distinguished Chancellor who for so many years has committed Germany to democracy and freedom and progress, and to come here in the company of my fellow American, General Clay, who has been in this city during its great moments of crisis and will come again if ever needed.

Two thousand years ago the proudest boast was '*civis Romanus sum*'. Today, in the world of freedom, the proudest boast is *Ich bin ein Berliner*.

I appreciate my interpreter translating my German!

There are many people in the world who really don't understand, or say they don't, what is the great issue between the

free world and the communist world. Let them come to Berlin.
There are some who say that communism is the wave of the
future. Let them come to Berlin. And there are some who say in
Europe and elsewhere we can work with the communists. Let
them come to Berlin. And there are even a few who say that it is
true that communism is an evil system, but it permits us to
make economic progress. *Lass' sie nach Berlin kommen*. Let
them come to Berlin.

Freedom has many difficulties and democracy is not perfect,
but we have never had to put a wall up to keep our people in, to
prevent them from leaving us. I want to say, on behalf of my
countrymen, who live many miles away on the other side of the
Atlantic, who are far distant from you, that they take the
greatest pride that they have been able to share with you, even
from a distance, the story of the last eighteen years. I know of no
town, no city, that has been besieged for eighteen years that still
lives with the vitality and the force, and the hope and the
determination of the city of West Berlin. While the wall is the
most obvious and vivid demonstration of the failures of the
communist system, for all the world to see, we take no
satisfaction in it, for it is, as your Mayor has said, an offense not
only against history but an offense against humanity, separating
families, dividing husbands and wives and brothers and sisters,
and dividing a people who wish to be joined together.

What is true of this city is true of Germany – real, lasting
peace in Europe can never be assured as long as one German out
of four is denied the elementary right of free men, and that is to
make a free choice. In eighteen years of peace and good faith,
this generation of Germans has earned the right to be free,
including the right to unite their families and their nation in
lasting peace, with good will to all people. You live in a defended
island of freedom, but your life is part of the main. So let me ask
you as I close, to lift your eyes beyond the dangers of today, to
the hopes of tomorrow, beyond the freedom merely of this city of
Berlin, or your country of Germany, to the advance of freedom
everywhere, beyond the wall to the day of peace with justice,
beyond yourselves and ourselves to all mankind.

Freedom is indivisible, and when one man is enslaved, all are
not free. When all are free, then we can look forward to that day
when this city will be joined as one and this country and this
great Continent of Europe in a peaceful and hopeful globe.
When that day finally comes, as it will, the people of West Berlin
can take sober satisfaction in the fact that they were in the front
lines for almost two decades.

All free men, wherever they may live, are citizens of Berlin, and, therefore, as a free man, I take pride in the words *Ich bin ein Berliner*.

Chapter Six

Quotation at head of chapter: *Willy Brandt: Portrait and Self-Portrait*, Klaus Harpprecht (Abelard-Schuman, London, 1972).

1. Interview with author.
2. *Berlin: Von der Frontstadt zur Brücke Europas*, Rainer Hildebrandt (Verlag Haus am Checkpoint Charlie, 1984).
3. Interview with author.
4. Hildebrandt, op. cit.
5. Ibid.
6. *Escape from Berlin*, Anthony Kemp (Boxtree Limited, 1987).
7. I have leaned heavily on *The Ugly Frontier*, David Shears (Chatto & Windus, 1970), as well as *Escape from Berlin* in re-creating this episode. Shears (ibid.) writes that 'one Dresden citizen who missed the last train to Berlin [after he received his message] took a taxi all the way from Leipzig. Completely exhausted, he reached the tunnel in time and made his escape.' Presumably this can't have been the same man who went to his rendezvous at Friedrichstrasse station.
8. Shears, ibid.
9. www.wall-berlin.org
10. Details of this particular escape are extremely vague, although the Isetta stands in the Museum at Checkpoint Charlie.
11. I'm indebted to Inge Donnell, the dogged translator, for shedding some unexpected light on this sad paragraph. The word used for sandwich was *Stullenpaar*, a Berlin expression which could be translated as 'doorstep' and seemed discordant in an official document.
12. This report was given to me by Hagen Koch, most fair of men, who wanted to demonstrate that there were violations on both sides, not just East. He gave me a second example, but it is in the next chapter.
13. Interview with author.
14. The Free German Youth was founded in 1946 as an 'anti fascist movement of all young people' (*German Democratic Republic*, Mike Dennis), but by 1952 was firmly part of the SED's structure. Membership was open to anybody from 14 to 25 and in 1982 had 2.3 million members. Every 'school, enterprise and university' had a Free German Youth organisation (Dennis).

It 'strove to mould young people as socialist personalities.'

15. Hagen Koch adds that: the following Border Regiments (*Grenz-regimenter*, abbreviated to *GR*) were deployed in the Border Command Mitte (*Grenzkommando Mitte*, Berlin): GR34, GR38, GR33, GR35, GR36, GR42, GR44. There were two Border Training Regiments (*Grenz-Ausbildungsregimenter*, GAR 39 and GAR 40) and one temporary regiment protecting the official crossing points (*Grenzübergangssicherungsregiment*).

     The main training area was called *Truppenübungsplatz Streganz*. The headquarters of the Border Guards was in Pätz, south of Berlin and the headquarters of the Border Command Mitte (Berlin) was in the Karlshorst district of East Berlin.

     The barracks of the respective regiments were: GR33 in Berlin-Treptow; GR34 in Groß-Glienicke; GR35 in Berlin-Rummelsburg; GR36 in Berlin-Pankow; GR38 in Hennigsdorf; GR42 in Heinersdorf; GR44 in Potsdam-Babelsberg; GAR39 in Berlin-Wilhelmshagen; and GAR40 in Oranienburg.

16. I have unashamedly used the television programme *First Tuesday* – which was made by Yorkshire Television and shown in November 1991 – for the whole of this episode, as well as one later in the book. The programme made me reflect on how ephemeral television is: professionally speaking, the contents were so moving and so profound that they deserved something more permanent. I hope the inclusion in this book goes some way towards that.

Chapter Seven

Quotation at head of chapter, given to the author by Egersdörfer.

1. *Germany and the Germans*, John Ardagh (Penguin Books, London, 1988). Apart from this lovely phrase, which I wish I'd thought of myself, he wrote that 'the area closest to the Wall has been left deliberately as a wasteland or semi-derelict jumble. So the first-time visitor arriving from West Berlin, by car at Checkpoint Charlie or by S-bahn at the Friedrichstrasse station, receives the initial impression of a city more shabby and shattered, indeed sinister, than it really is.'

2. Just as many Western people thought of the Russians as the Soviets, plenty of people East and West could not distinguish between the four entities making up Britain (England, Scotland, Wales and Northern Ireland) and simply called them the English. Quite what Glaswegian Peattie would have made of being called English does not bear contemplation. On my first trip to Berlin in

1970 I gave a lift to a British soldier who turned out to be Scottish. As we ran along the wire in the countryside he pointed to the Border Guards, guns drawn, supervising some workmen in the death strip. 'I don't hate them,' he said, '*I hate Rangers supporters. . . .*'

3. Document from the Hagen Koch archive.
4. *German Democratic Republic*, Mike Dennis (Pinter Publishers Ltd, 1988).
5. Interview with author.
6. Many of those who did escape, or emigrated legally, found themselves disorientated and sometimes lonely in the questing, more selfish West, as if they had found another subtly different no man's land. GDR papers sometimes published lists of those who had chosen to return home.
7. Quoted in *We Were The People*, Dirk Philipsen (Duke University Press, Durham and London, 1993).
8. Referred to in the GDR as the hinterland wall.
9. The military patrol jeeps were in fact adapted Trabants, but why they were called Kübels seems a mystery.
10. In anticipation of our interview (in January 2001) Egersdörfer had carefully written down some of the episodes he thought we'd be covering. He wrote Westberlin as one word quite naturally. The habits of a lifetime, literally, even if another lifetime altogether.
11. Interview with author.
12. *The Berlin Wall, Division of a City*, Thomas Flemming (Be.bra.verlag, Berlin-Brandenburg, 2000).
13. Interview with author.
14. Interview with author.
15. Interview with author.
16. Letter to author.
17. Interview with author.
18. Interview with author.
19. *The Fall*, Reinhold Andert and Wolfgang Herzberg (Aufbau-Verlag, Berlin and Weimar).
20. Drawn from a *UPI* report by Leon Mangasarian, August 1991.
21. *Daily Telegraph*, Sunday Magazine, 9 April 1978.
22. Ibid.

Chapter Eight

Quotation at head of chapter: *The Wall in My Backyard*, ed. by Dinah Dodds and Pam Allen-Thompson (University of Massachusetts Press, Amherst, 1994).

1. Irene Böhme, *Die da drüben* (Rotbuch Verlag, Berlin, 1982). I have used the translation in *Opposition in the GDR under Honecker 1971–1985* by Roger Woods and Christopher Upward (Macmillan Press Ltd, London, 1986).

2. Pensioners were not only allowed to cross but were not prevented from emigrating West if they wanted. In this way the FRG had to pay their pensions, relieving the GDR of that burden. See Chapter Six.

3. This account is based on the description in *Escape from Berlin*.

4. Associated Press.

5. Monica Brath used the old German name Chemnitz for the town in the south of the GDR which had been renamed, reflecting the communist desire to impose themselves, Karl-Marx-Stadt on 10 May 1953. To use Chemnitz was itself a statement of rejection – and she used it twice. Incidentally, in the 1970s and 1980s I used to goad GDR journalists working abroad by referring to it loudly as 'Chemnitz', to which they would reply, in unison, 'Karl-Marx-Stadt', almost as a reflex action.

6. Interview with author.

7. *Philby: the Spy who Betrayed a Generation*, Bruce Page, David Leitch and Phillip Knightley (André Deutsch, 1969).

8. Long after his and the GDR's fall, Birgit Kubisch heard Honecker interviewed and was astonished at how he used the old terminology as if nothing had happened. She could scarcely believe it. From every utterance he made then, and elsewhere, in his mind nothing *had* happened to disturb his creed.

9. I am entirely indebted to Yorkshire Television and their programme *First Tuesday* in November 1991 for this account.

10. *The Hidden Hand*, Jeffrey Gedmin (AEI Press, Washington, DC, 1992).

11. Interview with author.

12. Interview with author.

13. *The Berlin Wall*, op. cit.

14. *Unchained Eagle*, Tom Henegham (Reuters, Pearson Education, Harlow, 2000).

Chapter Nine

1. Interview with author.

2. Interview with author.

3. Interview with author.

4. Interview with author.

5. Interview with author.

6. Interview with author.

7. Interview with Birgit Kubisch. It is surely revealing that Stolz uses the word 'our' for a West German team, implying, as it does, that he regarded Germany as still one country. How many others did, and how many others didn't? And how many were in no man's land, not sure either way?

8. Courtyard does not carry the connotation it would in English: there were small courtyards with apartment buildings round them.

9. Birgit Kubisch explains: 'A typical GDR song that every child learned at school, approximate translation *Brothers, soar up to the sun, to freedom, a star is shining bright out of the dark past*. It refers to the hard times after the war.'

10. Interview with author.

11. There's a curious story that this evening of all evenings all the passport control commanders had been summoned to a meeting in the Ministry of the Interior, leaving their deputies in charge. In other words, the people who should have been taking the decisions weren't, and the people who shouldn't, were. . . .

12. I came across an amusing episode. A family lived near Bornholmer Strasse – they could see a tiny segment of the West if they leaned out of their window – and when the border seemed to be opening they decided that, since they walked their dog every evening, they might as well go that way. They were so sure the border wasn't really open that they took no identification papers with them. When they arrived and saw it was, they went to the passport control and explained that the only one of the three with any papers was the dog – they'd brought its licence – and therefore it was the only one of them entitled to go over. 'Tonight,' one of them announced, 'the dog is going to do its business in West Berlin.' They were waved through and the dog no doubt did.

13. Interview with author.

Chapter Ten

Quotation at the head of the chapter may well have originated as a German joke and been borrowed by an American, but either way that does not diminish how apt it is, and how perceptive. Wish I'd thought of it.

1. Interview with author.
2. Interview with author.
3. Interview with author
4. Interview with author.
5. Interview with author.
6. Interview with author.

Chapter Eleven

Quotation at head of chapter: *We Were The People*, Dirk Philipsen
(Duke University Press, Durham and London, 1993).

1. Interview with author.
2. Interview with author.
3. Interview with author.
4. Interview with author.
5. Interview with author.
6. Marina Brath worked in the Hotel Ahorn and was one of those
   Easterners who seemed to have adapted quickly and conclusively
   to the supposedly insurmountable problems encountered in the
   West. When she and her husband were taken to the FRG they flew
   on to West Berlin. I wondered what her first impression was. *All
   the lights*, she said, promising freedom and plenty. She glowed at
   the recollection of the moment.
7. Interview with author.
8. *Berlin Bulletin* (Education Branch, HQ Berlin Infantry Brigade for
   British Forces).
9. Interview with author. To recapture now the sense of the forbidden
   in crossing, and the disbelief that it had really happened and
   would become normality, was elusive then and has become more
   so as time has cemented the normality. The idea that it could be
   withdrawn as quickly as it had been granted is caught nicely here
   when she wondered if she really would be able to go back.
       As an aside, when the wall had been down for about three years
   I asked Birgit Kubisch how she felt about the new normality and
   she was ambivalent. She accepted that, physically, she could go
   whenever she wished but it still felt as if she was journeying
   somewhere else.
10. Interview with author. That Hering did not rush to the border but
    enacted the procedures to get the correct documentation reveals,
    perhaps, how deep the sense of such things was in the GDR (and
    the FRG, too . . .).
11. Interview with author. Birgit Kubisch was typical of many East
    Germans in that she knew what was wrong with her own country
    but regarded it as home, was not a little proud of it, and was very
    uneasy at abandoning everything to the West. Once, when we were
    walking across Alexanderplatz, she said with sudden vehemence,
    'The sun shone here, too! People went on holiday here, too! People
    made babies here, too! It wasn't a zoo!'
12. Interview with author.
13. Interview with author. After all he had seen in the war and after it,

Schabe became an absolute pacifist and we had a heated discussion about the possible consequences if, say, your country or your home was invaded. He remained adamant that his pacifism was non-negotiable and smiled because I didn't seem to understand.

14. Letter to author.
15. Interview with author.
16. Telephone interview with author. When Erdmute reached the point where she recounted promising her son that he would not have to wait until he was 65, her voice raised to a pitch of what I can only describe as angry sincerity.
17. Emphasising how everybody had a fascinating tale to tell, Gurtz was in a hotel I happened to be staying at.
18. Interview with author.
19. Interview with author.
20. Interview with author.
21. Interview with author. Steinstücken was more than an enclave with the unavoidable anomalies, it was frankly very odd indeed because the houses East and West were so close. At one point the rear gardens backed on to each with only the twin walls and the death strip separating them – about, I suppose, 12 feet wide. When the wall came down, people discovered that they had had neighbours for years just the other side of the street and, in one case, the same side of the street. When I went there in 1990, an American officer was showing a couple of guests round a broader area of the death strip and a GDR Border Guard patrol jeep approached. 'Don't worry,' he said. 'They won't shoot, they'll probably try and sell you their uniforms.'
22. Interview with author. The activities of the Stasi have been well documented, and this book isn't about that, but what they did cut so deep that new wounds are being diagnosed all the time. For example, as I was writing this chapter in November 2000, the London *Sunday Telegraph* carried a news story headed SECRET STASI DOSSIER SET TO SHAKE BERLIN. It began: 'A hitherto secret CIA catalogue of East German Stasi agents threatens to embarrass Berlin's political establishment after the disclosure that at least 120 spies worked, or are still working, for Germany's main parties.'
23. Broadening what Gerda Stern has just said, Diana Loeser, the Briton who embraced the GDR and lived there for so long, was utterly sincere about her beliefs and articulate in discussing them. I interviewed her where she was living in Potsdam: a heavy old stone house, darkened within. At the end of the interview she said that 'communism has failed *this time round. . . .*'
24. Interview with author.

25. *Daily Telegraph*, 9 December 2000.
26. Letter to author.
27. Interview with author.
28. Interview with author.
29. *The leap of hope that ended in despair*, Imre Karacs, *The Independent*, 24 June 1998.
30. Associated Press.
31. *The Herald*, Glasgow, 6 March 1997.

Bibliography

Alter, Reinhard and Peter Monteath. *Rewriting the German Past*. Humanities Press, New Jersey, 1997.

Andrew, Christopher and Vasili Mitrokhin. *The Mitrokhin Archive*. Allen Lane/ Penguin Press, London, 1999.

Annan, Noel. *Changing Enemies: the Defeat and Regeneration of Germany*. HarperCollins, London, 1995.

Ardagh, John. *Germany and the Germans*. Penguin Books, London, 1987.

Bailey, George. *Germans: Biography of an Obsession*. Free Press, New York, 1991.

——, with David E. Murphy and Sergei A. Kondraschev. *Battleground Berlin*. Yale University Press, New Haven and London, 1997.

Balfour, Alan. *Berlin: The Politics of Order 1737–1989*. Rizzoli International Publications Inc., New York, 1990.

Bearend, Hanna. *German Unification: The Destruction of an Ecomony*. Pluto Press, London and East Haven, CT, 1995.

Borneman, John. *After The Wall*. BasicBooks (a division of HarperCollins), 1991.

Bornstein, Jerry. *The Wall Came Tumbling Down*. Outlet Book Company Inc., 1990.

Bourke-White, Margaret. *"Dear Fatherland, Rest Quietly."* Simon and Schuster, New York, 1946.

Brandt, Willy. *My Road to Berlin*. Peter Davies, London, 1960.

Brogan, Patrick. *Eastern Europe 1939–1989*. Bloomsbury Publishing Ltd, London, 1990.

Byford-Jones, Lieutenant-Colonel W. *Berlin Twilight*. Hutchinson & Co. Ltd, London, undated.

Cate, Curtis. *The Ides of August*. Weidenfeld & Nicolson, London, 1978.

Childs, David. *The GDR: Moscow's German Ally*. Unwin Hyman, London, 1988.

Crampton, R.J. *Eastern Europe in the Twentieth Century*. Routledge, London and New York, 1995.

Davidson, Eugene. *The Death and Life of Germany*. Jonathan Cape, London, 1959.

Deloffre, Jacqueline and Hans Joachim Neyer. *Berlin Capitale*. Éditions Autrement, Paris, 1992.

Dennis, Mike. *German Democratic Republic*. Pinter Publishers, London and New York, 1988.

Dodds, Dinah and Pam Allen-Thompson. *The Wall in My Backyard*. University of Massachusetts Press, 1994.

Echikson, William. *Lighting the Night*. Pan Books, London, 1990.

Fest, Winfried. *The Wall, 13 August 1961–1987*. Press and Information Office of the Land of Berlin, 1986.

Flemming, Thomas. *The Berlin Wall, Division of a City*. Be.bra.verlag, Berlin-Brandenburg, 2000.

Forster, Thomas M. *The East German Army*. George Allen & Unwin Ltd, London, 1980.

Gablentz, O.M. von der. *Documents on the Status of Berlin, 1944–1959*. R. Oldenburg Verlag, Munchen, 1959.

Gay, Peter. *My German Question*. Yale University Press, New Haven and London, 1998.

Gedmin, Jeffrey. *The Hidden Hand*. The AEI Press, Washington, DC, 1992.

Gehlen, General Reinhard. *The Gehlen Memoirs*. William Collins Sons & Co. Ltd., London, 1972.

Gelb, Norman. *The Berlin Wall*. Michael Joseph, London, 1986.

Government of the Federal Republic of Germany. *Violations of Human Rights, illegal Acts and Incidents at the Sector/Border in Berlin since the Building of the Wall (13 August 1961–15 August 1962)*. Published on behalf of the Government of the Federal Republic by the Federal Ministry for All-German Questions, Bonn and Berlin, 1962.

Grant, R.G. *The Rise and Fall of the Berlin Wall*. Magna Books, Leicester, 1991.

Gray, Richard T. and Wilkie, Sabine. *German Unification and its Discontents*. University of Washington Press, Seattle and London, 1996.

Gympel, Jan and Wernicke, Ingolf. *The Berlin Wall*. Jaron Verlag GmbH, Berlin, 1998.

Hafner, Katie. *The House at the Bridge*. Scribner, New York, 1995.

Harpprecht, Klaus. *Willy Brandt: Portrait and Self-Portrait*. Abelard-Schuman, London, 1972.

Harrison, Hope M. *Ulbricht and the Concrete 'Rose': New Archival Evidence of the Dynamics of Soviet–East German Relations and the Berlin Crisis, 1958–1961*. Cold War International History Project, The Woodrow Wilson Center, Washington, DC, 1993.

Heller, Deane and David. *The Berlin Wall*. Frederick Muller Ltd, London, 1964.

Henderson, the Rt Hon. Sir Neville. *Failure of a Mission*. Readers Union Ltd by arrangement with Hodder & Stoughton, London, 1941.

Heneghan, Tom. *Unchained Eagle (Germany after the Wall)*. Reuters, Pearson Education, Harlow, 2000.

Hertle, Hans-Hermann. *Chronik des Mauerfalls*. Ch. Links Verlag, Berlin, 1999.

Hildebrandt, Dr Rainer. *Es Geschah an der Mauer*. Verlag Haus am Checkpoint Charlie, 1984.

——. *Berlin: Von der Frontstadt zur Brücke Europas*. Verlag Haus am Checkpoint Charlie, 1984.

——. *Von Ghandi bis Walesa*. Verlag Haus am Checkpoint Charlie, 1993.

Isherwood, C. *Goodbye to Berlin*. Minerva, London, 1989.

Jarausch, Konrad H. *The Rush to German Unity*. Oxford University Press, New York and Oxford, 1994.

——, and Volker Gransow. *Uniting Germany*. Berghahn Books, Providence, RI, 1994.

Kemp, Anthony. *Escape from Berlin*. Boxtree Ltd, London, 1987.

Laufer, Peter. *Iron Curtain Rising*. Mercury House, San Francisco, 1991.

Leonhard, Wolfgang. *Child of the Revolution*. William Collins Sons & Co. Ltd, London, 1957.

Le Tissier, Tony. *Berlin Then and Now*. After the Battle, London, 1992.

Lippert, Barbara and Rosalind Stevens-Ströhmann. *German Unification and EC Integration*. The Royal Institute of International Affairs, Pinter Publishers, London, 1993.

Lippmann, Heinz. *Honecker and the New Politics of Europe*. Macmillan Co., New York, 1972.

Maaz, Hans-Joachim. *Behind the Wall*. W.W. Norton & Co., New York and London, 1995.

MacDonogh, Giles. *Berlin*. Sinclair-Stevenson, London, 1997.

Marsh, David. *The Germans: Rich, Bothered and Divided*. Century, London, 1989.

McCauley, Martin. *The German Democratic Republic since 1945*. Macmillan Press, London, 1986.

McDermott, Geoffrey. *Berlin: Success of a Mission?* André Deutsch, London, 1963.

McDougall, Ian. *German Notebook*. Elek, New York and London, 1953.

Mercer, Derrik (ed.-in-chief). *Chronicle of the 20th Century*. Longman, London, 1988.

Millar, Peter. *Tomorrow Belongs to Me*. Bloomsbury Publishing Ltd, London, 1992.

Möbius, Peter and Helmut Trotnow. *Mauern sind nicht für ewig gebaut*. Verlag Ullstein GmBh, 1990.

Mount, Ferdinand (ed.). *Communism*. A Times Literary Supplement Companion, Harvill, London, 1992.

Naimark, Norman M. *The Russians in Germany*. Belknap Press of Harvard University Press, 1995.

Nelson, Walter Henry. *The Berliners*. Longmans, Green and Co. Ltd, London, 1969.

Newman, Bernard. *Behind the Berlin Wall*. Robert Hale Ltd, London, 1964.

Oberdorfer, Don. *The Turn*. Jonathan Cape, London, 1992.

O'Donnell, James P. *The Berlin Bunker*. Arrow Books, London, 1979.

Petschull, Jürgen. *With the Wind to the West*. Hodder & Stoughton, London, 1981.

Philipsen, Dirk. *We Were the People*. Duke University Press, Durham and London, 1993.

Pond, Elizabeth. *Beyond the Wall*. Brookings Institution, Washington, DC, 1993.

Press and Information Office of the Land of Berlin. *The Wall and How it Fell*. 1994.

Prittie, Terence. *Willy Brandt: Portrait of a Statesman*. Weidenfeld & Nicolson, London, 1974.

Read, Anthony and David Fisher. *The Fall of Berlin*. Hutchinson, London, 1992.

——. *Berlin: The Biography of a City*. Pimlico, London, 1994.

Schaffer, Gordon. *Russian Zone*. Published for the Co-operative Press by George Allen & Unwin, London, 1947.

Scholze, Thomas and Falk Blask. *Halt! Grenzgebiet!* BasisDruck Verlag GmbH, Berlin, 1992.

Shears, David. *The Ugly Frontier*. Chatto & Windus Ltd, London, 1970.

Shirer, William. *Berlin Diary*. Hamish Hamilton, London, 1941.

——. *The Rise and Fall of the Third Reich*. Pan Books Ltd, London, 1971.

Smith, Ken. *Berlin: Coming in from the Cold*. Hamish Hamilton, London, 1990.

Steele, Jonathan. *Socialism with a German Face*. Jonathan Cape, London, 1977.

Steinberg, Rolf (ed.). *Berlin im November*. Nicolaische Verlagsbuchhandlung, Berlin, 1990.

Stern, Carola. *Ulbricht, a Political Biography*. Pall Mall Press, London, 1965.

Wolf, Markus, with Anne McElvoy. *Man without a Face*. Jonathan Cape, London, 1997.

Woods, Roger and Christopher Upward. *Opposition in the GDR under Honecker, 1971–1985*. Macmillan Press Ltd, London, 1986.

Zubok, Vladislav M. *Khrushchev and the Berlin Crisis (1958–1962)*. Cold War International History Project, The Woodrow Wilson Center, Washington, DC, 1993.

The Death Strip: The Toll

Note: known fatalities are indicated by *f* following the date in brackets.

Behnke, Wolfgang (22.8.85*f*) 252
Beilig, Dieter (2.12.71*f*) 216
Berger, Dieter (13.12.63*f*) 183
Bittner, Michael (24.11.86*f*) 253–5
Blass, Barbara Hildegard (12.1.62*f*) 154
Block, Willi (7.2.66*f*) 199
Böcker/Boecker, Peter (1.11.84*f*) 247
Böhme, Peter (18.4.62*f*) 155
Brandes, Dieter (9.6.65*f*) 195
Bruckner, Axel (3.9.61*f*) 135
Brueske, Klaus (18.4.62*f*) 155
Burkett, Rudolf (Apr. 1983*f*) 246
Buttkus, Christian (4.3.65*f*) 194

Cyrus, Heinz (10.11.65*f*) 197

Döbler, Hermann (15.6.65*f*) 195
Dullick, Udo (5.10.61*f*) 138

Ehrlich, Friedhelm (2.8.70*f*) 212
Eich, Klaus-Peter (12.10.61*f*) 138–9
Einsiedel, Horst (15.3.73*f*) 218

Fechter, Peter (17.8.62*f*) 164–72, 245,
 260, 348–9, 353
Forgert, Hedwig (April 1963*f*) 176
Frank, Horst (29.4.62*f*) 155
Freie, Lothar Fritz (4.6.72*f*) 245
Freundenberg, Winfried (3.3.89*f*) 259–60
Friese, Christin-Peter (25.12.70*f*) 215

Gadegart, Alice Paula Olga (10.12.84*f*)
 249
Garten, Klaus (18.8.65*f*) 197

Gaudian, Christian (5.2.89) 259
Gertzki, Manfred (27.4.73*f*) 218
Glöde, Wolfgang (10.6.62*f*) 159
Gneiser, Rainer (28.7.64*f*) 188
Gomert, Klaus (20.7.73*f*) 218
Graupner, Ernest (29.4.62*f*) 156
Gross, Rene (21.11.86*f*) 253
Gueffroy, Chris (5.2.89*f*) 124, 259

Haberlandt, Lutz (27.5.61*f*) 159
Halli, Norbert (2.4.75*f*) 229
Hanke, Fritz (1963) 175
Hannemann, Axel (5.6.62*f*) 159
Hartmann, Jörg (15.3.66*f*) 199
Heike, Walter (22.6.64*f*) 188
Heinemann, Ursula (19.8.61) 125
Held, Philipp (11.4.62*f*) 155
Hennig, Lothar (4.11.75*f*) 231
Heyn, Walter (27.2.64*f*) 187
Hinz, Melita (18.12.62*f*) 174
Hoff, Roland (29.8.61*f*) 135
Hoffmann, Wolfgang (15.7.71*f*) 215

Jercha, Heinz (27.3.62*f*) 155
Jirkowski, Marietta (22.11.80*f*) 242

Kabelitz, Rolf-Dieter (7.1.71*f*) 215
Kahl, Hans-Jürgen (3.12.64*f*) 193
Kayser, Gerhard (27.10.61*f*) 146
Kelm, Erna (11.6.62*f*) 159
Kirste, Anna (Nov/Dec. 1973*f*) 218
Kittel, Walter (18.1.65*f*) 197
Kluge, Klaus-Jürgen (13.9.69*f*) 207
Kollender, Michael (25.4.66*f*) 201–2

Körner, Horst (15.11.68*f*) 205
Kreitloff, Peter (23.1.73*f*) 218
Kreitlow, Peter (24.1.63*f*) 175
Krug, Siegfried (6.7.68*f*) 205
Krüger, Ingo (10.12.61*f*) 154
Krzemien, Ulrich (3.3.65*f*) 194
Kube, Karl-Heinz (16.12.66) 204
Kühl, Werner (24.7.71*f*) 215
Kuhn, Erich (26.11.65*f*) 197
Kullack, Horst (1.1.72*f*) 216
Kutscher, Horst (15.1.63) 175

Lange, Johannes (9.4.69*f*) 207
Lehmann, Lothar (17.11.61*f*) 151
Liebke, Rainer (3.9.86*f*) 253
Lis, Leo (20.9.69) 207
Litwin, Gunter (24.8.61*f*) 135
Lunzer, Bernd (4.10.61*f*) 138
Lupke, Gustav (6.11.66*f*) 204

Mader, Manfred (21.11.86*f*) 253
Mädler, Peter (26.4.63*f*) 162
Märtens, Elke (10.6.66*f*) 203
Marzhan, Willi (19.3.66*f*) 199
Meixner, Hans-Peter (1963) 176–7
Mende, Herbert (8.7.62*f*) 162
Meyer, Michael (13.9.64) 188–9
Mispelhorn, Wernhorn (18.8.64) 188
Mueller, Rudolf (18.6.62) 160–1
Müller, Heinz (19.6.70*f*) 209
Müller, Otto (14.3.62*f*) 155
Mund, Ernst (4.9.62) 174
Muschol, Dr Johannes (16.3.81*f*) 243
Muszinski, Wolf-Olaf (Mar. 1963*f*) 176

Niering, Burkhard (5.1.74*f*) 218–19
Nittmeier, Hans-Joachim (1.12.62) 174
Noffke, Siegfried (28.6.62) 161

Petermann, Peter (25.4.66*f*) 201
Philipp, Adolf (5.5.64*f*) 188
Probst, Werner (14.10.61*f*) 140
Proksch, Silvio (25.12.83*f*) 246
Puhlfüss, Wolfgang (8.10.69*f*) 207

Rassmann, Hans-Joachim (2.9.61*f*) 135
Räwel, Hans (1.1.63*f*) 174–5
Reck, Ottfried (27.11.62) 174
Richter, Hartmut (Jan. 1966) 198–9, 203–4
Sahmland, Max Willi (27.1.67) 205
Schleussner, Lothar (14.3.66*f*) 199
Schmidt, Heinz (29.8.66*f*) 204
Schmidt, Lutz (12.2.87) 255
Schmidt, Michael (1.12.84*f*) 247–8
Schmiel, Doris (19.2.62*f*) 154
Schmock, Klaus (18.7.70*f*) 212
Scholz, Elmar (1.4.69*f*) 206
Scholz, Peter (June 62) 159
Schöneberger, Heinz (26.12.65*f*) 198, 206
Schröder, Falk (29.9.87*f*) 256
Schröter, Klaus (4.11.63*f*) 182
Schultz, Paul (25.12.63*f*) 184
Schulz, Dietmar (25.11.63*f*) 182
Schulze, Eberhard (30.3.66*f*) 199
Schulze, Frieda (Sept. 1961) 137
Schulze, Klaus (7.3.72*f*) 217–18
Schuman, Konrad (Aug. 1961) 107–8, 111
Schwietzer, Dietmar (16.2.77*f*) 234
Segler, Olga (25.9.61*f*) 137
Seling, Günter (30.9.62*f*) 174
Semmler, Günter (13.1.72*f*) 216
Siekmann, Ida (22.8.61*f*) 133
Sokolowski, Heinz (25.11.65*f*) 197
Steinhauer, Ulrich (4.11.80*f*) 242
Stephan, Joachim (21.11.66*f*) 204
Stretz, Paul (29.4.66*f*) 202, 203

Tharau, Margit (1963) 176–7
Thiem, Gerald (7.8.70*f*) 212
Thomas, Max (May 1962) 156
Trabant, Hildegard (18.8.64) 188

Urban, Peter (?18.11.87*f*) 256
Urban, Rudolf (19.8.61*f*) 124, 259

Walzer, Anton (8.10.62*f*) 174
Weckeiser, Dieter (18.2.68*f*) 205
Weise, Henry (17.5.75*f*) 231

Weser, Hans-Dieter (23.8.62*f*) 173
Weylandt, Manfred (14.2.72*f*) 217
Wiedenhöft, Günter (5.12.62*f*) 174
Wohlfahrt, Dieter (9.12.61*f*) 153–4
Wolff, Hans-Joachim (26.11.64*f*) 193
Wolscht, Norbert (28.7.64*f*) 188
Wroblenski, Eduard (26.7.66*f*) 203

Unnamed escapees:
(23.5.62) 156, 158
(57 tunnellers: 3–5.10.64) 189–92
(2 Border Guards: Aug. 1985) 252

Unnamed fatalities:
(5.10.61) 138
(18.10.61) 140
(31.10.61) 151
(17.11.61) 153
(20.11.61) 153
(1.1.62) 154
(3.4.62) 155
(22.6.62) 161
(29.7.62) 162
(4.9.62) 174
(Nov. 62) 174

(1.11.62) 174
(16.4.63) 176
(26.3.64) 187
(1.1.65) 193
(19.1.65) 193
(1.5.67) 205
(1.1.70) 209
(21.6.74) 223
(2.7.84) 246
(18.8.87) 256
(16.4.89) 260

Other casualties:
  Children (drowned)
  Cetin, Mert (5.5.75) 229
  Koc, Cengiz (30.12.72*f*) 218
  Krobot, Siegfried (14.5.73*f*) 218
  Savoca, Guiseppe (17.6.74) 223

  East German Border Guards
  Göring, Peter (23.5.62) 158, 171–2
  Huhn, Reinhold (18.6.62) 159, 160,
    171–2
  Schmidtchen, Jörgen (18.4.62) 155
  Schulz, Egon (5.10.64) 192–3

Index

Adalbertstrasse 103

Adenaur, Chancellor Konrad 29, 50, 54, 113–14, 121, 122, 134, 179

ADN (official GDR press agency) 33, 37, 43

  East German communiqués 38–9, 46

Albertz, Heinrich (Chief of Staff, West Berlin) 27, 45

Alexanderplatz 70, 211

American army in Berlin

  Emergency Operations Center 163

  Flag Patrols 184–5

  Military Liaison Mission 42

  Military Police 145, 269

  Mitchell Suite (observation office) 262, 282, 287, 291

  travel instructions 185–7

  see also Battle Group

American Berlin Mission 20, 23, 27, 37, 63

  friction with Washington 72–3, 109

  see also Berlin Task Force

American Sector 6, 7, 44

Amrehn, Franz (Deputy Mayor, Berlin) 47, 65, 112

Andropov, Yuri 245, 246

ARD (West German television) 283, 294

Ardagh, John (author) 208

Associated Press 248, 252, 253, 275

Ausland, John (Berlin Task Force) 23, 24, 53, 61–2, 65, 66, 69, 73, 107, 118

  on autobahn problems 181–2

  and 'Clay' problem 150–1

  and Fechter killing 172–3

  Kennedy briefing (Aug. 1962) 173–4

  and US Battle Group 127

Austro-Hungarian border opening 262

autobahn link 109, 209–10

  convoy procedures 182

  as escape route 239

  movement of US Battle Group 125–8, 150

  problems 181–2

  transit agreement 213, 239

  US military instructions 185–7

Axel Springer 160, 245

Babelsberg 338–9

Bailey, George (US journalist) 21, 48

Baker, Jim 343

Bakewell, Joan (BBC) 347

Bark, Dennis L. (US student) 164–7, 172, 212, 245, 341

Battle Group (US) 118–19, 125–31, 150

BBC World Service 58, 282, 302, 308

Behrendt, Kurt 11, 136, 151, 183, 195–7, 235–6, 338–9

Benner, Astrid 269, 271, 272, 274, 279–81, 294, 300, 318

  coping with Adler 'siege' 305–6, 307, 311, 314

Bentz, Bill (US infantry) 162–4, 184–5

Berlin 4

  airlift 8, 9, 117, 151

  East–West contrasts 89, 133, 181, 184, 185, 208, 210–11, 314–15, 330, 351–3

  first Christmas 153–4

  Four Power status 9–10

  inter-zonal trade 100–1

  Kennedy's view of 86–7

  sectors 6

  telephone links 102, 105, 215, 216

  see also East Berlin; West Berlin

Berlin Bulletin 325–6

Berlin Museum (East and West) 332–3

Berlin Task Force (US) 15, 66
  formation 24
  meetings 52, 101, 117–19
Berlin Treaty 8, 64, 236
Berlin Wall 1–3,181, 198, 208
  American reaction 71, 149–50
  building/rebuilding of 28, 106–8, 116,
    151, 181, 183
  demolition and disappearance 307,
    322–3, 338, 339, 343–4
  GDR exhibitions for Westerners 175
  property ownership problems 107
Berlin Wall, The (Flemming) 230
Berlin–Washington time gap 65–6
Bernau 42, 54
Bernauer Strasse 1, 3, 11, 21, 40, 49, 56,
    57, 67, 89, 224, 225–6
  closure of U-bahn station 51
  death strip creation 111, 140
  escapes 58, 59, 100, 107–8, 111, 137,
    189–92, 253
  attempts/fatalities 124–5, 133, 137,
    138
  forced evacuation 111, 116, 124, 137,
    139
  opening of Wall 305, 330–1
  reunification 336, 349
  screens 139, 153
  sealing of houses 111, 114, 120
Bernhard, Jens (Border Guard) 253
Bilt Zeitung 103
Bittner, Irmgard 254–5
Black Forest 19
Blake, George 62
Boenisch, Peter (FRG spokesman) 248
Bohlen, Charles (US State Department)
    118
Böhme, Irene (author) 243–5
Bonn (Government) *see* Federal Republic
    of Germany (FRG)
Bonn University 111
border closure 29–30
  Allies' inaction 105
  effects on public transport 92
  first indications 38–40
  and Four Power Agreement 20

Honecker's orders 30–1
  installation of barbed wire barriers 44,
    47–8, 49, 57, 63
  manning 199–202
  passport controls 19, 277, 294
  People's Police timetable 33
  and Politburo meeting 29–30
  reopening of borders 261–8, 279,
    294–303
Border Guards (GDR) 32, 38, 199, 200,
    237
  checkpoint controls 277
  duties 201–2, 218–25
  and Fechter killing 172, 348–9
  and Gueffroy killing 124, 259, 347
  personnel and equipment 200–1
  and reopening of borders 294,
    299–300, 317, 328, 329
  trials (post-unification) 348–9
Border Police
  East Berlin 42, 110, 119, 199, 200
  West Berlin 110
Bornholmer Strasse 103, 270
  reopening of borders (9–10.11.89)
    276–8, 283, 287, 288–9, 289–90,
    294, 296–9, 331
Boyes Lyon, Maj-Gen F.C. 209
Brandenburg Gate 17, 21, 35, 38, 67,
    134, 232–3, 255, 299
  closure to traffic 42, 43, 45–6, 52–3,
    54, 76, 105
  and insurrection fears (12/13 Aug.)
    83–5, 91, 96–7
  reopening 302, 312–13
Brandenburg (town) 27, 63, 76
Brandt, Willy (Mayor, West Berlin) 27,
    29, 36, 47, 50, 55, 59, 61, 181,
    189
  and border closures 64–5, 89, 115
  as Chancellor 207, 223, 245
  JFK's visit 178
  LBJ's visit 122, 123, 124
  letter to Kennedy (16.8.61) 112–13,
    118
  West Berlin address (16.8.61) 111–12
Branson, Sir Richard 349

Brath, Peter and Marina, escape attempt 249–51, 324–5
Brezhnev, Leonid 213, 245
British army in Berlin 119, 129
 4th Royal Tank Regiment 93
 Military Police 44, 272, 273
 Olympic Stadium barracks 44, 129, 299
 and reopening of borders/checkpoints 325–6, 331–2
 Royal Green Jackets arrest 194
British Government, Foreign Office 54, 87
British Mission, Berlin 44
British Sector 6, 7, 8, 100, 272, 299
 patrol 273–4
 Soviet war memorial 116–17
Brown, Sgt Nathaniel (US army) 278–9, 282, 314
Bulgaria 9
Bundy, McGeorge 15
Burkhardt, Jacqueline 10, 148, 302
Byford-Jones, Lt-Col W. 8–9

Café Adler 262, 269, 272, 274, 279, 281, 291, 292, 293, 300
 'siege' 305–7, 311, 314
Carl Zeiss Jena 11
Carter, Jimmy (US President) 241
Cash, Frank (Berlin Task Force) 15, 24, 61, 62, 66, 173, 180
 and inter-zonal trade 100–1
 on Kennedy 149–50
 LBJ's visit to Berlin 121–2, 123–4, 127
Ceauşescu, Nicolae (Romania) 251
cemeteries 49, 225
Central Intelligence Agency (CIA) 21, 27, 28
Chancellery, Berlin 4
Chausseestrasse checkpoint 133, 270, 277, 300, 305, 337
Checkpoint Charlie 3, 135, 160, 177, 210, 212, 261–2, 273, 341, 342
 confrontation (Oct. 1961) 140–9
 escapes 185
 identification problems 162–4
 Lightner incident 140–5

Museum 335, 340–1, 346, 349
 opening of checkpoint 304–7
 passport control 277
 reopening of borders (9–10.11.89) 262–8, 279–83, 284–5, 287–8, 289, 290–3, 293–6, 299–301
checkpoints 133, 294–5
 opening 297, 299, 301–3, 337
Chernenko, Konstantin 246, 251
Church of Reconciliation 41, 111, 125, 140, 153, 225, 336
 destruction 226–7
 GDR expropriation 161–2
 rebuilding 349
CIA *see* Central Intelligence Agency
Clarke, Gen (US army) 134
Clay, Lucius D. (US general, retd) 101, 109, 118, 147
 Berlin appointment 136, 156
 and Checkpoint Charlie confrontations 144–5, 148
 visits to Berlin 125
Clayallee (American Mission) 152, 178
Cleveland, Earle (American Mission) 140
Clifton, Maj-Gen Chester V. (US army) 74, 126, 130
CNN news channels 61
Coblentz, Gaston (US journalist) 22
Combat Groups (*Kampfgruppen*) 200
command posts (*Führungsstellen*) 201
communism/communists in Germany 4–5, 6, 78–81
Couve de Murville, Maurice (French Foreign Minister) 48
Crampton, R.J. 8
crossing-points: manning prior to closure 40–1
Czechoslovakia 9, 198, 199, 261, 265, 267

Dahlem District, West Berlin 273, 278–9
Daly, John 48
Davis, Dick 118
Day, Arthur (Berlin Task Force) 24
de Gabory, Gen Olivier (French Mission) 248

de Gaule, President Charles 48
death strip 111, 116, 217, 225, 253, 256,
        338, 344
Delacombe, Maj-Gen Rohan (British
        commandant) 116–17
Dennis, Mick (author) 213
Deutschmark 9, 11, 13
Dick, Peter 235
Doherr, Anna-marie 17
Douglas-Home, Alec (British Foreign
        Secretary) 48, 54, 87, 120, 151
Dowling, Walter (US Ambassador) 23
Dreilinden 130, 187, 216
Dresden 208, 216, 265
Dulles, John Foster 23
Düsseldorf 10, 240

East Berlin 133, 208
    Allied access to 106
    border sealing responses 77–81
    Central Committee 50
    decree 109
    demonstrations 267
    insurrection (1953) 10
    opening up of checkpoints
        (9–10.11.89) 276–303
    passport controls 277
East Germany *see* German Democratic
        Republic (GDR)
Eberswalder Strasse 57
Ebert Strasse 48
Egersdörfer, Roland (Border Guard) 208,
        218–25, 253, 346
Eigenfeld, Frank 224
Einsatzgruppen (East German police) 99
Eiskeller enclave 162, 213, 235, 236–7,
        331
Emergency Operations Center (US army)
        56
enclaves 136, 235–6
escapes 89, 91, 109, 111, 125, 129, 130,
        131, 132, 133, 138, 140, 152–3,
        160, 176–7, 188–92, 193, 194–5,
        203–4, 247, 253, 258–9
    Border Police reports 68, 70, 93, 158,
        159–60

failed attempts 135, 240, 255, 259–60
fatalities 124–5, 135, 137, 138–9, 140,
        146, 153, 154, 155–6, 162, 164,
        174–5, 176, 182, 183, 193, 195,
        201, 202–3, 215, 218–19, 231,
        234, 242, 243, 247, 253, 253–5,
        256, 259, 260
    Fechter killing (17.8.62) 164–72
    first 58–9, 63, 87–8, 100
    Gueffroy killing 124, 259, 346–7
    incident sheet tallies 103, 104, 110,
        114, 120, 126
    organisers 240
    tunnelling 138, 154, 156, 159, 160,
        174, 189–93
European Security Conference (1970)
        213
evacuations of property (forced) 111,
        116, 124, 136–7, 138

Factory Fighting Groups (*Kampfgruppen*)
        26, 37, 80
    arming of 49, 67, 68, 70
    assembly at crossing points 39–40, 44
    complement figures 60, 67, 119
    and insurrection fears (12/13 Aug.) 85,
        91
Falkensee 36, 57, 111, 206, 237, 327, 331
    station 35, 43
Fechter killing and memorial 164–72,
        245, 285, 341, 342, 348–9, 353
Federal Merit Cross 340
Federal Republic of Germany (FRG) 9
    accord with Soviet Union and Poland
        (1970) 213
    Bundestag 120, 213
    Minister of Posts and
        Telecommunications 105
Fischer, Pastor Manfred 225–7, 305,
        336–8
Flemming, Thomas 230
Florin, P. (SED) 17
Four Power Agreement (1971) 125, 128,
        132
    and border closures 20, 55, 63–4, 292,
        295

and Fechter killing 168
infraction by East Germany 72, 74, 105
and military manoeuvres 128, 146
and Rusk's statement (13 Aug.) 74–5
Four-Power negotiations on Berlin (1970)
213
Frankfurt 11
Frankfurter Rundschau 17
Free Berlin radio station 97
Free German Youth (GDR) 54, 115, 120,
199
Freedom Bell 124
French Zone 6, 119
Friedrich, Rolf (Border Guard) 348, 349
Friedrichshain 40, 45, 60, 283–4
Friedrichstrasse (East Berlin) 33, 67–8,
70, 133, 160, 270
station 13, 29, 50, 51, 106, 234, 303,
318
white line (Hagen Koch's) 117, 141,
210, 212, 269
Frohnau 255
Fuchs, Wolfgang, 'Operation Tokyo'
189–93
Fulbright, William (US Senator) 20

GDR *see* German Democratic Republic
GDR television 88, 274
Gehlen, Reinhard (head, FRG security
service) 30
Gelb, Norman (US journalist) 24, 96, 136
German Democratic Republic (GDR)
9–10, 175–6
40th anniversary celebrations 261, 265
arrests for 'state crimes' 135–6
border clearances 105, 182
Central Committe meeting (18.10.89)
266–7, 272
Council of Ministers 268
decrees 109, 115, 132, 134
economy 181, 242–3
Foreign Ministry 16
government/police orders (13.8.61)
94–5, 96–7
identity cards, passes and permits 95,
104–5, 133, 226

insurrection fears 58–9, 69, 83–5, 87,
91, 96–7, 105, 120
military personnel numbers 119
opposition groups and demonstrations
96, 265
Politburo 29, 266, 267, 268, 348
shoot-to-kill policy 109, 132, 237–8,
248–9, 347
status and sovereignty 132, 213, 215,
223–4, 348
telecommunication links 102, 105,
215, 216
see also House of Ministries; Ministry
of the Interior
German Protestant Church Synod 20
Germany
and communism 4–5, 6
reunification 332–3, 341, 343
zoning 6
Gesundbrunnen 44, 67
Geue, Gisela (Fechter's sister) 348
glasnost 252
Glau, Daniel 286, 323, 345
Glau, Peter 25
Glienicker Bridge 135
Godek, Maj Bernie (US army) 261–5,
266, 273, 274, 278–9, 282, 287,
342
at Checkpoint Charlie (9.11.89) 290–3,
293–6, 299, 301, 304, 306, 314,
316, 317, 318
Gorbachev, Mikhail 251, 252, 255, 258,
262, 266, 267
visit to East Berlin 264–5
Gorlitzer Bahnhof 115
Gosen 303
Gotsche, Otto (Ulbricht's secretary) 79
Greathouse, Col John (US army) 279,
282, 287, 290, 291, 293, 299
Greis-Behrendt, Erdmute (Reuters) 31,
33, 48, 54, 57
arrest (13.8.61) 98–100
on reopening of borders 293, 311, 331
Schabowski press conference 275–6
visits to the West 231–3, 333–4
Grey, Dave (Joint Chiefs of Staff) 119

Grohmann, Klaus-Peter 34, 56–7, 100, 216–17, 336
Gromyko, Andrei 18
Grotewohlexpress (prisoner transport train) 199
Gueffroy, Chris, killing 124, 259, 346–7
Gutz, Erkhard (GDR army) 334–5

Hamilton, Brigadier 100
Hannover 47, 125, 209
Harrison, Hope M. 17, 18
Harzer Strasse: forced evacuation 136–7
Havel, River, escape 135
Heidelburg, US army headquarters 126, 127
Heinrich, Ingo 347
Heinrich-Heine-Strasse 103, 133, 205–6, 270, 277, 299
Helmstedt (Marienborn) 126, 127–8, 187, 209, 216
Helsinki Agreement (Aug. 1975) 224, 229, 232, 238
Hemsing, Al (American Mission) 37, 52, 67–8, 76, 89, 106, 121, 123
  Checkpoint Charlie confrontation 147
  Fechter killing 167
  Lightner incident 141–4
  post-border closures 134–5, 137
Hering, Rudiger 31, 33, 36, 57, 58, 105, 111, 206, 327–8, 344, 345
Hermlin, Stefan (writer) 78–9
Hildebrandt, Rainer 340
Hillenbrand, Martin (US State Department) 23–4, 62, 66
Hitler, Adolf 4, 6, 79, 179, 180
Holloway, Jerry (Berlin Task Force) 24
Home, Lord *see* Douglas-Home
Honecker, Erich 23, 30–1, 61, 79, 80, 88, 251, 252, 269, 350
  Central Committee meeting (18.10.89) 266–7
  Gorbachev visit 265, 266
  Schultz death investigation 193
  and shoot-to-kill policy 109, 237, 256
House of Ministries (GDR) 17, 29, 86
  escape 194–5

Howley, Frank (US commander) 118
human rights 112
Humboldt Canal: escape attempts 135, 138
Hungary 9
  opening of borders 261, 275
Hurd, Douglas 332, 343
Husak, Gustav (Czechoslovakia) 251
Huttner, E. 16

identity cards 104–5, 129–30, 133, 226
insurrection fears (12–13 Aug.) 58–9, 69, 83–5, 87, 91, 105, 120
intelligence services 62, 65
  Allied 21, 27, 28, 118, 148
Inter-Allied Governing Authority 6
International Court of Justice 15
International Press Centre 273
Intra-German Relations Ministry, Bonn 253
Invaliden cemetery 217
Invalidenstrasse checkpoint 93, 94, 133, 270, 277, 294, 301, 302, 303, 313
Isherwood, Christopher 37, 346

Jäger, Harald (passport control) 276–8, 287, 288–90, 296–9, 311–12, 331, 349–51
Johns, Col Glover S., Jnr (US) 127, 128, 130
Johnson, Lyndon (US Vice-President) 101
  visit to West Berlin 118, 119, 121–4, 130, 131
Johnson, Peter (journalist) 57–8, 66, 70, 85, 101, 104, 113, 122
  arrest (13 Aug.) 98–100
  Battle Group coverage 126
Jungpionier (children's organisation) 199

Kaiser Wilhelm Memorial Church 131
Kampfgruppen see Factory Fighting Groups
Kardar, Janos (Hungary) 251
Karl-Marx-Allee, East Berlin 302, 308
Karlshorst (Soviet headquarters) 152
Kellerbrücke 103

Kellett-Long, Adam (Reuters) 25–6, 33, 34, 37
  arrest (13.8.91) 98–100
  and Checkpoint Charlie confrontation 145–7
  Christmas 1961 154
  post-border closure 83–5, 106, 129
  pre-border closure 38–9, 42–3, 46, 54–5, 57, 60, 67, 69, 70–1
Kellett-Long, Mary 69, 75, 96
  diary entries
    on border closures 43, 86, 94, 99–100, 102, 105
    post-border closures 110–11, 134
Kennedy, Edward: visit to Berlin 155
Kennedy, John F. (US President) 22, 30, 34, 74, 131
  assassination (Nov. 1963) 205
  at Hyannis Port 30, 33, 34, 38, 73–4, 86, 131
  and Battle Group 119, 126
  Berlin strategy 20, 119, 136, 150–1, 173
  initial handling of crisis 66, 74–5, 86–7, 100–1, 109–10, 118
  and nuclear fears 73, 87, 119, 173
  and Rusk relationship 74–5
  and tank confrontation (Oct. 1961) 148–51
  Vienna Summit (June 1961) 13, 14, 16
  visit to Berlin (June 1963) 177–80
Kennedy, Robert: visit to Berlin 155
Khrushchev, Nikita (Soviet leader) 10, 12, 17, 19
  and border closure 18, 21–2, 23, 29, 53, 88, 101
  and tank confrontation 148–50
  and unilateralism 12
  Vienna Summit (June 1961) 13, 15, 16
Kiel 29
Klein, David (Berlin Task Force) 24
Kleinmachnow (East Berlin) 44, 152
Kleuhs, Alfred (Reuters) 126
Koch, Hagen 3, 27, 80, 117, 171–2
  manning the border 199–202
Kohl, Helmet (FRG Chancellor) 245, 316

Kohler, Foy (US Asst Secretary of State) 24, 66, 71, 72, 73, 117, 119, 127
Kohn, Elli (East Berliner) 78, 88
Kommandatura
  meetings 47–8, 64
  setting up 6–7
Konev, Ivan (Soviet marshal) 24, 26, 53
Köpenick 40, 45, 60, 219, 258, 285–6
Köpenickerstrasse 103
Krenz, Egon 265, 266, 267, 268, 272, 348, 350
Kreuzberg (West Berlin) 85
Ku-damm 31, 89, 131, 309, 310, 329
Kubisch, Birgit 258, 302, 308, 318, 323, 328–9, 349, 351–3
Kühnpast, Andreas 347
Kull, Peter (Border Guard) 239–40
Kurfürstendamm 335
Kvitsinsky, Yuli 16, 17, 18

Lazarev, (?)Anatoly Ivanovich 144
Le Carré, John 252
Ledwidge, Bernard 44, 45, 54, 61, 75–6
Lehrter station 29
Leipzig demonstrations 265
Leipziger Strasse 48, 212, 271, 272, 283
Lemmer, Ernst (West German minister) 50
Lenin, Vladimir 79
  statue 342
Lenne Triangle 235
Leonhard, Wolfgang 5, 6
Liaison Mission (US), Potsdam 52
Lichtenberg 40, 42, 60, 104, 249
Lichterfelde 56
Lightner, Alan (American Mission) 46, 72, 73, 101
  Checkpoint Charlie confrontation 140–5
Lightner, Dorothy 23, 140–5
Lochner, Robert (RIAS) 28
Loeser, Diana 27, 81
Loschek, Rudolf (Border Guard) 201–2

McDermott, Geoffrey (British minister) 45, 62, 64, 93, 116, 123
  and 'Clay' problem 151, 156

Mackay, Maj Ross (British army) 299

Macmillan, Harold (British Prime Minister) 48, 54, 98, 105

Magdeburg 128

Marienborn 128

Marienfelde Reception Centre 11, 13, 17, 21, 36

refugee numbers post-border sealing 93, 104, 114

Marienkirche, East Berlin 129

Marshall Aid 8, 9, 11

Marx-Engels-Platz 42, 289

Mateus 11, 231

Mautner, Martha (US Intelligence) 118

Meyer, Peter 247

Mielke, Erich (Stasi head) 18, 30, 193

Ministry of the Interior (GDR) 24, 40, 95, 97, 200, 267

incident reports 103, 169–72

travel restrictions decree 115

Ministry of State Security (GDR) *see* Stasi

Mitchell, Gen John (US commander in Berlin) 262

Mittag, Günter 267

Mitte district 40, 42, 49, 60, 64, 92, 226, 293

Mohnke, Maj-Gen Wilhelm 4–5

Moll, Günter (East Berlin Commander) 266, 267, 269, 271, 272, 273, 274, 288, 289, 342, 349, 351

at the checkpoint (9.11.89) 290–6, 299–301, 304–5, 306

Mongau, Katrin 320–3, 327

Moore, Corp Michael 93–4

Morgen Post 63

Morris, Donald (CIA) 27–8

Moscow 9, 11, 267

Moscow–East Berlin conflict 256

Muggelheim 31–2, 34

Muller, George (American Mission) 27, 37, 46, 47, 140, 148

and Battle Group 128, 130

and Brandt's letter to Kennedy 113

on building of Wall 134

Kommadatura meeting (13.8.61) 64–5

LBJ's visit to Berlin 118, 121, 122, 123, 127

on Washington problem 72–3, 109

Muller, Heiner (playwright) 78, 79

Murrow, Ed (US broadcaster) 76, 89, 118

National Border Protection System 200

National People's Army (*Nationale Volksarmee*) 200

NATO (North Atlantic Treaty Organization) 8, 71

Nazi party 80

Neitzold, Uwe 303

Neues Deutschland 34, 37, 53, 111, 229, 284, 303

New York Herald Tribune 22, 24, 178

New York Times 84, 94, 128, 129

news agencies 26, 33, 43, 233, 275

Nietzold, Uwe 283–4, 286, 313, 318, 323–4

Nikolai Church, Leipziger Strasse 272, 308

Nitze, Paul (Berlin Task Force) 24, 66, 119

Nixon, Richard (US President), visit to Berlin 205–6

Norwegian Military Mission 45

nuclear fears/caution 73, 87, 119, 163, 173

Nuremburg: Brandt electioneering speech 29

Oberbaumbrücke checkpoint 133, 270, 277, 300

Old Museum, East Berlin 324

Operation Tokyo (tunnel escape) 189–92

Ost, Friedhelm (FRG spokesman) 254

Ostbahnhof (East Berlin) 34

Ostmark 13

Ostpolitik 207, 213, 238

Owen, Henry (US Policy Planning) 119

Pan-European Picnic (8.8.89) 262

Pankow 40, 45, 60

Pätz (Border Police command post) 32, 43

peace treaty (East–West) 16–17, 21

Peattie, William 209

Peervukhin, Mikhail (Soviet Ambassador) 18

pensioners, visits to West 193, 231, 247, 331

People's Parliament (GDR) 24, 25–6

People's Police (GDR) 33, 35, 45, 47, 48, 119, 199, 200
  arming of 49, 68, 70
  first impacts of closure 95–6
  Headquarters' order (13.8.61) 96–7

perestroika 252

Peter, Col Erich (GDR Border Police) 31–2

Philby, Kim 252

Poland 9

Polgar, Tom (CIA) 28

Poser, Horst 240

Potsdam 42, 56, 63, 216

Potsdamer Platz 21, 47, 48
  construction of Wall 114
  erection of barrier 51, 84, 85, 100, 103
  sealing of S-bahn station 120

Powers, Gary (US pilot) 259

Prague: FRG Embassy 265, 267

Pravda 124

Prenzlauer Berg 40, 45, 60, 92, 98, 103

Prittie, Terence 28

Protestant Church in Germany Governing Council 115

Pruster, Horst 39–40, 78

Puhl, Hans Werner (US army) 188

Quadripartite Agreement 213, 215

Quai d'Orsay 23

Quasner, Wolf (escape organiser) 240

Radtke, Bodo (journalist) 11, 63, 96, 206

Raferty, Sgt Michael (US army) 282, 300, 312, 314, 317, 343
  legend of Helmut 319–20

Railway Police (East Germany) 199

railway system 234
  effects of border sealing 92
  see also S-bahn; U-bahn

Rainhold-Huhn-Strasse (Schüzenstrasse) 161

Raw, Albrecht (owner of Café Adler) 279, 280–1, 314

Reader's Digest 35

Reagan, Ronald (US President) 241
  visit to Berlin 255–6

refugees (East–West flow)
  final exodus (1989) 261–2, 265, 267, 275
  post-border closures 93, 114, 132
  prior to border closures 10, 12–13, 16, 17, 20, 22, 23, 24, 26, 28, 29, 36

Reichsmark 4, 9

Reichstag 6, 21

Reporter, The 21

Reuters news agency (Berlin) 25, 33, 35, 38, 57, 66, 67, 126, 145, 233, 293
  arrest of staff (13 Aug.) 98–100
  Schabowski press conference 275–6

RIAS radio station 42, 44, 55, 89, 97, 135, 231, 284–5

Richter, Hartmut 198–9, 229, 242, 243, 349

Riot Police (GDR) 38, 103, 199, 200

Roennebeck, Klaus 252

Rohrdorf 19, 20

Rontgental 42

Rostov, Walt (US Government) 66

Romania 9

Royal Air Force 4

Royal Navy Officers' Club 105

Rudow 330

Rudower Chaussee checkpoint 297

Rusk, Dean (US Secretary of State) 16, 22, 62, 66, 69–70, 71, 74–5, 109, 172
  and Battle Group dispatch 119
  initial reactions to Berlin crisis 87, 100
  on Kennedy visit to Berlin 179–80
  strictures on Berlin staff 72–3

Russian Zone 6, 7

S-bahn (metropolitan railway) system 3, 37, 43–4, 49, 68, 215
  closure of lines 50–1, 63, 92, 115

Sachsenweger, Heinz 27, 63, 76, 125, 332–3

Salbrecht, Hans-Heiner 252

Salinger, Pierre (White House press secretary) 30

Schaal, Hans-Juergen (judge) 348–9

Schabe, Martin 36, 236–7, 331

Schabowski, Günter (Berlin Party secretary) 266, 268, 348
  press conference (9.11.89) 272, 273, 274–5, 279, 287, 302

Schimke, Brigitta 56, 58, 129–30, 227–8, 230, 325

Schimke, Erhard 27, 38, 42

Schmidt, Helmut (FRG Chancellor) 245

Schneider, Lt-Gen (GDR police) 33

Schönefeld 66

Schönhauser Allee 25, 33, 43, 57, 66, 69

Schreiber, Erich (Border Guard) 348

Schultz, Astrid 42

Schultz, Klaus 29, 47, 48

Schultz, Peter (RIAS reporter) 8, 42, 44, 55, 91, 105, 152
  on division of families 230–1
  Fechter killing 168–9, 285
  reopening of borders/checkpoints 285, 313, 330–1

Schumann, Sgt Conrad (Border Police) 41, 56, 58
  escape 107–8, 111, 346

Schwarz, Karl 240

sectors *see* Zones

SED (Socialist Unity Party) 8, 18, 19, 213

Seeger, Pete 82

Segger, Brita 274, 289, 291, 300, 307–14

Segler, Olga 41

Senefelderplatz 230–1

Sens, Maj Manfred (Border Guard control) 276, 278, 288

Sharansky, Anatole (Soviet dissident) 259

Shepard, Cdr Tazewell (US naval aide) 30

Shevardnadze, Eduard (Soviet statesman) 343

Shevchenko, Arkady N. (Soviet diplomat) 62

Shishkin, Ivan (Soviet Embassy) 60

shoot-to-kill policy 109, 114, 132, 237–8, 248–9, 260, 347

Showalter, Wilbur (Berlin Task Force) 24, 66

Siekmann, Ida 41

Sindermann, Horst 25–6

Smyser, Richard (American Mission) 20, 46–7, 49, 50, 51–2, 53, 55, 61, 63, 118, 147
  Checkpoint Charlie confrontation 148–9

Solovyev, Col Andrei (Soviet commander) 105, 120

Sonnenallee 133, 270, 277, 294

Soviet army 40, 42, 200
  Pioneer Platoons 54
  tank movements (11–13.8.61) 52–3, 68

Soviet Union
  24th CPSU Congress (Mar. 1971) 213
  accord with Bonn (Aug. 1970) 213
  creation of buffer zone 9
  German invasion (1941) 9
  Presidium 17
  Soviet war memorial (West Berlin) 76, 116, 163–4, 172–3
  escape 152–3

Spandau 31, 35, 36, 71, 237

Spree, River 21, 33, 48
  child drowning incident 230
  escape attempts 138, 139, 154, 155, 174–5, 176, 193–4

Staaken checkpoint 43, 327–8

Staatsoper 145–6

Stadtautobahn 330

Stalin, Joseph 5, 10, 80

Stasi (secret police) 29–30, 31, 187, 193, 234, 300–1, 339, 347, 348, 349
  files 341
  opening of checkpoints 304, 331
  passport controls 277

Steinke, Ernest (RIAS) 284–5

Steinstücken enclave 136, 150, 151, 183, 213, 214, 235–7, 338
  escapes 195–7
  second homes 196–7

Stern, Carola (author) 176

Stern, Gerda (East Berliner) 78, 79, 88, 339–40

Stolz, Lutz 19, 20, 28–9, 34, 55–6, 93, 234
  opening of borders 285–6, 329–30
  visits to West Berlin 256–8

Stolz, Uta 19, 56, 340

Stoph, Willy (GDR Prime Minister) 266–7

Strauss, Franz Josef (Minister-President, Bavaria) 238

Stuttgart 19

Sydow, Ursula 241

tanks
  anti-tank barriers 147
  British 93–4
  Checkpoint Charlie confrontation 145–51
  Soviet 94, 102, 105

telephone links 102, 105, 215, 216

television
  border closure reports 56–7, 61
  border reopening reports 283, 291, 294
  GDR removal of aerials 115

Teltow Canal
  escapes 63, 89, 91, 109, 125, 203–4
  fatalities 138, 176, 246

Templehof, West Berlin 286–7

Thälmannpionior (youth organisation) 199

Thompson, Llewellyn (US Ambassador in Moscow) 75, 100

Thompson, Tommy (US) 182

Thurow, Sgt Rudi (Border Police) 42, 53, 54

Tiergarten 91

Toft, Chris (British Military Police) 272, 282, 299, 301, 305, 307, 310, 311, 312, 314

Transport Police (*Transportpolizei*) *see* Railway Police

travel
  Allies 144, 149, 185–7
  GDR pensioners 193, 231, 247

permits 95, 102, 104, 110, 133, 183, 216–17, 225–6
  relaxations 267, 274–303
  restrictions 115

Treptow 21, 31, 37, 40, 44, 45, 56, 60, 63, 67, 76, 353
  escapes 68, 70, 125
  forced evacuations 136–7, 138
  insurrection fears (12–13.8.61) 85
  Schabowski press conference (9.11.89) 276

Trinka, Frank 46–7, 49, 50, 51–2, 53, 55, 61, 63, 70, 75
  post-border closures 106, 151–2

Trivers, Howard (American Mission) 46, 142, 144, 152

U-bahn (underground railway) system 3, 9, 68, 234–5
  closure of stations 51, 92
  reopening 318, 337

Ulbricht, Walter (SED leader) 5, 6, 18, 19, 61, 85, 148, 213, 350
  and border closures 88–9, 101
  and communism 80
  and Fechter killing 172
  preparation for border closure 21–2, 23, 29
  and propaganda 175–6
  and refugee problem 12, 15
  retirement 213
  speech to Warsaw Pact meeting 20

underground railway system *see* U-bahn

United Nations 112, 229

United Press International (UPI) 43, 47

United States Air Force 4

United States Government
  despatch of Battle Group (Aug. 1961) 118
  National Security Action Memorandum (Oct. 1961) 173
  Pentagon 66, 146
  State Department 19, 21, 23, 61, 66, 101
  White House 15, 23, 66
  see also Berlin Task Force; Central Intelligence Agency; Washington

United States military
  Heidelberg 126, 127
  see also American army in Berlin
Unter den Linden 71, 211, 235, 258, 336
  and insurrection fears (12–13.8.61)
    83–5, 91
Urban, Rudolf (first escape victim) 124,
    259

vehicle permits 102, 104
Vienna Summit (June 1961) 13, 15, 118
Vogt, Wolfgang 254
von Braun, Sigismund 122
von Fritsch, Gen Werner 217
von Pawel, Col Ernest (US army) 56
von Scharnhorst, Gen Gerhard 217
Vopos (*Volkspolizei*) 134–5, 137, 144,
    199
  Lightner incident 140–5
  see also People's Police

Warsaw Pact countries 8
  meeting 16, 17, 19, 22
  support for East German action 64
Warsaw Pact (Treaty) 71, 213, 224
Warschauer Strasse 48, 67, 77, 145, 329
Washington 23, 100
  friction with Berlin Mission 109,
    117–18, 134
  nuclear fear 73, 87, 163, 173
  reaction to events (11–13.8.61) 55,
    61–2, 69, 71–3
  statement (12.8.61) 74
Washington Post 58
watchtowers (GDR) 116, 132, 353
  dismantling 339, 341
  personnel duties 201, 219–25
Watson, Maj-Gen Albert, Jnr 52, 56, 64,
    130–1

Watson, Maj (British army) 282
Wedding (West Berlin) 49, 226, 331
Weissensee 40, 46, 60
welcome money 324, 328, 329, 333
West Berlin 13, 133, 208, 210–11
  GDR entry permits 102, 104, 110,
    133, 183, 216–17, 225–6
  J.F. Kennedy visit (June 1963) 177–80
  morale 136, 150
  reactions to border closures 85–6,
    117
  Senate 47, 86, 97
  Soviet officers' access 162–4
Western Allies
  condemnation of shoot-to-kill policy
    248–9
  personnel travel papers 144, 149
  rejection of Khrushchev's ultimatum 19
Western media 77
Wolf, Markus (Stasi general) 21, 30, 62
Wollankstrasse 67, 70, 103
  escapes/fatalities 129, 130, 247–8
Woodcock, John 212
World War Three fears 134, 148
Wriezen 60
Wuthe, Birgit 315–16, 339

Year Zero 4
Yount, Sgt Michael (US army) 262–5,
    279, 287, 290, 291, 293–5, 305,
    316

ZDF television 294
Zehlendorf (West Berlin) 42, 44
Zeisar 187
Zhivkov, Todor (Bulgaria) 251–2
Zimmerstrasse 160, 164, 316
Zones/zones 6, 9, 92, 94, 225, 336–7
  see also Kommandatura